1993

From at least the eighth century and for about a thousand years the repertory of music now known as Gregorian chant, or plainsong, formed the largest body of written music, was the most frequently performed and the most assiduously studied in Western civilization. It lay at the root of all instruction in practical music, and in some sense is at the core of the enormous portion of notated music that survives today.

But plainsong did not follow rigid conventions. It seems increasingly clear that, whatever may have been intended with respect to uniformity and tradition, the practice of plainsong varied considerably within time and place. It is just this variation, this living quality of plainsong, that these essays address. In addition, much new information is made available on the study of local rites and practices, and on the liturgical matrix of important polyphonic repertories.

The contributors have sought information from a wide variety of areas: liturgy, architecture, art history, secular and ecclesiastical history and hagiography, as a step towards reassembling the tesserae of cultural history into the rich mosaic from which they came.

CAMBRIDGE STUDIES IN PERFORMANCE PRACTICE 2

Plainsong in the age of polyphony

CAMBRIDGE STUDIES IN PERFORMANCE PRACTICE 2

_____

General editor: PETER WILLIAMS

Editorial board:
OTTO BIBA, HOWARD MAYER BROWN,
PETER LE HURAY, ROBERT MORGAN,
R. LARRY TODD, ALEXANDER SILBIGER

Already published

1   Perspectives on Mozart performance *edited by* R. LARRY TODD *and*
PETER WILLIAMS

CAMBRIDGE STUDIES IN PERFORMANCE PRACTICE 2

Plainsong in the age of polyphony

Edited by
THOMAS FORREST KELLY

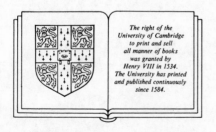

The right of the
University of Cambridge
to print and sell
all manner of books
was granted by
Henry VIII in 1534.
The University has printed
and published continuously
since 1584.

CAMBRIDGE UNIVERSITY PRESS

CAMBRIDGE   NEW YORK   PORT CHESTER
MELBOURNE   SYDNEY

Published by the Press Syndicate of the University of Cambridge
The Pitt Building, Trumpington Street, Cambridge CB2 1RP
40 West 20th Street, New York, NY 10011-4211, USA
10 Stamford Road, Oakleigh, Melbourne 3166, Australia

© Cambridge University Press 1992

First published 1992

Printed in Great Britain at the University Press, Cambridge

British Library cataloguing in publication data

Plainsong in the age of polyphony –
(Cambridge studies in performance practice).
1. Plainsong
I. Kelly, Thomas Forrest
782.292

Library of Congress cataloguing in publication data

Plainsong in the age of polyphony / edited by
Thomas Forrest Kelly.
      p.   cm. – (Cambridge studies in performance practice)
Includes index.
ISBN 0 521 40160 7
1. Chants (Plain, Gregorian, etc.) – History and criticism.
2. Church music – Catholic Church – 500–1400. 3. Church music –
Catholic Church – 15th century. 4. Church music – Catholic
Church – 16th century. I. Kelly, Thomas Forrest. II. Series.
ML 178.C5 1991
782.32'22 – dc20   90-25548 CIP

ISBN 0 521 40160 7 hardback

VN

CONTENTS

ILLUSTRATIONS

GENERAL PREFACE

No doubt the claim, heard frequently today, that 'authentic performance' is a chimera, and that even the idea of an 'authentic edition' cannot be sustained for (most) music before the last century or two, is itself the consequence of too sanguine an expectation raised by performers and scholars alike in the recent past. Both have been understandably concerned to establish that a certain composer 'intended so-and-so' or 'had such-and-such conditions of performance in mind' or 'meant it to sound in this way or that'. Scholars are inclined to rule on problems ('research confirms the following . . .'), performers to make the music a living experience ('artistry or musicianship suggests the following . . .'). Both are there in order to answer certain questions and establish an authority for what they do; both demonstrate and persuade by the rhetoric of their utterance, whether well-documented research on one hand or convincing artistic performance on the other; and the academic/commercial success of both depends on the effectiveness of that rhetoric. Some musicians even set out to convey authority in both scholarship and performance, recognizing that music is conceptual *and* perceptual and thus not gainfully divisible into separate, competitive disciplines. In general, if not always, the scholar appears to aim at the firm, affirmative statement, often seeing questions as something to be answered confidently rather than searchingly redefined or refined. In general, with some exceptions, performers have to aim at the confident statement, for their very livelihood hangs on an unhesitating decisiveness in front of audience or microphone. In the process, both sometimes have the effect, perhaps even the intention, of killing the dialectic – of thwarting the progress that comes with further questions and a constant 'yes, but' response to what is seen, in the light of changing definitions, as 'scholarly evidence' or 'convincing performance'.

In the belief that the immense activity in prose and sound over the last few decades is now being accompanied by an increasing awareness of the issues arising – a greater knowledge at last enabling the questions to be more closely defined – the Cambridge Studies in Performance Practice will attempt to make regular contributions to this area of study, on the basis of several assumptions. Firstly, at its best, Performance Practice is so difficult a branch of study as to be an almost impossibly elusive ideal. It cannot be merely a practical way of 'combining performance and scholarship', for these two are fundamentally different activities, each able to inform the other only up to a certain point. Secondly, if Performance Practice has moved beyond the questions (now seen to be very dated) that exercised performance groups of the 1950s and 60s, it can widen itself to include any or all music written before the last few years. In this respect, such studies are a musician's equivalent to the cry of literary studies, 'Only contextualize!', and this can serve as a useful starting-point for the historically minded performer or the practically minded scholar. (The Derridaesque paradox that there is no context may have already affected some literary studies, but context is still clearly crucial across the broad field of music, the original Comparative Literature.) Cambridge Studies in Performance Practice will devote volumes to any period in which useful questions can be asked, ranging from at least Gregorian chant to at least Stravinsky.

Thirdly, Performance Practice is not merely about performing, neither 'this is how music was played' nor 'this is how you should play it in a concert or recording today'. (These two statements are as often as not irreconcilable.) In studying all that we can about the practical realization of a piece of music we are studying not so much how it was played but how it was heard, both literally and on a deeper level. How it was conceived by the composer and how it was perceived by the period's listener are endless questions deserving constant study, for they bring one into intimate contact with the historical art of music as nothing else can. It is the *music* we fail to understand, not its performance as such, if we do not explore these endless questions. As we know, every basic musical element has had to be found, plucked out of thin air – the notes, their tuning, compass, volume, timbre, pace, timing, tone, combining – and they have constantly changed. In attempting to grasp or describe these elements as they belong to a certain piece of music, it could become clear that any modern re-realization in (public) performance is a quite separate issue. Nevertheless, it is an issue of importance to the wider musical community, as can be seen from the popular success of performers and publications (records, journals, books) concerned with 'authenticity'. In recognizing this practical importance, Cambridge Studies in Performance Practice will frequently call upon authoritative performers to join scholars in the common cause, each offering insights to the process of learning to ask and explore the right questions.

PETER WILLIAMS

ABBREVIATIONS

AH   Guido Maria Dreves, Clemens Blume, Henry Marriott Bannister, eds.,
         Analecta hymnica medii aevi, 55 vols., Leipzig, 1886–1922, repr. 1961
BL   British Library
BN   Bibliothèque Nationale
CAO   René-Jean Hesbert, *Corpus antiphonalium officii*, 6 vols., Rerum ecclesiasti-
         carum documenta, series maior, fontes 7–12, Rome, 1963–79
CMM   Corpus mensurabilis musicae
CS   Edmond de Coussemaker, *Scriptorum de musica medii aevi nova series*, 4
         vols., Paris, 1864–76, repr. 1963
CSM   Corpus scriptorum de musica
GS   Martin Gerbert, *Scriptores ecclesiastici de musica sacra potissimum*, 3 vols., St
         Blasien, 1784, repr. 1963
JAMS   *Journal of the American Musicological Society*
LU   *Liber usualis*, edited by the Benedictines of Solesmes, Tournai, Desclée,
         various editions
MGG   *Die Musik in Geschichte und Gegenwart*, ed. Friedrich Blume, 14 vols. plus
         supplement, Kassel, 1949–73
MQ   *The Musical Quarterly*
PL   Patrologiae cursus completus. Series latina, ed. Jacques-Paul Migne, 221
         vols., Paris 1878–90
RISM   *Répertoire internationale des sources musicales*
Note: The essays by Huglo, Robertson, and Bloxam in this volume cite
manuscripts using the abbreviation system of *The New Grove Dictionary of Music and
Musicians*, ed. Stanley Sadie, 20 vols., London, 1980.

INTRODUCTION

THOMAS FORREST KELLY

From at least the eighth century and for about a thousand years the repertory of music now known as Gregorian chant, or plainsong, was the most-heard, most-studied, and most-written music in Western civilization. It lay at the root of all instruction in practical music, and in some sense was also at the core of an enormous portion of the written music that survives to us.

This is not to say, of course, that plainsong was rigidly unvarying. It seems increasingly clear that, whatever may have been intended with respect to uniformity and tradition, the practice of plainsong varied considerably with time and place. It is just this variation, this living quality of plainsong, that we seek to address in the essays that follow.

Students of music history have often been tempted to view culture as a mosaic in time: one tile at a time, chant followed by 'primitive polyphony' followed by the great achievements of the school of Notre-Dame; *ars antiqua, ars nova*, Renaissance, and so on. But plainsong, though its repertory may have become essentially fixed, did not cease to be heard when polyphony began: it continued to be the only music heard everywhere and by everyone.

Chant scholars have worked long and hard, and have brought to light an enormous amount of information on liturgical and ecclesiastical matters, as well as questions of musical text and transmission. But at the same time it must be recognized that the vast majority of scholarship in chant has been concerned, naturally enough, with the question of origins, with the periods preceding and following the appearance of the first surviving manuscripts. In this context, questions of performance have naturally arisen; as the Gregorian chant was an indispensable part of the liturgy of the Roman Catholic Church until the Second Vatican Council, the process of 'restoring' the chant for modern use, largely begun by the Benedictines of Solesmes in the nineteenth century, and actively pursued by many scholars, was naturally concerned with performance, often with a practical end in view: the performance of medieval – or better, for their purposes, timeless – music by modern singers, amateur and expert.

The question of 'Gregorian rhythm' has been one of the most heated scholarly

1

discussions, and it has continued over many decades. The difficulties, of course, arise from many angles: paucity of evidence, interpretation of evidence, incompatibility of purpose. Chant manuscripts, with few early exceptions, do not generally intend to convey much instruction as to nuance of performance, beyond pitches and texts. They do, however, sometimes include such information for those able to interpret signs and signals whose primary intention is directed elsewhere. It is remarkable, however, that the same fragments of evidence can be used for support of opposing views; this is a phenomenon familiar to anyone who has ever argued, but it is particularly problematical in an area where so little evidence remains, and in which, therefore, each fragment of information takes on a surprising weight. Purposes also have varied; those who have wished to 'restore' chant to some kind of purity often leave unsaid what this restoration is, or in what the purity consists. The rhythmic theories of Dom André Mocquereau, expressed in print in his *Le nombre musical*, and in other ways in the 'rhythmic signs' of the Solesmes chant books and in the many very beautiful recordings by the monks of Solesmes, are a system that might almost be said to precede the evidence. With its arsis and thesis, its ictus, its indivisible rhythmic cells, this is essentially an aesthetic system devised by a former player of chamber music and applicable in many ways to any music. And it provides very beautiful performances of the notes of plainsong.

Likewise certain other attempts to reform or restore the performance of plainsong – the efforts of Agobard and Florus of Lyon in the ninth century, the Cistercian reforms of the later middle ages, the post-Tridentine revisions of the sixteenth century – are efforts to impose on a received repertory certain aesthetic norms that reflect more about their own time than about the timeless purity of a repertory now corrupted and in need of reform.

One of the problems, of course, is the question that arises repeatedly in our own historically oriented century: restore to what? There is no Sistine ceiling from which we can remove all non-Michelangelesque brushmarks, no autograph manuscript from which to restore a corrupt text, no first performance to reconstruct. This is a notion that has been confused from the very early written history of the chant. In many Carolingian illuminations, an original form of chant is posited: the dove of the Holy Spirit sings the first performance into the ear of St Gregory, and the neumes that Gregory in his turn inscribes on his tablet are the autograph manuscript: a picture of first performance and autograph manuscript in one. But of course the work of many scholars has made us keenly aware that plainsong consists of a series of layers from a variety of chronological and stylistic milieux, and that to peel back even one of these in order to reveal its antecedents provides an almost impossible task. Chant is of its time. It is just that its time is so long, and its beginning so obscure.

Scholarship has yet to address many specific questions of performance: how exactly is a Responsory performed? When did the practice begin of having the choir join in near the end of the Gradual's verse? What precisely is the relationship of prosula to melisma? How is an antiphon performed, when it is doubled, or triumphed, or neumed? And how do these matters change with time and place? We have much to learn about the sounds of chant. Much will be learned from the detailed study of surviving customaries and ordinals, which often give clear instructions for the performance of the liturgy: when these are used in conjunction with chant-books (as was their purpose), the results can be of great interest in re-creating the actions that generated the sounds of medieval ecclesiastical music.

Scholarly interest in the chant of later times (that is, after about the twelfth century) has had a few notable experts, but has largely been tangential to interest in polyphonic repertories. Later chant books have been used as quarries for polyphonic *cantus firmi*, and hence sometimes as locators in time and place for the origins of polyphonic compositions; otherwise such books have taken up much-needed space on library shelves, and have been consulted but little. It is only recently that later sources have come to be valued for the information they can add to our understanding of local and regional musical traditions.

The essays in this volume cannot address all of these questions, but they can serve to point directions for further research, and to indicate ways in which plainsong in later ages is an area worthy of careful study, not only for its own worth in time and place, but also as a valuable adjunct in the understanding of the full breadth of musical cultures.

In an opening essay, John Caldwell considers the contextual basis of comparison of plainsong and polyphony, dealing in turn with plainsong as such, plainsong in composition, and alternation practice. In addition to a broad survey of plainsong rhythm based on an observation of theoretical and practical consideration, Caldwell goes on to establish a conceptual framework joining plainsong and polyphony, and demonstrating, as he says, that questions of plainsong performance, at least in later centuries, cannot be divorced from the conventions of liturgical polyphonic composition.

Michel Huglo and Rebecca Baltzer investigate two different aspects of the very important practice of medieval Paris. Huglo's survey of the surviving chant books of the region points out some remarkable facts heretofore not noticed, and he considers the question of the mutual influence of plainsong notation and the notation of polyphony, often by the same scribes and for the use of the same singers. Rebecca Baltzer is concerned with the liturgy as it operates within a building: in this case a very important one. The path of processions in and around the cathedral of Paris in the early thirteenth century is reconstructed from surviving liturgical books; this information can be used to assist in mapping the building itself, as well as giving a physical picture of the unfolding of the liturgy throughout the year.

Elsewhere in France, the youth of Beauvais in the early thirteenth century performed the *Ludus Danielis*, one of the few works of medieval music-drama which is regularly revived in modern times. Margot Fassler gives us a new look at this work from a broadly conceived point of view, and situates its performance context, not so much in a building, as in a cultural complex that draws on popular traditions not easy to document. The result of her wide-ranging examination positions the play within its religious and social context, and provides recommendations for interpreting the play that will inevitably enrich our understanding of this masterpiece.

Anne Walters Robertson focuses her essay on one of the best-known pieces of fourteenth-century polyphony: the Mass of Guillaume de Machaut. She uses the readings of chant books to assist in localizing polyphony, and with the addition of archival and historical information, she is able to identify the place and purpose of the Mass within a specific building and a particular liturgical order.

Jennifer Bloxam, in her case-studies of *cantus firmi* in the works of Obrecht, is concerned with the sources of polyphonic *cantus firmi* as a means of dating and localizing specific polyphonic works; in this she succeeds, but she also considers other matters illustrating the relationship of plainsong to polyphony. In examining the manipulation of chant as *cantus firmus* Bloxam considers questions of pitch and of text underlay, and shows how a scribe unfamiliar with the source chant might make inappropriate alterations: local chants do not thrive on foreign soil. She thus shows how chant may be used as a corrective to polyphonic sources.

Richard Sherr demonstrates with a substantial amount of evidence at least one unwritten performance tradition in plainsong that can be reconstructed only through consideration of surviving polyphonic sources. And, as he says, if this practice influenced Josquin, it is worth knowing about. That singers should understand certain aspects of performance that are not regularly indicated in notation is no surprise to scholars of the chant, but that such practices can still be unearthed (and on a wide scale geographically) in the late fifteenth century, is an event of note, and a challenge to further study of polyphony as potential source material for performance practice of chant.

Iain Fenlon studies a newly established liturgical foundation of the sixteenth century, considering the complex of patronage that called it into being, and the many levels of past tradition and princely aspiration that create such a musical and liturgical complex. In considering the background of Santa Barbara at Mantua, Fenlon shows how the traditions of liturgy, plainsong, and polyphony may be fashioned into a new and composite whole for purposes that are at least partly political and social.

One fact emerges clearly from these essays: the study of chant is not a single discipline. The contributors have sought information in a wide variety of areas: liturgy, architecture, art history, history (secular and ecclesiastical), hagiography. The task is a daunting one, but the rewards are evident. It is also clear that much remains to be done, not only in each of these areas, but in the far more difficult task of reassembling the tesserae of cultural history into the rich mosaic from which they came.

PLAINSONG AND POLYPHONY 1250–1550

JOHN CALDWELL

The purpose of this essay is to examine the interaction between plainsong and polyphony during the later Middle Ages – in practice, in composition, and conceptually – in order to establish a framework for the solution of problems of performance and interpretation. It may help to clear the ground if a start is made with questions of terminology and definition.

I

'Plainsong' is simply the traditional English rendering of the Latin *cantus planus*, a term which arose during the thirteenth century out of the broader and more fundamental *musica plana*. *Musica plana* concerned the theoretical (or speculative) and practical study of music considered as a monophonic art. The speculative side was what was inherited from Boethius; the practical side involved such things as the study of the gamut and the eight modes (*toni*).[1] It is important to remember, however, that this 'practical' side of the course was still a branch of musical study; the music which the study was primarily intended to inculcate was known as *cantus planus*. In some sense the opposition between *musica* and *cantus* was analogous to the familiar one between *musicus* ('musician') and *cantor*, the *ars musica* as such being increasingly the property of the speculative enquirer. But the analogy is not quite complete, for while the word *musicus* was very generally confined to theorists, or at least composers, *musica* itself (and other adjectival uses such as *instrumenta musica*) could not be so easily divorced from the practice of the art.[2]

---

1 The term 'mode' will be retained here to denote the scale or tonality of a piece, in order to avoid confusion with the 'tone' (i.e. tune) of a psalm or other recitational chant. It must be remembered, however, despite the objections of Guido of Arrezzo (*Micrologus*, cap. x), that the overwhelming majority of writers in Latin used *tonus* in both senses.

2 For the bibliography of the *ars musica* see F.A. Gallo, 'Philological Works on Musical Treatises of the Middle Ages', in *Acta Musicologica* 44 (1972), 78–101 and M. Huglo, 'Bibliographie des éditions et études relatives à la théorie; musicale du Moyen Age (1972–1987)', *Acta Musicologica* 60 (1988), 229–72. For the *musicus* as composer see John (? of Afflighem), in *Johannes Affligemensis De musica cum tonario*, ed. J. Smits van Waesberghe, CSM 1 (Rome, 1950), cap. xvi.

Opposed to *musica plana* was *musica mensurabilis*, measured music, which similarly developed a body of theory. Although the general notion of measurement as applied to musical time is very ancient, the term *mensura* and the adjective *mensurabilis* acquired a technical sense only in the thirteenth century.[3] They were applied specifically to music in ternary rhythm, the *longa* being divided into three *breves*, the *brevis recta* or temporal unit being the *mensura* proper. Alongside *cantus planus* we find *cantus mensurabilis*, notably in the traditional title of Franco's treatise, *Ars cantus mensurabilis*, a work devoted to its study.[4]

It seems then that *cantus planus* and *musica plana* came to be so named in opposition to *cantus mensurabilis* and *musica mensurabilis*. They were applied to monophonic, 'unmeasured' music; but the technical meaning of *mensurabilis* should warn us against too literal an interpretation of *planus*. The terminology, quite apart from the fact that it took no account of secular monophony,[5] also left *discantus* in an anomalous position. The term *discantus* arose in the thirteenth century to describe techniques of composition other than pure (i.e. sustained-note) *organum*. At its simplest it consisted of elementary two-part note-against-note counterpoint without specific time-values. In later pedagogical tradition the supplied part, against which another was to be added, itself came to be known as the *cantus planus* or plainsong; yet *discantus* was to begin with always treated as a part of *musica mensurabilis*. This was presumably because such elementary instruction was seen merely as a preliminary to the genuinely measured forms of *conductus*, *clausula*, and motet; but the equation of the standard plainsong note at first with the *brevis* and later with the *semibrevis* of measured music enabled a rapprochement with mensural music to be made, however complex the added parts might be.

II

This introductory survey of terminology leads us to the question of plainsong rhythm. The appearance of the term *cantus planus* in the thirteenth century has

---

3 See W. Gurlitt in *Abhandlungen der geistes- und sozialwissenschaftlichen Klasse*, Jg. 1954 (Wiesbaden, 1955), pp. 651–77; a study by the present writer is in preparation.

4 *Franconis de Colonia Ars Cantus Mensurabilis*, ed. Gilbert Reaney and André Gilles (n.p., 1974). This title derives from the incipit in Milan, Bibl. ambr., MS D5 inf. (14th c.), fol. 110v; other manuscripts have 'ars mensurabilis musyce' (St-Dié, Bibl. mun., MS 42, explicit on fol. 53v), 'ars musice mensurate' (Tremezzo, Bibl. Sola Cabiati, (MS without shelf number, fol. 3r) or no title or explicit at all.

5 Johannes de Grocheio (*c.* 1300) distinguished between *musica simplex* or *civilis*, also called *vulgaris*; *musica composita* or *regularis* or *canonica*, also called *musica mensurata*, and *musica ecclesiastica*. E. Rohloff, ed., *Die Quellenhandschriften zum Musiktraktat des Johannes de Grocheio* (Leipzig, [1972]), p. 124. Jerome of Moravia refers to *cantus ecclesiasticus, firmus*, or *planus* (cap. 24; see *Hieronymus de Moravia, O.P. Tractatus de Musica*, ed. S.M. Cserba, Freiburger Studien zur Musikwissenschaft 2 (Regensburg, 1935), p. 173).

sometimes given rise to the belief that the chant then shed an earlier rhythmical complexity at this period; but as we have seen, it need mean no more than that it lacked the ternary organization of *musica mensurabilis*. In fact quite a reasonable case can be made out for the view that the rhythmic character of plainsong did not radically alter between the ninth and sixteenth centuries. It was never, during this long period, metrically regular,[6] though there were attempts from time to time to respect the quantities of the Latin, at least in syllabic chant. In the later Middle Ages, a definite correlation between the values of mensural music and the note-shapes used in plainsong emerged; when used in polyphony these were strictly interpreted, but there is no need to believe that they normally were so in monophonic chant. A brief résumé of the attempts to put plainsong into a rhythmic straitjacket may be of use at this point.

Several Carolingian or post-Carolingian theorists asserted that ecclesiastical chant was to be sung in strict time, using two values in the ratio 2 : 1; and the author of the *Commemoratio brevis de tonis et psalmis modulandis* went so far as to say that all melody should be strictly measured.[7] But this can hardly be taken literally, since the structure of melismatic chant is scarcely amenable to the application of strictly measured durations, and its notation resists interpretation in terms of exact values, despite several attempts in that direction.[8] The best explanation of the Carolingian view is to see it in the light of its protagonists' rediscovery of classical literature and the revival of grammar that went with it. There was a renewed interest in the structures of the language, and a concern for orthography and pronunciation.[9] The correct delivery of liturgical texts was of paramount importance, and the relevance of this to chant will have been primarily in the sphere of antiphonal psalmody. The recitational tones were almost wholly syllabic, and the accompanying antiphons largely so; and these were by far the most important part of the daily liturgical round. The *Commemoratio brevis* is about little else, and it is surely understandable that the author should extrapolate his view of psalmody into a general statement about melody.

This respect for the quantity of the syllables was maintained throughout the Middle Ages. The *accentuarii* attached to English missals and breviaries shortly before the Reformation attest to this;[10] for it was through knowledge of the

---

6 For some exceptional contrary instances see below.

7 The main evidence concerning chant rhythm was first assembled by P. Wagner in his *Neumenkunde* (2nd edn, Leipzig, 1912), pp. 353–80. For the *Commemoratio brevis* see the edition by T. Bailey (Ottawa, 1979), p. 106.

8 Wagner, *Neumenkunde*, pp. 409 ff.; J.W.A. Vollaerts, *Rhythmic Proportions in Early Medieval Ecclesiastical Chant* (Leiden, 1958).   9 Wagner, *Neumenkunde*, p. 354.

10 *Breviarium ad usum insignis ecclesiae Sarum*, ed. F. Procter and C. Wordsworth, 3 vols. (Cambridge, 1879–86), vol. 3, after col. 1120, with a list of some of the publications to which it was attached, p. (ii).

quantity that the position of the accent was determined. But it is clear that it was directed primarily at the reader, and by extension to the cantillation of recitational and other syllabic chants at the most. The later medieval notation of such chants appears to reflect this concern, though its details do not seem always to correspond strictly to the grammatical quantities (see Example 1.1).[11]

Example 1.1   *Missale ad vsum ecclesie Sarisburiensis* (Paris, 1555, Preface for Lent), with variants from the editions of 1534 (Paris) and 1555 (London)

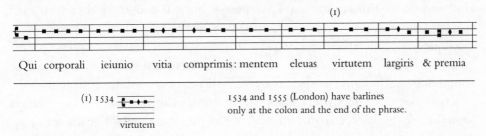

(1)

Qui corporali   ieiunio   vitia   comprimis: mentem   eleuas   virtutem   largiris & premia

(1) 1534

virtutem

1534 and 1555 (London) have barlines only at the colon and the end of the phrase.

In general there could be no equation between the shapes of the plainsong characters and mensural values before the middle of the thirteenth century, because until then a correlation between shape and value had not entered the notation even of avowedly mensural music. Nor had the ligature-patterning of polyphonic 'modal' notation been imitated in chant. It is to Jerome of Moravia that we owe the idea that the values in plainsong should correspond to certain equivalents in mensural music; but even he falls short of saying that the *figura* or shape of the note in plainsong invariably indicates its value.[12] The consequences of his doctrine were never fully realized in plainchant notation, and the situation was complicated by the continual slowing down of nominal tempo in mensural music. Already Jerome has to explain that the *tempus* of the *moderni* is worth three *tempora* of the *antiqui* (in the *organa* of Leoninus and Perotinus, for example). He was not to know that his own equations would soon be hopelessly out of date.

Briefly, Jerome says that all notes of plainsong, with certain exceptions, are equal

11 Cf. *Missale ad usum insignis et praeclarae ecclesiae Sarum*, ed. F. Dickinson (Burntisland, 1861–83), col. 598, based on the edition of 1526. Some earlier editions use only rhombi.

12 Jerome is unusual, though not unique, in regarding mensuration as the foundation of both plainsong and *discantus*: 'Cum autem modus cantandi omnem cantum ad musicam mensurabilem pertineat . . .' (ed. Cserba, p. 180: cf. the discussion of the *Quatuor principalia* and Hothby below). After giving the *figurae* of the *longa*, *brevis*, and *semibrevis* in turn he then defines the *longa* itself as worth two modern *tempora* (=6 ancient *tempora*), the *longior* as worth three, and the *longissima* as worth four. The *brevis*, *brevior*, and *brevissima* are worth one *tempus*, two *instantiae* and one *instantia* respectively. These distinctions could not have been fully reflected in the notation of his day, nor do they correspond to any other known hierarchies of values from the period for *musica mensurabilis*. The *semibrevis* is not defined, though later discussion seems to equate it with the *brevior*.

in length and are worth one *tempus* of the *moderni*. The first note, if it is the *finalis* of the mode, is a *longa*, worth two *tempora*. The second note of a syllable (if it has more than one note) is also a *longa* unless it is itself preceded or followed by a *longa*. A *plica*, ligated or otherwise, is a *longa*, except for the shape known as the *plica brevis*. The penultimate note is a *longa*, and the final note is worth two, three, or four tempora according to the context. There follow some suggestions for the interpretation of neumes of more than three notes, and for various ornaments including the *flores* or vibrato. Jerome's interpretations of those neumes come closest to the rhythms of mensural polyphony, but it is doubtful if they were ever widely followed. His values, transcribed in descending neumes, are given in Example 1.2.[13] Nor is there any evidence that notators attempted to express his ideas visually. Single notes continued to be written as square (tailed or untailed) or rhomboid, and ligatures in their conventional forms according to their melodic function, not according to any supposed rhythmic value they might have. But his remarks are of historical importance in linking the standard plainsong note (however written) to the *brevis* of his day, implying a tempo of perhaps M.M. 80.

Example 1.2   Jerome's suggested interpretation of neumes

Johannes de Grocheio stated that ecclesiastical chant was 'not precisely measured' (as opposed to being not measured at all, which he regarded as a philosophical impossibility).[14] Elsewhere he says that the Kyrie and the Gloria were sung in perfect longs in the manner of the *cantus coronatus*,[15] which certainly by his day implies exceptional slowness. But an equation with the *brevis* for other forms of plainsong was probably understood, even though the correspondence might not be exact.

Somewhat in the tradition of Jerome lies the anonymous English Franciscan author of the *Quatuor principalia musice* (colophon dated 1351), who asserts that everyone wishing to sing expertly should 'keep his measure'. All *cantus planus* should be performed in the fifth or the sixth mode, i.e. in (perfect) longs or in breves. But he then goes on to describe innumerable variants, both ornamental and

13 It is possible, though by no means certain, that the values for five, six, and seven or more notes should be assimilated to the mensural framework of those for four.

14 Rohloff, *Die Quellenhandschriften*, p. 124.

15 Ibid., p. 162. The *offertorium*, too, was to be sung 'ad modum ductiae vel cantus coronati' (p. 164).

rhythmic, of this basic procedure. We may guess that at this date even the equation with the *brevis* was purely nominal, the reference to the modes being an archaism to which lip-service was also paid in the discussion of *musica mensurabilis* later on.[16]

The historical connection with the mensural *brevis recta* or *tempus* is revealed in the fourteenth century by the frequent use of this value for polyphonic *cantus firmi* and by the occasional use of ordinary plainsong notation to indicate a string of mensural *breves* in a *cantus firmus*.[17] But the slowing down of nominal tempo, and the variable value of the *tempus* in *ars nova* theory (French and Italian) began to make it inappropriate as a yardstick for ordinary use. Under these circumstances (though the exact chronology has not been charted), the ordinary *nota simplex* of plainsong (however written) came by the early fifteenth century to be the equivalent of a *semibrevis*. It was also open to notators, as we shall see, to reserve the square *punctum* for the *semibrevis*, the tailed *punctum* for the *longa*, and the rhombus for the *minima*, and thus to create a simple form of measured 'plainsong' written in a form of diminution.[18] It was only rarely, however, that a truly mensural idiom was created. But the theoretical equation of the *nota simplex* with the *semibrevis*, in the fifteenth and early sixteenth centuries, is validated by its use as such in *cantus firmi*, just as it had been in terms of the *brevis* in the fourteenth. And again, as in the fourteenth century with the *brevis*, so now the equation with the *semibrevis* lost what general significance it may have had as a guide to performance because of the slowness and variability of that time-value. But the plainsong signs retained their currency as a simplified form of *semibrevis* notation in which the difficulties of perfect mensuration were eliminated (as in 'stroke' notation and many forms of tablature), and created a suitable impression of liturgical propriety when used for the *cantus firmi* of functional polyphony. In such cases the five-line staff would be used and the rapprochement between plainsong and polyphony would be visually complete. Whether the same *semibrevis* unit would operate throughout an *alternatim* work written in this way is a difficult question, but there must at least be the presumption that an approximate equality was maintained in the case of the *semibrevis* in *tempus imperfectum diminutum* and the single notes of the plainsong.[19]

16 The discussion of chant rhythm occupies ch. lviii of the *Tertium Principale* (CS 4, pp. 251–4).
17 The *brevis* is invariably used as the unit for the notes of the *cantus firmus* in the liturgical keyboard music of the Faenza Codex (Faenza, Bibl. com., MS 117; see *Keyboard Music of the Late Middle Ages in Codex Faenza 111*, ed. D. Plamenac (CMM 57, n.p., 1972). The use of plainsong notation for a *cantus firmus* may be sampled in an anonymous 'Benedicamus domino' from Paris, BN, MS ital. 568 (*c.* 1400), reproduced and discussed in W. Apel, *The Notation of Polyphonic Music 900–1600* (Cambridge, MA, 1953), pp. 378–80. In both cases the actual value of the *brevis* depends on the mensuration.   18 See the examples quoted below from Dufay's hymns.
19 The adoption of *tempus imperfectum diminutum* in the later fifteenth and early sixteenth centuries as a standard signature had the effect of enhancing the appropriateness of the *semibrevis* as the equivalent of the basic plainsong value.

In the Lyons *Contrapunctus* of 1528, for example, [20] the chants are written in plainsong notation in both the monophonic and the polyphonic sections, mostly in square notes but retaining the rhombus in the *climacus*. The rhombus here retains the same *semibrevis* value as the other notes. In some English sources, however,[21] the rhombus is treated as *minima*, the *punctum* and *virga* alike as *semibrevis* value and the *plica* (𝅘) as *brevis*. These are the values, together with the dotted square note, adopted by Marbecke in his *Booke of common praier noted* (1550). They could also be used for polyphony as a whole, and this restricted range of note values was sufficient for 'plainsong' Masses by Henry Petyr (though his is not so named), Taverner, and Sheppard.[22] The two latter survive only in mensural notation, but they could well have been conceived in terms of plainsong notation interpreted in this way.

Hints of a still more complex form of plainsong measurement are to be found in certain treatises and plainsong manuscripts of the fifteenth and sixteenth centuries. John Hothby, the English Carmelite who settled in Ferrara, propounded a threefold system based on the *modus*, *tempus*, and *prolatio* of mensurable music.[23] The first used mainly the *virga* and the square *punctum*, the second the *punctum* and the rhombus, the third the rhombus and the *minima*. Minims he said to be very rare, except in the 'Credo cardinalis' and certain plainchant Glorias. The rules he gives for the observation of the durations do not seem very practicable, since they depend on the recognition of perfect or imperfect mode, time, or prolation; and it is not made clear how this is to be achieved. Hothby's main concern is to demonstrate the derivation of polyphony from plainsong,[24] but the more widespread existence of a quasi-mensural treatment of plainsong, in Italy at least, cannot be ruled out.

A number of sources bear out Hothby's remark about the use of the *minima* in the 'Credo cardinalis', though this value is sometimes merely a substitute for the rhombus; but instances of the rhombus beside the *minima* also occur.[25] There are

20 *Contrapunctus*, ed. D.A. Sutherland, 2 vols., *Recent Researches in the Music of the Renaissance 21–2* (Madison, WI, 1976).

21 E.g. London, BL, Add. MS 17802–5 (the Gyffard part-books, *c*. 1560), in the anonymous settings of the *Te Deum* and *Asperges me* at the beginning of the collection.

22 Cf. F.Ll. Harrison, *Music in Medieval Britain* (London, 1958), pp. 197 ('playneson of fyve partes'), 279–80 (Petyr), 280–90 (Taverner, Sheppard); H. Benham, *Latin Church Music in England 1460–1575* (London, 1977), pp. 110–11 (polyphonic music in 'plainsong' notation, including Petyr's Mass, in London, BL, Add. MS 5665 (the 'Ritson' MS) and Cambridge, Magdalene College, Pepys MS 1236). The Ritson polyphony of this type uses only the *plica* (= *brevis*) and square *punctum* (= *semibrevis*).

23 *La calliopea legale*, ed. E.H. de Coussemaker, *Histoire de l'harmonie au moyen âge* (Paris, 1852), pp. 349; see sections 72–112. See also A.W. Schmidt, *Die Calliopea legale des Johannes Hothby* (Leipzig, 1897).   24 *La callipea*, section 111.

25 Wagner, *Neumenkunde*, p. 377. The *minima* with downward stem does not seem to represent a different value from that with upward stem. See also *Graduale Pataviense (Wien 1511)*, facs. ed. C. Väterlein, *Das Erbe deutscher Musik 87* (Kassel, etc., 1982), fols. 289v–292v: three Credos, using rhombus and *minima* as well as elements of standard *Hufnagel* neumes.

Example 1.3   Example of handwritten music in the Mozarabic *Missale mixtum* (1500)

Be-ne-di-ctus   es.

even occasions on which the *semiminima* is used, for example in the handwritten music in the Mozarabic *Missale mixtum* of 1500 (see Example 1.3).[26] This is a subject that plainly requires further investigation.

This very selective review of the evidence[27] strongly suggests that an equal-note performance of plainsong was the accepted norm throughout the Middle Ages. In the thirteenth century the standard duration was equated with the *brevis*, and later with the *semibrevis*; but these equations can never have meant absolutely fixed durations for the notes of plainsong, and it was only for limited periods and in particular contexts that they reflected, even approximately, their actual value. Refinements of this basic equality were founded either on a theoretical view of melodic context (Jerome) or were based on the variant shapes of the plainsong symbols. Hothby falls between two stools, propounding a theoretical system linked to patterns of note-shapes that simply do not occur in the standard sources.

Over and above these theoretical postures lay a much older concern for the proper pronunciation of Latin in the liturgy, whether read or sung. This too modified the notation of equality;[28] but it applied only to syllabic, or nearly syllabic, chant. In the later Middle Ages this concern was translated, not always very accurately or convincingly, into the notation.

In the circumstances the idea that the *cantus planus* of the thirteenth century represented a fundamental transformation seems misguided. There has always been

26 Transcribed from the copy in the British Library (IB 53535, *olim* c.17.c.2), fol. 222r. The use of the *semiminima*, together with dotted values, goes beyond even Hothby and gives the notator a range of possibilities akin to those envisaged by Jerome. Nevertheless, this music is not fully mensural; but mensural hymns do occur in at least one closely contemporary source, Cardinal Ximenes's *Intonarium toletanum* (Alcalá de Henares, 1515; not a Mozarabic book as is sometimes assumed), discussed with a facsimile and a few transcriptions by H. Anglés, 'Early Spanish Musical Culture and Cardinal Cisneros's Hymnal of 1515', in J. LaRue *et al.*, eds., *Aspects of Medieval and Renaissance Music: A Birthday Offering to Gustave Reese* (New York, 1966, repr. 1978), pp. 3–16. I am grateful to Mr Bruno Turner for drawing my attention to this source and furnishing photographs. Cf. the fifteenth-century examples discussed below and Examples 1.4 and 1.5.

27 Further theoretical sources of interest are referred to by Wagner, *Neumenkunde*, pp. 373–80.

28 It should be remembered that the latin word 'aequus' and its cognates do not necessarily refer to durational uniformity. Thus in the *Commemoratio brevis* we read: 'De cetero ante omnia sollicitius obseruandum ut aequalite diligenti cantilena promatur' (ed. Bailey, p. 102); in the next paragraph we are told that all *brevia* (short notes or syllables – the neuter plural implies *tempora*) and all *longa* are to be equally short or long respectively: 'Verum omnia longa aequaliter longa[sicut] brevium sit par brevitas, . . . Omnia quae diu ad ea quae non diu legitimis inter se morulis numerose concurrant.'

a predisposition towards equality in non-syllabic chant, despite the wealth of nuance implied by the notation of the early manuscripts. The Cistercian reforms of the twelfth century seem to have been directed in part to the elimination of such nuance, and to judge from its disappearance from the later manuscript tradition the Cistercian ideals of evenness and gravity were widely imitated outside the order.[29] With the thirteenth century came the possibility of giving theoretical expression to the notion of temporal equality; but at the same time, as if to compensate for the loss of the older subtlety, theorists like Jerome and, later, Hothby drew up elaborate schemes for varying the durations. Their views, together with the evidence of the notations, are not to be ignored. But it seems unlikely, with some well-defined exceptions (some to be noted below), that the principle of equality was widely disturbed in practice. On the whole we are justified in stressing the continuity rather than the variability of plainsong performance.

III

Plainsong was initially the foundation of all polyphonic composition. In the late eleventh century we first come across the composition of polyphonic *versus* (or *conducti*), sometimes based on pre-existing monophonic compositions of the same type, sometimes on melodies newly composed. We also see at this time the earliest bitextual compositions, and the birth of the sustained-note style.[30] All of these, separately and in combination, compromised the existing conceptual and formal equivalence of plainsong and polyphony.

The adoption of the sustained-note style in plainsong-based music caused a dichotomy between the chant as used in such pieces and the chant as normally sung, particularly when the two alternated as part of the same liturgical form. On the technical level it became necessary to reformulate the discipline associated with the homorhythmic style, and for this purpose the word *discantus* was adopted.[31] As a technical discipline it began with simple consonant progressions by way of

---

29 There is an excellent discussion of the Cistercian reforms in C. Page, *The Owl and the Nightingale* (London, 1989), pp. 155–70. That the neumes did not of themselves convey a variety of durations is surely demonstrated by the simultaneous use of different signs in note-against-note polyphony; see for example the facsimiles of the now destroyed Chartres fragments, especially MSS 130 and 109, in score, in *Paléographie musicale*, vol. 1 (Solesmes, 1889) plate 23; vol. 17 (Solesmes, 1958), cahier 4, plate 16, and cahier 5, plates 5, 6; described in A. Holschneider, *Die Organa von Winchester* (Hildesheim, 1968), pp. 64–5.

30 The earliest manuscript to exhibit these features is Paris, BN, lat. MS 1139 (*c.* 1100), from St Martial. On the troped 'Benedicamus domino', 'Stirps Iesse', see J. Handschin, 'Über den Ursprung der Motette', *Bericht über den musikwissenschaftlichen Kongress . . . Basel 1924* (Leipzig, 1925), pp. 189–200, using this manuscript and Paris, BN, lat. MS 3549.

31 The word *discantus*, meaning literally 'divided song', seems not to have been in use before the thirteenth century. It is defined laconically in the *Discantus positio vulgaris* as 'diversus consonus cantus' (*Hieronymus de Moravia, O.P. Tractatus de Musica*, ed. Cserba, p. 189).

preparation for genuine composition. As a style, it covered everything that could not be described as 'pure' (i.e. sustained-note) *organum*. When pure *organum* fell into disuse, *discantus* become more or less synonomous with polyphonic composition, written or improvised, from elementary exercises to the most elaborate conceptions.[32] In practice, moreover, despite the non-mensural (or at least semi-mensural) character of the initial teaching, *discantus* could only exist in terms of the developing mensural system.

The continuing practice of note-against-note *organum* overlapped with the development of *discantus*, so that it is not always easy to distinguish between the two.[33] But the characteristics of composed *discantus* stemmed from the possibilities inherent in neume-against-neume *organum* when the number of notes was not identical between the parts; and by the time the theoretical concept of *discantus* was formulated, the rhythmic style of the Notre-Dame composers was well established. *Organum purum* was still very much alive, but *discantus* already commanded a wide range of rhythmic values, effectively from *duplex longa* to *semibrevis*, and governed the upper parts of *organum triplum*, and *quadruplum* as well as all other music in two or more parts.

From the separable *discantus*-sections of *organum* arose the motet, exploiting the dichotomy between the text associated with the tenor and that of the upper part or parts and initiating the medieval use of plainchant unrelated to the main text. That music for the most part does not concern us here; it is liturgically functional polyphony, whether based on plainsong or not, that we must now briefly consider, beginning with the Ordinary of the Mass.

Originally tied to its liturgical place by style and by its foundation on plainsong, the polyphonic Ordinary eventually attained complete musical self-sufficiency. The earliest settings of separate movements, often troped, were based on pre-existing plainsongs;[34] in the fourteenth century such movements, whether or not

---

32 Tinctoris defines *discantus* as follows: 'Discantus est cantus ex diversis vocibus et notis certi valoris aeditus.' (*Dictionary of Musical Terms* [*Terminorum musicae diffinitorium*], ed. and transl. C. Parrish (London, 1963), p. 24).

33 The structural change whereby the chant melody came to occupy the lower of the two parts, resulting in final cadences on the octave, had already occurred by 1100 in connection with note-against-note style. (This change was of course irrelevant to the continued practice of parallel *organum*, in which each voice in effect carried the chant, and to strict voice-exchange music, in which each part necessarily had the same range.)

34 There are troped and untroped Kyrie and Sanctus settings, and troped Gloria and Agnus settings, in the eleventh-century Winchester repertory alongside settings of the Proper of the Mass. The style of these, and of the antiphonal chants of the Proper, is indistinguishable from that of the responsorial settings (which in any case include 'solo' and 'choral' sections) and continued to be largely so down to the middle of the fifteenth century. This is presumably because *all* polyphony was in any case entrusted to small groups, irrespective of whether they represented 'cantors' or 'choir' (see below). Both simple and elaborate techniques of setting a plainsong (except for the specialized case of sustained-note *organum*) were available for either function.

they were grouped together to form a 'Mass', might be independent of any plainsong but were still governed formally by liturgical considerations. In this context a polyphonic composer was simply doing in 'multiple harmony' what was still being done monophonically in plainsong.[35] Plainsong-based and freely-composed movements might be placed side by side, as they are in Guillaume de Machaut's Mass. The rationale was already provided by the great variety of plainsong settings of the Ordinary texts; and polyphony simply expropriated the licence, the choice of mode being in both cases completely free. In the fifteenth century methods of musical unification, including the single *cantus firmus*, were brought into play, and the integrated form pursued its own course thereafter; but throughout the fifteenth and early sixteenth centuries the humbler approach to the polyphonic Mass persisted.[36]

In the later Middle Ages a great variety of compositional options for the setting of liturgical texts emerged, though convention sometimes dictated the choice. Thirteenth-century settings of responsorial chants provided polyphony for the parts to be sung by cantors, the choral sections being sung in plainsong. A sense of structure was provided by the alternation between pure *organum* and *discantus* in the polyphonic sections themselves. In later compositions of this type the element of pure *organum* fell into disuse, but the opposition between solo polyphony and choral plainsong long persisted – hence, indeed, the use of the word *Choral* in German as a synonym for plainsong.[37] But when the choirs themselves began to cultivate polyphony there naturally arose a tendency to reverse the arrangement of the material.[38]

Such forms as antiphonal psalmody and hymnody are of course inherently choral in conception. The notion of a 'choir', however, should be based on the idea of function rather than on that of numbers. The larger choirs of the later Middle Ages were the descendants of smaller groups of *clerici*, sometimes as few as three or four, whose liturgical function was not (or not only) that of 'cantors' in responsorial chant but also to provide, often in a very humble way, a polyphonic 'equivalent' to the appropriate plainsong in the largely 'choral' portions of chant. Sometimes they performed 'antiphonally' in alternation with plainsong; sometimes the entire form

35 The term is Walter Odington's; see *Walter Odington's 'Summa de Speculatione Musicale'*, ed. F.F. Hammond, CSM 14 (n.p., 1970), p. 43.

36 This may be seen in the cultivation of the Proper of the Mass, for example in cycles such as those in the Trent MSS (see D. Fallows, *Dufay* (London, 1982), pp. 188–90), in 'plenary' Masses containing both Ordinary and Proper, in Masses 'De beata virgine', and in their separate components; in general, such items, if grouped together, show liturgical rather than musical unity.

37 This may stem equally, however, from the restriction of almost all polyphony to small groups, as discussed below. In Hothby's *Calliopea legale*, 'canto corale' refers to polyphony.

38 See M.F. Bukofzer, 'The Beginnings of Choral Polyphony', in his *Studies in Medieval and Renaissance Music* (New York, 1950), pp. 176–89.

was sung in polyphony.[39] The polyphonic Ordinary of the Mass was itself a product of this principle. In these cases the later enlargement of the 'choir' necessitated no change of method, in contrast to the situation that obtained with regard to responsorial chant.

It is in the humbler forms of antiphonal polyphony that the underlying unity of polyphonic and monophonic method can most readily be appreciated. It was not necessary for the fulfilment of this humble functionalism that plainsong should be incorporated into the texture; what was important was that the technique should match the function and the occasion. If alternation with plainsong were part of the scheme, then the tonality of the polyphony must be compatible with it. Otherwise the tonality need only be consistent with extrapolated, plainsong-derived norms; in other words, it must be 'in a mode' and, as regards the psalmodic forms, in the equivalent of a plainsong tone.[40] As a half-way-house to complete musical independence, a plainsong-derived *cantus firmus* such as a faburden or a square might be present.[41]

In point of fact this approach to liturgical composition continues an unbroken tradition from the earliest days of polyphony. Simple note-against-note polyphony had not ceased to be written down when techniques advanced further, and polyphonic improvisation 'super librum' was never abandoned.[42] The understandable interest shown by modern investigators in the development of St-Martial

39 A good impression of antiphonal variety may be seen from the Magnificat cycle in the Modena MS (Bibl. Estense, α.X.1.11, henceforth ModB). The methods adopted include alternation *a3/a2* or vice versa; *a3*, fauxbourdon/Contra; polyphony/plainsong; the same from verse 2 onwards (i.e. both verses 1 and 2 are polyphonic, enabling the work to end polyphonically); and *a2/a3/a4*.

40 The Magnificats of ModB are each assigned to a specific tone, and the appropriate intonation formula is provided.

41 For faburden see below, and note 46; 'squares' are mostly single parts from polyphonic works (sometimes arising as counterpoint against a *cantus firmus*) expropriated for independent polyphonic use. The phenomenon has been treated hitherto as exclusively English, but there may turn out to be continental analogues. See H. Baillie, 'Squares', *Acta Musicologica*, xxxii (1960), 178–93.

42 The written survivals are catalogued in *RISM* B IV, *Handschriften mit mehrstimmiger Musik des 14., 15. und 16. Jahrhunderts*, ed. K. von Fischer and M. Lütolf (Munich–Duisburg, 1972). B IV$^{3-4}$ includes the 'primitive' polyphony of the fifteenth and sixteenth centuries (for two two-part settings of the 'Gloria Patri' with variant endings, from a MS of Johannes (Cotto), see Huglo, 'Bibliographie', pp. 255–6). For improvisatory techniques see esp. S. Fuller, 'Discant and the Theory of Fifthing', *Acta Musicologica*, 1 (1978), 241–78; J. Dyer, 'A Thirteenth-Century Choirmaster: The *Scientia Artis Musicae* of Elias Salomon', *MQ* 66 (1980), 83–111: the discussion of parallel *organum* (possibly ornamented), based on the text in GS, vol. 3, pp. 57–61, is on pp. 94–103. The English fourteenth-century material includes *Quatuor principalia musicae*, IV, ii, (CS, vol. 4, p. 294) and Anonymus I (CS, vol. 3, p. 361), which are closely related and represent a development of the method described by Elias Salomonis. See now also *Le Polifonie primitive in Friuli e in Europa: Atti del congresso internazionale Cividale del Friuli, 22–24 agosto 1980*, Miscellanea Musicologica 4, ed. C. Corsi and P. Petrobelli (Rome, 1989).

and Notre-Dame has sometimes obscured this thread running throughout the history of medieval polyphony. But in the later Middle Ages we sense a change of ethos based partly on mensural character and partly on the development of a harmonic approach to tonality.

So far as mensural character is concerned, as we have seen, developments in polyphonic technique broke the earlier automatic identity between polyphonic and chant rhythm. The more sophisticated forms of polyphony went their own way, and the humbler forms were obliged to adapt themselves as best they could to the new climate. There was a lengthy period during which little was done, but from the early fourteenth century onwards even the simplest types of composed liturgical polyphony were normally expressed in terms of the prevailing mensural system.

The position with regard to the tonal structure of functional polyphony is somewhat analogous. As soon as polyphony broke away from an essentially parallel structure its motivation became at least potentially harmonic, whatever the melodic independence of the parts.[43] Tonal unity between the parts, or between the outer parts if there were more than two, was ensured by the *occursus* on to the unison or octave. (When the *occursus* is on to the fifth, the effect is of bitonality.) In the meantime, however, functional parallelism was not lost: it is described for example by Elias Salomonis and in two English fourteenth-century treatises.[44] But in the fourteenth century we find the beginnings of a rapprochement, since the purely contrapuntal movement came to be adapted, at least to some extent, to the prevailing 'harmonic' norms of most written polyphony.

The sense in which two different attitudes to polyphonic composition might lead to the same result can be illustrated from the phenomenon of bitonality just mentioned. This will inevitably arise if two outer parts move to a cadence on a perfect fifth: a familiar instance from the work of a polished composer occurs in Binchois' 'Files a marier'.[45] The same effect is endemic in parallel movement at the fifth (or indeed at the fourth at a period when the fourth was regarded as a perfect consonance). But such parallelism had long vanished from the cadential movement of the outer voices in written composition, and the fifth from the lowest part was normally consigned to an inner part (as in the characteristic Burgundian 6–3 cadence). In English faburden (and some continental analogues) the plainsong, being in the middle voice, provides this fifth at cadences, a conceptual rather than an

---

43 Contrapuntal theory is based on the notion of the acoustic compatibility of the parts (whether or not they are also melodically independent); harmonic theory (in the modern sense) is dependent on the idea of tonal unity in the vertical structure as a whole. There is no harmonic theory properly speaking in the Middle Ages and Renaissance, not because contemporaries could not imagine 'chords' as entities but because the concept of a harmonically unified tonality found no theoretical expression, even in Tinctoris or Glareanus.   44 See note 42 above.

45 Ed. W. Rehm, *Die Chansons von Gilles Binchois*, Musikalische Denkmäler 2 (Mainz, 1957), no. 55. Many of the cadences in Machaut's Mass exhibit the same phenomenon.

aural bitonality that is also found in a great deal of written English music of the period 1380–1460. It may have been an instinctive attraction to tonal unity that led to a reinterpretation of the structure of faburden, whereby the plainsong came to be regarded generally as being in the top rather than the middle voice.[46]

Continental *fauxbourdon* was sung from two mensurally notated parts from the outset, the plainsong if present being in the top voice and the middle voice being added in parallel fourths below.[47] Faburden, by contrast, was improvised in all three voices direct from a plainsong book; but the resulting sound was similar, and the evidence is that such improvisation was subjected to the rhythmic criteria of mensural polyphony. (This no doubt took some practice, but faburden was not always regarded as a wholly straightforward skill.)[48] Fauxbourdon or faburden was the fundamental form of functional polyphony from the early fifteenth century onwards, though it is really a special instance of techniques current for at least a century before and was already being modified in written composition by sophisticated variation such as that which substituted the V–I cadence (by dint of part-crossing) for the standard II⁶–I.

The 'technology' of faburden and fauxbourdon has often been studied, as has the emergence of a clearer sense of harmonic tonality in the early fifteenth century.[49] But the significance of fauxbourdon/faburden as a paradigm for late medieval tonality has been less often appreciated. By virtue of its homogeneity of rhythm, its clear separation of vocal lines, and its equation of tonal direction with frequent 6–3/8–5 cadences, it provides at one and the same time the closest possible approach to a 'harmonization' of plainsong and to a self-sufficient tonality of harmony. On this lowest form of late medieval polyphonic life all subsequent developments in tonal integration ultimately depend.

---

46 On faburden see the epoch-making article of B. Trowell, 'Faburden and Fauxbourdon', *Musica Disciplina* 13 (1959), 43–78; also his 'Faburden – New Sources, New Evidence: A Preliminary Survey', in *Modern Musical Scholarship*, ed. E. Olleson (Boston, MA, 1978), pp. 28–78; and F.Ll. Harrison, 'Faburden in Practice', *Musica Disciplina* 16 (1962), 11–34.

47 This at least is the normal structure. There are examples of the two lower parts only being given (e.g. Binchois, 'Ut queant laxis', in J. Marix, *Les musiciens à la cour de Bourgogne* (Paris, 1937), p. 226), and of the lowest part only (Munich, Bayerische Staatsbibl., MS Clm 14274 (*olim* Mus. 3232a), fol. 96r; cf. C. Wright, 'Performance Practices at the Cathedral of Cambrai 1475–1550', *MQ* 64 (1978), 295–328, quoting Cambrai, Bibl. mun., MS 29, fol. 159r (cf. note 57). (The top part of Wright's example on p. 318 should also be in square brackets; the dotted minims and whole-bar rests should be minims and crotchet rests.)

48 Cf. the difficulties experienced at Southwell in 1484: 'Dominus Thomas Cartwright cantat faburdon tali extraneo modo quod ceteri chorales nequent cum eo concordare' (*Visitations and Memorials of Southwell Minster*, ed. A.F. Leach (London, 1891), p. 46, cited Harrison, *Music in Medieval Britain* (London, 1958), p. 175).

49 Cf. H. Besseler, *Bourdon und Fauxbourdon* (Leipzig, 1950); C. Dahlhaus, *Untersuchungen über die Entstehung der harmonischen Tonalität* (Kassel and Basel, 1967).

IV

It will now be clear that the relationship between plainsong and polyphony was complex and varied. Liturgical polyphony always had some sort of relationship with plainsong: at the very least a shared set of tonal assumptions and a liturgical function in common with that of the plainsong it replaced. If it was actually based on a plainsong or faburden the relationship varied according to the technique adopted: the variables include such things as the place of the chant in the vocal texture (with the possibility of migration), its written pitch-level, and its rhythmic layout (including such choices as isorhythmic or isochronous presentation, and in the latter case the choice of a uniform note-value). All this potential variety had a bearing on the total effect in the case of *alternatim* structures.

Polyphony destined for alternation with plainsong was not necessarily itself based on plainsong, though it usually was, even if the dependence was sometimes a remote one. The underlying principle was one of tonal unity: a transposed *cantus firmus*, for example, usually implies a comparable transposition in the accompanying plainsong, although in practice certain difficulties may arise, such as variable transpositions in the same piece, or a *cantus firmus* whose tonality is at variance with that of the *cantus/tenor* matrix. Manuscripts do not normally transmit the chant itself, and do not necessarily transpose it to the 'correct' pitch when they do; it is the business of the editor and performers to locate and supply plainsong at the appropriate pitch, in the appropriate version, and in the appropriate style of performance.

The responsorial forms are *alternatim* by nature, so to speak; after the Winchester troper, in which polyphony is supplied in full, it is difficult to think of settings in which either the choral or the solo sections are not consigned to plainsong. Even in the case of a versicle such as 'Benedicamus domino' or 'Ite missa est', with their response 'Deo gracias', the same principle applies.[50]

The responsorial settings of the Notre-Dame manuscripts represent the apogee of a long tradition; in them the temporal dichotomy between the pace of polyphonic declamation and that of the plainsong rises to an extreme – they were after all composed 'to enlarge the divine service'[51] – and tonal unity is all that remains.

In the case of the antiphonal, or potentially antiphonal, forms much more

---

50 In the 'Benedicamus domino' of the Office the versicle is for cantors, and may be polyphonic; the response is choral (the plainsong responses 'Deo dicamus gratius' to the two Benedicamus by Dufay (*Minor Liturgical Works*, vol. 5 of *G. Dufay: Opera Omnia*, ed. H. Besseler, CMM I, V (Rome, 1966), nos. 9–10) are given in ModB). In the Mass the 'Ite missa est' or 'Benedicamus domino' as the case may be was sung by the deacon and the response 'Deo gratias' was choral. Polyphonic settings (such as Machaut's) are properly of the response, although some manuscript evidence appears to equate the polyphony with the versicle.

51 'Pro divino servitio multiplicando': F. Reckow, ed., *Der Musiktraktat des Anonymus 4*, 2 vols. (Wiesbaden, 1967), vol. 1, p. 46.

latitude existed. Either the full text could be set, or the polyphony could alternate with plainsong. In the latter case, the polyphonic singers occupied the function of one side of the choir. Whether the plainsong or the polyphonic singers started off depended on local custom: in England, for instance, the plainsong choir always led.[52] The question is complicated by variant conventions regarding the intonation. The intonations to the Gloria and Credo of the Mass were invariably sung by the celebrant (with what degree of musical success one cannot say), and that of the Magnificat at Vespers usually was. Other intonations were sung by the appointed ruler or rulers of the choir (the 'cantors' of our previous discussion), but their phrases were sometimes set polyphonically. In any case, liturgical convention varied at different times and places as to what chants should begin with an intonation; and of course the convention applied whether or not the rest of the polyphony was *alternatim*. The openings of the Sanctus and Agnus Dei were often left to be intoned, and if freely composed were sometimes supplied with 'bogus' intonations in our manuscripts.[53] Intonations, unlike complete *alternatim* plainchant verses, were often written into the manuscripts, usually against the voice bearing the *cantus firmus* if there were one.[54]

There are, of course, exceptions to the rule that plainsong sections were not normally incorporated into polyphonic manuscripts. One such example, quoted in Example 1.4, is from Cambrai, Bibliothèque municipale MS 29; this is the first verse of the Compline hymn 'Cultor Dei memento'; the rhythm given to the plainchant is exactly that given to the fauxbourdon bass of verse 2.[55] Further evidence is

Example 1.4   The first verse of the Hymn *Cultor Dei memento*, from Cambrai, Bibliothèque municipale MS 29, fol. 159

52 In organ settings, the reverse arrangement prevailed. On the continent, practice varied: in Dufay's hymn-cycle the plainsong leads, except in hymns of three verses.
53 Cf. Dufay's Mass 'Sine nomine'; Bennet, Sanctus and Agnus in Bologna, Civico museo bibliografica-musicale, MS Q 15, fols. 26v–28r (*olim* 24v–26r).
54 This is often the top voice, as in the Magnificats, antiphons, and other liturgical works in ModB.
55 See above, note 47. The first two notes are obscure in pitch and rhythm but are confirmed by the layout of verse 3, which is again in mensural plainsong. The penultimate bar accommodates a hypermetric syllable in the underlay: the suggested sharp seems to follow from the fauxbourdon cadence in verse 2. The hymn has eight verses in all.

provided by Dufay's cycle of hymns, the most complete version of which is in the Modena manuscript.[56] In two cases, 'Conditor alme siderum' and 'Vexilla regis prodeunt', the tunes are given a quasi-mensural form, and the conclusion that they were intended to be so sung is inescapable, the equations being *virga* = *brevis*, square *punctum* = *semibrevis*, rhomboid *punctum* = *minima*, with ligatures to correspond (Example 1.5). The other plainsongs could be interpreted as a series of *breves* (perfect or imperfect according to the surrounding polyphony); that is, they consist of separate notes looking like *longae*, or groups that are best interpreted as ligatures consisting of *longae*.[57] But the effect of singing them in this way would be undeniably stilted, and it is by no means certain that this was intended. More probably the notes would have been sung slowly and equally, but not as slow as the perfect *brevis* (the usual mensuration of the polyphony being *tempus perfectum*). It is something of a mystery why only two chants should be given a notation which is not only unequivocal in itself but corresponds to the rhythmic character of the polyphonic treatment.

The transposition of a *cantus firmus*, or failing that the cadential tonality in the polyphony, is important evidence for the pitch of the alternating plainsong.

Example 1.5   Plainsongs in Dufay's cycle of hymns
(a)   ModB, fol. 4r

(b)   ModB, fol. 9v

56 ModB, fols. 4r–24r (*olim* 1r–21r).
57 The literal Franconian interpretation of these ligatures (when they do not explicitly consist of *longae*) would lead to absurd results.

Uniformity of tonality is important, though vagaries in cadential patterns and their polyphonic treatment can lead to apparently awkward intervals between the end of one verse and the start of the next.[58] Magnificats, and other pieces based on psalm-tones, can be problematic, since the *differentia* which is being harmonized may well not end on the *finalis* of the tone, and the polyphony may not quote it recognizably at all. Sometimes however the manuscript sources themselves indicate the tone.[59] While tonal unity between plainsong and polyphony is axiomatic, its expression may be unfamiliar to an investigator not deeply immersed in contemporary convention. In the case of English compositions based on the faburden of the chant, an added difficulty is that of deciding whether it is 'thirds' faburden (lying mostly a third below the original plainsong) or 'sixths' faburden that is represented.

As we have seen, a problem is created when the tonality of the chant as quoted in the polyphonic setting is at variance with that formed by the *cantus/tenor* framework. This difficulty (of which 'thirds' faburden is merely a special case) is particularly apparent in English liturgical compositions of the fourteenth and fifteenth centuries, though in most cases the problem is confined to the choice of pitch for the intonation. The usual solution is to assume that the pitch of the plainsong should be that of the polyphonic *cantus firmus*, and to regard the resulting tonal dichotomy as an extrapolation of what is inherent in the polyphony itself.[60] This seems perfectly valid for this period (though the occasional adoption of variant pitch-levels for the *cantus firmus* adds a further dimension to the question), and the problem virtually disappears thereafter, particularly if faburden is assumed to be 'sixths' faburden (as seems normally to have been the case).[61] Of course there is

58 See below for the problems raised by *cantus firmi* given at pitches other than that of the 'harmonic tonality' of the setting.

59 This is so, for example, in the case of the Magnificats in ModB. But later English polyphonic settings, which are usually based on the faburden, rarely do so; and tone 1, for example, can look very like tone 6.

60 This happens rather more rarely on the Continent. Dufay's hymn 'Audi, benigne conditor', for example, paraphrases the chant, a fifth up, in the contratenor, which thus cadences a fifth above the tenor. The plainchant verses in ModB, however, are given at the untransposed pitch. The evidential value of this is diminished by the fact that plainsongs are often (not always) quoted at the original level even when transposition is obviously required; but in this case the alternation may well have taken place at the notated pitch, which corresponds to the harmonic tonality of the polyphonic setting.

61 English settings of the Te Deum, both vocal and for organ, are particularly complex, for a double transposition was adopted to accommodate the different tessitura of certain verses. It is certain, nevertheless, that the faburden in these is 'sixths' faburden (i.e. in line with the harmonic tonality), since their tonal schemes correspond to those of the vocal settings by Taverner and Sheppard, which adopt the chant throughout. Since the organ and the vocal versions set odd and even verses respectively, it is clear in either case which plainsong verses are to be sung in a particular transposition. See my articles 'The Pitch of Early Tudor Organ Music', *Music and Letters* 51 (1970), 156–63, and 'The "Te Deum" in Late Medieval England', *Early Music* 5 (1978), 188–94.

much tonal manipulation of plainsong in later medieval music – Dufay's 'C major' harmonization of 8th-tone plainsongs in his Mass 'Ecce ancilla domini' is an instructive example – but these are devices of musical structure using 'alien' *cantus firmi*, and not of the treatment of the liturgically appropriate plainsong for functional use.

As a general rule, notwithstanding the problem addressed in the preceding paragraph, plainsong *cantus firmi* were presented at the pitch at which they would have been sung monophonically, or at the octave above; transpositions represent an attempt to bring the *cantus firmus* within a reasonable vocal tessitura. It is usually maintained that medieval polyphonic notation, like that of plainsong, was purely relative;[62] but a number of factors suggest that, in the fifteenth century if not before, an approximation to an absolute standard was being gradually reached. One of these is the ever widening range of the music; another is the phenomenon of transposition itself (i.e. of the mode in which a piece is written, with consequent transposition of the *cantus firmus* if present); the use of extreme low or high written tessitura (with the possible consequence of *conscious* upward or downward transposition by singers); and the use of instruments, the organ being potentially the strongest influence on the establishment of absolute pitch. A study of organ alternation reveals that, in certain contexts at least, the conventions of written pitch were manipulated to ensure a suitable pitch-level for the alternating plainsong.

It is not known for certain when the practice of organ alternation arose, but there seems to be definite evidence from the early fourteenth century.[63] Written repertories arise only at the very end of that century or in the early fifteenth. The Faenza Codex of *c.* 1400 includes settings of the Kyrie and Gloria of the Mass, of the 'Benedicamus domino', of the hymn 'Ave maris stella', and perhaps of other liturgical tenors as yet unidentified. Some German fragments, and a few items in the Buxheim Organ Book, are the principal evidence from the fifteenth century. For the most part (and certainly in the case of the Faenza and Buxheim manuscripts) these were not documents to be used at the desk of a chamber organ, even a small positif. The main contents are secular, and the liturgical items are included only for the purposes of demonstration and practice, possibly on a clavichord with pedals.[64] Liturgical organ music was mostly improvised, largely no doubt with the aid of formulae derived from such textbooks as Paumann's *Fundamentum organisandi* (of which the Buxheim manuscript itself contains three different versions).

62 See, for example, R. Bowers, 'The Performing Pitch of English 15th-Century Church Polyphony', *Early Music* 7 (1980), 21–8.

63 There is a vivid description in Dante's *Purgatorio*, ix. 142–5, of what seems to be *alternatim* performance of the Te Deum.

64 See my article, 'Two Polyphonic Istampite of the Fourteenth Century', *Early Music* 18 (1990), 371–80.

The theory of organ participation was that it occupied the place either of one side of the choir or of the cantors (or rulers). This seems to be reflected in two of the favourite choices for the location of the medieval organ, namely the north side of the choir and on the *pulpitum* or screen at its entrance from which the solo parts of the responsorial chants at Mass could be sung.[65] This is not to say that the function was necessarily determined by the location, however, and in small churches, and in the chapels of large churches, the location will have been largely a matter of convenience. Such instruments were usually very small, but relatively large instruments also existed;[66] presumably they too were used for alternation, as well as for performing the preludes, transcriptions of vocal polyphony, and variations on liturgical themes that were beginning to invade the church organ repertory.[67]

When the organ was used as a substitute for liturgical chant, the words associated with it were apparently lost, although there is evidence from the early sixteenth century onwards that the liturgical texts might be audibly recited, or even sung, during the instrumental music.[68] But this probably represents a reforming tendency that culminated with the Council of Trent, and we must assume that prior to 1500, and not infrequently thereafter, the performance of the chant itself was a sufficient guarantee of acceptability. For that reason genuinely liturgical organ music is almost invariably a setting of the appropriate chant or of a surrogate such as the faburden, though the technique by which it is represented might be somewhat allusive.[69]

The basic method, as found in the Faenza manuscript, was simply to quote the plainsong, usually untransposed,[70] in the lower part, each note having the value of a

---

65 F.Ll. Harrison, *Music in Medieval Britain* (London, 1958), pp. 204, 207, 209–14.

66 A number of large instruments are described in the annotations to the treatises of Henri Arnaut de Zwolle (Paris, BN, lat. MS 7295, fols. 131v–135r (see the edition by G. Le Cerf and E.R. Labande, *Instruments de musique du XVe siècle: les traités d'Henri-Arnaut de Zwolle et de divers anonymes*, Paris, 1932).

67 For example the settings of 'Da pacem' in Schlick's *Tabulaturen etlicher Lobgesang* (Mainz, 1512).

68 See E. Higginbottom, *The Liturgy and French Classical Organ Music*, 2 vols. (PhD dissertation, University of Cambridge, 1978/9), vol. 1, pp. 54–6, citing the *Acta Capitulorum Generalium Ordinis Praedicatorum*, 9 vols. (Rome, 1898–), vol. 4, pp. 136 and 261 (for the years 1515, 1536). The legislation was repeated at the Council of Milan (1565) and in the *Caeremoniale Episcoporum* (Rome, 1600).

69 The use of the faburden as *cantus firmus* is frequent in English *alternatim* organ music for the Office. It is possible that the vocal verses in such cases should be sung in improvised faburden rather than in unharmonized plainsong. Ornamentation of the *cantus firmus*, described by Morley as 'breaking the plainsong', was equally applicable to a faburden (see note 72).

70 The two settings of 'Benedicamus domino', untitled in the manuscript, transpose the second-mode chant up a fourth (CMM 57, nos. 25 and 48). The melody used was one of those proper to the Office rather than to the Mass (though there was some degree of interchangeability in this regard); these settings are therefore more likely to represent the versicle than the response 'Deo (dicamus) gratias'.

brevis in the chosen mensuration, which normally varied from one section to another in an *alternatim* work. The same technique is used in the earliest German sources; but the Magnificat tones were usually handled more freely (only isolated verses, or pairs of verses, exist from the fifteenth century), and in the Buxheim book we find freely ornamented *cantus firmi*, for example in *alternatim* settings of the 'Salve regina'.[71]

The rhythmically free treatment of plainsong gained ground in Germany, Italy, and France in the early sixteenth century. English composers, however, were wedded to an isochronous presentation: even where the *cantus firmus* is highly ornamented or based on the faburden (or both), it proves to consist essentially of a series of notes of identical value.[72] The plainsong could be quoted in any voice of the texture and is often transposed; the choice of basic note-value ranged from the minim to the dotted breve. This, with the fact that an *alternatim* cycle may begin and end with the organ, seems to disprove the notion that the plainsong verses should derive their speed from the adjacent polyphonic presentation.[73]

The transpositions of the plainsong in the organ repertory sometimes stem from nothing more than a desire for technical variety, as witness the successive settings of the Marian Offertory 'Felix namque' by the English sixteenth-century composer Thomas Preston.[74] But at other times the variants seem to be designed to accommodate the practical requirements of the singers of the plainsong verses. The existence of two different transposing schemes in English settings of the Te Deum appears to relate to different sizes and hence pitch-standards in the contemporary organ.[75] The same is true of continental settings of the 'Salve regina' for the evening antiphon-ceremony. The settings in the Buxheim manuscript are pitched on D,

71 *Das Buxheimer Orgelbuch*, ed. B.A. Wallner, 3 vols., *Das Erbe deutscher Musik* 37–9, (Kassel, 1958–9), nos. 72 and 73. Of the four Magnificat verses given in the MS the first, no. 24, bears a resemblance to verses 1, 4, 7, and 10 of Dufay's 'Magnificat octavi toni' (*Opera omnia* 5, no. 34); but this is probably a coincidence due to the use of a similar compositional procedure (although with the substitution of Contratenor for fauxbourdon). In no sense can this organ version be described as a 'source' of Dufay's composition. The second Magnificat, no. 77, sets the first verse and the third, 'Quia respexit', on the basis of approximately one note of the plainsong to each perfect *brevis*.

72 Within each note in the chosen duration the plainsong pitch had to be sounded at least once, with certain exceptions: see T. Morley, *A Plaine and Easy Introduction* (London, 1597), p. 96. The principle is not observed in the sole surviving English organ Magnificat: *Early Tudor Organ Music: I*, ed. J. Caldwell, Early English Church Music 6 (London, 1966), no. 4.

73 As proposed by Mother Thomas More, 'The Performance of Plainsong in the Late Middle Ages', *Proceedings of the Royal Musical Association* 92 (1965/6), 121–34, a valuable pioneering study nevertheless.

74 London, BL, Add. MS 29996, fols. 53v–60r (*Early Tudor Organ Music: II*, ed. D. Stevens, Early English Church Music 10 (London, 1969), nos. 13–19), perhaps for the daily Lady-Mass (another setting in this collection, no. 12, does not belong to this set).

75 See my article 'The Pitch of Early Tudor Organ Music'.

corresponding to the untransposed plainsong.[76] The limited available evidence suggests that the standard contemporary organ sounded a tone or minor third higher than at the present day. Later settings, such as that of Arnolt Schlick, are in G minor or occasionally A minor. Schlick's own information suggests that his favoured type of organ, descending to written *F*, sounded a tone or so lower than today's standard.[77] The two pieces of evidence, taken together, suggest that in terms of modern pitch a *finalis* on *f* or thereabouts would be appropriate.

The point about these correlations is not that they need have been exact or of universal applicability. It is sufficient that they would have yielded a performable pitch-level for the accompanying vocalists. In the case of the 'Salve regina' settings the assumption has been, first, that conventions of vocal performance did not greatly change over (say) 50 years or more, and, second, that in the early sixteenth century the type of organ preferred by Schlick was widely adopted, at least throughout the Holy Roman Empire. Both assumptions seem reasonable. What is perhaps surprising is that the evidence, if it is reliable, suggests a plainsong range rather higher (i.e. *eb–f′*) than would seem natural or comfortable for the average male voice.[78] But that is no reason to reject it. It is precisely by means of unexpected results such as this that advances in understanding are possible.

As it happens, a similarly high range emerges in connection with the Te Deum transpositions mentioned above. What is more, the assumed correlations also work reasonably well for the surviving vocal polyphonic settings.[79] In England, a preference for a high plainsong tessitura might be related to the move already mentioned from 'thirds' to 'sixths' faburden. For that matter three-part faburden, rather than monophonic plainsong, might conceivably have been employed in alternation with the organ. Whatever we may choose to make of the evidence, it seems clear that standardized organ pitch in the late Middle Ages had a strong bearing on the performing pitch of plainsong and on the written conventions of vocal polyphony. Plainsong was not normally transposed in writing, and there was

---

76 *Buxheimer Orgelbuch*, nos. 72–3.

77 These calculations were first published by A.J. Ellis in the *Journal of the Royal Society of Arts* (March and April, 1880); the 'Buxheim' pitch was suggested by pipe-lengths of historic organs as given in M. Praetorius, *Syntagma musicum*, vol. 2, and that of Schlick's favoured type of instrument by the information given in his *Spiegel der Orgelmacher und Organisten* (Mainz, 1511). The calculations were disputed by A. Mendel (see the reprint of his and Ellis's articles, *Studies in the History of Musical Pitch* (Amsterdam, 1968)), but subsequently reaffirmed (as regards Schlick) by W.R. Thomas and J.J.K. Rhodes in *The Organ Yearbook* 2 (1971), pp. 58–76.

78 This range, expanded outwards to something like *Bb–g′* in modern terms, is the outcome of the suggestions made by Schlick in his *Spiegel* for the written pitch-level of organ pieces presenting *cantus firmi* in various modes (see table in the Appendix on pp. 30–1).

79 See my article 'The "Te Deum" in late Medieval England', where the question of alternation of the organ with vocal polyphony is also considered.

no absolute necessity for a purely monophonic item to be related in pitch to an external standard. Choirs devoted entirely to plainsong, as many monastic communities were, may have had little or no contact with polyphony of any kind, and hence no concept of such a standard. But the evidence from some kinds of organ music, and from the unusually precise indications of Schlick, is that in certain quarters at least the preference was for a pitch corresponding to the tenor part in polyphony, and that this had been forced upwards by the early sixteenth century to accommodate a distinctly lower bass-line.[80]

v

Enough has been said to establish the point that questions of plainsong performance cannot be divorced from the conventions of liturgical polyphonic composition. Even when not based on plainsong, church polyphony was governed by norms of modality that place it within a comparable framework. The convention of alternation absolutely necessitated an accommodation between the two media in the sphere of rhythm and pitch. Plainsong shadowed the developing mensural system without ever quite belonging to it. It requires the greatest tact to bring it into line with contemporary mensural practice, but a useful rule-of-thumb would be to relate each note to one half or one third of the prevailing *mensura*.[81] To the *mensura* later corresponded the *tactus*, a double motion of the hand; and it does not seem sensible to relate every plainsong note to so long a duration, though it might be done for chants of special solemnity or gravity. This rule gains support from a good deal of early fifteenth-century polyphonic writing, from the measured plainsongs quoted above, and from the later frequent equation of the plainsong note with the *semibrevis* of *tempus imperfectum diminutum*.

The practice of alternation with polyphony, whether for organ or for voices, is even more significant as regards pitch. Though the evidence is unambiguous only from the early sixteenth century (if then), it does convey a message which it would be unwise to disregard, at least for the period from the early fifteenth century on. We shall not be far wrong if we posit, for the *finales* of each of the eight modes in

---

80 The general question of the evolution of vocal ranges is immensely complex and far beyond the scope of this essay. An attempt has been made by Bowers in the article cited above (note 62), and subsequently in the *Journal of the Royal Musical Association* 112 (1987), 38–76, to address the question as regards England, but it needs to be looked at from a European perspective.

81 This is in itself a complex topic. For the late thirteenth century the theoretical possibility of treating the *longa perfecta* as the *mensura* provides our suggestion with its rationale; if the *brevis recta* is treated as the *mensura*, that would correspond to the single plainsong note as Jerome says. In the fourteenth and early fifteenth centuries the *mensura* is normally the *brevis*; later in the fifteenth century it is so in diminution, but is otherwise the *semibrevis*.

turn, the following pitches at $a' = 440$: f, f, g or d (depending on the range of chant), $g, eb, ab, f,$ and bb or f. As already indicated, the outside limits of vocal range required on these assumptions would be in the region of $Bb–g'$; and for a lengthy chant of exceptional range a change of pitch-level could always be accommodated, at least if polyphonic practice is any guide.[82]

But even beyond the scouring of polyphonic practice for its information-content, the modern performer of late medieval plainsong, having located and transcribed the available versions nearest to the period and location of the desired reconstruction, will do well to ponder on the ethos of contemporary composed polyphony. Liturgical music was a widely diversified yet fundamentally unified whole, and its polyphonic manifestation is an extrapolation into the sphere of 'multiple harmony' of the underlying presumptions of plainsong composition. The singers of *canto figurato* had been trained in *canto plano*, and they carried with them into the higher sphere the very foundations of their musical consciousness.

82 In addition to the conventions of English descant already mentioned we may note the dual transposition system of English Te Deum settings (see the article mentioned in note 79), and the change of pitch-level apparently signalled in the last, incomplete, verse of the fragmentary setting (presumably by Thomas Preston) of the Sequence 'Fulgens praeclara'. In my dissertation (British Museum Additional Manuscript 29996: Transcription and Commentary (D.Phil. dissertation, Univ. of Oxford, 1965), vol. 2, pp. 119–20) I argued that the last two chords of this verse were a make-shift cadence by a later scribe and that in reality the completed verse would have ended with a cadence on *B*, corresponding to a new transposition down a 7th (after 12 verses based on the plainsong down a 4th). The curious reader may verify the reasonableness of this argument by consulting the work in *Early Tudor Organ Music: II*, pp. 31–7, and comparing it with the plainsong on pp. 131–2.

Appendix: Choice of pitch-level for *cantus firmi* after Schlick (1511, chapter 2)

A: on organ descending to F^1

Mode[2]	Finalis[3]	Transposition	Example	Range[4]	Modern equivalent
I	g	up 4th	Salve regina	d–g′	c–f′
			Ave maris stella	f–g′	eb–f′
			Gaudeamus	f–f′	eb–e′b
			Vita sanctorum[5]	f–f′	eb–e′b
(II	g	up 4th	—	d–f′	c–e′b)
III	a	up 4th	Pange lingua	g–g′	f–f′
			A solis ortus	g–g′	f–f′
			Hostis Herodes	g–g′	f–f′
	e	at pitch	higher-pitched chant	(e–e′	d–d′)[6]
(IV	a	up 4th	—	d–f′	c–e′b)[7]
V	f	at pitch	—	(e–f′	d–e′b)
VI	bb	up 4th	—	(f–f′	eb–e′b)
VII	g	at pitch	—	(f–g′	eb–f)
(VIII	? c′	up 4th	—	(g–g′	f–f′)
	or ? g	at pitch	—	(d–d′	c–c′))
(VI)	f/c′	(at pitch)	Laus tibi Christe[8]	(c–a′	Bb–g′)
			Psallite regi[8]	(c–a′	Bb–g′)
(VII/VIII)	g	(at pitch)	Benedicta sit semper[9]	(c–g′	Bb–f′)
			Et in terra summun[9]	(d–a′	c–g′)

B: on organ sounding a 5th lower[10]

Mode[2]	Finalis[3]	Transposition	Example	Range[4]	Modern equivalent
I	d	at pitch	—	(A–d′	c–f′)
III	e	at pitch[11]	—	(d–d′	eb–e′b)
VII	c	down 5th	—	(Bb–c′	db–e′b)

1 On this organ the pipes sounding F (manuals and pedals) were approximately $6\frac{1}{2}$ feet long, sounding $E\flat$ or slightly lower depending on assumptions made about scaling and wind-pressure.

2 Bracketed modes are not mentioned by Schlick: details are speculative.

3 Schlick's discussion does not refer to key-signatures, which are not used in tabulature; in standard notation transposition up a 4th, and the untransposed mode V, would call for one flat; the transposed mode V would normally call for two.

4 Where no specific example is given, a standard range is given in brackets.

5 Presumably Melody 423 in *Die Hymnen I*, ed. B. Stäblein, Monumenta Monodica Medii Aevi 1 (Kassel and Basel, 1956).

6 Not many mode III chants rise above *d'*; Schlick is thinking more in terms of tessitura than overall range.

7 Antiphons in the transposed mode IV on *a* would of course require no further transposition; similar considerations apply, *mutatis mutandis*, to other transposed modes.

8 These two very similar Sequences of exceptional range may be thought of as being in mode VI, initially untransposed, subsequently transposed. Schlick does not suggest any change from the written pitch, but it would have been possible to set the 'untransposed' section on *b♭* as for standard mode VI, reverting to performance at pitch or down a tone for the 'transposed' section. Contemporary versions may be seen in the *Graduale Pataviense* (see note 25 above), fols. 238r–239v ('Laus tibi, Christe, qui es creator', for S. Mary Magdalene), and 249r–250v ('Psallite regi', for the Beheading of S. John the Baptist).

9 These are considered by Schlick to be in mode VIII, reverting to I. They are however firmly in the *tetrardus*, but with *b* flats here and there. One of the advantages of the *F* organ for Schlick was that such chants could be played at pitch, retaining the mi/fa opposition at *b/b♭* rather than transferring it to the less convenient *e/e♭* or *f♯/f♮*. See *Graduale Pataviense*, fols. 209v–210v ('Benedicta semper sancta sit', Sequence for Trinity Sunday), and fols. 176v–177r (Gloria 'in summis festivitatibus'). The setting of the Gloria by Hans Buchner (*Hans Buchner; Samtliche Orgelwerke*, ed. J.H. Schmidt, 2 vols. (Das Erbe deutscher Musik 54–5, Frankfurt, 1974), vol. 1, no. 8) is down a tone on *F*; Buchner's choice of location for his *cantus firmi* requires further careful study, as does that of Isaac in the *Choralis Constantinus*.

10 The note *c* sounded at the same pitch as the *F* of Schlick's preferred organ, i.e. a major 6th below modern pitch. However, if '4-foot' stops (i.e. $3\frac{1}{4}$-foot at *c*) were used as the foundation, the pitch would be a minor 3rd higher and Schlick's recommendations would apply. His preference for the *F* organ was partly because it necessitated fewer cadences on *a*, G sharp being too high in chords of E major to make a satisfactory leading note (or 3rd of a final chord).

11 But the organist was to transpose down a tone, presumably to avoid the use of G sharps; perhaps the same applied to high-pitched mode III chants when played on the *F* organ.

2

NOTATED PERFORMANCE PRACTICES IN PARISIAN CHANT MANUSCRIPTS OF THE THIRTEENTH CENTURY

MICHEL HUGLO

Historians of music often seem to show little interest in the period which stretches from the birth of Parisian polyphony to the beginnings of the *Ars nova* in the first decades of the fourteenth century. What is more, specialists in the musical interpretation of neumatic notations are generally reticent on this period, though it encompasses the appearance, the development, and the decline of square notation on a staff of four red lines. In fact, however, it is in this very notation that the first attempts at discant and Parisian organum were transcribed.

The oldest treatise on Parisian organum (now in the Vatican Library), written and notated about 1170 using red staves traced freehand,[1] gives more than two hundred examples of improvized organum as a function of the melodic context of the *cantus*. This is a treatise that notates its examples using connected points written by a cursive hand: it is not a liturgical book. The oldest examples of liturgical pieces in two voices appear in a Parisian *Mariale*[2] which must have been written in the reign of Philippe-Auguste: the notation of the discant is composed of linked small squares analogous to those found in the contemporaneous chant books of Paris, Chartres, Autun, and elsewhere.

In the course of the thirteenth century, the dimensions of the *nota quadrata* and of the red four-line staff are gradually enlarged, and easily allow reading at a distance:

---

1 Vatican City, Biblioteca Apostolica Vaticana, MS Ottoboni 3025: colour facsimile by Irving Godt and Benito Rivera, 'The Vatican Organum Treatise', in *Gordon Athol Anderson, 1929–1981; In Memoriam von seinen Studenten, Freunden und Kollegen*, Musicological Studies 39, 2 vols. (Henryville, PA, 1984), vol. 2, pp. 264/1, 264/10. Facsimile of fol. 46 in Craig Wright, *Music and Ceremony at Notre Dame of Paris, 500–1500* (Cambridge, 1989);, p. 337, figure 27.
2 Paris, BN, Nouv. acq. lat. MS 186: description with facsimile in Michel Huglo, 'Les débuts de la polyphonie à Paris: les premiers *organa* parisiens', in *Aktuelle Fragen der musikbezogenen Mittelalterforschung*, Forum musicologicum 3 (Winterthur, 1982), pp. 122–34 and plates 5–6.

the quarto-format chant book, and even more clearly the noted choir breviary in folio format,[3] can be read by three or four singers, as can be verified in the miniatures of many psalters[4] and books of polyphony of the thirteenth century, such as that found in W2.[5] The *cantus supra librum* became a concrete reality.

At the end of the anonymous Vatican treatise, the author gives as examples three liturgical pieces in organum: the Alleluia-verse *Hic Martinus* for the feast of St Martin (11 November); the responsory *Operibus sanctis* for St Nicholas (6 December) which appears in the liturgy of St Maur-des-Fossés[6] but not in that of the cathedral of Notre-Dame; and finally the responsory *Petre amas me* which is found both at Notre-Dame and St Maur (formerly St Pierre-des-Fossés) at the end of a nocturn.[7]

In the notation of these pieces in organum we can see a distinction between virga (written cursively **◣**) and punctum, but also the isolation of these virgas in the tenor by means of vertical lines: in other words, a first attempt at modal notation. On the other hand, the plicas deriving from two liquescent neumes (the *epiphonus* and the *cephalicus*[8]) seem not to have been used. Finally, the direct, or *custos*, which indicates at the line-end the placement of the first note of the next line, is not found in any of these examples, although it had been used in staffless Aquitanian and Beneventan notations since the tenth century.

This absence of the custos in the manuscripts of Parisian polyphony before the fourteenth century is not inexplicable. In fact, the custos was not used in the square notation of manuscripts copied north of the Loire before the middle of the thirteenth century because this sign was unknown to the copyists and cantors who transcribed liturgical chant into square notes on staves.

Indeed, a rapid survey of the notated manuscripts of the dioceses of Sens and Paris shows that no custos by an original hand is found in any Parisian manuscript from the end of the twelfth century until the end of the fourteenth.

---

3 Paris, BN, lat. MS 15182: see Victor Leroquais, *Les bréviaires manuscrits des bibliothèques publiques de France*, 6 vols. (Paris, 1934), vol. 3, p. 260.

4 Günther Haseloff, *Die Psalterillustration im 13. Jahrhundert* (n.p., 1938). The word 'ALLELUIA' can be read on a book placed on a lectern before two cantors in copes, drawn in a French manuscript of the thirteenth century (US-BAw 123, fol. 214v): see Lilian W. Randall, *Medieval and Renaissance Manuscripts in the Walters Art Gallery, Volume I: France 875–1420* (Baltimore, MD, 1989), p. 102.

5 D-W Helmstedt 1099. Facsimile in Luther Dittmer, *Wolfenbüttel 1099 (1206)*, Publications of Medieval Music Manuscripts 2 (New York, 1960).

6 *CAO*, vol. 2, no. 150a; vol. 4, no. 7324.

7 See the comparative table in Huglo, 'Les débuts' (above, note 2), p. 102.

8 David Hiley, 'The Plica and Liquescence', in *Gordon A. Anderson, 1929–1981*, vol. 2, pp. 379–91; Mark Everist, 'Theoretical Presentation of Plicae', in *French 13th-Century Polyphony in the British Library* (London, 1988), p. 14, table 1.

Notated manuscripts of Paris and Sens, twelfth to fifteenth centuries

The dates in the following list are established according to *Le Graduel romain. Edition critique par les moines de Solesmes*, vol. 2, *Les sources* (Solesmes, 1957); Leroquais, *Les Bréviaires manuscrits* (see note 3); and, for decorated manuscripts, Robert Branner, *Manuscript Painting in Paris during the Reign of St. Louis* (Berkeley, CA, 1977).

Twelfth century
  F–Pn 17296: Antiphoner of Saint-Denis; facsimile in *CAO* 2, plate XII
  F–Pn 12044: Antiphoner of St Maur-des-Fossés

Twelfth century (late)
  F-Psg 93: Missal
  F-Pn 13254: Gradual of St Maur-des-Fossés

Thirteenth century (early and first half)
  F-Pn 1112: Missal from about 1225;[9] facsimile in Craig Wright, *Music and Ceremony at Notre Dame of Paris, 500–1500* (Cambridge, 1989), p. 56, figure 9
  F-Pn 15616: Missal
  F-Psg 1259: Missal

Thirteenth century (middle)
  I-BA (Bari), San Nicola MS 1: Missal from the Sainte-Chapelle du Palais, executed in the 'Bari atelier' (Branner, p. 229); facsimile in René-Jean Hesbert, ed., *Le prosaire de la Sainte-Chapelle*, Monumenta musicae sacrae 1 (Macon, 1954)
  F-Pn 1107: Missal of Saint-Denis, after 1254, executed in the atelier of the 'Cholet group' (Branner, p. 228; facsimile in *MGG*, vol. 4, cols. 1307–10)
  F-Pn 9441: Missal from the same atelier at the famous I-Fl Plut. 29.1; that is, the atelier of Johannes Grusch (Branner, p. 222), but notated by a different scribe[9]

Thirteenth century (without further precision)
  F-Pn 748: Breviary
  B-Br 1799 and 4334: processionals[10]
  F-Pn 13253: Gradual of St Maur-des-Fossés

9 Collated for the edition by Edward H. Roesner, *The Magnus Liber Organi of Notre Dame*, vol. 1: *The Parisian Organa Tripla and Quadrupla* (Monaco, in press).
10 These two processionals were dated at the end of the fifteenth century by Joseph Van den Gheyn in his *Catalogue des manuscrits de la Bibliothèque Royale de Belgique*, 13 vols. (Brussels, 1901), vol. 1, p. 402, on account of the foundation of bishop Guillaume Charretier (d. 1472) added at the end; they were reassigned to the thirteenth century by Victor Leroquais, *Le Bréviaire de Philippe le Bon* (Paris, 1929), p. 232. I owe this reference to Rebecca Baltzer's April 1985 paper 'Performance Practice: The Notre Dame Calendar', to appear in *Das musikgeschichtliche Ereignis 'Notre-Dame'*, ed. Wulf Arlt and Fritz Reckow (Wolfenbüttel, forthcoming).

F-Pn 14194, fols. 169–212: antiphoner (fragmentary)

F-Pn 15182: choir Breviary, folio format[9]

F-Pn 15615: Missal:[9] executed in the 'Life of St Denis atelier' (Branner, p. 225)

Thirteenth century (second half)

F-Pn 830: Missal of St Germain l'Auxerrois, executed in the 'Bari atelier' (Branner, p. 229); the custos, formed like a 2 with an ascending tail, seems to have been added in the fifteenth century

Thirteenth century (end)

F-Pa 197: Gradual of St Victor, between 1270 and 1297

F-Pn 1028: Breviary of Sens

F-Pn 13255: Gradual of St Maur-des-Fossés

Fourteenth century:

F-Pn 1337: Gradual of Paris[9]

F-Pa 203: Missal; facsimile in Solange Corbin, *Repertoire de manuscrits médiévaux contenant des notations musiciales*, vol. 3 (Paris, 1974), plate XLI

F-Pn, nal 2649: Missal, first quarter of the fourteenth century; summary description in *Bibliothèque de l'Ecole des Chartes* 130 (1972), 511–12

GB-Lbl, Add. 16905: Missal; facsimile in *Paléographie musicale*, vol. 3, plate 204A

GB-L Victoria and Albert museum: Missal of Saint-Denis

F-Pn 1337: Gradual[9]

F-Pn 10482: Breviary[9]

F-Pn 110: Gradual

F-Pm 411: Missal of Notre-Dame, from around 1380; facsimile in *Paléographie musicale*, vol. 3, plate 207

F-Pu 705: Missal; the custos has been added by a very recent hand

Fifteenth century

F-P Arch, nat, L 499: coronation Mass for Henry VI Plantagenet at Notre-Dame in December 1431; facsimile in Wright, *Music and Ceremony*, p. 210, figure 20

F-Pa 204: Missal of the Confraternity of St Sebastian; facsimile in Wright, *Music and Ceremony*, p. 136, figure 15, and p. 137, figure 16

US-BAw 302: Missal, copied probably from F-Pn 15615

These last two missals are related by their musical variants, but also by the fact that they are the only missals among those mentioned here which preserve the offertory-prosula *Laetemur gaudiis*,[11] a vestige of the *Officium stultorum* of January 1 at the

---

11 *AH* 49, p. 313, no. 615; see David G. Hughes, 'The Sources of *Christus manens*', in Jan LaRue et al., eds., *Aspects of Medieval and Renaissance Music: A Birthday Offering to Gustave Reese* (New York, 1966), pp. 423–34; Wulf Arlt, *Ein Festoffizium des Mittelalters aus Beauvais*, 2 vols. (Cologne, 1970), Editionsband, pp. 5–6.

cathedral of Notre-Dame which bishop Odo of Sully retained in the liturgy of the Chapter by his decree of 1198.

About 1233, a few years after the copying of the Florence manuscript in the workshop of Jean Grusch, Humbert de Romans, the General Master of the Dominican Order, caused to be drawn up the archetype Codex of all the liturgical books of his order. The preface to the antiphoner describes in detail the norms for notation, and insists on the custos by describing it, in the absence of any appropriate term to designate it:

Puncta enim directiva, posita in fine linearum ad inveniendum ubi prima nota sequentis lineae debet inchoari, diligenter a notatoribus observetur.[12]

[The indicator point, placed at the end of each line in order to find where the first note of the next line is to begin, must be carefully observed (in the transcription) by the notators.]

This recommendation stands out more clearly in the light of the antiphoner of the Franciscans, drawn up in Italy shortly before that of the Dominicans, which is entirely silent on this 'detail' of staff notation, since the custos had been in general use in southern Italy since the tenth century. It was the Dominicans, then, who retailed this sign throughout Europe with their liturgical books, while the churches of the secular orders and of the Benedictines did not adopt it in their monophonic and polyphonic books until the fifteenth century or later. There is, however, one exception among the polyphonic collections of the thirteenth and early fourteenth centuries: the Darmstadt manuscript,[13] which regularly uses the custos at the ends of lines; the manuscript comes from the Dominican convent of Wimpfen.

The Anonymous IV of Bury St Edmunds, who at the end of the thirteenth century describes the staves in books of 'ecclesiastical chant', seems to suggest that, in books of polyphony, the four-line staff reserved for the tenor included a sign at the end, 'ut in canto plano, propter cognitionem primi puncti alterius lineae

12 Michel Huglo, 'Règlement du XIIIe siècle pour la transcription des livres notés', in *Festschrift Bruno Stäblein zum 70. Geburtstag*, ed. Martin Ruhnke (Kassel, 1967), p. 124. The complete text is presented below in the Appendix to this chapter (pp. 43–4). For the dating of the Dominican regulations I have adopted that proposed by Kenneth Levy, 'A Dominican Organum Duplum', *JAMS* 27 (1974), 185, note 14.

13 Darmstadt, Hessische Landes- und Hochschulbibliothek, MS 3471, described in Gilbert Reaney, *Manuscripts of Polyphonic Music*, RISM B IV 1 (Munich–Duisburg, 1966), pp. 75–9; facsimile of fol. 6v in Heinrich Besseler and Peter Gülke, *Schriftbild der mehrstimmigen Musik*, Musikgeschichte in Bildern, Band III: Musik des Mittelalters und der Renaissance, Lieferung 5 (Leipzig, 1976), table 16. It would be interesting to extend the study of this matter to include all the manuscripts in black notation of the Ars Antiqua and the Ars Nova, using the lists given in Everist (above, note 8), pp. 64–5, and particularly in Hendrik van der Werf, *Integrated Directory of Organa, Clausulae, and Motets of the Thirteenth Century* (Rochester, NY, 1989), pp. 159–60.

quatuor linearum'[14] ['as in plainsong, for the identification of the first note of the next system of four lines'].

It is true that the standard custos of the Dominicans looks more like a virga than a punctum, but the prescription of 1255 had no intention of descending to these realms of subtle distinction of technical vocabulary. Any classification of the variety of custos-forms encountered in the thirteenth and fourteenth centuries must begin with the virga-form, as follows:

Vertical custos
    downward tail   ❚ ❚ ❚
    upward tail   ♩ ♩♩♩ ♩ ♩
Oblique custos   ♩♩ ♩ ♩
    reversed   ↳
    beaked (rare in northern Europe) ⟋
Other various custodes   ■ ⬙ ♩
Late forms   ⟆ ⟲ ⟁

The Dominican notators who follow the directives of the 1254 regulations habitually use as custos a vertical virga with a downward tail: this virga–custos is sometimes written a little beyond the staff, in the side margin, probably to avoid confusion with the final virga of the same staff.

The first form of virga with ascending tail is never used in Parisian manuscripts as a custos, but it is sometimes used as a long ascending plica, as, for example, in the Bamberg and Montpellier manuscripts. Franco admits this form along with the usual rounded form:

Plica longa ascendens est quaedam quadrangularis figura, solum tractum gerens a parte dextra ascendentem, ut hic ◢, vel magis proprie duos, quorum dexter longior est sinistro, ut hic ◗.[15]

[The long ascending plica is a certain quadrangular figure, bearing a single line ascending on the right, like this ◢, or more properly two, of which that on the right is longer than that on the left, like this ◗.]

This form was not created by the notators of *cantus mensurabilis* to whom Franco is speaking, but was borrowed from plainsong. The square plica, indeed, can be seen

---

14 Fritz Reckow, *Der Musiktraktat des Anonymus 4*, Beihefte zum Archiv für Musikwissenschaft 4, vol. 1: Edition (Wiesbaden, 1967), p. 60. The phrase *sicut in cantu plano*, coming from an English author from Bury St Edmunds, would suggest an examination of manuscripts of plainsong from the British Isles, since the Sarum chant books had been renewed at the beginning of the century.

15 *Franconis de Colonia, Ars cantus mensurabilis*, ed. Gilbert Reaney and André Gilles, CSM 18 (n.p., 1984), pp. 41–2.

as a sign of liquescence in F-Pn 15615, particularly on the word *alleluya* (fols. 16v, 19v, 304, 333, etc.), and also in the related fifteenth-century missal US-BAw 302; it is seen also, but rarely, in the noted breviary Pn 15182; finally, it is found in the genealogy according to Matthew in the noted missal Pn 9441, on the diphthong of *autem*. Here as elsewhere, Franco is speaking of the signs ('figures of notes') used in his time at Paris, though he does say that the normal ascending plica is preferable.

It is not surprising to encounter in noted Parisian missals the occasional use of other figures normally used in the notation of measured music, such as the ligatures ‌ for the *clivis* or ‌ for the *torculus*: both are found in the noted missal of Notre-Dame Pn 9441. In fact, the *notatores* of the time – probably cantors – accomplished their task in the same fashion whether they were writing plainsong or polyphony.

The square notation of the twelfth century and later makes no distinction between simple notes which plot the melodic line and ornamental notes which indicate both a pitch and a particular mode of expression or embellishment. In the contemporaneous staff notation of the Low Countries and the Rhineland, the notators had succeeded in indicating these ornamental notes on the staff: there was no confusion for the singers. In square notation, on the contrary, the group ‌ can have several different meanings: simple *scandicus* (two *tractulus* plus *virga*), *scandicus* with emphasis on the second note (*virga* plus *pes*), *salicus*, or a quilismatic group. We might imagine that the cantors corrected from memory the lack of precision in the notation;[16] but would it not be better to acknowledge that the ornaments, so necessary to a 'horizontal' melodic line, became unperformable when a piece of plainsong became the foundation and underpinning of the 'vertical' edifice of organum?

The study of vertical strokes in plainchant is enhanced by the comparison of *cantus planus* and *cantus mensurabilis*. Vertical strokes measuring the lengths of silences appear at the same time as the signs indicating the duration of notes. It is, however, more difficult to determine the moment of arrival of the division-strokes that mark a pause or a simple breath between the phrases and sub-phrases of the ornate chants of the Mass or the Office. Shortly before 1254, the Franciscan regulations for transcription[17] prescribed a double vertical bar after the intonations of pieces, and at their ends to indicate the place where the choir is to resume. But nothing more.

The examination of Parisian noted missals and breviaries must be undertaken *in vivo* and not on microfilm, for these strokes are extremely fine. Division-strokes are

---

16 Michel Huglo, 'Tradition orale et tradition écrite dans la transmission des mélodies grégoriennes', in *Studien zu Tradition in der Musik: Kurt von Fischer zum 60. Geburtstag*, ed. Hans Heinrich Eggebrecht and Max Lütolf (Munich, 1973), pp. 31–42.
17 See the fifth paragraph of these regulations in the Appendix to this chapter, p. 44.

used regularly beginning in the fourteenth century. By the sixteenth century, however, printed chant books place them on the staff between words of the text: they have no deeper function than to facilitate the simultaneous reading of text and notation, and certainly do not indicate that a pause should be made after each word!

The study of notation leads naturally to the study of melodies: not in their original state, but in the state in which they are transmitted in the age of Parisian polyphony. In such an analysis it is important to consider only Parisian manuscripts to the exclusion of other witnesses of the plainsong tradition, even those generally considered 'the best witness of the Gregorian tradition'. In practice, such a comparison should include notated Parisian missals; naturally, the only surviving gradual from the cathedral of Paris;[18] and finally, the notated books of Saint Victor, even though, in the thirteenth century, the Augustinian canons of the Left Bank had distanced themselves from the canons of the Chapter of Notre-Dame.[19]

This comparison, which I have undertaken by using large comparative tables, reveals for the Parisian tradition as a whole a remarkable unity in the transmission of chant, from the end of the twelfth century through the middle of the fourteenth, and sometimes later still. One also discovers differences of detail, which, following the lead of philologists with their classical texts, we call 'variants'.

This term of 'variant' in medieval music is entirely justified for the chant tradition of the religious orders of the twelfth and thirteenth century which imposed on their cantors an extremely rigid norm of reference: the *exemplar*[20] or *correctorium* according to whose text it was obligatory to remove errors of transcription by means of a double or even triple collation. This painstaking work was to be accomplished by members of the order for themselves, and was not confided to lay persons, 'who corrupt almost everything they write or notate'.[21]

In the scriptorium of the cathedral of Paris – as indeed in other cathedrals – it is the canons who copied, on parchment purchased each year at the *foire du Lendit*, their own liturgical books, though they consigned to competent nearby decorators in the Cité or the Left Bank the decoration and illumination of the books. This

---

18 F-Pn 1337: this manuscript is the only known Parisian gradual. The rubrics for Lent (fols. 36–7, 38, 111, 113, 125) refer without question to the choir of canons of the *maioris ecclesiae beatae Mariae* with or without the bishop presiding in choir. For Maundy Thursday, a rubric (fol. 113v) refers to the *Liber processionum*. Naturally, all these rubrics could have been recopied for a gradual destined for one of the great parishes of Paris. Note that the vertical strokes, occupying two or three spaces of the staff, separate neumes of three, four, or five notes, but they are not used to mark the syllabic articulation or words.

19 See my report on an article by Margot M. Fassler ('Who was Adam of St. Victor? The Evidence of the Sequence Manuscripts', *JAMS* 37 (1984), 233–69) in *Scriptorium* 42 (1988), p. 44*, no. 169.

20 The term appears in the regulations of both the Franciscans and the Dominicans (see Appendix). It derives from the practice of producing university books by *pecia*.

21 See the Franciscan regulation, Appendix, no. 4b.

resulted in certain differences in quality between contemporaneous books: thus, for example, in the processionals at Brussels, Brussels 1799 is much more carefully made than Brussels 4334. At Notre-Dame, there is no *exemplar* or *correctorium*: the canons, who dedicated their entire lives to singing the liturgy, knew perfectly well how to choose one choirbook over another for recopying.

The case of noted missals and breviaries for the use of the parishes of Paris is somewhat different: these books evidently reproduce the usage of the cathedral, except for the insertion of a proper piece for a parochial confraternity,[22] but they are usually transcribed, decorated, and notated, by hired artisans, who were eager to get to the end of their task . . .

Nevertheless, the variants that arise from the comparison of Parisian noted missals cannot all be attributed to hired copyists. Certain variants are the result of the 'wear and tear' of time, for example variant no. 4 (see Example 2.1), which shows a reduction of the *tristropha* or of long values in general: likewise, the cadential *pressus* becomes a simple *clivis*. Other variants show the singer's natural propensity to fill in the disjunct intervals of a climacus (variant no. 1): this sort of 'filling the void' is extremely widespread beginning with the thirteenth century. Another interesting case is that of the repetition of a motive (variant no. 3) or indeed of a whole short phrase: thus in the Alleluia-verse *Diffusa est*, the Parisian gradual repeats as an echo a whole melisma of the composite 'neuma' on the word *beneDIxit* (variant no. 6). This final case poses the question of freedom of improvization in liturgical chant: would not a virtuoso cantor have given in to the pleasure of impressing his auditors by the emphatic repetition of a handsome motive in this melody?

The problem of the B-flat allows us to see the great distance that separates the surviving notated text from the chant as it was performed in the thirteenth century. There is no unanimity in the notation of B-flat, but it goes without saying that, though a notator may fail to mark it, the singer who has performed this piece for a lifetime will sing the B-flat without even looking at the notated book.

Variant no. 5 (Example 2.1) shows a case of transposition for the versus *Crucifixum* sung in two voices in many French and German churches from the twelfth century onward.[23] In Paris, the missal of Saint Germain l'Auxerrois (F-Pn

---

22   Thus the Parisian fourteenth-century missal, US-BAw 124, described in Rendall, *Medieval and Renaissance Manuscripts* (above, note 4), p. 179, no. 67, includes on fol. 283 the proper prosa *De sancto Fiacro* 'Lucernae novae specula' (*AH* 8, p. 128), which does not belong to the series of prosas used in the choir of Notre-Dame (US-BAw 302).

23   Michel Huglo, 'Structure et fonction de l'antienne de procession a deux voix Crucifixum', *Bericht über den Internationalen musikwissenschaftlichen Kongress Berlin 1974*, ed. Hellmut Kühn and Peter Nitsche (Kassel, 1980), pp. 90–2.

Example 2.1   Examples of variants

830) is the only manuscript which notates the versus on C, as in the Florence manuscript (fol. 25v) where the piece appears in three voices.

The examination of all these variants has led musicologists to compare the tenors of organa with the plainsong versions contained in Parisian manuscripts. For Heinrich Husmann, the study of liturgical and musical variants shows that the *Magnus liber organi* was composed by compiling Parisian sources, with the addition of peripheral influences; it thus reveals older portions along with more recent layers dating from around 1220.[24]

By re-examining the verse *Pascha nostrum* of the Eastern Alleluia and the pieces which Husmann attributed to composers foreign to Notre-Dame, Craig Wright

24 Heinrich Husmann, 'The Origin and Destination of the Magnus Liber Organi', *MQ* 59 (1963), 311–30; 'The Enlargement of the Magnus Liber Organi', *JAMS* 16 (1963), 176–203.

reached much more reserved conclusions: 'The variants are simply too numerous and too complex to draw a connection between the *Magnus liber organi* or sections of it to any one church among the three that originally constituted the Parisian chant tradition.'[25] He concludes that the *Magnus liber organi* was already constituted by the time of Leonin and that the Florence manuscript 'most closely agrees with the cycle of chants preserved in the plainsong manuscripts emanating from the cathedral'.[26] The critical edition of the *Magnus liber organi* by Edward H. Roesner,[27] which compares in detail each organum with the slightest variants in the Parisian sources, confirms this judgment, and at the same time opens a new path in the critical analysis and the interpretation of these variants.

In the Carolingian epoch, the transmission of the liturgical chants of each church was the unique responsibility of the cantor, or rather of two cantors, who gave each other mutual assistance in cases of memory lapses. After the creation of neumatic notation, the cantor's memory remained the indispensable link in the transmission of the repertory.

With Guido of Arezzo, inventor of staff notation, the training of a cantor was reduced from ten years to three months: nevertheless, the capacity of his memory was as prodigious as before, for he was to interpret, with all its nuances of style, a chant which he rehearsed from a notated book in the regular weekly *recordatio*. Still, he always kept a book with him in choir, in case of a memory lapse.

In the thirteenth century, the situation is different: the dimensions of books and of musical staves increase considerably;[28] the notated book '*ad memoriae subsidium*' has become a lectern-book. The Dominicans, in the middle of the century, include in their list of liturgical books the *pulpitarium*, the choir-book containing the portions sung by cantors as soloists. In the choirs of cathedrals and monasteries, the gradual and the antiphoner, readable from a distance, remain open during the office before the cantor who rules each side of the choir.

The transmission of chant reposes henceforth on the notated book: hence the precise recommendations to notators found in the prefaces to antiphoners and in musical treatises. However, at the beginning of the fourteenth century the *notator* is not listed among Parisian 'artisans du livre',[29] perhaps because that speciality is confused with that of the copyists, or perhaps with that of the cantor. This double

---

25 Wright, *Music and Ceremony*, p. 250.   26 Wright, *Music and Ceremony*, p. 258.

27 *The Magnus Liber Organi* (above, note 9), Commentary to the Plainchants.

28 Michel Huglo, *Les livres de chant liturgique*, Typologie des Sources du Moyen Age occidental 52 (Turnhout, 1988), pp. 92–5.

29 The ordering of university processions found in the *Livre de la nation de Picardie* (F-Psg 1655; 14th century) specifies that artisans engaged in book-manufacture – parchment-makers, copyists, illuminators, and binders – should follow the chancellor of the university.

function of cantor and notator, well known in the age of neumatic notation, may perhaps be the key which will allow us to explain the diversity and the 'personality' of these variants fixed on parchment as witnesses of the art of chant in the age of the Parisian polyphony of the thirteenth century.

(Translation by Thomas Forrest Kelly)

Appendix: Thirteenth-century regulations concerning the transcription of chant books

Reproduced from Michel Huglo, 'Règlement du XIIIe siècle pour la transcription des livres notés', in Martin Ruhnke, ed., *Festschrift Bruno Stäblein zum 70. Geburtstag* (Kassel, 1967), p. 124.

FRANCISCANS   DOMINICANS

(Statutum Ordinis Minorum)   (Statutum Ordinis Praedicatorum)
Ista rubrica ponatur in prima pagina
gradualium singulorum

rules for   1 a) In primis injungitur fratribus ut
notation   de cetero tam in gradualibus quam in   1 In antiphonariis
                    antiphonariis nocturnis et aliis   et gradualibus et aliis libris cantus
                    faciant notam quadratam   fiant notae quadratae
                    et quattuor lineas   cum quattuor lineis
                    rubeas sive nigras
                 b) et littera aperte et distincte
                    scribatur, ita quod nota congrue super
                    suam litteram valeant ordinari
                 c) et fiant lineae modo debito   debito modo
                    distantes, ne nota hinc inde   distantibus, ne nota hinc inde
                    comprimatur ab eis   comprimatur ab eis.

                 2 Secundo, quod custodiant
                    eandem litteram, eandem notam   2 Nullus scienter litteram aut notam mutet
                    cum suis legaturis,   sed teneantur
                                                                  litterae et notae
                    easdem pausas   et virgulae pausarum.

Exemplar | 3 Puncta etiam directiva, posita in fine linea-
                                                            | rum ad inveniendum ubi prima nota se-
                                                            | quentis lineae debeat inchoari, diligenter a
                    quae in exemplaribus correctis cum | notatoribus observetur.
                    magna diligentia continentur, nihil
                    scienter addito vel remoto.

                 3 Tertio, quod quenlibet librum
Correction   post exemplaria *ter* ad minus,
                    antequam ligetur   4 Antequam legatur
                    vel ponatur in choro   vel cantetur
                                                              de cetero in quocumque libro de novo scri-
                                                              bendo, prius liber *bis* ad correcta exem-
                                                              plaria
                    corrigant (corrigatur) ⟶ corrigatur.
                    diligenter tam in littera quam in nota

FRANCISCANS

ne ista opera, sicut solitum est,
propter defectum correctionis corrumpatur.
Idem dicimus de Ordinariis Breviarii
et Missalis et Missalibus etiam postquam
ea habuerint.

Copyist chosen
in the Order
(no seculars)

4 a) Quarto, ut postquam habuerint correcta
Gradualia, Ordinaria praedicta et Missalia,
faciant Officium secundum quod in eisdem
continetur.

b) [Quinto quod] Nec faciant huiusmodi
opera scribi vel notari a secularibus aliqua
ratione, si habere valeant Fratres Ordinis
qui haec scribere [poterunt] et notare nove-
rint competenter. Quod si nesciunt addis-
cant et cogantur ad hoc per suos superiores,
quia seculares omnia fere quae scribunt vel
notant corrumpunt.

Intonation and
final reprise

5 Item notandum quod quandocumque cantor
vel cantores aliquid incipiunt ad Graduale
pertinens, dicunt usque ad duas pausas
simul junctas. Cum autem duo qui cantant
versum gradualis vel alleluia vel ultimum
versum tractus pervenerint ad duas pausas
ultimas simul junctas, chorus complet resi-
duum quod sequitur et non plus.

6 Item notandum quod alia *alleluia* quae no-
tata sunt in marginalibus gradualium, in-
juguntur introitibus inter Pascha et Pente-
costen tantum.

3

THE GEOGRAPHY OF THE LITURGY AT NOTRE-DAME OF PARIS

REBECCA A. BALTZER

Few musicologists would question the statement that the cathedral of Paris was one of the most important churches in Europe in the Middle Ages. As musicologists, we would love to pierce the veil of history and behold at first-hand the workings of liturgy, music, and ceremonial, especially during that half-century from about 1180 to 1230 when Notre-Dame polyphony enjoyed its greatest renown. A substantial portion of the great Gothic cathedral of Paris was complete by the early years of the thirteenth century, and services had been held in the new edifice since at least the early 1180s, if not sooner. Art historians have produced significant studies about the building and the various stages of construction, but there are still many aspects of the cathedral's original interior that are not clear from the available documentary sources.[1]

Fortunately, the liturgy itself is a relatively untapped mine of information about the geography of the cathedral, for it can tell us much about the location of early altars to a number of saints, places visited in procession, and the various sites at which polyphony was sung. The liturgy also gives explicit acknowledgement of the relation of the cathedral church to other Parisian churches, both monastic and secular, since Paris was one of the cities other than Rome that developed an elaborate stational liturgy of its own.[2]

Nonetheless, it is one of history's ironies that because of the importance of Notre-Dame of Paris in French national life, the surviving documentary record of this most central of French cathedrals in its early years is woefully incomplete. Both the library and the treasury of Notre-Dame fell victim to the destructions of the French Revolution. As one unfortunate result, liturgical manuscripts of cathedral use are virtually non-existent before the early thirteenth century; those that do survive did

---

1 For the most recent study of the building campaign of Notre-Dame, see Caroline Bruzelius, 'The Construction of Notre-Dame in Paris', *Art Bulletin* 69 (1987), 540–69; relevant earlier studies are cited. A handy summary of the chronology of construction can be found in Henry Kraus, *Gold Was the Mortar: The Economics of Cathedral Building* (London, Henley, and Boston, 1979), p. 18.
2 See Roger E. Reynolds, 'Liturgy, Stational', *Dictionary of the Middle Ages*, ed. Joseph Strayer *et al.*, vol. 7 (1986), pp. 623–4, and also the studies cited in note 6 below.

so in large part because they belonged to individuals and institutions other than the cathedral. Books for the Office are particularly sparse, for no medieval antiphonals are extant and only a few noted breviaries from the thirteenth and fourteenth centuries are still to be seen. The earliest extant ceremonial from Notre-Dame is apparently the one produced by Martin Sonnet, a canon of the cathedral, in 1662.[3]

From the thirteenth century, the types of books closest to ceremonials in terms of the information they supply about liturgical performance practice are pontificals and processionals.[4] Both tend to offer more ceremonial detail than either missals or breviaries do about those features of the liturgy that fall within their special spheres of responsibility. And even though we have no missals or breviaries from the twelfth century, a number of the surviving books copied in the thirteenth century represent a liturgical practice no later than the early years of the thirteenth century or even before.[5] Hence there is still something to be learned about the liturgical practices from the time of Leonin and Perotin when such books are viewed from this perspective.

Not surprisingly, it is the commemoration of saints in the liturgy of Notre-Dame that tells us most about ecclesiastical geography. Whenever a saint was memorialized (other than as part of a Mass), three items were required: an antiphon (or

3 Martin Sonnet, ed. *Caeremoniale Parisiense ad usum omnium ecclesiarum collegiatarum, parochialium et aliarum urbis et diocesis Parisiensis. Iuxta sacros et antiquos Ritus sacro-sanctae Ecclesiae Metropolitanae Parisiensis* (Paris, 1662). Thirteenth- and fourteenth-century noted breviaries include Charleville, Bibl. Mun., MS 86; Paris, Bibl. Univ., MS 1220; Bari, Archivo della Basilica de S. Nicola, MS 3 (81); Paris, BN, MS lat. 10482; and BN, MS lat. 15181–15182. Covering only the winter part of the year (the *pars hiemalis*) are Paris, Bibl. Mazarine, MS 343; BN, lat. MS 15613, London, BL, Add. MS 37399, and Bari, Archivio della Basilica di S. Nicola, MS 1 (7). Only the summer portion (*pars aestivalis*) is found in Paris, BN, lat. MS 748 and Bibl. Mazarine, MS 344. Paris, BN, lat. MS 16308 includes only the temporale, and Paris, Bibl. Univ., MS 178 includes some musical items for the Office (mainly hymns) but is not a complete breviary.

4 The most informative Paris pontifical is Montpellier, Bibl. Interuniversitaire, Section Médecine, MS 399, from the first half of the thirteenth century. The only two surviving medieval processionals are Brussels, Bibl. Royale Albert Ier, MSS 1799 and 4334, both copied in the 1270s but representing a liturgical state of the 1220s. I have had more to say about the thirteenth-century date of these manuscripts in a 1985 paper, 'Performance Practice, the Notre-Dame Calendar, and the Earliest Latin Liturgical Motets', forthcoming in *Das musikgeschichtliche Ereignis 'Notre-Dame'*, ed. Wulf Arlt and Fritz Reckow (Wolfenbüttel: Herzog August Bibliothek, forthcoming).

5 White Bibl. Ste-Geneviève, MS 93 is a Paris missal of the late twelfth century, I do not consider it to be of cathedral use, for its Mass formularies differ on numerous feasts from the 'standard' cathedral liturgy, and it includes no specifically Parisian feasts. Norman Smith hints at much the same conclusion in his comparison of the list of feasts included in its sanctorale with those in the calendar of BN, lat. MS 1112, from the end of the first quarter of the thirteenth century. See his 'The Parisian Sanctorale ca. 1225', *Capella Antiqua München: Festschrift zum 25 jährigen Bestehen*, ed. Thomas Drescher, Münchner Veröffentlichungen zur Musikgeschichte, Band 43 (Tutzing, 1988), pp. 247–61. Surviving manuscripts which represent a liturgical state earlier than that of lat. 1112 include, among others, the missals Rome, Bibl. Casanatense, 1695; London, BL, Add. MS 38723; and Paris, BN, lat. MS 862, though all were copied later in the thirteenth century than BN, lat. MS 1112.

sometimes a great responsory), a versicle with response, and a collect appropriate for the saint. Since Notre-Dame was the Virgin's church, she was commemorated far more frequently than any other saint, for the majority of processions at Notre-Dame ended with a memorial to the Virgin as the participants returned to their places in the choir. Usually they sang the antiphon or responsory from memory as they approached and entered the choir; once they took up their assigned positions, the versicle and the collect were performed. The next service of the day then followed.

Lesser saints in the Paris calendar received only a memorial commemoration during the principal Office of the day; their material was taken entirely from the common of saints and was performed in choir at the end of Vespers and Lauds. Saints who were important enough to have their own feast day were memorialized on the eve of the feast and sometimes during the octave following their day. But under certain special conditions, quite a number of saints in the Paris liturgy were memorialized in processions. These were the saints who had altars in the cathedral and/or who were the *tituli* of other churches in the city.[6]

It was in the 1230s that the original walls of the nave of Notre-Dame began to be moved outward to create side-chapels between the buttresses. These chapels were then endowed by the nobility, the burghers, and the guilds of Paris and provided income for chantry priests; often their altars were dedicated to saints especially esteemed by the donors. Some years later, the same procedure of expansion was followed in the apse, creating the radiating chapels of the choir and further enlarging the interior space.[7] Prior to these changes, the plan of the cathedral before 1230 had the shape seen in Figure 3.1.[8]

6 The titular churches visited on their saints' days by the clergy of Notre-Dame included Saint-Christophe, Saint-Éloi and Saint-Barthélemy on the Ile-de-la-Cité; SS Gervais-et-Protase, Saint-Paul, Saint-Martin-des-Champs, Saint-Laurent, and Saint-Merry on the Right Bank; and Sainte-Geneviève, Saint-Victor, Saint-Étienne-des-Grès, and Saint-Benoît on the Left Bank. Thus instead of simply memorializing these saints at Notre-Dame, the choir and celebrant of the cathedral processed to the appropriate titular church usually for the services of Terce, Mass, and Sext, jointly observed by the cathedral and the titular clergy. For discussion of these processions, see Baltzer, 'Performance Practice', cited in note 4 above. On other occasions such as the weekdays of Lent, Palm Sunday, and the Rogation Days, these and other churches also figured on processional routes to and from Notre-Dame. See Pierre Maranget, 'Les Stations de Carême à Paris', pp. 47–54 of *Miscellanea Giulio Belvederi* (Vatican City, 1954), and Craig Wright, *Music and Ceremony at Notre Dame of Paris, 500–1500* (Cambridge, 1989), pp. 339–41.

7 Establishment of the chapels has been most extensively discussed by Henry Kraus, 'New Documents for Notre-Dame's Early Chapels', *Gazette des Beaux-Arts* 74 (1969), 121–34. In vol. 76 (1970), p. 271, of the same journal, Kraus provides a summary 'Plan of the Early Chapels of Notre-Dame de Paris' with their dedications and dates. Craig Wright, *Music and Ceremony*, p. 8, reproduces Marcel Aubert's ground plan of the cathedral (as expanded to form the chapels) with the medieval and modern dedications of the chapels; these differ in some particulars from those of Kraus.

8 This drawing is my own, based on the twelfth-century plan of Notre-Dame in Marcel Aubert's *Notre-Dame de Paris, sa place dans l'histoire de l'architecture du XIIe au XIVe siècle* (Paris, 1920; 2/e

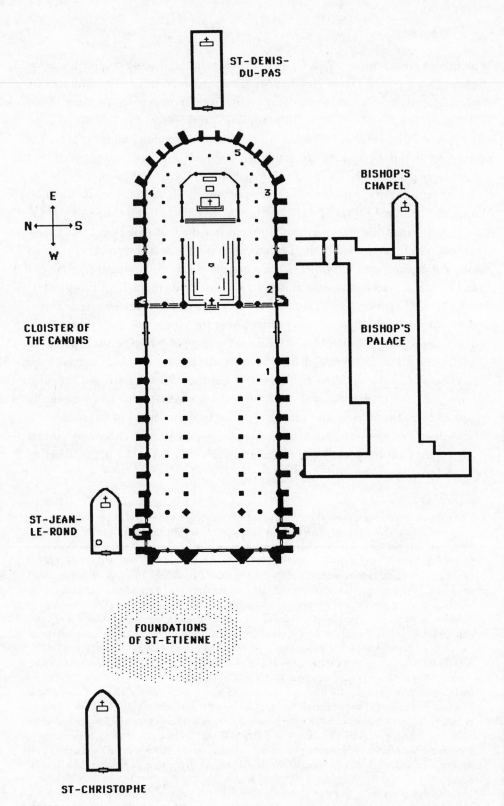

Figure 3.1   Plan of Notre-Dame before 1230, with the bishop's palace and surrounding churches

Also shown in Figure 3.1 are the satellite churches which made up the cathedral group: the baptistery, Saint-Jean-le-Rond, no doubt still in its original place since the circular shape but not its original name had changed; the oratory of Saint-Denis-du-Pas directly east of Notre-Dame; the little church of Saint-Christophe, slightly to the west; and between Saint-Christophe and Notre-Dame, the ruins of the original Merovingian cathedral of Saint-Étienne. The bishop's palace, with its double (two-storey) chapel, stood on the south side of Notre-Dame, between the cathedral and the Seine, and the cloister of the canons occupied the space to the north. Altars to the saints were located not only in Notre-Dame itself, but also in Saint-Jean-le-Rond, Saint-Denis-du-Pas, and Saint-Christophe, and all were visited in processions on numerous occasions throughout the church year.

On two days of the year, Maundy Thursday during Holy Week and All Saints' Day (November 1), more than a dozen altars were ceremonially visited in procession and their saints were each memorialized. It is these processions that are particularly informative about the location of various altars. But before we follow them out of the choir, let us first see how the participants in a procession lined up. Earlier on Maundy Thursday (*Feria V in cena domini*) at the Mass of the Holy Oils, there was a ceremony for the blessing of the holy oils which included a procession. Notre-Dame's two surviving thirteenth-century processional books – which, Jacques Handschin suggested, were probably intended for the cantor and the succentor – describe the procession which formed at the sacristy in this manner.[9]

Preceded by the master of the boys, two boys singing the versus *O redemptor*; they are followed by four more boys who respond to them. After them come four subdeacons; after the subdeacons four deacons; after the deacons, two boys carrying candles; after them one boy with a cross. After the cross, two subdeacons and two deacons carrying a pallium *extensum*. Beneath the pallium, two canon priests wearing albs and chasubles, one carrying oil and the other balsamum. After the pallium, two boys with candles and another with a cross; subsequently, the archpriest. Next to the priests, two boys with thuribles, one on the right and the other on the left.

1929), p. 36, with additional details of both the cathedral and the adjacent buildings from a wide variety of other sources. The most important of the latter are Adrien Friedmann, *Paris, ses rues, ses paroisses du moyen âge à nos jours* (Paris, 1959), p. 111; Bruzelius (see note 1 above); Michel Fleury, 'La cathédrale mérovingienne Saint-Étienne de Paris: plan et datation', pp. 211–21 of *Landschaft und Geschichte: Festschrift für Franz Petri zu seinem 65. Geburtstag*, ed. Georg Droege *et al.* (Bonn, 1970); André Marty, *L'Histoire de Notre-Dame de Paris, d'après les estampes, dessins, miniatures, tableaux exécutés au XVe, XVIe . . . et XIXe siècles* (Paris, 1907); and Victor Mortet, *Étude historique et archéologique sur la cathédrale et le palais épiscopal de Paris du VI. au XII. siècle* (Paris, 1888). The one misleading feature of this composite plan is that all the buildings appear to be built on exactly the same east-west axis; their actual orientations were not so well aligned.

9 See Jacques Handschin, 'Zur Geschichte von Notre-Dame', *Acta musicologica* 4 (1932), 13–14. For the Latin text of the procession at the Mass of the Holy Oils, see Appendix 1 on p. 61, the translation is my own.

The [two] boys begin the versus [*O redemptor*] and all proceed around the ambulatory outside the choir to the door which is at the entrance to the choir next to the stall of the dean, and there they progress to the altar under the gaze of the bishop, with the deacons and subdeacons arranged in the manner of a crown before the altar.

After the bishop blessed the holy chrism, the procession returned with the chrism to the middle of the choir and then to the sacristy, singing the remaining verses of *O redemptor*.

The sacristy was reached through one of the bays on the south side of the ambulatory;[10] since the dean's side of the choir was also the south side, it is likely that the procession made a complete circuit counterclockwise through the ambulatory before entering the choir by the south door between the choirstalls and the sanctuary area that surrounded the altars. The bishop's chair (as well as his stall in choir) was also located on the south side of the choir, though the processional rubrics do not make clear whether the bishop awaited the arrival of the procession seated on his *cathedra* or from a position at the altar.

Post prandium – after the main meal on Maundy Thursday, all the altars were ceremonially washed, beginning with the altars in the sanctuary area. As the processional rubrics describe this occasion,[11]

After the main meal the canons assemble in the principal church of Holy Mary [Notre-Dame] and the altars are washed by a priest and two deacons wearing albs. The procession makes its way to each of the altars, first to the altar of the Trinity, where the antiphon *Te invocamus* is begun by the cantor. The versicle *Benedicamus patrem et filium cum sancto spiritu*; the collect *Omnipotens sempiterne deus, qui dedisti famulis tuis in confessionem vere fidei eterne trinitatis gloriam agnoscere* . . .

Then [the procession] comes to the altar of Holy Mary, singing the antiphon *Sancta Maria*. The versicle *Post partum*; the collect *Famulorum*.

Then the procession makes its way to the altar of St Marcel, where the antiphon *O dulce decus* is begun. The versicle *Ora pro nobis beate Marcelle*; the collect *Exaudi domine preces nostras, quas in sancti Marcelli confessoris tui atque pontificis* . . .

Then it goes to the altar of St Mary Magdalene where the antiphon *Maria ergo* is sung. The versicle *Dimissa sunt ei peccata multa*; the collect *Largire nobis clementissime pater quod sicut beata Maria Magdalena* . . .

Then the procession ascends to the altar of the apostles Peter and Paul, singing the responsory *In monte oliveti* and its verse *Verumptamen*. The antiphon *Gloriosi principes* follows. The versicle *In omnem terram*; the collect *Deus cuius dextera*.

Then [the procession] comes to the altar of SS Cosmas and Damian singing the antiphon *O veneranda*. The versicle *Letamini in domino*; the collect *Deus qui nos concedas sanctorum martirium tuorum Mauricii sociorumque eius* . . . There follows the antiphon *Gaudent in celis*

10 See note 13 below.   11 For the Latin text, see Appendix 2 on pp. 61–2.

anime; the versicle *Exultent iusti* and the collect *Presta quesumus omnipotens deus ut qui gloriosos martires Chosmam et Damianum fortes* etc.

Then it goes to the altar of St Michael the Archangel, singing the antiphon *Laudemus dominum*; versicle *Stetit angelus*; collect *Deus qui miro ordine angeli* . . .

Then the procession descends, singing the responsory *Tristis est anima [mea]* and its verse *Ecce*. Afterwards it enters Saint-Jean-le-Rond, where the antiphon *Inter natos* is begun. The versicle *Fuit homo missus a deo*; the collect *Presta quesumus omnipotens deus ut familia*.

There follows a memorial of St John the Evangelist by means of the antiphon *Valde honorandus est*, the versicle *Constitues*, and the collect *Ecclesiam tuam*. There follows a memorial to St Martin by means of the antiphon *Ora pro nobis*, the versicle *Iustum deduxit*, and the collect *Deus qui populo tuo eterne salutis beatum Martinum* . . . There follows a memorial to Ste Geneviève by means of the antiphon *O felix*, the versicle *Diffusa est gratia*, and the collect *Exaudi nos deus*.

Then the procession makes its way to Saint-Denis-du-Pas, singing the responsory *Amicus* and its verse *Bonum*. There follows the antiphon *O beati Dyonisi*; the versicle *Tradiderunt corpora* and the collect *Deus qui beatum Dyonisium*.

Then the procession returns [to Notre-Dame] and the deacon prepares himself for the solemn reading of the Gospel in choir. After the reading comes the sermon. After the sermon the canons assemble in chapter, and there a benediction is made over bread and wine . . .

This lengthy description prompts several observations, with the plan of Figure 3.1 in view. The first altar visited was the easternmost one in the sanctuary, the altar of the Trinity, in acknowledgement that God came first and foremost. Next, the procession went to the main altar, the first and largest in the sanctuary (marked with a cross in Figure 3.1); this was the altar of the Virgin, whose cathedral it served. Third in line was the altar 'between the two altars' (as the space is described elsewhere in the processionals), this one dedicated to the most important confessor bishop in the Paris calendar, St Marcel. His reliquary, refurbished in the middle of the thirteenth century at great expense, was on a high platform between the altars of the Virgin and the Trinity.

After the memorial to St Marcel, the procession most likely moved due west through the choir and out its central door beneath the cross.[12] Not far away in the nave, the altar to Mary Magdalene was probably located in the first bay of the south

12 While the medieval enclosure of the choir with its elaborate choirscreen (or jubé) was not completed until the fourteenth century, some sort of choirscreen with a cross over its central door certainly existed prior to the fourteenth century, as the processional rubrics from the early thirteenth century make abundantly clear. Remnants of a pre-fourteenth-century stone choirscreen, still kept in a storeroom at the cathedral, are mentioned by Wright, *Music and Ceremony*, p. 340, note 104. On the fourteenth-century enclosure of the choir, see Dorothy Gillerman, *The Clôture of Notre-Dame and Its Role in the Fourteenth Century Choir Program* (New York and London, 1977).

aisle (marked by the number 1 in Figure 3.1), since this was the bay which was later expanded into her chapel. Following the commemoration of this saint, the procession then *ascended* to the altar of SS Peter and Paul; this can only mean that the procession moved from the level of the nave up the steps into the ambulatory. After the creation of the radiating chapels of the choir, the chapel to SS Peter and Paul was the first one on the right (south) side of the ambulatory (marked by number 2 in Figure 3.1); there is no reason to doubt that the original altar of the apostles was against the outer wall of this first bay, later enlarged into a full chapel.

Two other altars were located in the ambulatory, since they were both visited before the procession descended back to the level of the nave. At least one (and perhaps two or three) of the bays on the south side provided access to the sacristy, the treasury, and the bishop's palace from the choir.[13] Probably farther east, St Maurice and his companions shared an altar with SS Cosmas and Damian, perhaps (at number 3 in Figure 3.1) just before the first turning bay towards the southeast. On the northeast side of the ambulatory (at number 4), directly opposite the suggested location for the martyrs' altar, was the altar of St Michael, since that bay was later expanded into his chapel.

When the procession descended from the north side of the ambulatory, it probably moved west through the nave and out one of the doors of the west front to enter Saint-Jean-le-Rond, the site of the baptismal font. The first memorial there was of course for John the Baptist, but three other saints – John the Evangelist, Martin, and Geneviève – also had altars in the baptistery, or perhaps shared the main altar with the *titulus* of this church, John the Baptist. In contrast to this multiplicity, only St Denis had an altar in Saint-Denis-du-Pas, which was no doubt reached by an outside route from Saint-Jean through the area of the cloister along Notre-Dame's north side. When the procession returned from Saint-Denis-du-Pas to the choir of Notre-Dame, no indication of the route is given, but other occasions mention a return through the courtyard of the bishop's palace, in which case the participants probably went into the cathedral through what later became the south transept door and re-entered the choir through its centre door beneath the cross.

The chants prescribed for this lengthy procession included not only thirteen antiphons but also three great responsories with verses – the first one sung when the procession ascended to the altar of Peter and Paul, the second on the trip from the ambulatory of Notre-Dame to Saint-Jean-le-Rond, and the third for the passage

---

13 There was undoubtedly a door in the third bay that led to the bishop's palace; this paralleled the canons' door (which later became known as the Porte Rouge) in the third bay of the north ambulatory. Some twentieth-century plans of the cathedral show a door to the sacristy in the second bay and a door to the treasury in the fourth bay on the south side, but we cannot be certain that this was the case in the late twelfth and early thirteenth century. The bishop's palace was torn down in 1831.

from Saint-Jean-le-Rond to Saint-Denis-du-Pas. While the antiphons were drawn
from various positions in the Offices of the saints being commemorated (primarily
Vespers and Matins), the three responsories all came from the first nocturn of
Matins that began Holy Thursday. Except for the cantor and the succentor (or their
designated substitutes), members of the choir did not carry books in procession.
Even so, none of the three responsories nor the thirteen memorial antiphons were
written out in the processional books; they were expected to be memorized and
recalled on cue.

On All Saints' Day, the procession that visited all the altars followed Second
Vespers. In this position, an extra item was added to the commemoration of each
saint, namely, a performance of the Magnificat in the tone of the antiphon or
responsory selected to honour that saint. In most cases the same chant and collect
prescribed on Maundy Thursday were called for again on All Saints', but after the
memorials at the three altars in the sanctuary area, the procession divided into two
halves, and each went its separate way:[14]

After Vespers the cantor or the succentor begins the antiphon *Te invocamus . . . .iiii.* Amen.
Ps. *Magnificat.* Then the whole procession comes singing to the altar of the Trinity. The
psalm having been finished, the antiphon *Te invocamus* is begun again. There follows the
collect *Omnipotens sempiterne deus, qui dedisti . . .*

Then the whole procession comes to the altar of Holy Mary singing *Sancta Maria . . . .iiii.*
Amen. Ps. *Magnificat.* The psalm having duly been finished, the antiphon is begun again.
There follows the collect *Famulorum . . .*

Then is begun the antiphon *O dulce decus . . . .iiii.* Amen. Ps. *Magnificat.* And thus goes the
chorus on its way, singing, to the altar of St Marcel. The psalm having been finished, the
antiphon *O dulce* is begun again. There follows the collect *Exaudi domine preces nostras . . .*

Then two processions are made and the right one goes to the altar of St Mary Magdalene
singing *Maria ergo . . . .iii.* Amen. *Magnificat.* The psalm having been finished, the antiphon
Maria is begun again. There follows the collect *Largire nobis . . .*

Then the right choir procession ascends to the altar of the Apostles Peter and Paul, singing
[the respond] *Isti sunt due olive. .vii.* Amen. *Magnificat.* The psalm having been finished, the
[responsory] verse *In omnem terram* is sung. Afterwards the end of the respond, *Quia lingua,* is
begun again. There follows [the collect] *Deus cuius dextera.*

Then is begun [the antiphon] *O veneranda. .i.* Amen. *Magnificat.* And [the procession]
comes singing to the altar of St Maurice. The psalm finished, the antiphon is begun again.
There follows [the collect] *Deus qui nos concedis.* Afterwards a memorial is made of SS
Thosmas [sic, for Cosmas] and Damian by means of the antiphon *Gaudent in celis,* without
the *Magnificat.* [The versicle] *Letamini in domino*; [the collect] *Presta quesumus omnipotens deus
ut qui.*

Then is begun [the respond] *Te sanctum dominum. Magnificat .i.* Amen. And thus [the

14 For the Latin text, see Appendix 3 on pp. 62–4.

procession] comes singing to the altar of St Michael. The psalm finished, [the responsory verse] *Cherubin* is sung. There follows the collect *Perpetuum nobis* . . .

Then the procession descends and returns to the choir singing the responsory *Styrps iesse*, the versicle *Post partum*, and [the collect] *Famulorum* [for the Virgin]. This procession awaits the procession of the left side of the choir, which goes from the altar of St Marcel to Saint-Christophe, singing the respond *Gloriosi*. Ps. *Magnificat*. .i. Amen. The [responsory] verse *Fulget*. [The repetenda] *Qui non distulit*; the collect *Letetur ecclesia*.

Then the procession comes to Saint-Jean and, upon entering the walls of the church, the respond *Inter natos* is begun. Ps. *Magnificat*. .i. Amen. The [responsory] verse *Fuit homo missus qui viam*; the collect *Presta quesumus omnipotens deus ut familia*.

After[wards] a memorial is made of St John the Evangelist by means of the antiphon *Valde honorandus*, without the *Magnificat*. The versicle *In omnem terram*; the collect *Ecclesiam tuam*. There follows a memorial of St Martin by means of the antiphon *Ora pro nobis*. The versicle *Iustum deduxit*; [the collect] *Deus qui populo tuo* . . . There follows a memorial to Ste Geneviève by means of the antiphon *O felix*. The versicle *Diffusa est gratia*; the collect *Exaudi nos deus*.

Then to Saint-Denis-du-Pas; the respond *Preciosus* is sung. Ps. *Magnificat*. ii. Amen. The verse *Adleta* [sic, for *Athleta*]. [The repetenda] *Nunc iam*. There follows the collect *Presta quesumus omnipotens domine ut qui gloriosus*.

Then the procession returns to the choir singing the antiphon *Tota pulchra*, the versicle *Post partum*, and the collect *Deus qui salutis* [for the Virgin]. Then the priest begins the antiphon *Placebo*. Vespers of the dead having been finished, Compline of All Saints' is sung as on the vigil.

Thus in this processional commemoration of all the saints – or at least those who had altars – the altar of St Christopher in the little church of Saint-Christophe was the only one added to those visited on Maundy Thursday. But instead of a memorial antiphon, a great responsory with its verse was prescribed for several saints: Peter and Paul, Michael, Christopher, John the Baptist, Denis, and for the Virgin when the right half of the procession returned to the choir. Once again, a large number of chants was required – ten antiphons and six great responsories, plus the *Magnificat* in the various tones, and though both halves of the choir did not have to sing all sixteen chants and ten *Magnificats*, they were required to know by memory the ones they did sing.

If those saints who had altars were commemorated in processions on Maundy Thursday and All Saints' Day, what happened on their individual feast days? Instead of being memorialized in choir after Vespers and/or Lauds, these saints had a procession to their altar, marked by a single candle which burned there throughout the feast from First Vespers through the final service of Compline the next night.[15]

15 The candle burning at the saint's altar before the reliquary (ante capsam sancti vel sanctorum) is mentioned in a document on the lighting of the church copied at the end of the Grand Obituary of Notre-Dame, Paris, BN, lat. MS 5185cc, fol. 336. Though not in the main thirteenth-century hand of the manuscript, this material was added sometime later in the same century.

The saints whose feasts were ranked nine lessons – Geneviève (3 Jan.), Maurice and his companions (22 Sept.), and Cosmas and Damian (27 Sept.) – had a procession to their altar for a memorial after Vespers on the eve of the feast. The saints whose feasts were of higher rank, duplex or semiduplex – John the Baptist (24 June), Mary Magdalene (22 July), Michael (29 Sept.), Denis (9 Oct.), and Martin (11 Nov.) – had memorial processions to their altar after both First Vespers and Lauds, thus at the same time that memorials were normally performed in choir. As part of the Vespers procession, the *Magnificat* was again sung; as part of the Lauds procession, the *Benedictus*, similarly framed by an antiphon or great responsory and followed by a collect. Each of these processions then ended with a commemoration of the Virgin as the participants returned to their places in the choir. On the feast of SS Peter and Paul (29 June), not only were there processions after First Vespers and Lauds; there was a third procession to their altar after Second Vespers, which took the place of First Vespers for the Commemoration of St Paul (30 June).

A special exception to the rule was the feast of St Christopher (25 July), which at Notre-Dame was outranked by the feast of St James the Apostle on the same day. As a result, Christopher were merely memorialized in the mother church, but of course he took precedence in his own church, Saint-Christophe. Rubrics in the processional manuscripts indicate that on the vigil of St Christopher, at the beginning of the second psalm at Vespers for St James, the succentor came down from his stall in the choir of Notre-Dame and convoked several other clerics. He led them to Saint-Christophe, where they sang Vespers for St Christopher, while the mother church continued with Vespers for St James. At the end of First Vespers in the cathedral, there was a procession from Notre-Dame to Saint-Christophe; it used the same items to commemorate Christopher as those prescribed on All Saints' Day. On the return from Saint-Christophe to Notre-Dame, nothing was sung until the procession entered the cathedral; then came the antiphon *Tota pulchra*, the versicle *Post partum*, and the collect *Famulorum* for the Virgin. On the feast day itself, at the beginning of Mass for St James, a priest went with a deacon, subdeacon, two boys with candles and a cross, and a number of canons or clerks to Saint-Christophe to celebrate Mass and then Sext for St Christopher.[16]

---

16 Brussels, Bibl. Royale, MS 1799, fol. 113–113v; MS 4334, fols. 112v–113.

In vigilia sancti Xpistofori ad vesperas, incepto secundo psalmo, descendit succentor de stallo suo in chorum et, convocans quosdam de clericis, duxit eos ad sanctum Xpistoforum et cantantur ibi vespere ab eis. In maiori autem ecclesia, facta memoria sanctorum, fit processio. In eisdem vesperis ad sanctum Xpistoforum et cantatur Responsorium *Gloriosi.* Ps. *Magnificat. .i.* Amen. V. *Fulget.* Oratio *Deus qui beatum Xpistoforum virtute constantie in passione roborasti . . .* In reditu nichil cantatur usque ad introitum beate Marie, sed tunc incipitur A. *Tota pulchra.* v. *Post partum.* Oratio *Famulorum.*

In die festi in maiori ecclesia, cantata tercia et incepta missa, vadit sacerdos revestitus per medium chori ad sanctum Christoforum, precepdentibus eum diacono et subdiachono et duobus pueris cum cereis et cruce, et sequentibus eum pluribus tam canonicis quam clericis, cantatur ibi missa. Qua finita et cantata .vi., redit processio.

The three feasts of the Holy Cross – its Invention or Finding (3 May), the Exaltation (14 Sept.), and the Reception of (a fragment of) the Cross at Notre-Dame (always celebrated on the first Sunday in August) – also had memorial processions to 'the altar' of the Holy Cross. The Invention and the Reception of the Cross had a procession after First Vespers; the Exaltation had processions after both First Vespers and Lauds. Their destination was probably the crucifix at the west door of the choir, which was regularly the place for a station at the procession after Terce on Sundays and on the most important feast days. Even though the choirscreen or jubé, with its spiral staircases up to the pulpits and the cross over the entrance to the choir, was not completed until the fourteenth century (see note 12 above), the rubrics from early in the thirteenth century frequently indicate that a station was made *ante crucem*, and it was here that the verses of processional responsories were sung in organum on the most important feasts.[17]

We may take three of the Marian feasts as an example. On the Purification (2 Feb.), the Assumption (15 Aug.), and the Nativity of the Virgin (8 Sept.), there were no processions after First Vespers and Lauds; instead *the* procession of the day was the procession after Terce, immediately before the main Mass of the day. Normally such processions were a Sunday phenomenon; if a saint's day coincided with Sunday, an antiphon or responsory honouring that saint was prescribed to be sung on the return of the procession, which otherwise honoured the Lord's day. But on these three feasts of the Virgin, there was a procession after Terce no matter what the day of the week.[18]

As the procession made its way, either an antiphon or the respond portion of a great responsory for the Virgin was sung: the antiphon *Responsum accepit Symeon* on the Purification, the respond *Styrps iesse* on the Assumption, and the respond *Solem iusticie* on the Nativity BVM. Then the procession made a station before the cross at the west entrance to the choir and the verse of the same chant was 'organized', or sung in polyphony by the chosen soloists. Because of the inherent difficulties of the music, processional polyphony was quite sensibly performed when the procession had halted, not while it was moving. The rubrics specified that four singers organize the verse *Hodie beata virgo Maria* (O 6) on the Purification and the verse *Cernere* (O 19) on the Nativity BVM, since those feasts had duplex rank.

But on the Assumption, when the whole choir processed wearing silk copes, the verse *Virgo dei* of *Styrps iesse* (O 16) required six singers – the maximum number,

17 Apart from processions, the normal place for singing organum during Vespers, Matins, and Mass was at the eagle lectern in the centre of the choir (see Figure 3.1).

18 For further on these processions and their rubrics, see Baltzer, 'Performance Practice', cited in note 4 above, and 'How Long Was Notre-Dame Organum Performed?' in *Beyond the Moon: Festschrift Luther Dittmer*, ed. Bryan Gillingham and Paul Merkley (Ottawa: Institute of Mediaeval Music, 1990), pp. 118–43.

since the Assumption was the only saint's feast (along with Christmas, Easter, and Pentecost) of annual rank. Following the soloists' polyphony, choirboys performed the versicle, answered by the full choir, and the collect for the day was intoned by the celebrant. Then, even though the procession had been entirely devoted to the Virgin, it was still concluded by the 'standard' Marian commemoration prescribed on major feasts: the antiphon *Alma redemptoris mater*, the versicle *Post partum virgo*, and either the collect *Deus qui salutis* or the collect *Famulorum*.

Two additional points should be made about this kind of procession. Since the procession had only to go from the choir to the cross at the west door of the choir as the respond or antiphon was sung, it is again likely that a complete circuit around the ambulatory was made. This was clearly the case on the return of the procession while *Alma redemptoris* was being sung, for the rubrics state: 'In reditu per choream antiphona *Alma*.' The feminine noun *chorea* (with accusative *choream*) referred to the ambulatory surrounding the choir; the masculine noun *chorus* (with accusative *chorum*) referred to the choir itself (as in 'Tunc processio intratur in chorum').[19]

Secondly, of the more than a dozen Marian chants prescribed in these memorials to the Virgin at the ends of processions, *Alma redemptoris* was the only one not drawn from a regular position elsewhere on a feast of the Virgin. Most of the antiphons were taken from Vespers of the Assumption and the Nativity of the Virgin – *Tota pulchra es*, for instance, was the fourth antiphon of First Vespers on the Assumption. *Alma redemptoris*, by contrast, made its first appearance in the Paris liturgy in the processionals rather than in a breviary. It was copied in both processionals for the end of the procession after Terce on Christmas Day, and it was thereafter prescribed for the Terce procession on seven other major feasts: Easter, Ascension, Pentecost, the three major Marian feasts, and St Denis. This processional usage is the only prominent position in the Paris liturgy in the thirteenth century for any of the four 'standard' Marian antiphons. At Notre-Dame *Alma redemptoris* had no association with the end of Compline in the twelfth and thirteenth centuries, and the other three Marian antiphons were largely absent.[20]

Interestingly enough, when *Alma redemptoris* was copied for the Christmas procession, it was immediately and directly followed by the prosa *Alle resonent omnes ecclesie . . . luya*, which at first glance looks like an Alleluia prosula, but its paired versicles mark it as a prose. In the thirteenth century this piece appeared also in the elaborate Offices for New Year's Day at Sens and at Beauvais, but each time in a different position. At Sens, it came at the beginning of First Vespers, just after

19 See Yvonne Rokseth, 'Danses cléricales du XIIIe siècle', *Études historiques III: Mélanges 1945*, Publications de la Faculté des Lettres de l'Université de Strasbourg, Fascicule 106 (Paris, 1947), p. 96, note 3.

20 According to Craig Wright, *Music and Ceremony* (see note 6 above), pp. 108–9, singing a Marian antiphon at the end of Compline did not begin at Notre-Dame until about 1330.

the conductus *Orientis partibus* and the troped *Deus in adiutorium*; in Second Vespers, it immediately followed the opening *Deus in adiutorium*. At Beauvais *Alle resonent* appeared in the procession after First Vespers as a prosa following the antiphon *Ibo michi* for the *Magnificat* performed during the procession; it appeared again following *Alma redemptoris* as part of the elaborate Marian commemoration that concluded Second Vespers.[21] The Beauvais melody, however, has a number of varients from the version used at Paris and Sens.

The thirteenth-century Paris pontifical now in Montpellier (see note 4) includes a musical cue for *Alma redemptoris* along with *Alle resonent* fully notated at the end of the Terce procession on the Purification of the Virgin. (This occasion was included in the pontifical because the bishop had a direct role in the ceremony during the procession.) On folio 134v the rubric reads: 'Dein[de] processione ad chorum redeunte: incipit precentor A[ntiphona *Alma redemptoris*] que cantetur cum hac prosa que sequitur.' Villetard (*Office de Pierre de Corbeil*, 131–2) mentioned a similar pairing of these two chants in a Sens pontifical of the thirteenth century, Sens, Bibliothèque Municipale, MS 12, fol. 96. (Paris was, of course, part of the ecclesiastical province of Sens in the Middle Ages and for several centuries thereafter.) In Paris in the last quarter of the thirteenth century, *Alma redemptoris* and the prosa *Alle resonent* were also copied together in Paris, BN, lat. MS 10482, fols. 349v–350, for use at the end of processions; this is their only appearance in a Paris breviary from the thirteenth century. During that century, in sum, *Alma redemptoris* was notated in three Paris liturgical books, Brussels 1799 and 4334 and Paris, BN, lat. MS 10482; *Alle resonent* was also included in these three books (though the melody went noticeably astray in Brussels 1799) and in Montpellier 399. The Paris processional version of *Alma redemptoris*, which has a number of variants from the melody known today, is given along with the prose *Alle resonent* from Brussels 4334 in Example 3.1; the inclusion of the *seculorum amen* indicates that the *Gloria patri* was also intended as a regular item in this position.[22]

One important saint who has remained conspicuously absent from this discussion

---

21 For Sens, see Henri Villetard, ed., *Office de Pierre de Corbeil* (Paris, 1907), pp. 131–2 and 178. For Beauvais, see Wulf Arlt, ed., *Ein Festoffizium des Mittelalters aus Beauvais in seiner liturgischen und musikalischen Bedeutung*, 2 vols. (Cologne, 1970), Editionsband, pp. 19–20, 154, and 204–5; Darstellungsband, pp. 84 and 156. See also Handschin's comments in 'Zur Geschichte von Notre-Dame', *Acta musicologica* 4 (1932), 51.

22 The choice of the seventh-mode *seculorum amen* in the processionals seems ill-advised. The *seculorum amen* in lat. 10482, which incidentally follows the prosa rather than the antiphon, accords better with the transposed fifth mode of both chants, since it has the pitches E E C DE D C. (Montpellier 399 gives no indication of a *seculorum amen*.) Paris, BN, lat. MS 10482 also presents a better textual understanding of *Alle resonent*, for it ends properly with *omnes luya*; Brussels 1799 has *omnes Alleluya* with no notes above the redundant *Alle-*, while Brussels 4334 omits *omnes* and uses the whole word *Alleluya*. I have adopted the reading of BN, lat. MS 10482 at that point as the correct one.

Example 3.1   *Alma redemptoris mater* with prosa *Alle resonent . . . omnes luya*

Brussels, Bibliothèque Royale, MS 4334, fols. 3–3v

* MS: resonet
† MS: alle-

so far is the one whose namesake church was the first cathedral of Paris, St Stephen
the protomartyr. The remains of the foundations of the Merovingian cathedral of
Saint-Étienne lay between Saint-Christophe and Notre-Dame (see Figure 3.1); they
are today outlined in white stone on the cathedral parvis. The obit of Bishop Odo
of Sully indicates that by the time of his death in 1208 there was an altar to St
Stephen at Notre-Dame, which Aubert located in the apse at number 5 in Figure
3.1,[23] but it was evidently too recent to figure in the memorial processions of

23 Aubert, *Notre-Dame de Paris, sa place* (see note 8 above), p. 141; Henry Kraus in 'New Documents
    for Notre-Dame's Early Chapels', *Gazette des Beaux-Arts* 74 (1969), 131, determined that the
    earliest mention of it was in 1208. Bishop Odo's obit appears in BN, lat. MS 5185cc, fol. 240v–241;
    in Benjamin Guérard, *Cartulaire de l'église Notre-Dame de Paris*, 4 vols. (Paris, 1850) vol. 4, pp.
    108–9; and in Auguste Molinier, *Obituaires de la province de Sens*, vol. 1: *Diocèses de Sens et de Paris*
    (Paris, 1902), p. 152.

Maundy Thursday and All Saints' Day as outlined in the two processional books. However, St Stephen was commemorated in a number of processions that visited other churches in Paris, such as those on Palm Sunday, the Sunday before Ascension, and the immediately following three Rogation Days, in a manner that surely represents an earlier practice – one that originated before the destruction of the cathedral of Saint-Étienne.

At the end of the Greater Litany on the Sunday before Ascension and again on the first Rogation Day (Monday), when the procession returned to the Ile-de-la-Cité, the titular saint of virtually every church of the Cité was commemorated, for a total of a dozen saints are listed with the incipit of an antiphon for their commemoration. The last three in order are St Christopher, St Stephen, and the Virgin; clearly the old cathedral of Saint-Étienne was the church intended for Stephen, located as it was between Saint-Christophe and Notre-Dame. On the second and third Rogation Days, the returning procession sang the antiphon *Civitatem istem* as it crossed the bridge to the Cité and then commemorated Ste Geneviève (whose church Sainte-Geneviève-des-Ardents was on the rue Neuve), St Christopher, St Stephen, and the Virgin.[24] Thus the processional commemoration of titular saints must date at least from the time when Saint-Étienne was still standing, and it represents an earlier practice than the processional commemoration of saints who had altars in the new Gothic cathedral. And while St Stephen continued to be commemorated outside the Gothic Notre-Dame at the site of the first cathedral (since this was a well-entrenched liturgical custom), at least thirty-five to forty years must have elapsed before an altar dedicated to him was established (by 1208) inside the new cathedral. Even then there was no immediate reflection of this and other such changes[25] in the processional commemorations, for liturgical conservatism also dictated that older liturgical manuscripts remain in use even though they might be outdated in a number of ways. Just as thirteenth-century polyphonic theory retained many of the old ideas along with the new and wove them seamlessly together (thereby offering some reassurance to traditionalists), the liturgy and its geography in the time of Leonin and Perotin represented a complex layering of features both ancient and new. Only with patient and meticulous archaeology applied to both the physical and the written monuments can we hope to sort them out.

---

24 Brussels 1799, fols. 67v, 76v, 82, and 88v; Brussels 4334, fols. 69, 77, 82–82v, and 89–89v.
25 Aubert in *Notre-Dame de Paris, sa place*, pp. 138–9, cites documentary evidence that there was an altar to St Nicholas as early as 1186; several other saints had altars by about 1220.

Appendix 1: Procession at the Mass of the Holy Oils on Maundy Thursday, from Brussels, Bibl. Royale, MS 1799, old fol. 31–31v; also in MS 4334, fols. 31–2

Dum autem hec aguntur, duo canonici presbiteri induti albis et casulis sollempnibus veniant in sacrarium, quorum unus deportabit ampullam *Olei* et alter ampullam *balsami*. Similiter autem et omnes diaconi et subdiaconi qui assistebant episcopo in missa preter maiorem diaconum et subdiaconum veniant et ordinetur processio in hunc modum. In prima fronte processionis: Precedente magistro puerorum, ponantur duo pueri cantantes versus *O redemptor*. Illos autem duos secuntur alii quatuor pueri respondentes eis. Post istos statuantur, quatuor de subdiaconis. Post subdiaconos quatuor de dyaconis. Post diaconos, duo pueri portantes cereos. Post illos puer cum cruce. Post crucem, duo subdiaconi et duo diaconi, portantes pallium extensum. Sub pallio duo presbiteri canonici induti albis et casulis, quorum unus portet *Oleum* et alter *Balsamum*. Post pallium duo pueri cum cereis et alter cum cruce, subsequente archipresbitero. Iuxta presbiteros, duo pueri cum thuribulis, unus a dextris et alius a sinistris.

Hiis itaque ordinatis: incipiant pueri versus et procedant omnes per circuitum extra chorum usque ad portam que est in introitu chori iuxta stallum decani, et fiat statio ad singulos versus, et ita progrediantur usque ad altare ante conspectum episcopi, et ordinatis in modum corone ante altare diaconis et subdiaconis. Duo presbiteri accedant ad episcopum existentes sub pallio, et benedicat episcopus *Crisma*. Facta autem benedictione regrediantur omnes per medium chori reportantes *Sanctum Crisma*. Et redeant ad sacrarium ab altara parce [*sic*: parte] ecclesie cantando residuos versus de *O redemptor sume carmen temet continentium* . . . [noted; cf. LU, p. 665].

Appendix 2: Procession for the washing of the altars on Maundy Thursday, from Brussels, Bibl. Royale, MS 1799, old fols. 33–34v; also in MS 4334, fols. 33–5

Post prandium conveniunt canonici in maiori ecclesia beate Marie, et lavantur altaria per unum sacerdotem et duos diaconos revesticos [MS 4334: revestitos] in albis, et vadit processio ad singula altaria, primum ad altare trinitatis, ubi incipitur a cantore A. *Te invocamus*. v. *Benedicamus patrem et filium cum sancto spiritu*. Oratio. *Omnipotens sempiterne deus: qui dedisti famulis tuis in confessionem vere fidei eterne trinitatis gloriam agnoscere* . . .

Tunc venitur ad altare beate Marie cantando antifonam sequentem, A. *Sancta Maria*. v. *Post partum*. Oratio. *Famulorum*.

Tunc vadit processio ad altare sanci Marcelli ubi incipitur antifona sequens, A. *O dulce decus*. v. *Ora pro nobis beate Marcelle*. Oremus. *Exaudi domine preces nostras, quas in sancti Marcelli confessoris tui atque pontificis* . . .

Tunc itur ad altare beate Marie Magdalene ubi cantatur antifona *Maria ergo*. v. *Dimissa sunt ei peccata multa*. Oratio. *Largire nobis clementissime pater quod sicut beata Maria Magdalena* . . .

Tunc ascendit processio ad altare apostolorum Petri et Pauli cantando R. *In monte oliveti*. V. *Verumptamen*. Sequitur A. *Gloriosi principes*. v. *In omnem terram*. Oratio. *Deus cuius dextera*.

Tunc venitur ad altare sanctorum Cosme et Damiani cantando antifonam *O veneranda*. v. *Letamini in domino*. Oremus. *Deus qui nos concedas sanctorum martirium tuorum Mauricii sociorunque eius* . . . Sequitur ibidem antifona *Gaudent in celis anime*. v. *Exultent iusti*. Oratio. *Presta quesumus omnipotens deus ut qui gloriosos martires Chosmam et Damianum fortes* etc.

Tunc itur ad altare sancti Michaelis archangeli cantando antifonam *Laudemus dominum*. v. *Stetit angeli*. [Oratio] *Deus qui miro ordine angeli* . . .

Tunc descendit processio cantando R. *Tristis est anima*. V. *Ecce*. Postea intratur ad sanctum Johannem rotundum, ubi incipitur A. *Inter natos*. v. *Fuit homo missus a deo*. Oratio *Presta quesumus omnipotens deus ut familia*.

Sequitur memoria de sancto Johanne evangelista per antifonam *Valde honorandus est*. v. *Constitues*. Oratio. *Ecclesiam tuam*. Sequitur memoriae de sancto Martino per A. *Ora pro nobis*. v. *Iustum deduxit*. Oratio. *Deus qui populo tuo eterne salutis beatum Martinum* . . . Sequitur memoria beate Genovefe per A. *O felix*. v. *Diffusa est gratia*. Oratio. *Exaudi nos deus*.

Tunc vadit processio ad sanctum Dyonisium de passu, cantando Respons. *Amicus*. V. *Bonum*. Sequitur A. *O beate Dyon[isi]*. v. *Tradiderunt corpora*. Oratio. Oremus. *Deus qui beatum Dyonisium*.

Tunc redit processio, et preparat se diaconus ad legendum evangelium sollempniter in choro. Quo lecto, fit sermo. Post sermonem conveniunt canonici in capitulo et fit ibi benedictio super panem et vinum . . .

Appendix 3: Procession after Second Vespers on All Saints' Day, from Brussels, Bibl. Royale, MS 4334, fols. 121v–124, and MS 1799, fols. 122–4

Post vesperas cantor vel succentor incipit [antifonam] *Te invocamus* . . .iiii. Amen. Ps. *Magnificat*. Tunc venit tota processio cantando ad altare trinitatis. Finito psalmo, reincipitur [A.] *Te invocamus*. Sequitur [oratio]. Oremus. *Omnipotens sempiterne deus, qui dedisti famulis tuis in confessione vere fidei eterne trinitatis* . . .

Tunc venit tota processio ad altare beate Marie cantando *Sancta Maria . . .iiii.* Amen. [Ps.] *Magnificat.* Iusti finito psalmo, reincipitur A. Sequitur oratio *Famulorum tuorum . . .*

Tunc incipitur Ant. *O dulce decus . . . .iiii.* Amen. [Ps.] *Magnificat.* Et sic venit utque [inserted: corus] sua via cantando ab altare sancti Marcelli. Finito psalmo, reincipitur [A.] *O dulce.* Sequitur oratio. Oremus. *Exaudi domine preces nostras quas in sancti Marcelli confessoris tui atque pontificis sollempnitate . . .*

Tunc fiunt due processiones et vadit dextera ad altare beate Marie Magdalene cantando *Maria ergo . . . .iii.* Amen. [Ps.] *Magnificat.* Finito psalmo, reincipitur A. *Maria.* Sequitur [oratio]: *Largire nobis clementissime pater quod sicut beata Maria Magdalene . . .*

Tunc ascendit processio dextri chori ad altare apostolorum Petri et Pauli cantando [R.] *Isti sunt due olive.* vii. Amen. [Ps.] *Magnificat.* Finito psalmo, cantatur V. *In omnem terram.* Postea reincipitur finis R. *Ouia lingue.* Sequitur [oratio] *Deus cuius dextera.*

Tunc incipitur [Ant.] *O veneranda.* i. Amen. [Ps.] *Magnificat.* Et venitur cantando ad altare sancti Mauricii. Finito psalmo, reincipitur A. Sequitur [oratio] *Deus qui nos concedis.*

Postea fit de sanctis Thosma [*sic*] et Damiano memoria per antifonam *Gaudent in celis,* sine *Magnificat.* [though it is cued musically nonetheless.] [v.] *Letamini in domino.* [Oratio] *Presta quesumus omnipotens deus ut qui.*

Tunc incipitur [Responsorium] *Te sanctum dominum.* [Ps.] *Magnificat* .i. Amen. Et sic venitur cantando ad altari sancti Michaelis. Finito psalmo, cantatur [V.] *Cherubin.* Sequitur oratio *Perpetuum nobis tue miserationis presta subsidium quibus et angelica . . .*

Tunc descendit [in 1799; 4334: ascendit] processio et redit in chorum cantando R. *Styrps iesse.* v. *Post partum.* [Oratio] *Famulorum.*

Ista processio expectat processionem [1799: processiol] sinistri chori que vadit ab altare sancti Marcelli ad sanctum Xpistoforum [Christoforum] cantando R. *Gloriosi.* Ps. *Magnificat.* .i. Amen V. *Fulget. Qui non distulit.* Oratio *Letetur ecclesia.*

Tunc venit processio ad sanctum Iohannem, et in ingressu claustri ecclesie, incipitur R. *Inter natos.* Ps. *Magnificat.* .i. Amen. v. *Fuit homo missus qui viam.* Oratio *Presta quesumus omnipotens deus ut familia.*

Post fit memoria de sancto Iohanne evangelista per antifonam *Valde honorandus.* sine *Magnificat.* v. *In omnem terram.* Oratio. Oremus. *Ecclesiam tuam.*

Sequitur memoria de sancto Martino per antifonam *Ora pro nobis.* v. *Iustum deduxit.* Oremus. *Deus qui populo tuo eterne salutis beatum Martinum . . .*

Sequitur memoria de sancta Genovefa per antifonam seq. A. *O felix.* v. *Diffusa est gratia.* Oratio. *Exaudi nos deus.*

Tunc eundo ad sanctum Dyonisium de passu cantatur R. *Preciosus*. Ps. *Magnificat.* .ii. Amen. Versus *Adletha* [*sic*]. *Nunc iam*. Sequitur Oratio. Oremus. *Presta quesumus omnipotens domine ut qui glo[riosus]*.

Tunc redit processio in chorum cantando antifona *Tota pulchra*. v. *Post partum*. Oratio. Oremus. *Deus qui salutis*.

Tunc sacerdos incipit A. *Placebo*. Finitis vesperis mortuorum, cantatur completorium de omnibus sanctis sicut in vigilia.

4

THE FEAST OF FOOLS AND *DANIELIS LUDUS*: POPULAR TRADITION IN A MEDIEVAL CATHEDRAL PLAY

MARGOT FASSLER

INTRODUCTION

Since its revival by Noah Greenberg in 1958, the Daniel play from Beauvais has been central to modern understanding of liturgical drama and its performance practice. This is the play singled out for mention again and again in textbooks on music history and appreciation, with photographs of the Greenberg production sometimes included to exemplify what early music–dramas may have looked like and even sounded like.[1] There are more performing editions of *Daniel* than of any other liturgical drama; it is far and away the most frequently recorded of them all; and it undoubtedly still appears in live performances more regularly and often than any other medieval drama with music. In fact, this is one of the few works in the medieval repertory with a documentable modern performance history, a history which would make a worthy study in its own right.[2] It is no wonder that modern audiences know it better than any other single work composed in the twelfth and thirteenth centuries, from sequences, conductus and rhymed offices to organa and motets.[3]

Early versions of this essay were presented at the annual meeting of the Medieval Academy in Toronto, 1987 and at a colloquium sponsored by the History Department of Princeton University in 1988. This final version was read by Peter Jeffery and profited from his comments. The paper is dedicated to my teacher and friend, Mary H. Marshall, Professor Emerita at Syracuse University.

1 See, for example, the photographs in *Listen* by Joseph Kerman (New York, 1980), p. 86, one of which depicts instrumentalists playing on either side of Darius the Mede.

2 For a brief introduction to this history, see Harry Haskell, *The Early Music Revival: A History* (London, 1988), pp. 109–11.

3 The Beauvais *Daniel* is presented in music history books as a work of extraordinary popularity with modern audiences. See Donald J. Grout and Claude V. Palisca, *A History of Western Music*, 4th ed. (New York, 1988), p. 73. Greenberg's edition inspired countless performances: *The Play of Daniel: A Thirteenth-Century Musical Drama*. Based on transcriptions by Rembert Weakland; narration by W.H. Auden (New York, 1959).

The wide acceptance of *Danielis ludus* in modern times leads to speculation about its meaning as an individual play, and, indeed, about its place within the broad category of works to which it belongs. There is nothing like it in the Latin West before the twelfth century – no dramatic art with this particular blend of learnedness and popular appeal, an appeal so strong that it has proved capable of being transmitted from a remote age to our own. It is surprising, then, that even the most basic questions about *Daniel* have rarely been asked, and certainly never sufficiently answered.[4] Perhaps because its prologue, which states that the play was written 'by the youth of Beauvais', provides rare and welcome information, scholars have been content not to concern themselves with larger issues raised by the play. But the fact that *Daniel* was, like the Circumcision Office contained in the same manuscript, put together at Beauvais cathedral really says very little about the work itself.[5] Indeed, the prologue raises more questions than it answers and provokes rather than satisfies: Who were these 'youths' who wrote the Daniel play and why would they have done so? What authorities would have encouraged such an enterprise? Who performed *Daniel*? Is it a Christmas play or a play for some other feast? Is it comic or serious? And most importantly, what is this play really about?

This paper will suggest answers to these questions, first by positioning the play within the liturgical, religious, and social circumstances surrounding it, and second through offering a new reading of the play and its music, one that develops from considering the apparent historical forces shaping its structure and message. The argument, in short, is that *Danielis ludus* is a Feast of Fools play; that the staging, the texts and music, the particular choice of Old Testament characters, and the narrative, all serve to illustrate the themes of misrule prominent in other aspects of Feast of Fools celebrations. But, although *Daniel* is a *ludus*, that is, a sporting or jocular entertainment, it is not ultimately irreverent. Instead this is a play written by ecclesiastical reformers, as was the Circumcision Office that accompanies it in manuscript.[6] It permits folly and discord, but within an orthodox context, and its

4 The sole exception is Jerome Taylor's provocative 'Prophetic "Play" and Symbolist "Plot" in the Beauvais *Daniel*', *Comparative Drama* 11 (1977), 191–208.

5 London, BL, MS Egerton 2615 is a much studied manuscript. Not only does it contain one of two fully noted Circumcision Offices from the early thirteenth century and the Daniel play, it also contains a small but important repertory of polyphonic works. The Circumcision Office has been edited by Wulf Arlt with extensive commentary: *Ein Festoffizium des Mittelalters aus Beauvais in seiner liturgischen und musikalischen Bedeutung*, 2 vols. (Cologne, 1970). The polyphony is edited in a forthcoming monograph by Mark Everist. The Circumcision Office and the *Danielis ludus* were inscribed by the same hand and had the same notator. See Arlt, Darstellungsband, p. 26, for a description of the sections of the manuscript.

6 The Circumcision Offices from Sens and Beauvais, which do not appear until the early thirteenth century, are surely attempts at reforming the Feast of Fools. They are more elaborate than the

goals are to suppress certain aspects of well-established popular traditions by bringing them into the church and containing them within larger liturgical and exegetical traditions.

This new interpretation of the Daniel play is offered to performers in the hope that it will embolden them in their attempts to recreate this early thirteenth-century masterpiece. When one studies and performs early drama, it is as important to consider the spirit in which a work was written as it is to know technical facts about what performing forces to use, or how to solve questions of rhythmic interpretation or *musica ficta*. Can it be imagined that we could perform *Così fan tutti*, for example, or *Aida* if we knew as little about their historical circumstances as we have known about *Daniel*? Yet such a complete lack of understanding has been the norm not only for this play, but for numerous other large-scale religious music-dramas from the late twelfth and thirteenth centuries. Historians can serve performers well by helping to explain what obscure repertories meant to those who created them. This kind of knowledge can stimulate the performing imagination, and can often widen ranges of interpretive possibilities.[7] And there is no single thing more important for convincing and lively performances of antique music than a firm sense of what the piece was about during the period of its original conception.

Thus although *Daniel* was conceived centuries ago in a culture very different from our own, there are ample clues both within its history and within its texts and music to account for its peculiar dramatic structure and to demonstrate the specific purposes for which it was created. Knowledge of these, in turn, will suggest that *Daniel* should not be used as a model for other dramas from the period, or at least not for all of them. Like all large-scale religious plays from the late twelfth and early thirteenth centuries, *Daniel* is made up of traditional elements, texts drawn from scripture, music borrowed from the liturgy, and ceremonial gestures. Here, however, these have been drawn together to serve a special occasion: the gathering of cathedral canons and townspeople to witness the annual storming of their

---

plans for any other feast, undoubtedly to fill the entire day with acceptable texts and music and to leave no room for the scurrilous songs and hee-hawed responses found in the popular tradition. David Hughes suggests that 'with so much ritual to organize and so much music to rehearse and perform, the celebrating clerics would have neither time nor energy to get into trouble'. See 'Another Source for the Beauvais Feast of Fools', in *Music and Context: Essays for John M. Ward*, ed. Anne Dhu Shapiro and Phyllis Benjamin (Cambridge, MA, 1985), p. 14.

7 This paper takes a more positive attitude toward the relationship between performer and historian than is frequently expressed in the scholarly literature. After reading *Authenticity and Early Music*, ed. Nicholas Kenyon (Oxford, 1988), for example, one comes away with a grim list of the several ways historians shackle performers and dampen their spirits. But the study of history should not be held accountable either for rigid scholars or dull performances. When these exist, there are other reasons for them, reasons that frequently have little to do with knowing about history.

cathedral during the Feast of Fools. No other day in the church calendar produced such circumstances, and no other celebration could have given rise to a play such as *Daniel*.

CLERICAL IDENTITY AND THE CHRISTMAS OCTAVE

The celebration of 25 December in commemoration of Christ's birth has been important in the West from at least the fourth century.[8] Although the Nativity is celebrated in many eastern rites on 25 December, the feast never achieved in the East the prominence afforded it in the Roman rite, where it came to join Easter and Pentecost as a third major pillar sustaining the temporal cycle.[9] The period of penance before Christmas, sometimes known as 'St Martin's fast', slowly settled into an Advent of four Sundays, which by the twelfth century commonly marked the opening of the church year in liturgical books and calendars.[10] Just as the time before Christmas formed a kind of 'second Lent' in the medieval liturgical year, the period after Christmas was a time of great rejoicing. But the quality of the joy and its modes of expression were different in character from those of the post-Easter period.

The weeks immediately following 25 December were filled with a variety of associations for worshippers, lay and clerical, and were particularly important in French cathedral towns from the twelfth century on, especially in places where there were great numbers of secular clergy and students in minor orders. This was a

8 A Roman calendar, the Chronograph of 354, which was probably prepared in 336, begins and ends the liturgical year with 25 December. It has long been taken as the first evidence that Christmas was well-established in Rome by the early fourth century. Some scholars now believe that the establishment of 25 December as Christmas can be pushed even earlier, and the long held belief that Christmas was founded 'as a Christian adaptation of the pagan Roman winter solstice festival, the *Natalis solis invicti*', (established by the Emperor Aurelian in 274) is now seriously questioned. See Thomas Talley, *The Origins of the Liturgical Year* (New York, 1986), pp. 88–90.

9 There is great variety in the celebration of Christ's Nativity in eastern churches. The Armenian rite, for example, following the ancient use of Jerusalem, continues to celebrate the Nativity on 6 January. The dependence of the Armenian calendar upon that of Jerusalem is discussed in Charles Renoux, 'Casoc et Tonakan Arméniens: dépendance et complémentarité', *Ecclesia Orans* 4 (1987), 168–201. In the Greek church, however, Christmas is one of seven feasts of the Lord, all of which are of relatively equal importance and are to be distinguished from Easter. One of the four major fasts of the year precedes Christmas, which also has a Vigil Mass and six days of afterfeast. See *The Festal Menaion*, trans. Mother Mary and Archimandrite Kallistos Ware (London, 1977), pp. 42–6.

10 See Antoine Chavasse, *Le Sacramentaire Gélasien* (Tournai, 1958), pp. 413–17; Walter Groce, 'Die Adventsliturgie im Lichte ihrer geschichtlichen Entwicklung', *Zeitschrift für katholische Theologie* 76 (1954), 257–96 and 440–72; and Francis X. Weiser, *Handbook of Christian Feasts and Customs: The Year of the Lord in Liturgy and Folklore* (New York, 1958), pp. 49–59.

time not only to celebrate the birth of Christ and commemorate early events in his life; the week after Christmas was also a time for medieval clerics to celebrate their Offices and to proclaim their identities within the communities they served all year. The feast of the Deacon St Stephen on 26 December, belonged to the deacons; the feast of the Apostle St John on 27 December to the priests; the feast of the Holy Innocents on 28 December to the acolytes; and the Circumcision on 1 January (or sometimes 6 January or 13 January) to the subdeacons.[11] Medieval ordinals and other service books demonstrate that each of the orders was given extra liturgical responsibilities on the days designated as their own and, furthermore, that the feasts were often highly decorated with special texts and music. No manuscript better illustrates this practice than Laon, Bibl. municipale, MS 263, a troper-proser, with a small group of plays, from Laon Cathedral.[12] Here, although rubrics are sparse, one finds stunning examples of the lavish ceremony and music medieval clerics created for the time that belonged specially to them: the Christmas Octave and the days immediately after it.[13]

The musically elaborate festivities following Christmas were, by the twelfth century, augmented through religious plays as well. These dramas tended to be more elaborate than those miniature Nativity dramas, modelled after the Easter sepulchre scene, with crib in place of tomb and midwives instead of angels, found on Christmas day itself.[14] These larger works, which celebrated the coming of the three kings, or the slaughter of the innocents and the flight into Egypt, required the motion of processions. Unlike small-scale Nativity plays, which seem usually to have been enacted within the choir, characters from the larger plays – the Magi, for example – came out from the choir and into the nave where everyone could see them, sometimes following a star pulled on a string. A major character in Magi and

---

11 For an introduction to these feasts and their significance for members of the clergy, see Arlt, *Ein Festoffizium*, Darstellungsband, pp. 42–51. A fuller historical explanation of the various clerical orders, their social status, duties, and privileges can be found in René Metz, 'L'accession des mineurs à la cléricature et aux bénéfices ecclésiastiques dans le droit canonique médiéval', *Recueil de mémoires et travaux publié par la Société d'histoire du droit* 9 (1974), 553–67; and Roger Reynolds, *The Ordinals of Christ from Their Origins to the Twelfth Century* (New York, 1978).

12 This manuscript is the subject of my forthcoming paper, 'The Sequences of Laon in the Twelfth Century'.

13 For discussion of the music for St Stephen, feast of the deacons, in Laon, Bibl. municipale, MS 263, see David G. Hughes, 'Music for St. Stephen at Laon', in *Words and Music: The Scholar's View. A Medly of Problems and Solutions compiled in Honor of A. Tillman Merritt* (Cambridge, MA, 1973), pp. 137–60. Special music for St Stephen at Salisbury is discussed in Ruth Steiner, 'The Responsories and Prosa for St. Stephen's Day at Salisbury', *MQ* 56 (1970), 162–82.

14 See Karl Young, 'Officium pastorum: A Study of the Dramatic Developments within the Liturgy of Christmas', *Transactions of the Wisconsin Academy of Sciences, Arts, and Letters*, 17/1 (1912), 299–396.

Innocents plays was Herod, the mad and raging king, who represented authority gone beserk.[15]

Much of the dramatic and musical art created for the weeks immediately following Christmas must be understood in the context of the clerical celebrations proper to the season; these include both activities properly contained within the liturgy and, in most cases, officially sanctioned by local authorities, and also those that were 'ever lurking on the outskirts of the liturgy'.[16] Through this art, the special offices, the plays, and the organum, a tightly organized and carefully governed community won the psychological release that allowed the rest of the year to turn smoothly. It is only to be expected, then, that abuses of various kinds (or, at least, what were termed 'abuses' by reformers of the twelfth and thirteenth centuries) were common during this part of the liturgical year. The practice of granting clerics special privileges during the days belonging to them was, in some places, extended to allow boys and youths chances to take over ecclesiastical authority for a time, to become themselves like the masters, cantors, and bishops who controlled them and their activities within the choir and at school. A thirteenth-century ordinal from the cathedral chapter at Padua describes at length the activities of the 'boy bishop' on Holy Innocents day and will serve as an example here of the types of activity found during this week in many European cathedral towns.[17]

Because there are two sets of instructions for the opening description of first Vespers, the passage demonstrates that every year did not have its 'Episcopellus' or 'little bishop''.[18] When there was not an Episcopellus, the acolytes were honoured by allowing certain of their numbers to wear chasubles, to distribute candles and books to scholars, and to intone an antiphon. But when there was an Episcopellus, the procedure was much more elaborate: the boy bishop processed from the sacristy, vested, and attended by his court who wore chasubles, and preceded by

---

15 In thirteenth-century Padua, Herod and his retinue invaded the choir with wooden spears, while certain of his attendants beat the bishop, canons, choir members, and even the men and women present in the church, with an inflated bladder. See Padua, Bibl. Capitolare, MS S, fols. 58r–58v; the relevant passage is in Karl Young, *The Drama of the Medieval Church*, 2 vols. (Oxford, 1933), vol. 2, pp. 99–100. The ordinal from Padua will be discussed further below.

16 Karl Young, *Drama*, vol. 2, p. 100.

17 The text is published in Karl Young, *Drama*, vol. 1, pp. 106–9 and in Vecchi (as below). For a description of the manuscript, see Dondi Orologio, *Dissertazione sopra li Riti, Disciplina, Costumanze della Chiesa di Padova sino al xiv Secolo* (Padua, 1816), p. 3 and Giuseppe Vecchi, *Uffici drammatici padovani*, Biblioteca dell''Archivum Romanicum', ser. I, 41 (Florence, 1954). Edmund K. Chambers has a full chapter dedicated to boy bishop ceremonies in *The Mediaeval Stage*, 2 vols. (Oxford, 1903), vol. 1, pp. 336–71.

18 Boy bishops were usually elected on the feast of St Nicholas (6 December), patron saint of children and particularly beloved by young scholars. See Charles Jones, *The Saint Nicholas Liturgy and its Literary Relationships (Ninth to Twelfth Centuries)* (Berkeley, 1963).

persons bearing the processional cross, the thurible, and candles. The entire entourage went to the altar of Holy Daniel for the singing of the responsory 'Centum quadraginta', a chant from the Office of Holy Innocents.[19] The new bishop then went up to the altar of Daniel and an acolyte censed him, as well as the acolytes who would rule the choir, the canons, clerics, and scholars. When the responsory had been sung, an acolyte intoned the antiphon for the Magnificat, 'Istorum est enim regnum celorum'.[20] The new little bishop said the closing prayers and blessed the clergy and the people, who were apparently present for this unique ceremony.

Throughout the rest of the night and the following day, the Episcopellus carried out his duties with all the energy of youth. The entire time was coloured by events emphasizing role-reversal and demonstrating that, as at first Vespers, the laity had a keen interest in these events. After first Vespers, for example, the boy bishop processed wearing his mitre to the real bishop's house. As he entered, the antiphon 'Sinite paruulos' was sung,[21] and subsequently the new bishop and the 'old bishop', the crowd of canons, clerics, scholars, and laity were blessed and sat down. The boy demanded that the 'old bishop' account for his management of church goods and property. Then the little bishop served wine, acting the part of host, and all drank. On the following day, the Episcopellus blessed the clergy and people upon several occasions and performed all the ceremonial functions of bishop, except celebrating Mass. He received an oblation from the people and visited other churches and monasteries, where some ceremonial drinking took place. This was a festival for the entire town and all its churches, but the children who served the cathedral must have especially welcomed this time of attention, extra food, and small gifts. It was

19 The text of this Responsory comes from Apocalypse 14: 3–4 and describes the one hundred and forty thousand who will rule the world with the Lamb at the end of time. These are virgins who have not 'been defiled with women'. The text is appropriately positioned in the Paduan ceremony, for 'an innocent' is about to rule.

   An altar dedicated to Blessed Daniel is not out of keeping with traditions in Eastern-rite churches, nor apparently with those of some Italian centres. In the Greek church, the feast of Daniel the Prophet is kept on 17 December. Johan Beleth, writing in Paris in the mid-twelfth century, knew that Daniel and other Old Testament character were honoured with their own feasts in the Greek church and in Verona. See his *Summa de Ecclesiasticis Officiis*, ed. Herbert Douteil, Corpus Christianorum, Continuatio Mediaevalis 41 A (Turnhout, 1976), p. 244.

20 This antiphon was sung on feasts of more than one martyr, and at the Dedication of the Church. The full text ('Istorum est enim regnum celorum qui contempserunt vitam mundi, et pervenerunt ad premia regni et laverunt stolas suas in sanguine agni') refers to the rewarding of the saints as described in Apocalypse 7: 9–17. The Innocents were interpreted both in the liturgy and in medieval exegesis as representing the martyrs of the church. The opening of the text resonates with Matthew 19: 13–15 and Mark 10: 13–16, Jesus' welcoming of the children, and thus is particularly fitting for the ceremony of the boy bishop.

21 This antiphon, whose text comes from Mark 10: 14, is well chosen, creating a welcome for the children as they entered the bishop's house.

customary in the fifteenth and sixteenth centuries to issue lead coins to be distributed as souvenirs on this occasion.[22]

REFORMING THE FEAST OF FOOLS

The smooth transition of the bishop's office to a boy and back again in medieval Padua is only an example of the various kinds of role reversals that took place during the twelve days of Christmas, some of which were hardly so well-ordered. There is ample evidence from many medieval towns, particularly in France and England, that the day given over to the subdeacons, usually 1 January, the feast of the Circumcision, gave church officials the greatest cause for worry.[23] The *festum subdiaconorum* was called by other names as well: *festum stultorum, fatuorum* or *follorum, festum baculi*, and *asinaria festa*.[24] It was the feast of asses, of fools, of the seizing of the cantor's rod, the baculus. If there were to be a 'Feast of Fools', it usually took place on the subdeacon's day, and because this usually fell on the Circumcision, it often coincided with the celebration of the New Year, a day of special feasting and merriment among the townsfolk as well.[25] Much can be learned from contrasting the description of the Episcopellus in thirteenth-century Padua with well-known descriptions of the Feast of Fools in twelfth- and thirteenth-century Paris.[26] The traditions are similar: roles are deliberately reversed to give young persons a chance to govern themselves and the church for a brief time, and the people are spectators and participants in these events, sometimes themselves reversing roles by dressing up as clerics. In Paris, where there was a boy-bishop ceremony as well, great attention was focused by the clergy and the people upon the

22 The best iconography of the boy bishop and the Feast of Fools is found on surviving examples of these lead coins. The subject has been studied by Marcel Jerôme Rigollot, *Monnaies inconnues des évêques des innocens, des fous, et de quelques autres associations singulières du même temps* (Paris, 1837). Rigollot included numerous drawings of coins and documentation taken from classic works on the Feast of Fools.

23 The evidence for the great popularity of the Feast of Fools and other similar activities in medieval France is presented most thoroughly in Jean Bénigne Lucotte Du Tilliot, *Mémoires pour servir à l'histoire de la Fête des Fous* (Geneva, 1741). Du Tilliot had access to a wealth of archival materials some of which are no longer extant. His work has served as the basis for all subsequent discussions including the invaluable synthesis of Edmund Chambers found in *The Mediaeval Stage*, vol. 1, pp. 276–371.

24 See Charles Du Fresne Ducange, *Glossarium mediae et infimae latinitatis* (Paris, 1840–50) under 'Festum asini', 'Kalendae', and 'Festum fatuorum'.

25 Prohibitions of pagan festivities on the first day of the year date back to the second century. An indication of the scope and strength of the literature on the subject is found in Chambers, *The Mediaeval Stage*, vol. 2, pp. 290–306: Appendix N: 'Winter Prohibitions'.

26 *Music and Ceremony at Notre Dame of Paris: 500–1550* by Craig Wright (Cambridge, 1989) reached my hands only after this paper was written. A cursory reading of pages pertaining to the Feast of Fools in Paris offers no disagreements with arguments presented here.

day the subdeacons took control of the choir. The event took place on 1 January, New Year's day, and was a Feast of Fools. The surviving evidence regarding the Parisian celebration was recorded not in an ordinal, as at Padua, but in a variety of writings ranging from sermons and treatises to official documents, often written by reformers who wished, if not to abolish Parisian Feast of Fools activities, at least to restrict and contain them.

Displeasure with the feast did not begin at the end of the twelfth-century, as Chambers and others have argued.[27] Already at mid-century Richard of St Victor complained bitterly about clerical New Year's celebrations in the city, discussing them as if they were traditional.[28] Clerical capers held within the church itself must have existed in the city by at least the first half of the twelfth century.[29]

But today, more than other days of the year, they concentrate upon fortune tellings, divinations, deceptions, and feigned madnesses. Today they outdo each other in turn with offerings by observation of silly or superstitious intent. Today, having been seized up by the furies of their bacchant-like ravings and having been inflamed by the fires of diabolical instigation, they flock together to the church, and profane the house of God with vain and foolish rhythmic poetry in which sin is not wanting but by all means present, and with evil sayings, laughing, and cacophony . . . and many applaud with the hands of priests, and the people love these things.[30]

27 The documents Chambers cites in *The Mediaeval Stage* concerning the Feast of Fools in Paris (from Beleth, to Bishop Odo of Sully, to councils edited in Domenico Mansi, *Sacrorum conciliorum, nova et amplissima collectio*) have formed the basis for all subsequent writings on the subject.
28 Sermon literature in general has not been explored in the rich tradition of scholarship concerning the Feast of Fools. The severe tone of many Circumcision sermons and their themes of paganism and abuses of the flesh were clearly directed at the festivities so commonly connected with 'Kalends', the New Year's celebrations. Honorius Augustodunensis suggested to the clerics he addressed in the *Speculum ecclesiae* that they not preach on the Circumcision: 'In octavis Domini rarius debes sermonem facere, ne vilescat, et ut verbum Dei parcius dictum auditoribus dulcescat', PL 172, col. 839.
29 Although Richard does not call these events a Feast of Fools, it seems from his description that this is what he is talking about: these events take place in the cathedral, are carried out for the applause of clergy and the people, and are decorated with 'stultiloquiis rhythmicis'.
30 Translated from the text as found in PL, vol. 177, col. 1036:

Hodie namque sortilegiis et divinationibus, vanitatibus et insaniis falsis prae caeteris anni diebus intendunt. Hodie donis ad invicem vanae et superstitiosae intentionis observatione se praeveniunt; odie [*sic*] debacchationis suae furiis rapti, et instigationis diabolicae flammis accensi ad ecclesiam convolant, et vaniloquiis ac stultiloquiis, quibus peccatum non deerit imo aderit rhythmicis quoque dictis nefariis, risibus, et cachinnis domum Dei profanant . . . et nonnulli sacerdotum plaudunt manu et populus diligit talia.

Although the one hundred sermons, among which this work is printed, were attributed to Hugh of St Victor by the editors of the *Patrologia Latina*, they are really by his student Richard. The attribution of this sermon collection to Richard was made by Jean Châtillon in *Liber exceptionum: Texte critique avec introduction, notes et tables* (Paris, 1958).

Richard points derisively to the secular clergy of Paris as darkened images of what they should be: instead of providing models for how the people should live, they are models of how the people should not live.[31] And it was only to their great misfortune that the people found pleasure in this guise of misrule.

To have won the intense disapproval of the prior of St Victor was a serious matter in the mid-twelfth century. During the twelfth century the Gregorian Reform movement (named for Pope Gregory VII) came to triumph throughout France, and the church focused ever greater energy upon ridding the secular clergy of lay influence. Throughout the first half of the twelfth century, the Victorines were responsible for the defence and promotion of the ideals of the Gregorian reform throughout the city of Paris. In fact, in the early 1130s they had attempted to reform the cathedral canons, that is, tried to persuade them to give up their property and worldly ways and adopt the common life and the Rule of St Augustine.[32] Like Bernard of Clairvaux, another reformer and close ally of the Victorines, Richard was in close contact with the popes throughout the mid-century, and was a constant friend to those Parisian bishops who favoured keeping the secular clergy in line. Richard's outrage at the Parisian Feast of Fools celebrations no doubt made itself felt in Rome, even if only as one cry among many.[33]

Discussion of the Feast of Fools in the scholarly literature traditonally begins with the writings of Johan Beleth, a Parisian theologian who wrote in the third quarter of the twelfth century, a younger contemporary of Richard of St Victor.[34] In his *Summa de ecclesiasticis officiis* Beleth described the scope and significance of these feasts:

The feast of the subdeasons, which we call *of fools*, by some is executed on the Circumcision, but by others on Epiphany or its octave.

And four 'tripudia' are made in the church after the Nativity of the Lord: to wit, of deacons, of priests, of boys, that is, of those of the least age and rank, and of the subdeacons, whose ordo is unspecified. It is so made because sometimes it has been counted among the sacred orders, sometimes not, thus expressly from this is understood that it might not have a special time and might be celebrated with a confused office.[35]

---

31 In the opening of this same sermon, Richard charges the clergy to be true pastors of the flock. See col. 1034 C and D.

32 The attempt failed. See discussion in Margot Fassler, *Gothic Song: Augustinian Ideals of Reform and the Victorine Sequences*, chapter 8 (forthcoming).

33 In fact, Richard of St Victor was in close contact with Rome during the final years of his life as he worked to rid St Victor of a corrupt abbot. See the introduction to Jean Châtillon's edition of *Super exiit edictum seu 'De tribus processionibus'* by Richard of St Victor (Tournai, 1951).

34 For an introduction to Beleth's life and works, see Douteil's edition (above, note 20), pp. 29–36.

35 See *Summa de Ecclesiasticis Officiis*, cap. 72, (ed. Douteil, pp. 133–4):

Capitulum 72
    Festum subdiaconorum, quod uocamus *stultorum*, a quibusdam fit in circumcisione, a quibusdam in Epiphania uel in octauis Epiphanie.

Beleth makes it clear that each of the orders had its own 'tripudium' in Paris. This word signified a celebration with dancing in ancient Rome, and it seems to have preserved these connotations in the Middle Ages.[36] Wulf Arlt cites an informative passage from the younger Cambridge songbook to demonstrate activities connected with the tripudium of the boys on Innocents day:

> Rejoicing with great joy
> Our boys
> Sing with a tripudium
> On account of this birthday celebration.
> For the honour of the Innocents
> Let lyres and drums sound out;
> May the subject of glad mind
> Be song and instruments.
> By law of the feast
> With the heavenly curia
> May we rejoice
> And be glad
>   Eya!
> May the joke and the joy of the laugh,
> Peace and grace
> With everlasting joy
> Be our familiar friends.[37]

Beleth points to several features of clerical tripudia as he knew them, one of which is especially important here. He mentions that the feast of the subdeacons is without 'ordo', that is, without a specified plan for its Office.[38] Offering an

Fiunt autem quatuor tripudia post natiuitatem Domini in ecclesia: leuitarum, sacerdotum, puerorum, id est minorum etate et ordine, et subdiaconorum, qui ordo incertus est. Vnde quandoque adnumeratur inter sacros ordines, quandoque non adnumeratur, quod exprimitur in eo, quod certum diem non habet et officio celebratur confuso.

36 See Wulf Arlt, *Ein Festoffizium*, Darstellungsband, pp. 42–3 for discussion of 'tripudia' and bibliography on the subject of ecclesiastical dance.

37 Magno gaudens gaudio/nostra puericia/psallat cum tripudio/propter hec natalia./Ad onorum Innocentum/sonent lire, timpana,/lete mentis argumentum/cantus sit et organa./ Iure festi/cum celesti/ curia/gratulemur/et letemur/ eya./Nostra sint familia/iocus et leticia/risus, pax et gratia/cum perenni gloria.

See Wulf Arlt, *Ein Festoffizium*, Darstellungsband, p. 43.

In the Middle Ages, it was believed that a person's state at the opening of the year presaged the future: great joy on New Year's Day, for example, portended a state of well-being throughout the year. 'Lux hodie, lux leticie', a text sung at the opening of both the Beauvais and Sens Circumcision Offices, has this sentiment in mind when warning that no sadness of any kind is to be permitted.

38 In the later Middle Ages, Masses for the Circumcision were usually two, one the 'Puer Natus' of Christmas and the other 'Vultum tuum' in honour of the Virgin Mary. See further discussion of the Marian themes proper to the feast in Wulf Arlt, *Ein Festoffizium*, Darstellungsband, pp. 38–9.

allegorical explanation, Beleth says this signifies the uncertain status of the subdeacons, who have sometimes been counted among the major clergy and sometimes not.[39] Indeed, the status of subdeacons was somewhere between the lesser ranks held by the boys the higher orders of deacon and priest, and the rites of ordination reflect the differences between the subdiaconate and the other major orders.[40] As Chambers has argued, however, the distinctions between the various degrees of subdeacon, deacon, and priest, blurred in many cathedral chapters.[41] Important and highly placed canons were 'subdeacons', as numerous charters from the twelfth century attest. Over time the tripudium of the subdeacons came to belong to the minor clergy, to those who studied at the school or were paid to serve in the choir.

There is confirmation that the Parisian custom of not having a specific ordo for the Office of the Circumcision existed elsewhere in northern French cathedrals.[42] Ordinals of Chartres Cathedral, one dating from the early twelfth, and the other from the early thirteenth century, both indicate that the feast of the subdeacons was, or could be, kept empty.[43] The 'Ordo Veridicus' states: 'In Octabis Domini, festum subdiaconorum sine ordine.'[44] In Chartres, Bibl. municipale, MS 1058 this suggestion is repeated, but with modification: 'Vespere de octabis domini, et fit festum subdiaconorum sine ordine quid quisque melius.'[45] At Chartres in the early twelfth century, parts of the Circumcision Office were left without specific instructions that the subdeacons might make their own feast, and in the early

39 Until the fifth century the subdiaconate was counted among the minor orders; after this time, it slowly became one of the higher ranks.

40 René Metz writes in the *Dictionary of the Middle Ages*, vol. 3 (New York, 1983), p. 442:

> There is an essential difference between the subdiaconate and the three higher orders. The subdeacon's ordination is carried out in the same manner as that of the minor orders, by a prayer of benediction (*cheirothesia*) and the delivery of the objects symbolizing the function: the chalice and paten, the vestments, and the book of epistles. For the other major orders the laying on of hands (*cheirotonia*), by which the sacrament of the order is truly transmitted, intervenes.

41 See *The Mediaeval Stage*, vol. 1, pp. 324–5.

42 In many places, it was customary to adopt elements of the Christmas Office for the Circumcision, but Beleth's description of the 'ordo-less' feast was incorporated into the late thirteenth century *Rationale Divinorum officiorum* by Durandus of Mende, as if the practice were ongoing. I have consulted the edition of the *Rationale* printed in Naples, 1859. The passage in question is in Book VII, cap. 42, p. 714.

43 The earlier of these two books, the Ordo Veridicus, is the now-missing Châteaudun, Arch. Hôtel-Dieu MS 13. Fortunately, a handwritten copy made by Yves Delaporte circulates freely throughout the scholarly community, thanks to Pierre Bizeau, diocesan archivist. The thirteenth-century Chartrian ordinal, Chartres, Bibl. municipale, MS 1058 was destroyed in 1944, but is available in a modern edition prepared by Delaporte, who knew the original manuscript very well. See *L'ordinaire chartrain du XIIIe siécle*, Société Archéologique d'Eure-et-Loir: Mémoires 19 (Chartres, 1953).

44 Delaporte's copy, p. 6.   45 *L'ordinaire chartrain*, p. 88.

thirteenth century this was still true.[46] These ordinals offer evidence for what an early twelfth-century ordinal from Notre-Dame of Paris, if one had survived, might have said about the Octave of Christmas. And we know as well, from the evidence of Johan Beleth that this ordo-less feast was filled by an improvized 'ordo fatuorum'. The discussion of the feast by Beleth and the indication of the Chartres ordinals of a feast 'sine ordine', demonstrate the lack of an elaborate written-out Office for the Circumcision in late twelfth-century Paris and in twelfth-century Chartres.

Beleth was a major source for William of Auxerre who wrote in the early thirteenth century. William's words on the subject of reform are of major importance here. He believed in reforming abuses through well-ordered, Christian substitutes that would succeed as replacements because they could offer some, but not all, of the most popular features of the abuse. The special feasts for clerics following Christmas were successful attempts to substitute Christian feasts for pagan customs proper to the time around New Year. William compared the institution of these feasts replacing pagan customs to another reform: the writing of new sporting or mirthful plays (*ludi*) to replace older ones. 'In the same way', he says, 'ludi, which are against the faith [the church], changed into ludi which are not against the faith'. Clearly William knew of some tradition of religious drama that was thought to have grown out of secular 'ludi', plays with humour.[47]

The call for reform implicit in Richard of St Victor and ideas about reform in William of Auxerre are signs of the times, indications that reformers and other high-minded churchmen were fed up with the Feast of Fools and other popular displays of misrule during the Christmas Octave in Paris and elsewhere. At the very close of the twelfth century, Bishop Odo of Sully, spurred on by a papal legate, attempted to reform the Feast of the Subdeacons in Paris. His decree has been much-studied by students of Parisian organum for it offers explicit instructions about the singing of polyphonic responsories in the Office.[48] The connection between polyphony and the Parisian Feast of Fools has been underscored by the fact that the

---

46 The tradition of special clerical celebrations during the Christmas Octave and on other feasts as well was apparently particularly strong in the diocese of Chartres. See Du Tilliot, p. 27.

47 'Et si ista die ab ecclesia quadam fiant praeter fidem, nulla tamen contra fidem. Et ideo ludos qui sunt contra fidem permutavit in ludos qui non sunt contra fidem. Et hoc fecit [ecclesia] premittendo.' The passage from his *De officiis ecclesiasticis* is as cited in Henri Villetard, *Office de Pierre de Corbeil (d. 1222)* (Paris, 1907), p. 63.

48 The decree is printed in Benjamin Guérard, *Cartulaire de l'église Notre Dame de Paris*, 4 vols. (collection des cartulaires de France 4–7), vol. 1 (Paris, 1850), pp. 71–5. Odo of Sully was the close relative of and successor to Maurice of Sully, an important reformer who instituted an influential new vernacular sermon collection based upon the sermons of Richard of St Victor. See Charles A. Robson, *Maurice of Sully and the Medieval Vernacular Homiliary* (Oxford, 1952).

poet Leoninus, now thought to have been the famed composer of polyphony as well, spoke of the feast as a time for meeting a friend and celebrating.[49]

Bishop Odo's decree is important here because it singles out the features of the Feast of Fools celebrations most disliked by the reformers in Paris and demonstrates, through the banning of specific items, what the unreformed celebrations might have been like.[50] From the prohibitions in the decree, one can suppose what must have happened during Feast of Fools celebrations in Paris, at least some of the time: instead of the orderly transferral of power from bishop to boy observed in Padua, the transferral of the cantor's power to a 'subdeacon', (probably an elected chief of the choir vicars or other minor clergy) was marked by disorder at every turn. The bells must have pealed in strange ways;[51] rhythmic poetry was sung; there were impersonations; strange lights filled the church.[52] The Lord of the Feast was led with riotous procession both to the church and afterward to his house where, if traditions in other cathedral towns are any guide, there was probably some sort of drinking bout.[53] The youth elected to be the Lord may have processed in the cantor's ceremonial cope, and brandished his rod of authority. Vespers, Compline, Matins, and Mass were filled with aberrations in texts and music. The 'deposuit' of the Magnificat of second Vespers, the point at which the Lord of Fools had to relinqiush his borrowed rod, was sung again and again, perhaps to underscore his return to being a mere chorister, or perhaps, as Chambers suggested, to mark the introduction of next year's Lord of the feast.[54] Canons and clerics must have been

---

49 The quotation from Leoninus is mentioned in much of the Feast of Fools' literature. See, for example, Chambers, *The Mediaeval Stage*, vol. 1, p. 276. On the identity of Leoninus see Craig Wright, 'Leoninus, Poet and Musician', *JAMS* 39 (1986), 1–35.

50 Scholars have scrutinized the signatures on Odo's decree to find the names of the reformers responsible for instituting a new Ordo for the subdeacons in Paris. Chambers suggested that the dean of the Chapter during this reform, Hugo Clemens, who reformed the Feast of St John the Evangelist, was a moving force behind the Parisian reform. But it has been more commonly assumed that Petrus de Corbolio was central to the reform: in 1198 he was a canon at Notre Dame in Paris and therefore signed the bishop's decree. Subsequently, he became archbishop of Sens, and there instituted a Circumcision Office which he apparently helped to design. For discussion of Petrus and his career, see Villetard, *L'office*, pp. 51–61.

51 'In vigilia festivitatis, ad vesperas, campane ordinate, sicut in dupplo simplici, pulsabuntur', Guérard, p. 74. Du Tilliot, p. 17, describes the wild May Day celebrations carried on by the clerics of Evreux, reporting that the festivities were announced by the ringing of all bells in the cathedral.

52 'Rimos, personas, luminaria herciarum, nisi tantum in rotis ferreis et in penna, si tamen voluerit ille qui capam redditurus est, fieri prohibemus', Guérard, p. 74. Chambers translates the passage 'There are to be no chansons, no masks, no hearse lights, except on the iron wheels or on the penna at the will of the functionary who is to surrender the cope', *The Medieval Stage*, vol. 1, p. 277. Apparently the cantor or succentor was to retain control of many aspects of the feast.

53 'Statiumus etiam ne dominus festi cum processione vel cantu ad ecclesiam adducatur, vel ad domum suam ab ecclesia reducatur', Guérard, p. 74.

54 See Chambers, *The Mediaeval Stage*, vol. 1, p. 278. The sung text refers to deposing the powerful.

seated in some sort of reverse order in their stalls for the celebration, and the entire ecclesiastical establishment was, for one day, turned inside-out.

The decree of Odo of Sully forbade all these things, and more as well, and may have led to the composition of a complete ordo for the feast of the subdeacons like that from Sens, an ordo which would have allowed the subdeacons special liturgical privileges, including the taking of the baculus, the farcing of the Epistle (the reading they were responsible for at Mass), etc., but stripped the service of its accustomed frivolities and drinking.[55] Though no such ordo survives from Paris, had one existed it would have been in accord with the type of reform described by William of Auxerre. It still permitted the reversal of roles so pleasing to the minor clerics – one of their number still ruled the choir – but it removed the many excesses to which the reformers objected.[56]

Two attitudes toward reform of the Christmas Octave predominated in the early thirteenth century, and Richard of St Victor and Petrus of Corbolio represent them. Richard would have ended all such activities, believing that clerics should not, under any circumstances, behave beneath the dignity of their offices. Had he been given the chance, he undoubtedly would have reformed the Feast of Fools by abolishing it completely. Various decrees promulgated by Rome in the early thirteenth century by Pope Innocent III and by a number of local church councils, including one in Paris in the early thirteenth century, are cast in this mould: the Feast of Fools and other such festivals were to stop, and those who persisted in such abuses would face excommunication or other penalties.[57] But in the Circumcision Office of Sens, Petrus de Corbolio permitted certain activities of the Feast of Fools as long as they were purged of their most offensive features. And there were clearly many within the ranks of the secular clergy during the twelfth and thirteenth centuries who would have sided with his attitudes. These men promoted the various forms of art created for the Christmas Octave during the late twelfth and early thirteenth centuries, including elaborate Circumcision Offices such as those of Beauvais, Sens and, later, Le Puy, as well as dramas for the Innocents, the Prophets'

---

55 The loss of extra income, special meals, and other privileges associated with the feast clearly caused great outcry among the minor clerics. One year later, the bishop decreed that they would be paid for the loss of the Feast of Fools, but that payment would cease if the abuses returned, and his successor renewed this decree in 1208. See the *Constitutions* of Odo of Sully, PL, vol. 212, cols. 72 and 92; Guérard, pp. 358–9.

56 Villetard, *L'office*, pp. 62–3, offered an astute analysis of the nature of this reform: 'Ainsi donc, la fête des Fous n'est pas abolie, mais réglementée, et l'autorité ecclésiastique espère par ces concessions tarir la source des désordres. Elle ne considère pas comme mauvaise en soi l'institution de la fête des Fous, mais, respectant ce que cette coutume populaire avait de respectable, elle se borne à la dégager des pratiques impies qui la déshonorent.

57 For reports of these councils and the various places in Mansi where they may be found, see Chambers, *The Mediaeval Stage*, vol. 1, p. 279.

Play of Rouen, and the Daniel play from Beauvais. Perhaps these moderates believed Feast of Fools ceremonies to be too firmly embedded in the popular culture to be removed and chose not to fight battles they could not win. And if this was indeed the case, history proved them right: the absolute restrictions imposed by Pope Innocent III and others in the early thirteenth century seem only to have fanned the fires of abuse.[58]

WHY A *LUDUS DANIELIS*?

In the mid-nineteenth century Maurice Sepet, citing two texts which refer to the birth of Jesus in the Beauvais Daniel, concluded that the work was designed for performance during the Christmas season. Sepet was most concerned with how there came to be a play for Daniel at Christmastime, given that liturgical plays based on Old Testament characters are rare in the twelfth and thirteenth centuries.[59] His reasoning was that the fifth-century sermon 'Contra Judeos, paganos, et Arianons Sermo de Symbolo', commonly read during the Office in and around Christmas, spawned dramatic readings of the sermon with members of the clerical community taking the parts of various prophets announcing the birth of Christ.[60] From these

---

58 In town after town, numerous documents attest to the extraordinary popularity of the Feast of Fools throughout France in the fourteenth through the seventeenth centuries. Many references can be found in Chambers' discussions mentioned above, most of which were taken from Tilliot and Rigollot. Chambers translates part of a letter from 1445 written by the Faculty of Theology at the University of Paris in protest of the Feast of Fools:

> Priests and clerks may be seen wearing masks and monstrous visages at the hours of office. They dance in the choir dressed as women, panders or minstrels. They sing wanton songs. They eat black puddings at the horn of the altar while the celebrant is saying Mass. They play at dice there. They cense with stinking smoke from the soles of old shoes. They run and leap through the church, without a blush at their own shame. Finally they drive about the town and its theatres in shabby traps and carts; and rouse the laughter of their fellows and the bystanders in infamous performances, with indecent gestures and verses scurrilous and unchaste.

> The entire document, which Chambers judged too 'scholastic' to print in full, can be found in Henri Denifle, *Chartularium Universitatis Parisiensis*, 4 vols., (Paris, 1891–7), vol. 4 (1897), p. 652. In the early seventeenth century, Jean Savaron wrote his *Traitté contre les masques*, which demonstrates that the tradition was still alive in his time and that reformers were still deeply disturbed by it. [I have consulted the third edition of this work, published in Paris in 1611.]

59 *Les prophètes du Christ* (Paris, 1878); this text was first published as a series of articles in *Bibliothèque de l'École des Chartes* (1867, 1868, and 1877): 28 (1867), 1–27, 211–64; 29 (1868), 105–39, 261–93; 38 (1877), 397–443.

60 Throughout the Middle Ages, this sermon was thought to be by Augustine and this gave it great authority. It is now attributed to the early fifth-century African Quodvultdeus. The text is printed in Young, *Drama*, vol. 2, pp. 126–31, as found in a late twelfth-century lectionary from Arles, Paris, BN, lat. 1018, fols. 129r–132v. For a more authoritative version, see *Opera Quodvultdeo Carthaginiensi episcopo tributa*, ed. R. Braun, Corpus Christianorum 60 (Turnhout, 1976), pp. 225–58.

dramatic readings the custom developed in some places of having a procession of the prophets, wherein each individual was summoned forth to speak his (or her) piece in appropriate costumes and with established gestures.[62] Sepet thought that because Daniel was always present in these readings and dramatic presentations, he came to have a play of his own. Although every stage of Sepet's hypothesis has been challenged in some way, still no new theory has come forth to replace it and *Daniel* has continued to be characterized as a Christmas play.[62] And this in spite of the fact that several scholars have suggested in passing that the work may have been associated with the Feast of Fools: after all, King Darius brays like an ass at one highly dramatic moment, and, of course, the play is contained in a manuscript with a Circumcision Office.[63]

Sepet's thesis that the character of Daniel became detached from the Ordo prophetarum and came to have a play of his own is probably, in a simple sense, true. It may well be through the sermon 'Contra Judaeos, paganos, et Arianos' and the *Ordo prophetarum* that Daniel first became associated with the Christmas liturgy and its traditions.[64] And, as has long been recognized, Daniel speaks his prophecy at the end of the Beauvais play as worded in the sermon rather than in the Vulgate.[65] But immediately one must ask why Daniel and Daniel alone, of all the prophets and other Old and New Testament characters found in the sermon and the dramatic scenes growing out of it, came to be celebrated with plays of such length? Why is there no play for Isaiah, for example, or for David, even though both are consistently included within prophets' scenes?

Equally problematic are the criteria governing the selection of scenes to be used in the play. The dramatic material in the biblical Book of Daniel is varied and plentiful, including the stories of Nebuchadnezzar, the three youths in the fiery furnace, and numerous dream scenes. Yet the particular parts of the book used in the Beauvais play, scenes from chapters 5, 6, and the apocryphal 14, were the same ones

61 Karl Young, 'Ordo prophetarum', in *Transactions of the Wisconsin Academy of Sciences, Arts, and Letters* 20 (1922), 1–82 remains the best study of this tradition.

62 For an evaluation of Sepet's theories regarding the development of *Daniel*, see Young, *Drama*, vol. 2, pp. 304–6. Although many of Septet's ideas regarding the history and development of liturgical plays have not worn well, still he offered brilliant insights at every turn and remains highly respected today.

63 See, for example, Chambers, *The Mediaeval Stage*, vol. 2, p. 60: 'It was perhaps intended for performance on the day of the *asinaria festa*.' Guatave Desjardins in this *Histoire de la cathédrale de Beauvais* (Beauvais, 1865), p. 121, said that *Daniel* was performed at the close of Matins for the Circumcision. He offered no proof for his supposition, and probably thought it was not necessary given that the play is written down at the end of a Circumcision Office; the same assumption is made by David Wulstan in *The Play of Daniel*, rev. ed. (Oxford, 1976), p. i.

64 Lectionaries from the later Middle Ages usually assign readings from Daniel and the minor prophets to November, not to Advent, Christmas, or Epiphany.

65 See Karl Young, *Drama*, vol. 2, pp. 304–5.

dramatized in the twelfth-century *Historia de Daniel Representanda* by Hilarius, the only other surviving Daniel play from the period.[66] The popularity of this particular narrative in the late twelfth and early thirteenth century is attested in the visual arts as well: Munich, Bayerische Staatsbibliothek, MS Clm 835, an English psalter with a fine series of illuminations, presents, among its scenes of the Daniel story, a series containing all the scenes of the surviving Daniel plays. Here are the drinking bout, the Queen and Daniel teaching the King, Balthasar's murder, Daniel as chief of Presidents, the evil counsellors, the prophet Habakkuk coming to the lion's den to feed Daniel, and finally the death of the plotters. (See Figures 4.1 and 4.2.)[67] Why were these scenes so popular in a play for this season?[68]

The answer to the question 'Why Daniel?' is undoubtedly that certain aspects of Daniel's story lent themselves perfectly to development within the clerical celebrations proper to the Christmas Octave. Daniel appealed not only to celebrating clerics, but also to men responsible for reshaping the Christmas Octave and its festivities, particularly the Feast of Fools, into worshipful celebrations. There is other direct evidence that popular traditions associated with the Feast of Fools were incorporated into plays. In the Rouen Prophets' Play, a work called *Ordo Processionis Asinorum secundum Rothomagensem Usum* in the manuscript, Balaam and his donkey get an expanded scene of their own.[69] Balaam rides an ass, spurring it until the person playing the part in costume complains. The scene is pure slapstick, but Balaam is converted after a fashion as well. This is precisely the kind of story a reformer working in the spirit of Petrus de Corbolio might have sought: foolery enters the church, but it is 'baptized' at the end.

There is evidence that such reformers were at work at Beauvais in the late twelfth and early thirteenth centuries, and that the Circumcision Office and the Daniel play are somehow the results of this reform. What the Feast of Fools celebration was like before the reform was indicated in a now-lost unofficial ordo or mock processional from Beauvais. The manuscript was apparently known to the seventeenth-century historian Pierre Louvet, whose writings about the source have formed the basis for

---

66 The Daniel play of Hilarius will be discussed further below.

67 For a description of the manuscript, see Nigel Morgan, *Early Gothic Manuscripts I: 1190–1250* (Edinburgh and Oxford, 1982), pp. 68–72.

68 The story of Habakkuk feeding Daniel as well as the stories of Suzanna, Bel, and the dragon, are part of the 'Theodotion-Daniel', and were translated by Jerome from the Greek and placed at the end of the Book of Daniel. For further explanation, see *The New Jerome Biblical Commentary* (Englewood Cliffs, 1990), pp. 419–20.

69 Rouen, Bibl. de la Ville, MS 384 is from the fourteenth century. Unfortunately, the play was copied without musical notation. For an edition of the text and bibliography, see Young, *Drama*, vol. 2, pp. 154–65.

Figure 4.1 Scenes from the story of Daniel as found in the Old Testament picture cycle: Munich, Bayerische Staatsbibliothek, MS Clm. 835 (Munich Psalter), fols. 106v and 107r

Figure 4.2   Scenes from the story of Daniel as found in the Old Testament picture cycle: Munich, Bayerische Staatsbibliothek, MS Clm. 835 (Munich Psalter), fols. 106v and 107r

all subsequent study.[70] Because the *Laudes regiae* contained references to King Louis VII of France (d. 1180) and to Adele of Champagne, whom Louis married in 1160, Louvet dated the manuscript to between 1160 and 1180. The booklet proved that the Beauvais Circumcision Office contained several of the outrageous features later reported in Paris and elsewhere: there was a drinking bout at the doors of the cathedral, and an ass was led into the church to the singing of 'Orientis partibus'.[71] The Mass and Office were carried out with traditional oddities, including censing the altar with pudding and sausage.[72]

The Beauvais Circumcision Office found in Egerton 2615 was prepared between 1227 and 1234, during the episcopate of Milo of Nanteuil, and thus during the beginnings of an ambitious building campaign for the cathedral of St Stephen.[73] It is more sober in character than the lost plan described by Louvet and more restrained than its slightly older contemporary, the Circumcision Office from Sens reformed by Petrus de Corbolio.[74] The very openings of the Sens and Beauvais offices point to the differences between them: although both begin with the festive 'Lux hodie, lux leticie', the feast is called 'asinaria festa' in the Sens version and 'presentia festa' at Beauvais. 'Orientis partibus', the famous prose of the ass, was used in both Sens and Beauvais during a procession to the reading of the tablet assigning the liturgical roles for the feast.[75] But the Beauvais Office does not have a conductus 'ad ludos' or a special piece to lead the youths to a festive meal, as at Sens. The outrageous conductus to the bacularius or staff-bearer, 'Nouus annus hodie' is also not found in the Beauvais Office.[76] In fact, the Beauvais Office retains the character of the earlier

---

70 Pierre Louvet, *Histoire et antiquitez du pais de Beauvais*, 2 vols. (Beauvais, 1631–5). For later discussions dependent upon this source, see Chambers, *The Mediaeval Stage*, vol. 1, p. 286; Arlt, *Ein Festoffizium*, Darstellungsband, p. 30; and David Hughes, 'Another Source', p. 16.

71 For an introduction to this famous piece see Henry Copley Greene, 'The Song of the Ass "Orientis partibus" with special reference to Edgerton MS.2615', *Speculum* 6 (1931), 534–49. The piece is edited in Villetard and Arlt as well.

72 See Chambers, *The Mediaeval Stage*, vol. 1, pp. 286–7. This mock censing was reported in Ducange under 'Kalendae'; and it is not possible to tell which manuscript the report refers to. Although the source remains uncertain, to have such a censing would certainly have been in character with other pranks.

73 See Gustave Desjardins, *Histoire de la cathédrale de Beauvais*, pp. 5–6. The rich printed archives available from Paris, Chartres, and other northern French cathedrals do not exist from Beauvais. The early dispersion of the cathedral library, which began in the second half of the sixteenth century, may account for this lack. For the history of the library at Beauvais, see Henri Omont, *Recherches sur la Bibliothèque de Beauvais* (Paris, 1914).

74 The two offices are closely related and stem from a common tradition. Wulf Arlt's edition of the Beauvais Office lists the sources for each piece and provides useful commentary; Villetard provides tables for the pieces in the Sens Office, but his commentaries are not extensive and are, of course, dated.

75 At Beauvais, the rubric reads 'Conductus quando asinus adducitur'. This could mean that the piece was left out when a donkey was not present.

76 For the text and music, see Villetard, *L'office*, pp. 184–5. The text is also edited in *AH* 20, p. 228.

book reported by Louvet only during the opening (described above), at the procession of the subdeacon to read the Epistle (when 'Orientis partibus' was sung in three parts), and just after Lauds, when all were to process before the closed doors of the church and sing the New Year's conductus 'Kalendas ianuarias' while the drinking of wine took place.[77] But in this last example, subsequent pages are missing, as if the ceremony were somehow cut short. Gone are the several chances to sing, dance, drink, and be merry, that once were undoubtedly found in the 'ordo-less' Office and are still present to a degree in the Sens Office. New Year's celebrations for the Beauvais Office were tamed into Christmas joys, directed at the Nativity and the honour of Christ and Mary.

The subdeacons' tripudium, their time for dancing, singing, and behaving like minstrels, still took place in thirteenth-century Beauvais, however. One finds the reformed version of this celebration in the Daniel play. Indeed, it is no coincidence that the very chapters chosen from the Old Testament story to make up the play allow for many of the abuses cited by Richard of St Victor and other twelfth and early thirteenth-century reformers. Here is a crowd of pagans who hold a drinking bout; here are mysterious divinations which must be interpreted; here are instruments, rhythmic singing, bizarre behaviour; and, apparently, a delighted audience of clerics and, perhaps, townspeople as well. The complicated ways in which the play, its action, texts, and music, allow both for a riotous tripudium and for its suppression by divine power can be best explained through the many clues surviving in the play itself. The creators of Daniel designed two worlds: one the courts of Babylonian kings, and the other the staid home of the devout Israelite Daniel. The contrasts between them are carefully marked through choice of music as well as texts. In fact, distinguishing the two planes of existence and the special music created for each indicates how early thirteenth-century clerics thought about the various styles of liturgical text and music then in circulation.

In the following analysis of Daniel's 'two worlds', I will refer as well to the twelfth-century Historia de Daniel Representanda by Hilarius.[78] Surely Young and

---

77 See Arlt, Ein Festoffizium, Editionsband, pp. 2, 90, and 239. The pages are missing after this rubric, so the Beauvais version of this piece is not known. At Sens, it was used as the 'conductus ad poculum' and so as a drinking piece. See Villetard, L'office, pp. 185–7 for the complete text and music.

78 Although I have consulted microfilms of the original manuscripts, I have used the texts of these plays as edited by Karl Young in Drama, vol. 2, pp. 276–86 and 290–301. The play of Hilarius is found in the sole surviving manuscript of his works, Paris, BN, lat. MS 11331, fols. 12v–16r. Unfortunately, the music was not provided. The music of the Beauvais play is easily transcribed, but most editors have taken the liberty of assigning various rhythmic patterns to the conductus repertory, a practice I will not follow. Just as this volume goes to press, a new edition of the writings of Hilarius has appeared: Walther Bulst and M.L. Bulst-Thiele, eds., Hilarii Aurelianensis versus et ludi, epistolae; Ludus Danielis Belouacensis; vol. 16 of Mittellateinische Studien und Texte, ed. Paul Gerhard Schmidt (Leiden, 1989); the volume includes a supplemental discussion by Mathias Bielitz, 'Bemerkungen zur Musik des Daniel-Spiels von Beauvais', pp. 120–79.

others are wrong in claiming that the two plays must be directly related, and that perhaps the Beauvais *Daniel* is a reworking of the *Historia*.[79] Although their plots and characterizations are similar, their texts are markedly different. In fact they are two independent attempts to accomplish the same end – allowing for popular elements of the Feast of Fools to be present through dramatizing a particular Old Testament story. Because they express the same ideas in somewhat different ways, sometimes drawing upon what seems to have been a common fund of associations, they suggest that the tradition of writing Daniel plays for the Feast of Fools was widespread; and one can tell much more about this tradition from studying the two works together rather than singly.

THE BABYLONIANS: CLERICS IN DISGUISE

Chapter 5 of the Book of Daniel begins simply and abruptly with a drinking party held by the Babylonian king Balthasar (Belshazzar in the Authorized Version of the Bible) for one thousand of his favourites. While caught up in these festivities, he orders that the vessels plundered from the temple of Jerusalem by his father Nebuchadnezzar be brought forth, so that the entire company, which includes the king's wives and concubines, might drink from them. As they drink, the Babylonians praise their gods of gold, silver, of bronze and iron, and wood and stone. But suddenly, a human hand appears and writes on the wall, behind the lampstand, where the king could see the words. Chapter 6 of the Book of Daniel begins abruptly as well: Balthasar has been murdered and Darius the Mede has become king of Babylon.

In the Vulgate the description of Balthasar's feast is concise, occupying but five verses of chapter 5; the taking over of the kingdom by Darius is expressed in a single terse sentence at the end of chapter 5. The Daniel plays turn these scenes into long processions of Babylonian kings with their courts. Thus, in the dramatic works the biblical story has been reshaped to allow for extravagances of the kind so often criticized by late medieval reformers: the acting clerics sing, dance, play instruments, and otherwise behave as citizens of Babylon, always the symbol of discord and confusion in medieval exegesis.[80] And the texts and music of these processions refer, sometimes obliquely, sometimes directly, to events connected with the Feast of Fools.

79 See Young, *Drama*, vol. 2, pp. 303–4.
80 In the commentary on the Book of Daniel forming chapter 32 of his *De sancta trinitate*, the twelfth-century Benedictine author Rupert of Deutz drew upon the Book of Revelation, saying that Babylon will be judged at the end of time as '. . . the city of the Devil, the city of confusion, a prostitute drunk with the blood of the holy ones . . .' See Hrabanus Haacke, ed., *Ruperti Tuitiensis 'De sancta trinitate' et operibus eius*, 4 vols., Corpus Christianorum, Continuatio Mediaevalis 21–4, vol. 23 (Turnhout, 1972), p. 1750, lines 504–5.

In the Beauvais *Daniel*, the procession of King Balthasar comes into the church while men and boys applaud and the singers outline the story of the play to follow.[81] The opening procession of the Hilarius play mentions the audience clapping: 'Resonent unanimes cum plausu populari.'[82] Both works seem to refer to the delight of the people, and perhaps even to a secular audience, of the type customarily entertained by the clergy on the Feast of Fools. In the Hilarius play, the opening conductus charges that special honour be paid to the king's sceptre. If the King were indeed a subdeacon elected to be a lord of the feast, then this sceptre might well have been the stolen cantor's rod, and the blaspheming king would have waved the traditional symbol of misappropriated rule (line 3 of Young's edition).

In the Satraps' conductus of the Beauvais Daniel play, 'Iubilemus regi nostro', the text describes the frolic while the music, discussed further below, associates the piece with the subdeacons. Just as in the *Historia*, references to singing, clapping, and playing instruments abound, while the Babylonians rejoice with disorderly clamour about the despoiling of holy places and 'Babylon applauds while laughing; Jerusalem weeps' (line 56). The objects required for this scene of the play were precisely those emblematic of the subdeacon's office. Among their major responsibilities were the care of the chalices used for communion at Mass and the care of vestments. Here they have 'stolen' the items traditionally placed in their care, as the pagan Babylonians stole the vessels from the temple in Jerusalem, and used them for a magnificent pagan drinking bout. Indeed, these 'subdeacons' have plundered the church and violated their sacred charge, just as prior to the reform they might have done for drinking bouts held outside the church or in someone's home on the Feast of Fools. But this banquet is different: it remains within the church and is cast in a play with strong moral messages. Its host, the Babylonian king Balthasar, who may well have been dressed in opulent vestments borrowed from the sacristry, is a parody of the bishop. But although he carouses and rages within the bishop's accustomed place and with familiar sacred vessels, he will die for his crimes.

The well-known music for this conductus does not occur only in *Daniel*. It is found as well in the late twelfth-century troper-proser Laon, Bibl. municipale, MS 263 from Laon cathedral (see Example 4.1).[83] Here the piece has a religious text

81 The rubric reads, 'While King Balthasar comes, his princes will sing this prose before him.' The prose is the famous conductus, which begins, 'Astra tenenti, cunctipotenti, turba virilis et puerilis contio plaudit.'

82 In this play, four of Balthasar's soldiers sing the conductus while the king comes with his court. Hilarius provides a cast of characters, which includes four soldiers to sing the opening processions. While they sing, it may be assumed that other members of the king's court behave in Babylonian mode.

83 The piece is found on fol. 123. This correspondence has not been previously identified. Several liturgical sources have been identified, however, and strong cases can be made for the sequence 'Fulgens preclara' as the source for 'Rex in eternum vive' and the St Nicholas sequence

Example 4.1 'Iubilemus cordis uoce', prosa for Epiphany from Laon 263, fol. 123r; a twelfth-century concordance for 'Iubilemus regis nostro' from *Danielis ludus*, Egerton 2615, fol. 96v

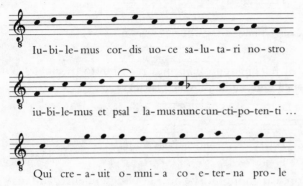

honouring the Son as the instrument of all creation.[84] The position of 'Iubilemus cordis uoce' at Laon is crucial: it was sung at Matins of the Epiphany, the day the subdeacons were specially honoured in the Office and Mass at Laon. The use of this melody both within a special Office designed for the subdeacons at Laon and in the Beauvais Daniel play points to the association the piece had for this particular tripudium and strengthens the argument that the Babylonians in *Daniel* were meant to be recognized as subdeacons in disguise.[85]. Yet further associations may well be buried in the tune itself, for both the opening and closing melodic phrases echo the familiar music of 'Orientis Partibus' (see Example 4.2).

Example 4.2(a)   Version B of 'Orientis partibus': tenor line of three-voice setting 'Conductus subdiaconi ad epistolam', Egerton 2615, fol. 43 (pitches adopted from Arlt's transcription)

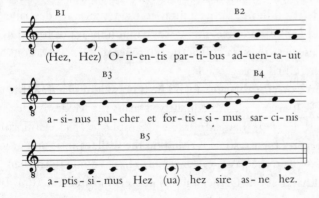

'Congaudentes exsultemus' for the conductus for Daniel with the same beginning (see discussion below). Wulstan has listed these and other more tentatively identified borrowings in his introduction to *The Play of Daniel*.   84 The text is edited in *AH* 54, pp. 255–6.

85 Although the texts are different, the two pieces are organized in the same fashion, with the first verses used as refrains throughout.

Example 4.2(b)   Opening pitches of 'Iubilemus regis nostro' resemble the opening of 'Orientis partibus', phrase B1 (darkened notes indicate resemblance)

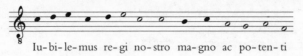

Iu- bi- le- mus re- gi no- stro ma- gno ac po- ten- ti

Example 4.2(c)   Cadence of refrain from 'Iubilemus regis nostro' resembles 'Orientis partibus', phrase B2 (darkened notes indicate resemblance)

Hec   sunt ua- sa re- gi- a qui- bus spo - li- a - tur

These borrowings were clear enough to be heard by the audience, and may have been used to strengthen the analogy between the subdeacons' traditional mis-behaviour and their scriptural parallel, the evil follies of Babylon. The argument could be made, of course, that these are mere formulae, and that their presence here and in examples cited below is insignificant; but the use of short melodic quotations of this sort and in this particular way is characteristic of late twelfth- and early thirteenth-century music and abounds in, for example, the Parisian sequence repertories. In fact, a musical pun is found in the Parisian version of the sequence 'Heri mundus exultavit' for St Stephen.[86] The penultimate strophe includes the phrase 'Augustinus *asser*it'. And here the familiar melody, that first used for 'Laudes crucis', has been altered to quote from 'Orientis partibus'.[87]

The procession of Darius the Mede with his entourage offered the youths of Beauvais another chance to become Babylonians. In the conductus 'Ecce Rex Darius', they are charged to play instruments of various types as they rejoice. Most importantly, the word 'tripudium' or its plural is used twice to describe the procession (lines 221 and 238). Of course, the word 'tripudium' is not found in the Book of Daniel, and its use here makes explicit the reference to the celebrations held by the clergy during the Christmas Octave.

The Fools must have a Lord for their feast, and he is present in *Daniel* as the two kings of Babylon, first Balthasar and, subsequently, Darius the Mede. As depicted in the Bible, both men are less than admirable examples of successful rulers. Balthasar, unable to interpret the mystical writing on the wall, cannot find anyone among his wise men to explain the passage. The Queen has to come to the banquet and tell the helpless Balthasar about Daniel and his powers of interpretation. Both plays emphasize the Queen through lavish processions, coming and going. In this

---

86 See the piece as edited by Eugene Misset and Pierre Aubry in *Les proses d'Adam de Saint-Victor* (Paris, 1900), pp. 229–31.   87 See Misset and Aubry, p. 231, strophe 11–12.

way, yet another opportunity is created for a group of 'Babylonians' to sing and play, and further, one of the youths could parade about dressed up as a woman, 'in vestitu deaurato' (lines 84–5). The numerous reports of clergy dressing up in female attire for the Feast of Fools indicate that such role reversals were typical of this day, and the Babylonian Queen provided a perfect opportunity for display of this sort. In addition, she is a very special 'woman': in *Daniel* and in the *Historia* the Queen is noted for her prudence and other characteristics proper to wise rule, thus offering a sharply drawn contrast with Balthasar's ineffectiveness. Because associating a woman with 'ratio', as in the *Historia*, is a reversal of standard medieval interpretations, this Babylonian Queen provides the play with yet another striking example of role-reversal, the basic theme of the Feast of Fools.

Darius the Mede is portrayed differently in the two plays under discussion. In the *Historia* he is 'iratus', even when he comes to console Daniel in the lions' den and does not reveal the despair at condemning Daniel found in the Beauvais play. This picture of Darius is doubtless a holdover from the common characterization of King Herod in the Innocents' plays and points to the early date of the Hilarius play, created, perhaps, before Daniel's tradition was well-established.[88]

Darius in the Beauvais play is close to scripture in his conception, except that here he becomes a veritable Lord of the Asses, at the very moment in the play when he is duped by jealous counsellors seeking to destroy Daniel. The scene begins with the plotters flattering King Darius, and their refrain is sung to music borrowed from 'Orientis partibus'. Thus direct address of donkey and of king have the same music (see Example 4.3).

Example 4.3 Cadential formula from the conductus for King Darius (fol. 102r) resembles 'Orientis partibus', phrase B4

Ec - ce rex Da - ri - us ue - nit cum prin - ci - pi - bus no - bi - lis no - bi - li - bus

When the king is fooled, he straightaway offers the decree potentially fatal to Daniel, but his music, with its odd reiterative passagework, echoes the 'hee-haw' of the ass in 'Orientis partibus'. This time reference is made to the extensive braying section found only in the version of 'Orientis' sung at the opening of the Office (see Example 4.4).

---

88 Young believed that Darius' anger demonstrated that his consolation of Daniel was ironic, an interpretation directly opposed to the biblical account (*Drama*, vol. 2, p. 288). When interpreting the play, it makes better sense to think of the King as frenzied or distressed, but not angry.

Example 4.4(a)   'Orientis partibus', version A, 'Conductus quando asinus adducitur', as in
Egerton 2615, fol. 1r and transcribed by Arlt

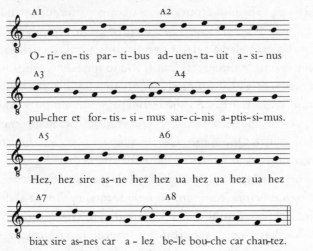

Example 4.4(b)   Braying motive, A6, a possible source for Darius' decree, fol. 105r; the
counsellors pick up on the music, fol. 105v

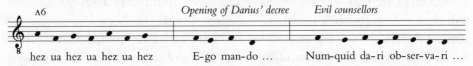

And then, to make the point strikingly clear, the king brays, using words and
music reminiscent of the Prose of the Ass (Example 4.5).

Example 4.5   The evil counsellors address Darius immediately after he is duped, fol. 105r;
Darius brays, revealing his condition, fol. 105r

Subsequently, the counsellors adopt the 'braying' motive, and it comes to unify
the entire scene. The Babylonians in their wickedness have become donkeys and
fools, and in their ignorance they do not realize that they are condemned. Yet
although the Daniel plays depict pagans, they fall far short of condoning them. This
Babylon is still the city of Apocalypse 18: 'the habitation of devils, and the hold of
every unclean spirit, . . . because all nations have drunk the wine of her fornication'.
Daniel the Prophet exposes the fools and, in so much as is possible in Old Testament
time, saves the leader of the kingdom from his own folly.

DANIEL THE PROPHET: THE IDEAL CLERIC

Just as the courts of Babylon offered the perfect opportunity for the subdeacons to become fools on 1 January, so Daniel offered the reformers who designed the play an excellent model for proper clerical behaviour. The Beauvais Daniel play is, indeed, the very sort of religious art described by William of Auxerre: a work redirecting abuses into a powerful religious statement, a statement that works because Daniel's character is strong enough to balance the weight of the Babylonian hordes. Daniel, in this play as in others, is a young man, wise beyond his years. In the *Ordo prophetarum* from Laon, Daniel is described as an 'adolescens, ueste splendida indutus';[89] at Rouen, he is clothed in a green tunic and has a youthful face;[90] at Beauvais, the conductus bringing Daniel to Balthasar describes him as 'in the glory of youth' (line 128); and in the prophets' play from the Anglo-Norman Play of Adam, Daniel has the appearance of youth, but the clothing of an old man.[91] In the midst of so many boisterous youths, Daniel stands out as the one who will not become a pagan on Kalends.

His talents are also of a sort particularly prized by clerics in minor orders: he is able to interpret difficult texts successfully and with apparent ease.[92] This ability gives him the potential for great power and financial reward. Because many young clerics in early thirteenth-century France attended cathedral schools and the then-emerging university of Paris in hopes of employment as clerks for secular institutions, Daniel would have been a character of immediate appeal. Yet his refusal to accept payments from King Balthasar makes him a model of the cleric who would remain steadfast in his vows, untempted by earthly pleasures, intent upon serving the church.[93] This need for clerics to ignore the temptations of the world is a common theme with religious reformers writing in the twelfth and thirteenth centuries, and for at least some of them, the prophet Daniel embodied their ideals. For Gerhoch of Reichersberg, for example, 'the prophet Daniel was not merely God's witness in a distant age and hostile environment, but he was also at

---

89 See the edition of this play in Young, *Drama*, vol. 2, p. 145.

90 See Young, *Drama*, vol. 2, p. 158.

91 See *Le Jeu d'Adam (Ordo representacionis Ade)*, ed. Willem Noomen (Paris, 1971), p. 69.

92 Daniel's ability to interpret difficult texts is the main theme of the opening conductus in the Beauvais play:

> Sed Danieli scripta legenti mox patuere
> que prius illis clausa fuere.

93 In Daniel 5: 17, the prophet says to the king, 'Thy rewards be to thyself, and the gifts of thy house give to another: but the writing I will read to thee, O king, and shew thee the interpretation thereof.' Both Daniel plays incorporate this denial into Daniel's speech to the king and make it a part of Daniel's conductus as well. See *Historia*, lines 188–220 and 136–8; and *Danielis ludus* lines 121 and 147–8.

one with the effects of praise and prayer active in the midst of the Babylon that tyrannized the twelfth-century church'.[94]

Daniel is a youth who is superior to his elders through the force of his talents and faith. He teaches kings; he knows more than the seniors, the wisemen at court.[95] He is the one figure in the play who can look back and forward across long stretches of time to understand the present, the goal of medieval scriptural exegesis.[96] And although knowing the future is not mentioned as one of Daniel's abilities by the Queen in the Bible, in both plays much is made of Daniel's 'futurorum prescia' at this point in the play.[97] For Daniel can not only read the writing on the wall and foresee the downfall of the king of Babylon, he can also look through time to the coming of Jesus.[98]

In spite of his strong beliefs, however, Daniel never chooses to undermine authority. Instead, he obeys the law of the land, though it is not his own, until the king asks that he surrender the one thing he cannot give up, worship of the living God. Daniel is ever humble, 'pauper et exulans', and when the Babylonians who escort him speak in a garbled language made up of Latin and Old French, Daniel defers to them.[99] Daniel's fearful lament just before being thrown to the lions is a moving testament against the pride and misguided leadership of king Darius, and depicts a historical type of Christ feeling the pangs of mortality.

In the Beauvais play, Daniel's exegetical abilities and faith are reflected in his music as well. His singing is the most elaborate in the play and the music written for him is frequently cast in a different style from that of the Babylonians. Coming and going in their seemingly endless processions, the Babylonians sing in sharply marked rhythmic poetry set to simple, immediately appealing melodies, some of

94 For discussion and further references, see Karl F. Morrison, 'The Church as Play: Gerhoch of Reichersberg's Call for Reform', in *Popes, Teachers, and Canon Law in the Middle Ages*, ed. James Ross Sweeney and Stanley Chodorow (Ithaca, NY, 1989), p. 135, where further references are cited.

95 In the Hilarius play, the wisemen are specifically called 'seniores'. Thus Daniel, in his wisdom, is a youth who has taken over the customary roles assigned to older men. But he takes them over in a proper and Godlike way.

96 For a discussion of time and exegesis in liturgical drama see Margot Fassler, 'The Representations of Time in *Ordo representacionis ade*', forthcoming in *Yale French Studies* (1991).

97 *Historia*, line 112. In a later conductus Daniel is described as 'Adest illi spiritus quo prenoscit omnia, et future penitus, tanquam sint presentia' (lines 217–20).

98 In *Danielis ludus* Daniel is seen upon several occasions as worthy of Christmas celebration because he was able to foretell the Nativity. 'Homo natus est in carne, qui creauit omnia, nasciturum quem predixit propheta facundia.' (The person is born in the flesh who created all things, whose coming birth was predicted by the eloquence of the prophet.) (lines 272–3).

99 The use of Old French here is symbolic. Young students and choir boys were not supposed to speak it in some places and could be fined for doing so. It is thus another of the play's licences. For discussion of a different use of vernacular in a religious play, see Fassler, 'The Representations of Time'.

which, I have shown, incorporate phrases from 'Orientis partibus'. Daniel, on the other hand, has sung to him, or sings himself, pieces of more serious character.[100]

The conductus for Daniel, 'Congaudentes celebremus' is loosely modelled after the sequence for St Nicholas which begins, both textually and musically, in the same way. Through this piece, Daniel comes to have his own sequence, a piece that reveals Daniel's sacred powers and praises God through the actions of the saint. It is probably no coincidence that a piece for St Nicholas was chosen as the textual and musical model for Daniel's 'sequence'. Nicholas was a patron saint of children and young scholars, and it was often on his day that boy bishops were elected.[101] The references to St Nicholas built into the conductus for Daniel associate the Old Testament figure with the protector of boys and youths. But Daniel, unlike the suffering youths in the Nicholas plays, has no St Nicholas to come to his rescue. He will be spared through miraculous intercession of a different kind.

At two points close to the end of the play, Daniel's music brings the style of liturgical chant to mind, and thus he seems to look ahead through Old Testament time to another age. On entering the pit, Daniel sings a quasi-'Kyrie eleyson' (lines 350–7). When he eats the meal provided by Habakkuk, he accepts the food in the name of God and sings 'alleluia'. The scene with Habakkuk, in spite of its comic overtones – the prophet is dragged in by the hair as the lions mill hungrily about – may well be an allusion to the sacramental meal served at Mass. Daniel receives the food and wine as a gift from God and praises God for his salvation from death. The power of his faith, in turn, serves as witness for King Darius and brings about his conversion.

Within *Danielis ludus* popular Feast of Fools activities are enacted as pagan festivals that insult the Judaeo-Christian God and threaten the youth Daniel with painful death. Daniel, who is profitably compared with the various troubled youths of the Nicholas plays, has enemies, the Fools and their follies. By the end of the play, some of them have suffered for their actions. But Darius the Mede, who was made a donkey earlier in the play, is won over to the side of order. When he intones the 'Te

---

100 It is difficult to say whether or not the symbolic use of music in the Beauvais play was found in the *Historia* as well: unfortunately the music does not survive for this earlier play. It does not appear, however, to incorporate the texts of any liturgical chants. Mathias Bielitz, 'Bemerkungen zur Musik des Daniel-Spiels', discusses the symbolic importance of the ranges and pitch levels found in the music of the various characters.

101 The numerous medieval plays for St Nicholas, which include the famous set in the Fleury playbook, are directly linked to the reverence accorded the saint by the children and youths in ecclesiastical establishments. For the view that the plays were written as school exercises, see O. Weydig, *Beiträge zur Geschichte des Mirakelspiels in Frankreich* (Erfurt, 1910), pp. 44–6. Young has edited several Nicholas plays in *Drama*, vol. 2. See his discussion there and further in his 'Concerning the Origin of the Miracle Play' in *The Manly Anniversary Studies in Language and Literature* (Chicago, 1923), pp. 254–68.

Deum laudamus' at the end of the Hilarius play, Darius, as Lord of the Fools, is about to relinquish his temporary rule over the minor clerics and return them to their rightful master.

It is tempting to suppose that the part of Daniel may have been acted by a young teacher of the boys who served throughout the year in some official capacity. Such persons would have helped prepare the play and its music and would have been the kind of authority figures who sympathized with the boys' needs for special festivities on New Year's Day. Gerhoch of Reichersberg recalled that as 'magister scholarum et doctor juvenum' at Augsburg cathedral in the early twelfth century, he was in charge of cathedral plays. The famous reformer later regretted that he encouraged the boys through the example of his own buffoonery.[102]

CONCLUSION

This essay has argued that the *Danielis Ludus* from Beauvais was specifically designed for the Feast of Fools. Performers recreating the work can use this knowledge to great advantage. The Babylonians are supposed to be comic characters, out of place in the ecclesiastical world in which they have been temporarily posited. To stage them playing musical instruments, dancing and revelling, and singing boisterously is in perfect keeping with the spirit of the play. The use of instruments in *Daniel* does not demonstrate some norm for the use of instruments in liturgical dramas: they are used here because they are so out-of-place in church, so pagan. And the Babylonian kings are buffoons and should be staged as such, not as frowning Hamlets with lofty purposes. Grotesque mime, such as having Balthasar knock his knees widly when confronted with the handwriting on the wall, is precisely the kind of gesture that can bring the play to life and serve its dramatic intentions. This was a play for a special occasion, and the tension between misrule and rightful rule built into the work requires attention from directors, actors, and singers.

Daniel is a stunning example of the medieval comic ideal, and to play it with a heavy hand throughout would be a real mistake. One must trust the play and the reformers who wrote it: the lofty character of Daniel, his moving testimony, his powerfully beautiful music, will put these Babylonians in their places. Thus although Darius the Mede is a braying ass before his conversion (and this point must be made clear in the directing, singing, and acting), he is won over by Daniel at the end, as in a sense, is the audience itself. This play bursts with youthful guffaws, with the lively merriment of a tightly ordered society that only got to laugh once or twice a year. It was a good laugh, and when it was over, there must have been a great sense of relief and a profound feeling of restoration and healing.

102 See Karl Morrison, 'The Church as Play', p. 135n.

Daniel was a play that served to bind a community together by allowing its members a common cup of good cheer. When speaking of the canons of Augsburg cathedral in the early twelfth century, Gerhoch of Reichersberg noted that they were rarely present as an entire body. An exception to this absenteeism was the Christmas Octave when all canons gathered to celebrate their offices and to see plays. During this time, they all slept in the dormitory and ate in the refectory.[103] It is no wonder that the Parisian canon Leoninus so looked forward to the 'Feast of the Rod' as a time when he would see a friend. This was the season when canons gathered in a community to witness plays and other entertainments and to see themselves 'roasted' through the enactment of various role reversals, including the Feast of Fools, when they would relinquish their stalls to underlings. Beleth reports that in some churchs, bishops and archbishops play with their clerics during December in the cloister, even lowering themselves to have a game of ball.[104]

Chambers suggested that the youths celebrating in the Feast of Fools were the choir clerks, the vicars choral, who were paid by the chapter to fulfill the canons' liturgical duties during the year.[105] This underclass of poorly paid young men in minor orders would have included many fine singers and students, and the plays they wrote and performed would have been given, in part, at least, to increase their own revenues and to show off their skills to the assembly who hired them. The spoofing of authority in both the Innocents plays and the Daniel plays, and the defence of young men and boys in trouble found in these plays (and in the Nicholas plays as well), undoubtedly reflect the self-image of the minor clergy and poor students. The plays plead for the social and economic needs of these young men and boys, all the while demonstrating to their benefactors and audience the great skill with which they carried out important musical and liturgical functions throughout the year. Of course Augustinian canons regular, such as Richard of St Victor or the mature Gerhoch of Reichersberg, who believed that cathedral canons should give up their property and live communally, would turn jaundiced eyes toward activities so intimately connected with the preservation of this system in the cathedrals.

If it is correct that *Danielis ludus* was designed for a reformed Feast of Fools celebration, then the play may well have been written and performed by the community of minor clergy at Beauvais cathedral, but under the supervision and with the blessings of higher authorities of the church. Its audience would have been made up of the entire collegiate community – assembled, as was traditional, to celebrate the Christmas Octave. But were the townspeople present as well? The

---

103 See discussion of this passage and further references in Morrison, 'The Church as Play', p. 135.
104 See his *Summa de ecclesiasticis officiis*, cap. 120, p. 223. According to Beleth, this playing is but one of many reversals common in popular custom during the month of December.
105 See Chambers, *The Mediaeval Stage*, vol. 1, p. 324.

Feast of Fools was the one day out of all the year that the clergy was most wont to entertain the people. And the composition of the audience would have been affected by this attitude, as well as by the time the play was scheduled during the liturgical round. *Daniel*, and other large-scale plays from the late twelfth and early thirteenth centuries, presumably could just as well be put on at the close of Vespers as at the close of Matins.[106] Because the people were likely to be present in the building at the time of Vespers, these circumstances increased the likelihood that the clergy would come out into the nave so that the people could witness their plays and entertainments. We must assume great fluidity in the traditions: sometimes plays would be staged for the people and sometimes not.

Indeed the musically complex *Danielis ludus*, with its constant and lengthy processions, may well have been performed, at least some years, in the nave of the church. Such a location would reinforce the themes of the work in several ways. During the twelfth and thirteenth centuries, massive rood screens were erected in northern French cathedrals, separating the choir and the clergy from the people.[107] This division of space created two worlds within the church, one sacred and sacramental, the other secular and of the people. Although the clergy often sang from the top of the rood screen or jubé, the opportunities for actual mingling between clergy and people were relatively few – restricted to those processions and stational liturgies when the ecclesiastical establishment would come forth from its walled enclave to celebrate in other parts of the church or of the town.[108] Thus at least some liturgical plays written for cathedrals stand as vivid witnesses to the festive occasions that would temporarily ignore the walls between clergy and people, and *Daniel* is a most likely candidate for being such a work. In plays staged in the nave, representatives from the musical and intellectual forces responsible for the enclosed cathedral liturgy came forth, both to entertain and to edify. Thus if *Daniel* is such a play, it mediates not only between minor clerics and canons, but also between people and clergy, and it makes fun of the rigid boundaries usually placed between these various groups.[109]

106 Just because 'Te Deum laudamus' follows a play is no proof at this late date that the work must have been performed at the close of Matins. By the late twelfth century, the singing of 'Te Deum' at the close of a play was a loosely held convention, which could be altered if the situation demanded. Hilarius said at the end of the *Historia* 'With the play being finished, if it was at Matins, let Darius begin the "Te Deum laudamus"; but if at Vespers, the "Magnificat anima mea Dominum".'

107 For an introduction to this subject, see Jean Mallion, *Le jubé de la cathédrale de Chartres* ([Chartres], 1964).

108 A picture of a fully developed stational liturgy emerges from the ordinals of Chartres. This liturgy is the subject of my forthcoming book on the liturgical life of Chartres cathedral in the eleventh, twelfth, and early thirteenth centuries.

109 In a plenary address before the North American Academy of Liturgy (St Louis, 1990), Ron Grimes discussed clowning within ritual action. This paper will presumably be published in the 'Proceedings' of the Academy.

Du Tilliot, writing in the mid-eighteenth century, spoke of the Feast of Fools as betokening the ignorance and barbarism of the centuries preceding the Italian Renaissance of the fifteenth century.[110] He failed to consider that the festivals and plays of the Feast of Fools were created at a time when much of cultural life still centred around local cathedrals with their liturgy and music, their frequent and lavish processions and ceremonies. There were popular traditions of all sorts that served to keep the clergy in touch with each other and with the people they ostensibly served. For, in the thirteenth century, at least, a cathedral, in some sense, still belonged to its people: 'they had helped erect it, with their sinew, with their wit, with their farthings and their pounds'.[111] *Danielis ludus*, with its deliberate mixture of the sacred and the secular, the serious and the comic, served to renew bonds too easily forgotten between masters and servants, teachers and students, clergy and people, God and man.

110 See Du Tilliot, p. 1.
111 Henry Kraus, *Gold Was the Mortar: The Economics of Cathedral Building* (London, 1979), p. xi.

5

THE MASS OF GUILLAUME DE MACHAUT IN THE CATHEDRAL OF REIMS

ANNE WALTERS ROBERTSON

Until the late eighteenth century, this epitaph in the nave of the cathedral of Reims marked the burial place of poet and composer Guillaume de Machaut and his brother Jean:

> Guillelmus de Machaudio . suusque Johannes frater.
> sunt in loco concordio . juncti sicut ad os crater.
> horum an[n]iversarium . est juxta petitorium.
> oratio de defunctis . diebus sabbathi cunctis.
> pro animabus eorum . amicorumque suorum.
> dicetur a sacerdote . celebraturo devote.
> ad roëllam in altari . missam quae debet cantari.
> pro quorum oratione . cum pia devotione.
> ad eorum memoriam . percepimus pecuniam.
> trecentorum florenorum . nuncupatorum francorum.
> suis exequ[u]toribus . pro emendis reddVdVdVbus.
> ad dicte misse crementum . reddituum et fomentum.

Portions of this article were presented at the fifty-fifth annual meeting of the American Musicological Society in Austin on 27 October, 1989. A Grant-in-Aid from the American Council of Learned Societies in 1988 and a Faculty Research Support Award from the University of Chicago in 1989 made it possible for me to carry out research in libraries and archives in Reims and Paris. I thank the staffs of the Archives de la Marne and of the Bibliothèque Municipale in Reims for their generous aid. Numerous colleagues assisted me in various ways, and I am pleased to acknowledge the help of Jennifer Bloxam, Howard Mayer Brown, Lawrence Earp, David Fallows, Barbara Haggh, Paula Higgins, Standley Howell, Peter Lefferts, Thomas Payne, Alejandro Planchart, Donna Sadler, Pamela Starr, Andrew Wathey, and Craig Wright. Professor Richard Helmholz of the Law School of The University of Chicago kindly advised me on legal issues connected with medieval testaments, and he, along with Jeremy Noble, gave me useful suggestions on the interpretation of the epitaph cited herein. I am particularly grateful to Daniel Leech-Wilkinson for his comments and for sharing with me sections of his forthcoming study and edition of Machaut's Mass. Manuscript abbreviations found here are based on the system used in *The New Grove Dictionary of Music and Musicians* (London, 1980).

in eadem presentium . solerter venientium.

hos fratres salvet dominus . qui tollit omne facinus.[1]

[Guillaume de Machaut and his brother Jean

have been joined together in the grave just as bowl to mouth.

Their anniversary is according to their petition:

a prayer for the dead will be said every Saturday

for their souls and for those of their loved ones

by a priest who will devoutly celebrate

the Mass which should be sung, by virtue of their prayer,

with pious devotion to their memory

at the altar near the *Rouelle*. We have received the sum

of three hundred *florins*, called *francs*,

from their executors for the purchase of revenues

for the growth of the revenues of the said Mass and for the nourishment

of those present and skilfully taking part in the Mass.

May the Lord who takes away all sin save these brothers.]

What was the nature of the 'Mass which [was] sung . . . at the altar near the *Rouelle*'? Did it include the movements of the renowned polyphonic Mass of Guillaume de Machaut?

The composer himself does not say, for nowhere in his voluminous writings does he mention the Mass. The two copies of the work apparently made during his lifetime and under his supervision (*Vg*, *A*)[2] differ in their designations of the piece.

---

1 F: RSc 1941, p. 94. The original epitaph still stood in the church in the early eighteenth century, at which time Charles Drouin Regnault copied it in the aforementioned manuscript, titled *Recueil choisi des épitaphes anciennes et modernes* (on F: RSc 1941, see Henri Loriquet, ed., *Catalogue général des manuscrits des bibliothèques publiques de France: Départements, t. 39 – Reims*, vol. 2/2 (Paris, 1906), pp. 998–9.) Another roughly contemporaneous transcription, introduced by the words 'Messe de Beate', was made by Canon of Reims Jean Weyen (F: RSc 1773, fol. 488v, no. 178). Weyen's reading differs slightly in three places: 1.1, 'Guillermus'; 1.3, 'anniversarium'; and 1.4, 'oratio *pro* defunctis'. Subsequent publications of the epitaph contain one or more errors in transcription and/or translation: Henry Vincent, *Les inscriptions anciennes de l'arrondissement de Vouziers ou rélatives à la région*, Epigraphie ardennaise (Reims, 1892), p. 266, no. 121; Henri Jadart, *Les inscriptions de la cathédrale de Reims*, Travaux de l'Académic Nationale de Reims 118 (Reims, 1907), 255–6; Armand Machabey, *Guillaume de Machault, 130?–1377: La vie et l'oeuvre musical*, 2 vols. (Paris, 1955), vol. 1, pp. 69–70; Jean Goy, 'Note sur la tombe de Guillaume de Machaut en la Cathédrale de Reims,' *Guillaume de Machaut: Colloque – Table Ronde (19–22 Avril 1978)* (Paris, 1982), p. 154; and Daniel Leech-Wilkinson, *Machaut's Mass: An Introduction* (forthcoming, Oxford, 1990). An abbreviated French translation is found in André Douce, *Guillaume de Machaut: Musicien et poète rémois* (Reims, 1948), p. 56. Machabey says that the epitaph disappeared from the church in the late eighteenth century: *Guillaume de Machaut*, vol. 1, p. 70.

2 Machaut MS *Vg*=US: NYw (no number), fols. 283v–296; MS *A*=F: Pn, fr. 1584, fols. 438v–451. The Mass is also included in F: Pn, fr. 1585 (MS *B*), fols. 281v–294; fr. 9221 (MS *E*), fols. 164v–170; ft. 22545–22546 (MS *F–G*), fols. 125v–133v. Part of the Ite missa est also exists

The earliest manuscript (*Vg*)[3] assigns the Mass to the Virgin Mary ('Ci commence la Messe de Nostre Dame'),[4] but this rubric recurs in no other source that transmits the work. Instead, the later manuscript *A* labels it 'La Messe',[5] while the three other manuscripts that include the Mass (*B, E, F-G*) omit titles altogether. The discrepancy between the rubrics in *Vg* and *A* calls in question the generally accepted assignment of the work to the Virgin. And Machaut's silence on the Mass even prompts us to ask whether he in fact wrote it for the cathedral in which he lived during much of the last four decades of his life.[6]

Not surprisingly, scholars have tried to explain the function of the Mass in terms of contemporaneous political and religious events, going in some cases well beyond the immediate cathedral environment. A legend arose in the eighteenth century that the work had been written for the coronation of Charles V in the church on 19 May 1364.[7] In the 1970s, Richard Hoppin theorized; that the musical emphasis placed on the words 'et in terra pax' in the Gloria might relate the Mass, at least

independently in I: Pu 1475 (*Pad A*), fol. [44] (4) (foliation as given in Kurt von Fischer and Max Lütolf, *Handschriften mit mehrstimmigen Musik des 14., 15. und 16. Jahrhunderts*, RISM, B/IV/4 [Munich, 1972], 1000). For evidence of a concordance for the Mass in a lost manuscript, see Lawrence M. Earp, 'Scribal Practice, Manuscript Production and the Transmission of Music in Late Medieval France: The Manuscripts of Guillaume de Machaut' (PhD dissertation, Princeton University, 1983), p. 16 (citing Lawrence Gushee).

3 François Avril has recently reassessed the dates of the principal Machaut manuscripts: *C* = 1350–6; *Vg* = 1370–2; *A* = 1370–7; *E* = *c*. 1390; *F–G* = 1390s ('Les Manuscrits enluminés de Guillaume de Machaut: Essai de chronologie', *Guillaume de Machaut: Colloque – Table Ronde (19–22 Avril 1978)* (Paris, 1982), pp. 117–33). Elizabeth Keitel had previously demonstrated that *B* likewise dates from 1370–2 ('The Importance of Machaut's paper Manuscript (Bib. Nat. F. Fr. 1585)', paper presented at the annual meeting of the American Musicological Society in Washington, DC, 1976, and 'La Tradition manuscrite de Guillaume de Machaut', in *Guillaume de Machaut: Colloque – Table Ronde (19–22 Avril 1978)* (Paris, 1982), pp. 82–9. Margaret Bent concludes that the contents of manuscript *B* were copied from *Vg*, except for Machaut's poem *La Prise d'Alexandrie*, which was transmitted from *B* to *Vg* ('The Machaut Manuscripts *Vg, B* and *E*', *Musica Disciplina* 37 (1983), 53–60). The nature of Machaut's relationship to the sources of his works written during his lifetime is treated in Earp, 'Scribal Practice', and 'Machaut's Role in the Production of Manuscripts of His Works', *JAMS* 42 (1989), 461–503.

4 A dim photograph of this folio of the manuscript, which is currently unavailable to scholars, can be seen in A. Beverly Barksdale, 'On the Planning and Arranging of Music Exhibitions', *Music Library Association: Notes* 10 (1953), 564. The title appears to be contemporaneous with the rest of the manuscript. (I am grateful to Lawrence Earp for his opinion on the date of this rubric.)

5 See the index of MS *A*.

6 Indeed, his silence is all the more resounding since it is likely that we possess the composer's complete extant poetic and musical *oeuvre*. Machabey treats Machaut's activities as canon of Reims in his *Guillaume de Machault*, vol. 1, pp. 13–83.

7 Gilbert Reaney reports that Abbé Lebeuf started this rumour, which has now been virtually discounted; see Reaney, 'Machaut, Guillaume de', in *The New Grove Dictionary* (London, 1980), vol. 11, p. 431, and Machabey, *Guillaume de Machault*, vol. 2, p. 114.

chronologically, to the Hundred Years' War, which for Reims culminated in the siege of that city in 1359–60.[8] Elizabeth Keitel, subsequently questioning the cyclic nature of the piece, suggested that it may not have been composed as a unit at all, but rather compiled 'in the finest southern [Avignon] tradition . . . from previously unrelated sections', perhaps for use in a Marian feast.[9] Most recently, Kurt Markstrom has speculated that 'the Mass was composed or compiled . . . during the early 1360s to serve as a votive offering to the Virgin for having answered the prayers of the city by sparing it from destruction by the English'.[10] Whereas valid observations can be found in these theories, no compelling reason for the existence of the work has yet emerged.

At the same time, the notion that Machaut's Mass was in fact intimately related to the ritual of Reims Cathedral – the composer's silence notwithstanding – remains virtually unexplored. In the early eighteenth century Charles Drouin Regnault, compiler of epitaphs and other curiosities from the cathedral, set the tone for all subsequent readings of the above epitaph for Guillaume and Jean de Machaut when he claimed that the brothers established the Saturday Mass for Mary which was sung weekly in Reims Cathedral:

Guillaume and Jean de Machaut were both brothers and canons of the church of Notre-Dame of Reims. They are the ones who founded the Mass of the Virgin that is sung on Saturdays in the aforementioned church, as explained in their epitaph which can be seen on the plaque near the altar of the *Rouelle* in the nave.[11]

Accepting this view, Machaut's biographer Armand Machabey tried to connect the polyphonic Mass with this Saturday service but offered little evidence to support his hypothesis.[12] That evidence does exist. A wealth of heretofore unexamined material from the archives of the medieval cathedral of Reims bears on the question. Service books from the church and architectural evidence, moreover, shed important light on the liturgical, musical, and spatial context in which Machaut worked. Evaluated singly and then collectively, these witnesses from Reims Cathedral offer an explanation of the nature of the 'Mass which [was] sung . . . at the altar near the *Rouelle*.'

---

8 *Medieval Music* (New York, 1978), p. 419. On the siege of Reims, see Pierre Desportes, *Reims et les rémois aux XIIIe et XIVe siècles* (Paris, 1979), pp. 550–62.

9 'The So-Called Cyclic Mass of Guillaume de Machaut: New Evidence for an Old Debate', *MQ*, 68 (1982), 323.   10 'Machaut and the Wild Beast', *Acta Musicologica* 61 (1989), 36.

11 'Guillaume et Jean de Machaux, tous deux frères et chanoines de l'église de Notre-Dame de Reims. Ce sont eux qui ont fondé la messe de la Vierge qu'on chante les samedis dans la susdite église. C'est ainsi que s'en explique leur épitaphe que l'on voit sur du cuivre proche l'autel de la Roëlle, à la nef' (F:RSc 1941, p. 94).

12 *Guillaume de Machault*, vol. 1, p. 70; vol. 2, pp. 114–15.

LITURGICAL EVIDENCE

The four isorhythmic movements of Machaut's Mass – Kyrie, Sanctus, Agnus Dei, and Ite missa est – are based strictly on well-known liturgical chants. It now appears, in addition, that the tenors of the Gloria and Credo are related to recognizable melodies as well. Jacques Handschin first stated that the tenor of the Credo bears some resemblance to the melody of the ubiquitous chant called Credo I in the Vatican edition,[13] and Daniel Leech-Wilkinson has recently proposed that the Gloria likewise paraphrases loosely the melody known as Gloria IV.[14] All of these chants were current in Europe in the fourteenth century,[15] but more importantly for the origin and destination of the Mass, they were present in the region of Reims as well.

To demonstrate that the melodies underlying the Mass correspond to the liturgy of Reims, we should be able to locate them in the Kyriale of the cathedral. Whereas the city of Reims is well represented by extant chants of the Ordinary of the Mass, the Kyriale of the cathedral itself survives in only one source, the notated missal F: RSc 224 (Table 5.1). This brief Kyriale of two folios includes three melodies each for the Kyrie, Gloria, Sanctus, and Agnus.[16] In the absence of other Kyriales from the cathedral, we must take into account the witness of manuscripts from nearby houses. Three Kyriales from other churches in the city of Reims and three from the neighbouring town of Châlons-sur-Marne in the diocese of Reims have survived.[17] These manuscripts, listed in Table 5.1, reveal which chants were current in the city

13 'Zur Frage der melodischen Paraphrasierung im Mittelalter', Zeitschrift für Musikwissenschaft 10 (1928), 542–3.   14 Leech-Wilkinson, Machaut's Mass.

15 Regarding the Agnus, on the other hand, Elizabeth Keitel states that 'the chant on which Machaut based his Agnus (Mass XVII) is absent in all Kyriales from the area, except in those compiled by the Franciscans' ('The So-Called Cyclic Mass', 315). In spite of this assertion, the Agnus was known in northern France. In addition to its appearance in F: Pn, lat. 842 from Châlons-sur-Marne, cited by Keitel and listed in Table 5.1 of this essay (see the discussion of the date of this manuscript in note 19 below), the melody is found in a Parisian gradual (F: Pn, lat. 1337, fol. 337v) and in a gradual from Saint-Corneille of Compiègne (F: Pn, lat. 16828, fols. 170v–171), both from the fourteenth century. Further concordances for this Agnus in other periods can be found in Schildbach, Das einstimmige Agnus Dei und seine handschriftliche Überlieferung vom 10. bis zum 16. Jahrhundert (PhD dissertation, University of Erlangen, 1967), melody 34.

16 The precise layout and content of this Kyriale can be seen in David Hiley, 'Ordinary of Mass Chants in English, North French and Sicilian Manuscripts', Journal of the Plainsong and Mediaeval Music Society 9/1 (1986), 49. The brevity of this Kyriale may be due to the fact that F: RSc 224 was apparently intended for use in the chapel of Saint Bartholomew, located in the south transept of the cathedral (see Diagram 5.1, letter 's'), rather than in the choir of the church; see Loriquet, ed., Catalogue général, vol. 1/1, pp. 205–7.

17 A distance of about twenty-five miles separates the two cities; see the map in Gallia Christiana, 16 vols. (Paris, 1715–1865), vol. 9 (1751), folded page at beginning of volume.

and its surroundings. The non-cathedral manuscripts moreover may supplement the information given in F: RSc 224 on the *Kyriale* of the cathedral, since, as we will see in the next section, the musical readings in most of these sources agree with those in F: RSc 224.

The tenors that Machaut chose for his Mass are accounted for in the sources from the area of Reims (Table 5.1),[18] and all the melodies appear together in the *Kyriale* of the missal from Châlons-sur-Marne, F: Pn, lat. 842.[19] Machaut probably knew these chants, having sung them in the course of his daily duties as canon in the cathedral. But why did he select the particular melodies that are found in the Mass, that is, Kyrie IV, Gloria IV, Credo I, Sanctus XVII, Agnus XVII (numbers as in Vatican edition)?

If the assignment of the Mass to Mary in the earliest manuscript (*Vg*) is correct, then the chants on which Machaut based the work should pertain to celebrations for the Virgin. By the late fifteenth and sixteenth centuries, the preferred *cantus firmi* for polyphonic ordinary settings for Mary were Kyrie IX, Gloria IX, Credo I, Sanctus XVII, and Agnus XVII,[20] the first two of these chants differing from the ones Machaut employed. But Renaissance composers did not universally adhere to this sequence of melodies, nor was there a standard formula for such services in Machaut's day.[21] For this reason, the chants that Machaut used in the Mass have to

18 Since the universal melody for Credo I was known virtually everywhere, I have not included it in Table 5.1.

19 Victor Leroquais shows that the original portion of F: Pn, lat. 842 was copied in 1325, and he states that the gathering containing the *Kyriale* (fols. 196–202v) is in 'another hand'; see *Les sacramentaires et les missels manuscrits des bibliothèques publiques de France*, 4 vols. (Paris, 1924), vol. 2, p. 209. The *conservateurs* of the Bibliothèque Nationale have kindly informed me that this gathering is later than 1325, but that it still probably dates from the fourteenth century, presumably the latter part. In her study of liturigcal sources from Reims, Keitel, on the other hand, seems to exclude this manuscript from consideration, implying that its 'later' *Kyriale* would have postdated Machaut ('The So-Called Cyclic Mass', 315, n. 28). Even if this particular *Kyriale* were added shortly after Machaut's death, we cannot rule out the evidence it supplies, for in view of the paucity of surviving sources from Reims, it is entirely possible that the *Kyriale* of F: Pn, lat. 842 witnesses melodies in use during Machaut's lifetime.

20 See Gustav Reese, 'The Polyphonic "*Missa de Beata Virgine*" as a Genre: The Background of Josquin's Lady Mass', in *Josquin des Prez: Proceedings of the International Josquin Festival-Conference Held at The Juilliard School at Lincoln Center in New York City, 21–25 June 1971*, ed. Edward Lowinsky and Bonnie Blackburn (London, 1976), p. 593.

21 Ibid. The fourteenth-century Marian formularies from two Parisian houses will also serve to illustrate this point. The cathedral of Notre-Dame in Paris used Kyrie IX, Gloria IX, Sanctus XVII, and Agnus II in the Saturday Mass for Mary, except when it fell within important octaves, at which times Kyrie XII, Gloria I and an appropriate Sanctus and Agnus from the feast were employed; see Craig Wright, *Music and Ceremony at Notre Dame of Paris, 500–1500* (Cambridge, 1989), pp. 86–7. The nearby royal abbey of Saint-Denis, on the other hand, employed Kyrie XII, Gloria XI, Sanctus XVII, Agnus IX in its Marian services; see Anne Robertson, *The Service Books of the Royal Abbey of Saint-Denis: Images of Ritual and Music in the Middle Ages* (Oxford, 1991), pp. 163–4.

Table 5.1. *Occurrence of chants from the Machaut Mass in manuscripts from Reims and Châlons-sur-Marne, 13th–15th centuries*

The movements of the Ordinary named here are the ones which appear as tenors in the Machaut Mass. In the standard catalogues, they are: Kyrie = Melnicki[1] no. 18; Gloria = Bosse[2] no. 56; Sanctus = Thannabaur[3] no. 32; Agnus = Schildbach[4] no. 34. Information on the Ite Missa Est is given on p. 110 below. The manuscripts are listed in approximate chronological order.

Manuscript	Type	Date	Usage	Chant	Folio	Rubric	Remarks
F:RSc 264	Gradual	13	St-Thierry, Reims	Kyrie IV	72	Item in precipuis festis	6th of 18 Kyries
				Gloria IV	73v	In precipuis	1st of 6 Glorias
				Sanctus XVII	75v	In precipuis sollemniatibus	2nd of 6 Sanctus
I:Ac 695	Troper, Proser	13/2	Troper probably in part from Reims	Kyrie IV	6		Trope *Cunctipotens genitor*
					9v		Trope *Rex virginum*
				Gloria IV	19		Trope *Regnum tuum solium o rex*
				Sanctus XVII	44v		
					47v		Trope *Sanctorum exultatio*
F:Pa 595	Missal/Breviary	13–14	St-Etienne, Châlons-sur-Marne	Kyrie IV	247	Item in totis dupplicibus	4th of 13 Kyries
				Sanctus XVII	243v	Item in totis dupplicibus	4th of 4 Sanctus
F:Pn, lat. 845	Missal	14/2	Châlons-sur-Marne	Kyrie IV	208v	In festis dupplicibus	5th of 6 Kyries
				Gloria IV	210		3rd of 3 Glorias
				Sanctus XVII	210v		1st of 2 Sanctus
F:RSc 224	Missal	14/2	Reims, Cathedral	Kyrie IV	246		2nd of 3 Kyries
				Gloria IV	246		1st of 3 Glorias
				Sanctus XVII	247		1st of 3 Sanctus
F:Pn, lat. 842	Missal	1325, Kyriale later 14th century	Châlons-sur-Marne	Kyrie IV	196v–7		Trope *Cunctipotens genitor*, 2nd of 3 Kyries

	Item	Folio	Rubric	Notes
	Gloria IV	197v		4th of 4 Glorias
	Sanctus XVII	198v–9	In terciis dupplicibus	This Sanctus paired with this Agnus.
	Agnus XVII	199	Same rubric as Sanctus above	
	Ite	126v		Follows a Canon of Mass that is rubricated 'De beata virgine Maria in Assumptione'
F: RSc 266 Gradual 15 St-Denis, Reims	Kyrie IV	66v	In minoribus sollemnitatibus[5]	This Kyrie paired with this Gloria.
	Gloria IV	67	Same rubric as Kyrie above	
	Sanctus XVII	69v	Rubric 'De beata Maria' at beginning of cycle	Sanctus and Agnus are part of an entire cycle (K-G-S-A)
	Agnus XVII	69v	Same rubric as Sanctus above	

[1] Margaretha Landwehr-Melnicki, *Das einstimmige Kyrie des lateinischen Mittelalters*, Forschungsbeiträge zur Musikwissenschaft 1 (Regensburg, 1955).

[2] Detlev Bosse, *Untersuchung Einstimmiger Mittelalterlicher melodien zum 'Gloria' in Excelsis Deo'*, Forschungsbeiträge zur Musikwissenschaft 2 (Regensburg, 1955).

[3] Peter Thannabaur, *Das einstimmiger Sanctus der römischen Messe in der handschriftlichen Überlieferung des 11. bis 16. Jahrhunderts*, Erlanger Arbeiten zur Musikwissenschaft 1 (Munich, 1962).

[4] See Note 15.

[5] This rubric encompasses duplex feasts. The Kyrie is preceded by the Kyrie *Fons bonitatis* (fol. 66), which is introduced by 'In majoribus sollemnitatibus', which includes the handful of highest feasts of the year (Christmas, Easter, Pentecost, Assumption, etc.). It is followed by a Kyrie that is rubricated 'Diebus dominicis et festis simplicibus'.

be examined one-by-one to determine the appropriateness of each for Marian celebrations. We have just seen that Machaut's Credo (I), Sanctus and Agnus (XVII) were sanctioned in masses for the Virgin in the High Renaissance. In addition, both the Kyrie and the Gloria that Machaut used (from Vatican Mass IV) had associations with Mary.

The connection of Kyrie IV with the Virgin seems to stem from its acquisition of the Marian trope *Rex virginum*, a text known in France as early as the twelfth century.[22] This trope appears in numerous monophonic and polyphonic settings of Kyrie IV,[23] and a fourteenth-century plainchant cycle rubricated for Marian solemnities in a gradual from Aosta includes the Kyrie *Rex virginum*.[24] As late as the end of the fifteenth century, the composers Juan de Anchieta and Pedro de Escobar still set this troped Kyrie in a polyphonic Mass for Mary.[25] Even the older and more customary trope for Kyrie IV, *Cunctipotens genitor*, was sung on feasts of Mary in the fourteenth-century Sainte-Chapelle in Paris.[26] Gloria IV, although not traditionally a Marian Gloria, was usually paired with this Kyrie.

The remaining movements of Machaut's Mass also have demonstrable connections with Mary. Sanctus and Agnus XVII were already firmly linked to Mary in France and Spain in the fourteenth century[27] and came to dominate in polyphonic Marian masses by the late fifteenth century, as noted above. The Ite missa est is derived not from an Ordinary chant at all, but rather from the melisma *O christi pietas* from the Saint Nicholas Antiphon *O christi pietas*, a popular fragment in the Middle Ages.[28] At least one French[29] and one German[30] source assign this Ite to

22 See Keitel, 'The So-Called Cyclic Mass', 316.
23 See Kyries; marked with ★ in List of Sources, on pp. 138–9
24 I: AO 9-E-17, as cited in Kurt von Fischer, 'Neue Quellen zum Einstimmigen Ordinariumszyklus des 14. und 15. Jahrhunderts aus Italien', in *Liber amicorum Charles van den Borren* (Anvers, 1964), p. 66; see also Reese, 'The Polyphonic "Missa de Beata Virgine"', 593; and Keitel, 'The So-Called Cyclic Mass', 316–17. Dominique Catta refers either to this or to some other manuscript from Aosta when he mentions a source from the 'Bibl. de Mgr Duc'; Catta, 'Aux Origines du Kyriale', *Revue grégorienne* 34 (1955), 176–8.
25 Edited in Higini Anglés, *Música en la Corte de los Reyes Católicos*, Monumentos de la Música Espãola 1 (Madrid, 1941), pp. 35–61; see also Reese, 'The Polyphonic "Missa de Beata Virgine"', pp. 594–5.
26 See the incipits for the four principal feasts of Mary in the ordinary F: Pn lat. 1435, fols. 72, 77, 126, and 151.
27 See the discussions of thirteenth- and fourteenth-century *Kyriales* in Schrade, 'The Cycle of the Ordinarium Missae', 92; Kurt von Fischer, 'Neue Quellen', p. 65; and Keitel, 'The So-Called Cyclic Mass', 314–17.
28 On this chant, see Robertson, *The Service Books of the Royal Abbey of Saint-Denis* pp. 197, 207–12, and '*Benedicamus Domino*: the Unwritten Tradition', *JAMS* 41 (1988), 29, 31, 32, 33, 35, 40, 42.
29 F: Pa lat. 201, fol. 9v ('festis marie virginis et commemorationibus'). This early fifteenth-century source is also cited in Keitel, 'The So-Called Cyclic Mass', 316.
30 D: DO 844 (fol. 231v), a Franciscan gradual of the thirteenth through fifteenth centuries, likewise

Marian celebrations, and the chant was also used in the Sarum rite on feasts of three lessons, which included the Saturday commemoration for Mary.[31]

Further corroboration of the Marian orientation of the chants that Machaut used in the Mass comes in the scant evidence of the manuscripts from Reims (Table 5.1). The Kyrie is troped with *Rex virginum* in the thirteenth-century compilation from Paris and Reims in I: Ac 695,[32] and the trope is rubricated 'De beata Maria' in a fifteenth-century Parisian missal found in the library at Reims.[33] The indication 'de beata Maria' in F: RSc 266 from Saint-Denis of Reims demonstrates that the Sanctus and Agnus were appropriate for Marian feasts by the early fifteenth century, and probably earlier as well. The unrubricated Ite in F: Pn, lat. 842 from Châlons-sur-Marne immediately follows a Canon of the Mass that is introduced by the title 'de beata virgine Maria in Assumptione'.

It appears, then, that each of the chants found in Machaut's Mass has a ready association with the Virgin. Moreover, since formularies of the Marian Ordinary were not fixed in the fourteenth century, Machaut's combination of these melodies in his Mass represents a possible grouping in a work intended for the Virgin. Thus the sole piece of contemporaneous evidence for the function of the Mass, the rubric

introduces this Ite with a Marian rubric. (I am grateful to William Eifrig for informing me of this source.)

31 See Robertson, *The Service Books of the Royal Abbey of Saint-Denis* p.209. The Ite also appeared in some memorial services (ibid.).

32 This manuscript was evidently copied from exemplars from different places. The first section of the book is a troper that contains chants for the Ordinary of the Mass and has characteristics pointing both to Reims and to Paris as place of origin. David Hiley states that 'it is impossible to say whether Assisi 695 has Reims or Paris items without studying variant readings in these and a wide range of other sources' (1981 source given below). The examination of two variant readings in Examples 5.1 and 5.2 of this essay shows that the Troper includes two versions each of the Kyrie (fols. 6, 9v) and Sanctus (fols. 44v, 47v) that are found in Machaut's Mass (Table 5.1). The different readings for each chant seem typical, respectively, of Reims (fols. 6, 44v) and of Paris (fols. 9v, 47v). It is probably safe therefore to accept the Reims readings as indication that at least part of the Troper of I: Ac 695 was taken from a model from that city. The second section of the manuscript comprises three prosers, the first of which probably comes from Saint-Nicasius, a Benedictine monastery under the control of the archbishop of Reims. The second and third prosers are evidently Parisian, the former perhaps from Saint-Victor, the latter possibly from Paris Cathedral. On I: Ac 695, see the edition of the text in Ulysse Chevalier, *Sacramentaire et martyrologe de l'abbaye de Saint-Rémy: Martyrologe, calendrier, ordinaires et prosaire de la métropole de Reims (VIIIe–XIIIe siècle), publiés d'après les manuscrits de Paris, Londres, Reims et Assise*, Bibliothèque liturgique 7 (Paris, 1900), pp. 358–94; and the discussions in Hiley, 'Rouen, Bibliothèque Municipale, MS 249 (A.280) and the Early Paris Repertory of Ordinary of Mass Chants and Sequences', *Music and Letters* 70 (1989), 477; Hiley, Further Observations on W1: The Ordinary of Mass Chants and the Sequences', *Journal of the Plainsong and Mediaeval Music Society* 4 (1981), 68; Gilbert Reaney, *Manuscripts of Polyphonic Music: 11th–Early 14th Century*, RISM B/IV/1 (Munich, 1966), p. 607; and Heinrich Husmann, *Tropen- und Sequenzenhandschriften*, *RISM* B/V/1 (Munich), 1964), pp. 167–9. Earlier literature on I: Ac 695 is cited in these works.

33 F: RSc 233 (fol. cccxlix).

'Ci commence la Messe de Nostre Dame' in *Vg*, may well reflect Machaut's wish that the work embellish a Marian feast or votive service.

What celebration might it have enhanced? Five major Marian festivals were solemnized at Reims in the fourteenth century: Purification (2 February), Annunciation (25 March), Assumption (15 August), Nativity (9 September), and Conception (9 December).[34] We will see further on, however, that there is good reason to eliminate the Marian feasts, which would have been sung in the choir of the cathedral, and to scrutinize instead the votive services for the Virgin, which were performed at side altars in the church. The epitaph for the Machaut brothers hints that the most likely Marian votive service was the Saturday Mass for the Virgin.

In fact, the format of the Saturday Mass in Reims Cathedral corresponds remarkably well to the content of Machaut's Mass. The five usual chants for the Ordinary of the Mass (Kyrie, Gloria, Credo, Sanctus, Agnus), along with the Ite missa est, were sung in all seasons except Advent and Lent. At these times, of course, the Gloria was omitted, and the Ite missa est was replaced by Benedicamus Domino.[35] The proper melodies for this Mass naturally varied according to the season of the year, and the two formularies given in the extant sources from Reims are *Rorate celi* and *Salve sancta parens* (Table 5.2). It may be no accident that Machaut's polyphonic Mass, like the Saturday Mass for Mary, contains all six movements of the Ordinary. So far, therefore, this service appears to be a possible destination for Machaut's Mass.

34 See the directions for these feasts in the ordinaires F: RSc 328 and F: RSc 329 from the thirteenth century, F: RSc 330 from the fourteenth century, and F: RSc 331 from the fifteenth century. The Feast of the Conception does not appear in the first hand of the calendars of most liturgical books of Reims until the fifteenth century, but it is included in the original hand of the thirteenth-century martyrology of Reims, Archives de la Marne, dépôt annex de Reims (hereinafter abbreviated AMR), 2G 661 (fol. 44), and in the texts of the thirteenth-century ordinaries mentioned above. It is evident, therefore, that the Conception of Mary was being celebrated in the cathedral by the mid-thirteenth century at the latest. Another popular feast, the Visitation of Mary (8 July), appears written by the second hand of only one fourteenth-century calendar from Reims (F: RSc 292) and was probably not celebrated in Reims during this period. One final late medieval festival for the Virgin, Mary of the Snows (5 August), was likewise adopted after the fourteenth century. This service appears in the second hand of the calendars of all the above manuscripts except F:RSc 331 (15th century), which contains the festival in the original hand, and it is absent from the texts of all fourteenth- and early fifteenth-century books. Keitel's suggestion that the Machaut Mass might be related in some way; to the introduction of this feast in the cathedral is thus unlikely, since there is no evidence that the feast was celebrated at Reims during his lifetime, Keitel, 'The So-Called Cyclic Mass', 322.

35 Instructions to this effect are found in the ordinaries of the cathedral: 'De beata Maria per adventum ad missam . . . Sabbato Gloria in excelsis non dicitur; sequentia dicitur *Ave maria* et Credo; Ite Missa Est non dicitur, sed Benedicamus; F: RSc 328, fol. 15v (published in Chevalier, *Sacramentaire et martyrologe*, p. 96); RSc 329, fol. 3v; RSc 330, fol. 16v; RSc 331, fol. 3v (on the dates of these sources, see note 34).

Table 5.2. *Propers for the Saturday Mass for Mary in Reims cathedral*

	Advent[1]	Other seasons[2]
Introit	Rorate celi desuper	Salve sancta parens
Epistle	Locutus est Dominus	Ab initio et ante secula
Gradual	Qui sedes Domine	Benedicta et venerabilis es
Alleluia	Ostende nobis Domine	Post partum virgo
Sequence	Ave Maria gratia plena	[not specified]
Gospel	Missus est angelus	Loquente jhesus ad turbas
Offertory	Ave maria gratia plena	Felix namque es sacra virgo
Communion	Ecce virgo concipiet	Beata viscera marie virginis

[1]Text incipits only given in the ordinaries from Reims F: RSc 328, fol. 15v (ed. in Chevalier, *Sacramentaire et martyrologe*, 96); RSc 329, fol. 3v; RSc 330, fol. 16v; RSc 331, fol. 3v.
[2]Texts and music found in the missal from Reims F: RSc 224, fols. 233–4.

Quite apart from the connection of the tenors of Machaut's Mass with services for the Virgin, the rubrics in Table 5.1 show that these melodies were also used on duplex feasts in Reims.[36] The dual allegiance of these chants both to Marian and to duplex celebrations was probably not contradictory. The rubric for Sanctus XVII in a mid-fourteenth-century missal from Saint-Denis in Paris ('dominicis diebus et festis dupplicibus et sabbato de beata maria ad magnam missam') shows that the same chant was assigned both to duplex services and to the Saturday Mass for Mary,[37] and it is possible that similar instructions were once found in service books from Reims. The Marian-duplex association may also reflect the fact that the five Marian festivals were duplex at Reims or that polyphony was normally used in feasts of duplex rank and higher. In most churches moreover services of duplex rank included the celebrations for saints whose remains were in the church. Reims

36 The Sanctus has the rubric 'terciis dupplicibus', a subcategory of duplex feasts, in F: Pn, lat. 842. A description of feasts 'in terciis dupplicibus', can be found in the ordinary from Châlons-sur-Marne, F: Pn, lat. 10579, fols. 12v–14. Jacques Chailley ignores the medieval rubrics for the Sanctus and Agnus that Machaut chose, and he relies on the modern designations which assign these two chants to Sundays in Advent and Lent. He concludes that the Sanctus and Agnus would not have been used with the Kyrie because of their 'penitential simplicity'; see Chailley, 'La Composition dans la messe de G. da Machaut', in *Guillaume de Machaut: Colloque – Table Ronde (19–22 Avril 1978)* (Paris, 1982), pp. 281–2. In manuscripts from Reims, this Ite survives only in F: Pn, lat. 842, where it is not specifically rubricated. In other houses, however, it is assigned most often to duplex feasts. (The liturgical placement of this Ite is treated in Robertson, *The Service Books of the Royal Abbey of Saint-Denis*, pp. 207–12.
37 GB: Lva 1346–1891, fol. 368 (see List of Sources).

Cathedral, one of the earliest churches in the West to be dedicated to the Virgin,[38] naturally possessed precious Marian relics.[39] Clearly the chants in Machaut's Mass, associated both with feasts of Mary and with festivals of duplex rank, were appropriate for a polyphonic work that might have been composed in honour of Mary, whose relics were the principal treasures of the church. And the composer's choice of melodies from those found in extant local service books supports the idea that the Mass was written for the cathedral of Reims.

MUSICAL EVIDENCE

Just as the selection of chants for Machaut's Mass seems consistent with the liturgy of Reims Cathedral, so the melodies stand in close agreement with the music of the church as well. A comparison of the tenors of the Mass with monophonic and polyphonic settings from France, England, Italy, and Spain shows that the chants adhere faithfully to melodies from the region of Reims. The similarities are most evident in Machaut's Kyrie and Sanctus, based on tunes which were widely disseminated in the late Middle Ages (see List of Sources on pp. 138–9).[40]

The tenor of the first section of the Kyrie[41] is remarkably close to versions of this chant found in English and Northern French manuscripts. In the first phrase,

38 See Donna Sadler-Davis, 'The Sculptural Program of the Verso of the West Facade of Reims Cathedral' (PhD dissertation, Indiana University, 1984), p. 2.

39 These included a shoe, a belt, some hair, and other clothing of the Virgin, in addition to some of the Holy Milk of Mary that nourished the Saviour; see Guillaume Marlot, *Histoire de la ville, cité et université de Reims, métropolitaine de la Gaule Belgique, divisée en douze livres contenant l'estat ecclésiastique et civil du païs*, 4 vols., (Reims, 1843–6), vol. 3, pp. 525–34; Charles Cerf, *Histoire et description de Notre-Dame de Reims*, 2 vols. (Reims, 1861), vol. 1, pp. 480–5; and Louis Paris, *La Chapelle du Saint-Laict dans la cathédrale de Reims* (Reims, 1885), pp. 14–20.

40 For the purposes of this detailed comparison, I have omitted the Gloria and Credo of Machaut's Mass, both of which heavily paraphrase their respective chants. Likewise excluded are the Agnus, which, though known in the fourteenth century in northern France, exists in only a few manuscripts, and the Ite missa est, which is transmitted with little variation from one source to another. Edward Kovarik briefly compares the tenors of Machaut's Kyrie, Sanctus, and Agnus with sources from different parts of Europe but without taking into account manuscripts from Reims and its immediate environs. He does conclude, however, that 'all three movements . . . are consistent with a French origin'; see Kovarik, 'Mid Fifteenth-Century Polyphonic Elaborations of the Plainchant *Ordinarium Missae*' (PhD dissertation, Harvard University, 1973), pp. 148–51.

41 A new edition of the Mass is forthcoming in Daniel Leech-Wilkinson, *Machaut's Mass*. Previous editions of the work include Heinrich Besseler, *Guillaume de Machaut: Musikalische Werke* (Leipzig, 1943), vol. 4, pp. 1–20 (ed. from Friedrich Ludwig's *Nachlass*); Guillaume de Van, *Guglielmi de Mascaudio Opera: La Messe de Nostre Dame*, CMM 2 (Rome, 1949); Leo Schrade, *Polyphonic Music of the Fourteenth Century* (Monaco, 1956), vol. 3, pp. 37–64; and Denis Stevens, *La Messe de Nostre-Dame* (London, 1973). A facsimile edition of the Mass is found in Friedrich Gennrich, *Guillaume de Machaut: La Messe de Nostre-Dame*, Summa Musicae Medii Aevi 1 (Darmstadt, 1957).

Example 5.1   Tenor of opening of Machant's Kyrie, compared with French, English, and Spanish sources. (For information on the manuscripts cited in the musical examples, see List of Sources, pp. 138–9.)

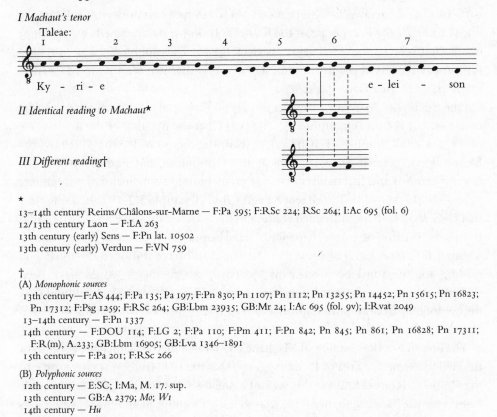

I *Machaut's tenor*

II *Identical reading to Machaut*★

III *Different reading†*

★
13–14th century Reims/Châlons-sur-Marne — F:Pa 595; F:RSc 224; RSc 264; I:Ac 695 (fol. 6)
12/13th century Laon — F:LA 263
13th century (early) Sens — F:Pn lat. 10502
13th century (early) Verdun — F:VN 759

†
(A) *Monophonic sources*
   13th century—F:AS 444; F:Pa 135; Pa 197; F:Pn 830; Pn 1107; Pn 1112; Pn 13255; Pn 14452; Pn 15615; Pn 16823;
      Pn 17312; F:Psg 1259; F:RSc 264; GB:Lbm 23935; GB:Mr 24; I:Ac 695 (fol. 9v); I:Rvat 2049
   13–14th century — F:Pn 1337
   14th century — F:DOU 114; F:LG 2; F:Pa 110; F:Pm 411; F:Pn 842; Pn 845; Pn 861; Pn 16828; Pn 17311;
      F:R(m), A.233; GB:Lbm 16905; GB:Lva 1346–1891
   15th century — F:Pa 201; F:RSc 266

(B) *Polyphonic sources*
   12th century — E:SC; I:Ma, M. 17. sup.
   13th century — GB:A 2379; *Mo*; *W1*
   14th century — *Hu*

differences from one source to another are minor except in one place. Machaut's fifth *talea* ends with G, and the first note of the sixth *talea* repeats G (Example 5.1). The Christe section likewise contains this double-G. The repeated Gs are by far the exception, not the rule, both in plainchant and polyphonic settings of this chant. We might speculate at first glance that Machaut himself doubled the G so that he would have seven complete *taleae*. But there is another explanation for the appearance of two Gs.

Example 5.1 shows that the handful of manuscripts transmitting the Kyrie with two Gs come from Reims and Châlons-sur-Marne, as well as from nearby Laon, a city likewise under the jurisdiction of the archbishop of Reims.[42] In contrast, the

42 Of the sources surveyed here, the only manuscripts with two Gs originating outside the immediate environs of Reims are F: Pn, lat. 10502 and F: VN 759, both early thirteenth-century missals from Sens and Verdun, respectively. F: Pn, lat. 10502 probably does not affect the

other thirty-odd monophonic and six polyphonic Kyries listed in Example 5.1 all
have one G. Surely this was the normal reading of the chant in Northern France and
England, whereas the double-G found in the region of Reims was a variant
particular to that area. When Machaut set out to compose his isorhythmic Kyrie, he
discovered that the first phrase of the Kyrie, as he knew it, contained twenty-eight
notes, precisely enough for seven perfect *taleae*. The double-G was not only
fortuitous in terms of the isorhythm, it was music that was familiar to Machaut –
music from Reims Cathedral.

Like the Kyrie, Machaut's Sanctus displays telltale variants which are particular
to the area of Reims (Example 5.2). The two Cs at the opening of the tenor voice
occur in a small number of manuscripts from the region of Reims, Châlons-sur-
Marne, Laon, Marchiennes, as well as the Dominican and Franciscan liturgies
(Example 5.2, II and III). In all other sources, including the majority of polyphonic
settings of this movement, the tenor begins *B-C* (Example 5.2, IV). It seems clear
that *C-C* was Machaut's intended reading in the Sanctus, for these notes reappear at
the third repetition of the word 'Sanctus'. Had he purposely changed the customary
opening *B-C* to avoid *B* at the outset, he could still have followed the usual *B-C*
reading for the third occurrence of 'Sanctus', where the *B* would have been
embedded more deeply in the polyphonic fabric. The fact that Machaut used *C* at
the beginnings of both phrases probably means that this was the reading he had in
his ear.

The identity of the opening of Machaut's Sanctus with the plainchant versions of
this melody from the area of Reims suggests that the *C-C* reading was exclusive to
the region of Reims. And yet this variant alone does not rule out all other possible
origins for the Sanctus, for we have seen that the Dominican and Franciscan books
likewise transmit the same incipit. A second musical peculiarity within this
narrower group of manuscripts (Example 5.2, II and III) demonstrates that the first
five notes of the tenor of Machaut's Sanctus were based on a reading traceable
directly to Reims and Châlons-sur-Marne. That variant is the fourth note *B* (= *B-
flat*) in Machaut's tenor, which appears in the four manuscripts from Reims and
Châlons-sur-Marne (Example 5.2, II). As in the case of the double-*C* reading, the *B*
is no accident – the note returns in the second phrase of Machaut's Sanctus and also
in the same four sources from Reims and neighbouring Châlons. Clearly the
opening succession of five notes in the Sanctus (*C-C-A-B-flat-A*) was distinctive to
Reims and Châlons-sur-Marne, and this reading is the version that Machaut knew

comparison, since it predates Machaut by a century and a half. The seventeenth-century copy of
another thirteenth-century gradual from Sens, F: SE 17, has a different reading altogether. F: VN
759 likewise is temporally removed from Machaut's day, although the double-G reading, if it
appeared in books from Verdun in the fourteenth century, can probably be explained by the
general proximity of Verdun to Reims, Laon, and Châlons-sur-Marne.

Example 5.2   Tenor of Machaut's Sanctus, first section, compared with French, English, and Italian sources

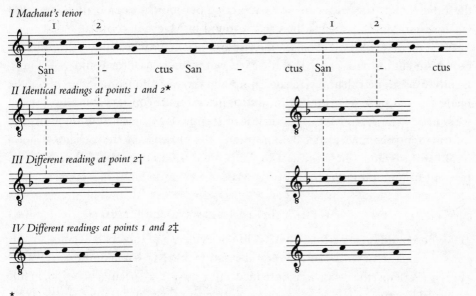

I Machaut's tenor

San — ctus   San — ctus   San — ctus

II Identical readings at points 1 and 2★

III Different reading at point 2†

IV Different readings at points 1 and 2‡

★
14th century Reims/Châlons-sur-Marne — F:Pn 842; Pn 845; F:RSc 224; RSc 266

†
(A) *Monophonic sources*
   12/13th century Laon — F:LA 263 (fol. 82v)
   13th century Verdun — F:VN 759
   13th century Reims — I:Ac 695 (fol. 44v)[1]
   13th century Dominican, Franciscan — GB:Lbm 23935; I:Rvat 2049
   13–14th century Châlons-sur-Marne — F:Pa 595
   14th century Marchiennes — F:DOU 114

(B) *Polyphonic sources*
   14th century Italy — I:Bc, Q 11

‡
(A) *Monophonic sources*
   12/13th century — F:LA 263 (fol. 82)[2]
   13th century — F:Pa 135; F: Pn 830; Pn 904; Pn 1107; Pn 1112;[3] Pn 15615; Pn 16823; F:RSc 264;[3] GB:Mr 24;[4]
      GB:Lbm 23935; I:Ac 695 (fol. 47v)
   14th century — F:LG 2; F:Pa 110; F:Pm 411; GB:Lbm 16905; GB:Lva 1346–1891

(B) *Polyphonic sources*
   13th century — *W1*
   14–15th century — GB:Lbm 462; Lbm 463; Lbm 40011B; GB:Ob D.R.3
   15th century — *OH*

[1] Reads C-C-C-A-A, both at the beginning and at the repetition.
[2] Reads C-A-A, both at the beginning and at the repetition.
[3] Reads B-C-A-F, both at the beginning and at the repetition.
[4] The reading in this Sarum missal is the standard one for Sarum sources. (I am grateful to Peter Lefferts for providing me with this information.)

as a consequence of his position in the cathedral. The preponderance of sources transmitting the beginning C-C-A-A and B-C-A-A (Example 5.2, III and IV), on the other hand, suggests that no manuscript outside the region of Reims and Châlons-sur-Marne contains the variant found in Machaut's Sanctus.[43]

What do these musical details in the Kyrie and Sanctus reveal about the music of the Mass? They do not prove that the Mass was written in or for Reims, of course. But they do suggest that if Machaut composed the work for some other house, he made no attempt to reflect the music of that place; on the contrary, the tenors of the Mass betray the regional musical dialect of Reims. Combined with the liturgical information presented earlier demonstrating the presence of these chants in local books from Reims, these musical findings point squarely to the cathedral as the place of origin and destination of the Mass.

THE ENHANCEMENT OF THE CHOIR IN REIMS CATHEDRAL

But who would have performed it? Without evidence of singers at Reims capable of executing such a work, one might still question that Machaut composed it for the church. Perhaps the Mass was intended after all for a specific occasion in the cathedral like the coronation of Charles V, an event for which trained singers from the royal chapel were undoubtedly on hand. Indeed, apart from the music of Machaut, Reims is not known as a centre of polyphony during or immediately after the composer's lifetime, nor does it seem to have nurtured a talent comparable to Machaut for centuries to come.[44]

43 Ideally, it would be desirable to compare the tenors of the Mass with sources from every place Machaut is known to have visited, including, for example, Verdun and Arras, where he received canonries in expectation in 1330 and 1332, respectively, as well as various cities in what is now Eastern Europe, where Machaut travelled in the entourage of John of Bohemia between 1327 and 1330 (see Machabey, *Guillaume de Machault*, vol. 1, pp. 23–31). The late thirteenth-century missal from Saint-Vaast of Arras F: AS 444 contains only one G in its Kyrie (Example 5.1). F: VN 759 from Verdun, on the other hand, does include the reading of the Kyrie with two Gs that Machaut used (Example 5.1), but the Sanctus in this same manuscript follows instead the version once-removed from that found in the Mass (Example 5.2). In similar fashion, a Bohemian gradual written for a congregation of Hussites in 1491 (A: Wn, serv. nov. 2657) contains the Sanctus variant C-C-A-B-flat-A-G-F, which is found in the region of Reims (see Kovarik, 'Mid Fifteenth-Century Polyphonic Elaborations of the Plainchant *Ordinarium Missae*', 757, source G: 3). Whereas the lateness and usage of this source effectively eliminate it as a factor in assessing the place of origin of Machaut's Sanctus, we cannot entirely rule out the possibility that Machaut may have come in contact with this reading of the Sanctus during his peregrinations in this region almost two hundred years earlier. But because the Kyrie in A:Wn, serv. nov. 2657 does not have the Reims reading cited in Example 5.1 (see Kovarik, 'Mid Fifteenth-Century Polyphonic Elaborations', 687, source G:3), we must conclude that the variants found in the mass result from Machaut's familiarity with the liturgy of Reims.

44 Reims had a distinguished musical life in the seventeenth and eighteenth centuries, numbering among its local talent the Clicquot family of organ builders, the famous organist Nicolas de

The city did nonetheless produce skilled soloists who proffered their abilities elsewhere in the late fourteenth and early fifteenth centuries. In 1391 Henri and Eynart le Fevre from Reims entered the Burgundian chapel choir, having previously served at the papal court in Avignon.[45] Gerard Le Fay and Jean Gobert from Reims were likewise members both of the papal choir in Rome and of the chapel of Leonello d'Este in Ferrara in the third and fourth decades of the fifteenth century.[46] As the premier ecclesiastical house in the city, the cathedral was probably responsible for the education of these and other singers who went on to the most prestigious musical establishments in Europe. This is all the more likely because the *maîtrise* that would have trained them was established in the cathedral in the late 1360s or 1370s. The first *maître des enfants*, Jean Roberti, may even have been active in this capacity during Machaut's lifetime, for he was succeeded by Jean Jayet on 29 August 1386,[47] only nine years after Machaut died.

Despite these indications of musical activity in the cathedral during Machaut's tenure, the first unequivocal mentions of polyphony in the divine service appear only in the 1460s. Guillaume Marlot, historian of Reims, writes that the chapter sent a *sçavant clerc* to Cambrai to learn *la musique* around 1462,[48] and Richard Berthelos, a priest of Noyon, was received as vicar of the cathedral and first *maître de musique* in 1477.[49] These reports, however, date from the seventeenth and eighteenth centuries, and they probably refer to polyphony sung in the main choir

---

Grigny, as well as Lully's assistant, Pascal Collasse. In the mid-eighteenth century, Henri Hardouin, *maître de chapelle* of the cathedral, formed a music society that grew into the Académie de Musique de Reims; see Hiley, 'Rheims', in *The New Grove Dictionary* (London, 1980), vol. 15, pp. 789–91.

45 Henri's tenure in the chapel began on 7 January, Eynart's on 2 May; see Craig Wright, *Music at the Court of Burgundy, 1364–1419: A Documentary History*, Musicological Studies 28 (Henryville, 1979), and esp. pp. 61, 63, 65, 79, 85, and 89.

46 Pamela Starr, 'Music and Music Patronage at the Papal Court, 1447–1464' (PhD dissertation, Yale University, 1987), pp. 126–7, 141–2, and 'The Ferrara Connection: A Case Study of Musical Recruitment in the Renaissance', *Studi Musicali* 18 (1989), 7–15; see also Lewis Lockwood, *Music in Renaissance Ferrara: The Creation of a Musical Center in the Fifteenth Century*, Studies in the History of Music 2 (Cambridge, MA, 1984), pp. 47, 48, 49, 61. In the realm of instrumental music, Jean de Reims and Regnaut Fresnel de Reims were organists at Notre-Dame in Paris in the fourteenth century; see Wright, *Music and Ceremony at Notre Dame*, pp. 148–9.

47 F: RSc 1777, no. 80, fol. 1, nos. 1, 2. No dates are provided for Jean Roberti.

48 Marlot, *Histoire de la ville, cité et université de Reims*, vol. 4, p. 219. A seventeenth-/eighteenth-century list of the *maîtres des enfans de choeur* likewise states: 'La musique fut introduite en l'Eglise de Reims vers 1462'; F: RSc 1777, no. 80, fol. 1.

49 'Richard Berthelos, prêtre de Noyon, dût à fondateur dans l'art de la musique la qualité de premier maître de musique de l'église de Reims, et fut reçu pour instruire les enfans de choeur, et comme vicaire de cette église sous les revenues ordinaires, le 30 juillet 1477. On lit dans les chartes de la nouvelle congregation qu'il fut chapelain dans cette année . . .'; F: RSc 1777, no. 80, fol. 1v, no. 9.

of the church. There is no reason to doubt that polyphony was heard elsewhere in the building much earlier. In other houses in the late Middle Ages, polyphony seems to have existed at side altars before it was officially used in the choir,[50] just as in the realm of painting and sculpture, new or innovatory works of art appeared first in the side chapels. Indeed, a choral establishment related initially to the side altars of Reims Cathedral received a substantial boost precisely during Machaut's tenure.

Throughout the thirteenth century, archbishops, canons, and wealthy lay persons had endowed services in the side chapels of the cathedral, and by 1274 some thirty-three chaplains were in residence.[51] A decade later the chapter realized 'that the divine service in the church was suffering from some defect and feared from like signs that it would suffer greater [defect] in the future.'[52] On 30 August 1285 the canons delegated to look into this matter hired twelve new vicars, of whom four were priests, four deacons and four subdeacons.[53] As in scores of other churches, this act was designed to provide persons not only to elevate the performance of services, but also to assist the canons, whose numbers on particular occasions in the fourteenth century rarely exceeded twenty-five or thirty,[54] by relieving them of some of their duties.

By the mid-fourteenth century even these measures were deemed inadequate, probably because the vicars lacked the one incentive that might have caused them to observe their duties more studiously – regular salaries. In 1340 Archbishop Jean de Vienne granted a chapter request, pending papal approval, to allow the money from a vacated prebend to be used for one year for the Office of Matins and other choir Offices, for which funds were insufficient.[55] Sometime before 1352 the chapter petitioned the Pope for a clarification of the status of the choral establishment, and on 1 February of that year Clement VI issued a bull which formally converted twelve chaplaincies, all at side altars in the church, to twelve vicarial posts.[56] He likewise established positions for four *pueri choriales*, stipulating that the vicars and boys appointed to these posts should be 'competently instructed

---

50 See pp. 136–7 below.

51 Desportes, *Reims et les rémois*, pp. 297–8 (citing AMR, 2G 408, no. 4).

52 '. . . quod prefata Remensis ecclesia circa divinum officium aliquem patiebantur defectum et majorem pati timebatur ex conjecturis versimilibus in futurum' (AMR 2G 410, no. 1).

53 'Volens remedium sibi possible super hoc adhibere ordinavit statuit in capitulo generali ad honorem et laudem divini nominis et ad cultus divini augmentum quod duodecim vicarii de novo in Remensi ecclesia crearentur, quorum quatuor in presb[yte]ratus, quatuor in dyaconatus, et quatuor alii in subdiaconatus officio ministrabunt . . .' (ibid.).

54 Desportes, *Reims et les rémois*, p. 297.   55 AMR, 2G 347, no. 8 (23 June).

56 Neither the chapter's request nor Clement VI's original bull have survived, but a *vidimus* of the latter from 25 August 1431 is extant (AMR, 2G 410, no. 5); see also Desportes, *Reims et les rémois*, p. 298. I am grateful to Pamela Starr for confirming that Clement's bull no longer exists in the pontifical registers in the Vatican Archives in Rome.

in the divine offices and in the ceremonies of this church'.[57] From now on, each vicar finally had his own benefice. This act marked the beginning of the *nouvelle congrégation* of Notre-Dame of Reims,[58] and it provided the much needed financial backing for the choir that would eventually sing polyphony regularly in the cathedral. By 1370 there were fifteen vicars,[59] and in 1384 the number of choirboys was raised from four to five.[60] The chapter clearly viewed Clement's proclamation as important; at least they copied it numerous times down to the eighteenth century.[61] And subsequent popes, in renewing this foundation, always refer back to this bull of 1352.

In the fifteenth century, papal foundations like that of Clement VI normally signal the formal establishment and regular funding of a choir of professional singers in a church. The intent of Clement's bull of 1352 and of similar fourteenth-century documents, however, is less obvious. Since Clement does not specifically state that the vicars and choirboys were to sing polyphony, it may be that they were not doing so. On the other hand, his bull certainly does not forbid the practice, and the silence of papal proclamations on the use of polyphony in this period may simply reflect the reticence of popes to countermand the restrictions on polyphonic singing in the church that had been imposed by John XXII in 1325. Whether Clement was giving tacit approval to the use of polyphony or not, the fact that his foundation is the one cited as authority for all subsequent documents shows that it was a turning point for the choir.[62]

Thus the bull is probably relevant to the execution at least of paraliturgical services in Reims Cathedral in the mid-fourteenth century. And if Machaut's Mass was intended as a votive service for a side altar, then the document provides evidence of the performing force of vicars and choirboys from which the singers of the work may have been drawn. Perhaps, therefore, the Machaut brothers' epitaph, in referring to persons who 'skilfully [took] part' in the performance of the Mass that they founded, is to be taken literally. That is, if this Mass included the movements of Machaut's polyphonic ordinary, then the *skill* of these performers was the art of polyphonic singing.

---

57 '. . . in divinis officiis et ejusdem ecclesiae ceremoniis competenter instructis' (AMR, 2G 410, no. 5).

58 Desportes, *Reims et les rémois*, p. 298; Cerf, *Histoire et description de Notre-Dame de Reims*, vol. 1, p. 478.   59 Desportes, *Reims et les rémois*, p. 298.

60 AMR, 2G 466, no. 1 (11 November 1394).

61 See the cartularies AMR, 2G 1650, fols. 342v–343v; AMR, 2G 1652, fols. 656–660; AMR, 2G 1654, fols. 26v–28, 270–271v. Six seventeenth-century copies of the bull are found in AMR, 2G 410, nos. 6–11; and there are references to it in three eighteenth-century documents which discuss the vicarial chapels (AMR, 2G 342, nos. 7, 9; 2G 1649, no. 25).

62 For examples of the effects of papal bulls on the performance of music in fifteenth-century churches, see Barbara Haggh, 'Itinerancy to Residency: Professional Careers and Performance Practices in 15th-Century Sacred Music', *Early Music* 17 (1989), 360.

ENDOWMENTS, WILLS, AND THE MACHAUT BROTHERS' EPITAPH

In 1355, just three years after Clement VI's bull concerning the choir, Jean de Machaut took up residence as a canon in the Cathedral.[63] There, as far as we know, Guillaume and Jean spent the remainder of their days in the service of the church. At some point the brothers, like other canons of Notre-Dame, undoubtedly made endowments and wills in the church.[64] We cannot know the precise contents of these foundations, for the epitaph for Guillaume and Jean is the only evidence of the arrangements they made prior to their deaths. Other extant foundations and testaments from fourteenth-century Reims nonetheless do shed light on the likely nature of the Machauts' provisions. Table 5.3 gives details of such endowments and wills in Reims Cathedral before, during, and after Machaut's tenure.

Foundations and wills were made by various levels of persons, including lay bourgeois, canons, and archbishops. These documents afforded a person the opportunity to officially set his spiritual health in order prior to his death. This was accomplished primarily through the establishment of one or more services that would be celebrated in perpetuity, or at least as long as the endowment continued to grow.[65] The liturgical portion of a foundation usually consisted in two parts: one that was to take effect immediately, and the other that would begin upon the death of the testator. An endowment might specify both portions of the foundation; a will dealt only with the latter. The contents of these endowments followed a standard pattern. They normally stipulated that an oration and one or more masses be performed at a certain altar in a church on designated days. The Mass was quite often dedicated to the Virgin to secure her intercession on behalf of the donor throughout the rest of his earthly existence. Upon his passing, this Mass was most often replaced with a commemorative, or *Requiem*, service.[66] In some instances, however, the original Marian Mass remained in place after the death of the founder,

---

63 Machabey notes that Jean received his prebend on 13 September 1355 (*Guillaume de Machaut*, vol. 1, p. 49 (citing AMR, 2G 1650, fol. 13)).

64 The use of the word 'executors' in the epitaph implies that the wills did exist; see H. Auffroy, *Evolution du testament en France des origines au XIIIe siècle* (Paris, 1899).

65 Foundations were common from the end of the twelfth century on, when the writing of wills became popular, and as the concept of Purgatory developed during the twelfth century; see Jean-Loup Lemaître, *Répertoire des documents nécrologiques français*, 2 vols., Recueil des historiens de la France, Obituaires 7–8 (Paris, 1980), vol. 1, pp. 23–4; Jacques Le Goff, *La naissance du purgatoire* (Paris, 1981), pp. 436–9, translated as *The Birth of Purgatory* (Chicago, 1984), pp. 326–8; and Lemaître, 'Obituaires, calendriers et liturgie paroissiale', *L'Eglise et la mémoire des morts dans la France médiévale, Communications présentées à la Table Ronde du C.N.R.S., le 14 juin 1982* (Paris, 1986), pp. 138–40. See the discussion of the relationship between foundations and music in Haggh, 'Music, Liturgy, and Ceremony in Brussels, 1350–1500' (PhD dissertation, University of Illinois at Urbana-Champaign, 1988), pp. 503–26.

66 Haggh, 'Music, Liturgy, and Ceremony in Brussels, pp. 511–16.

Table 5.3. *Foundations in Reims cathedral in the fourteenth and early fifteenth centuries*

The abbreviations used for money are as follows: l.t. = *livres tournois*; l.p. = *livres parisis*; f.F. (or simply f.) = *florins de France*; F = *francs d'or*; g.t. = *gros tournois*; s.p. = *sous parisiens*. The *livre tournois*, the *florin*, and the *franc* were all worth the same amount, that is, about 16 *sous parisis*. The *livre parisis* was slightly more valuable, comprising about 25 *sous tournois*. One *florin* was equal to about 10 *gros tournois*.¹ Unless otherwise stated, all ranks of persons are ranks of the Cathedral of Reims. The entries under 'Foundation' are sometimes divided into two parts: 1) portion to be carried out until death of founder; 2) portion to follow death of founder.

Date	Founder/Executor	Foundation	Altar	Frequency	Payment	AMR document
9 May 1309	executors of will of lawyer Gérard de Marlemont	Requiem Mass	in nave at choir entry	daily	income from 300 l.t., divided among 4 vicars	2G 410, nos. 3, 4
18 Jan. 1313	executors of will of Cardinal of St-Cyriaque Etienne de Suisy	anniversary		annual	income from 310 l.p.	2G 357, no. 2
4 Oct. 1315	Dean Nicholas de Ferrare (foundation)	1) BMV Mass 2) Requiem		annual (17 May) annual	8 l.t. per year	2G 357, no. 5 2G 1652, fols. 317–7v
2 Jun. 1316 (*vidimus* of 28 Feb. 1318)	*vidimus* of foundation of Canon of Reims and Archdeacon of Laon Adam of Nesle	BMV Mass 2 anniversaries	choir axial	2 days after death 1 service on anniversary and another 6 months later	income from property	2G 357, no. 6
30 Jul. 1325	chapter letter acknowledging foundation of Cardinal and Archdeacon of Reims Guillaume of Bray	anniversary		annual	income from 1000 l.t. = 40 l.p. per year	2G 357, no. 7
16 Apr. 1327	chapter letter acknowledging foundation of Canons Wermond and Adam de Cheilly	joint anniversary		annual	income from 100(=40+60) l.p. per year	2G 357, no. 8

Table 5.3 (cont.)

Date	Founder/Executor	Foundation	Altar	Frequency	Payment	AMR document
28 Aug. 1334 (vidimus of 6 Mar. 1408)	Vidimus of clause in will of Canon Jean de Monclin	chaplaincy consisting of 3 Requiems, 1 BMV Mass	Paul	weekly	income from 500 l.t.	2G 443, no. 1
2 Dec. 1336	chapter letter to Cardinal deacon Jacques Cajétan, St-George of Golden Fleece	Feast of St George		annual	10 l.p. per year, to be divided among canons who are present	2G 357, no. 9
9 Jan. 1341	Archbishop Jean de Vienne (foundation)	Saturday BMV Mass	BMV altar next to choir entrance (= Rouelle)	weekly	10 l., 8 s.p. per year	2G 357, no. 10
9 Dec. 1363 (regarding will of 20 Aug. 1349)	chapter letter concerning will of Dean Hughes de Juilly and subsequent provisions made by his executors	chaplaincy consisting of BMV Mass for souls of relatives and benefactors	Paul	1 March in the year of the installation of a new chaplain	income from property	2G 444, no. 1
		anniversary consisting of a chaplaincy for St Aubin	Rouelle		income from 60 l.p. plus other property	
16 Mar. 1368	chapter letter acknowledging executors of will of Canon Gérard d'Ambonnay	Mass	Bartholomew (his burial place)	daily	income from 800 f.F=30 l.p. per year	2G 357, no. 12
10 Jan. 1377	chapter letter acknowledging executors of will of Jean de Goussancourt, bourgeois of Reims	anniversary 6 Masses	choir Remy	annual weekly	6 l.p. per year 100 s., plus income from 450 f. per year	2G 357, no. 13

Date	Document	Item	Name	Frequency	Amount	Reference
May 1380	King Charles V (foundation)	1A) 2 Masses *submissa voce* for Holy Spirit and BMV		daily after Matins	60 l.p. per year, to be divided among all those present	2G 1550, no. 1
		1B) solemn Mass of Holy Spirit		1st day of each month	16 l.p.: 3 parts (?15 l.p.) divided among canons, remainder divided among others who are present	
		1C) Marian service, including special prayer for Charles	*Rouelle*	daily after Compline during Lent	18 s.p., to be divided among those who sing (*decantare*) the sequence and antiphon or responsory	
		2A) 2 Requiem Masses containing prayers for him	Remy	daily		
		2B) Requiem Mass		1st day of each month		
		2C) continuation of Marian service above with oration *de defunctis*				
11 Nov. 1384	chapter letter establishing 5th choirboy with money given by Archbishop Richard Picque of Besançon and anniversary for Richard	BMV antiphon, prayers *submissa voce*	Saint Lait	daily after Matins	500 F. (see below)	2G 466, no. 1
11 Nov. 1387	chapter letter acknowledging foundation of Archbishop Richard Picque of Besançon	anniversary Requiem Mass *submissa voca* for himself and relatives	*Rouelle*	daily	income from 500 F., precious objects, 48 F. for a house, other property	2G 408, no. 5

Table 5.3 (cont.)

Date	Founder/Executor	Foundation	Altar	Frequency	Payment	AMR document
22 Sep. 1389	Archbishop Richard Picque of Besançon (will)	Psalms		day of death and vigil of funeral	5 s.p. per vicar	2G 357, no. 14[2]
		Requiem Mass		day of funeral	2 g.t. to a priest	
		anniversary		annual	25 f.F. to be divided among canons	
22 Apr. 1392	chapter letter acknowledging foundation of Succentor Denis of Méry	1) BMV Mass	Rouelle	daily	income from 1000 F. and precious objects	2G 357, no. 15
		2) Requiem Mass				
24 Feb. 1407	Canon Laurent de Raillicourt (will)	'for augmenting the Mass of the Rouelle'	Rouelle		income from 200 f.	2G 357, nos. 17, 18
		obit			income from 200 f.	
		Ps. De profundis and oration de Requiem		daily after Compline	income from property	
3 Aug. 1411	chapter letter acknowledging foundation of Canon Jean le Verrier	2 Masses, plus Ora. Inclina domine aurem tuam	Saint Lait	on Assumption and on Sunday in octave of Trinity	income from 50 l.t., other objects, property	2G 357, no. 20
12 Dec. 1412	Archbishop Simon de Cramaud (foundation)	1) Mass of Holy Spirit	main	annually on 9 Dec.	600+100 s.p. per year	2G 357, no. 22
		2) Requiem Vigil and Mass				

[1] On medieval coinage in France, see Peter Spufford, *Handbook of Medieval Exchange* (London, 1986), pp. 164–87.
[2] Will also published in Varin, *Archives administratives*, vol. 3, pp. 731–75, and in *Gallia Christiana*, vol. 10 (Paris, 1751), cols. 68–74.

and an oration for the dead in his honour was added after his death to give the Mass the new dimension of a commemoration. The gift of a sum of money or piece(s) of land perpetuated the establishment through revenues that would accrue from the investment of the funds or from the rental of the property.

Combining this information on late medieval endowments and wills in Reims Cathedral with the text of the Machauts' epitaph, we can reconstruct the foundations that Guillaume and Jean probably made. The second part of their endowments, designed to go into effect after their deaths and probably reiterated in their wills, must have conformed precisely to the latter type just described. The epitaph calls first for the recitation of 'a prayer for the dead' for the Machauts. This oration was to be sung 'every Saturday', during 'the Mass' – that is, the weekly, Marian votive service – 'which should be sung, by virtue of their prayer, with pious devotion to their memory'. The new item in this foundation was the prayer that slightly altered the Saturday Mass, changing it from a service purely for Mary to a Marian-commemorative Mass in memory of the brothers after the deaths of Jean in 1372 or 1374[67] and of Guillaume in 1377. Canon of Reims Jean le Verrier recalls the Machauts' endowment several decades later and confirms that the brothers had chosen this type of Mass in which a prayer was appended to a service for Mary. In his foundation of 1411, he calls for the biannual performance of two Masses which, after his death, were to incorporate an oration just 'as is customarily said on Saturdays in the Mass of Blessed Mary at the *Rouelle* of the said church for the deceased Guillaume de Machaut, one-time canon of Reims'.[68]

The Saturday Mass itself already existed, of course, for the epitaph states that the executors were to provide three hundred *florins* 'for the purchase of revenues for the growth of the revenues of the said Mass'. The phrase 'growth of the revenues' does not mean that a Mass was newly founded after the Machauts died; it suggests instead that a service already in use had been supplied with further funds. This Mass, therefore, most likely formed the first part of the foundation that the Machauts made for the period prior to their deaths.

But was this service nothing more than the universally celebrated weekly Saturday Mass for Mary? Charles Regnault clearly thought so, for he stated in his eighteenth-century commentary on the epitaph, quoted earlier, that the Machaut brothers *founded* the Saturday Mass for the Virgin. We must remember, however,

---

67 There is some confusion about the year of Jean's death. Papal documents (summarized in Andrew Tomasello, *Music and Ritual at Papal Avignon* (Ann Arbor, 1983), p. 244) give 1372, whereas Jean Weyen (F: RSc 1773, fol. 291; cited in Machabey, *Guillaume de Machault*, vol. 1, p. 69) indicates 1374. I am grateful to Lawrence Earp for pointing out this discrepancy to me.

68 '. . . que consuevit dici diebus sabbatinis in missa de beata maria ad Roellam dicte ecclesie pro defuncto Guillermo de Machaudio quondam Remensis canonico'; AMR, 2G 357, no. 20 (see Table 5.3).

that by Regnault's time, Machaut had become a legend larger than life in the cathedral. It is hardly surprising that he and others in the seventeenth and eighteenth centuries would have believed that the Saturday Mass for the Virgin was Machaut's creation. We have seen that other dubious associations arose around this time, for it was in the eighteenth century that the theory connecting the Mass with the coronation of Charles V was proposed.

In fact the Machauts did not inaugurate the Saturday Mass for Mary. Not only had the service been celebrated in Reims Cathedral at least since the thirteenth century,[69] but during Machaut's very tenure, the location of the Mass was evidently transferred to the altar of the *Rouelle* in the nave by Archbishop Jean de Vienne in 1341 (Table 5.3). Recognition of Regnault's erroneous ascription of the foundation of the Saturday Mass to the Machauts opens two possibilities: either the brothers simply added money to perpetuate Jean de Vienne's endowment, or they embellished the Saturday Mass in some other way. We will see that there is good reason to hypothesize that the brothers transformed the Saturday Mass with the addition of Guillaume's polyphonic ordinary. And it is certainly no coincidence that the Machaut's stipulated that their Mass be sung 'at the altar near the *Rouelle*', the place which they likewise chose for their burials.

THE ALTAR OF THE *ROUELLE*

Two side altars in the fourteenth-century cathedral were associated with Mary. One was the chapel of the Saint Lait, so called because it reputedly housed a portion of the Holy Milk which had nourished the Saviour. This *oratorium* stood in the northern side of the cathedral, just to the west of the first circular chapel in the chevet (Figure 5.1, letter 'i').[70] In the time of Machaut, the altar of the Saint Lait was the site of a number of foundations, some of them in honour of the Virgin.[71] The other oratory, the altar of the *Rouelle*, took its name from the nearby round stone that stood in the centre of the nave.[72]

The *Rouelle* was singularly important in Reims Cathedral, intimately connected with earliest history of the church. This stone marked the spot on which Bishop

---

69 See the ordinaries of Reims F:RSc 328, fol. 15v (published in Chevalier, *Sacramentaire et martyrologe*, p. 96); and F:RSc 329, fol. 330.

70 On this chapel, see Paris, *La Chapelle du Saint-Laict*, and Cerf, *Histoire et description de Notre-Dame de Reims*, vol. 1, p. 127–33.

71 Treated in my forthcoming study of music and ritual at Reims Cathedral.

72 See Figure 5.1. On the location of the *Rouelle*, see L. Demaison, 'Les cathédrales de Reims antérieures au XIIIe siècle', *Bulletin monumental* 85 (1926), 75–7. The Latin word 'rotella' appears in the documents; it means a 'roundel' or 'disk'; see R.E. Latham, *Revised Medieval Latin Word-List* (London, 1965), p. 412.

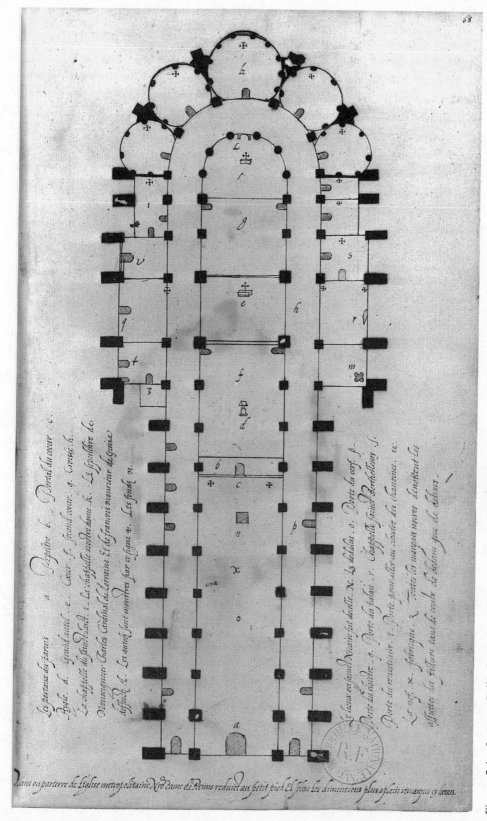

Figure 5.1 Jacques Cellier's drawing of Reims Cathedral (1580s): Paris, BN, MS français, 9152, fol. 68

Nicasius was said to have been decapitated by Vandal tribes in 406 or 407. His death reputedly occurred when the invaders forced the populace of Reims to take refuge in the pre-Merovingian church that stood on the location of the thirteenth-century Gothic Cathedral.[73] Positioning himself on the western threshold of the building, Nicasius perished defending his flock. The subsequent churches built around the old structure commemorated this venerable place by preserving the stone upon which Saint Nicasius fell.[74] No longer at the western end, the *Rouelle* now stood in the centre of the thirteenth-century nave in the sixth bay from the west facade.[75] The first extant drawing of the church by Jacques Cellier from the 1580s clearly shows 'le lieux ou sainct Nicaise fut décollé' (Figure 5.1, letter 'n'). Even today a marker in the pavement which has replaced the *Rouelle* reads 'In this place Saint Nicasius, Bishop of Reims, was beheaded and died a martyr in the year of our Lord 406' ('Hoc in loco Sanctus Nicasius Remensis Archipraesul truncato capite martyr occubuit Anno Domino 406').

At least three oratories stood in the nave near the *Rouelle*: the altars of Saint Nicasius, Saint Paul, and the Virgin Mary. The earliest of these, erected next to or above the *Rouelle*, appears to have been dedicated to Saint Nicasius[76] and was evidently constructed early in the fourteenth century. References to the *Rouelle*

73 On the martyrdom of Saint Nicasius, see *Bibliotheca Sanctorum* (Rome, 1967), vol. 9, cols. 854–8; and William Hinkle, *The Portal of the Saints of Reims Cathedral: A Study in Mediaeval Iconography*, Monographs on Archaeology and Fine Arts sponsored by the Archaeological Institute of America and the College Art Association of America 13 (College Art Association, 1965), pp. 19–22. Another legend holds that Nicasius was murdered by the Huns in 451; see Benedictine Monks of St Augustine's Abbey, Ramsgate, *The Book of Saints*, 5th ed. (New York, 1966), p. 521; and Herbert Thurston and Donald Attwater, eds., *Butler's Lives of the Saints* (New York, 1956), vol. 4, p. 558.

74 The principal monograph on the various buildings which have stood on the site of Reims Cathedral is Hans Reinhardt, *La cathédrale de Reims: Son histoire, son architecture, sa sculpture, ses vitraux* (Paris, 1963). See also the important studies of aspects of the cathedral in Robert Branner, 'Historical Aspects of the Reconstruction of Reims Cathedral, 1210–1241', *Speculum* 36 (1961), 23–37; Francis Salet, 'Le premier colloque international de la société française d'archéologie (Reims, 1er–2 juin 1965): Chronologie de la cathédrale', *Bulletin monumental* 125 (1967), 347–94; Jean-Pierre Ravaux, 'Les campagnes de construction de la cathédrale de Reims au XIIIe siècle', *Bulletin monumental* 137 (1979), 7–66; Sadler-Davis, 'The Sculptural Program'.

75 In the twelfth century, the *Rouelle* had been moved about ten metres to the east, but it was returned to the sixth bay of the nave when the Gothic church was built in the thirteenth century; L. Demaison, 'Les cathédrales de Reims', 75–7; see also Sadler-Davis, 'The Sculptural Program', 37, note 8.

76 There was another oratory to this saint in the chevet of the church since the twelfth century (see Figure 5.1, first chapel to the north [left] of the axial chapel; identified as Saint Nicasius' chapel in Cerf, *Histoire et description de Notre-Dame de Reims*, vol. 2, unnumbered page following p. 232). This chapel enjoyed numerous chaplaincies, the documents for which are preserved in AMR, 2G 430–2.

prior to the fourteenth century do not mention it,[77] but in 1335, Jean d'Escamps established a chaplaincy 'in honour of almighty God, of the Virgin Mary his mother, and of Saints Mary Magdalene and Mary of Egypt at the altar of Saint Nicasius in front of the *Rouelle* in the church of Reims'.[78] Several decades later, Canon of Reims Etienne of Juilly requested his burial in the nave of the cathedral in front of the altar of Saint Nicasius.[79]

Connections of the *Rouelle* with Saint Nicasius, however, are not as plentiful as the documents in which the stone is associated with the altars of Saint Paul and the Virgin to the left and right, respectively, of the entrance to the choir and against the rood screen (Figure 5.1). The first rood screen that can be firmly documented in the cathedral was the one erected in 1417 in front of the entrance to the choir.[80] This partition, some thirteen feet in depth, extended from the middle of the eighth bay of the nave to the middle of the seventh, terminating about eight feet to the east of the *Rouelle*. A somewhat less elaborate screen undoubtedly preceded it,[81] and the numerous contemporaneous mentions of the two altars on the left and right side of the entrance to the choir support the existence of this earlier screen during Machaut's lifetime. The altar on the left was dedicated to Saint Paul, and the one on the right, designated as 'the altar of the *Rouelle*' in the early fourteenth century, came to be known as 'the altar to Mary in front of the *Rouelle*'.[82]

Paraliturgical services and private endowments were made at these two oratories beginning in the fourteenth century,[83] and from the 1330s on, the altar of the *Rouelle* on the right side of the choir attracted numerous foundations. The importance of this place, precisely during Machaut's tenure in the cathedral, seems related to its increasing association with the Virgin Mary. We have already seen that Archbishop of Reims Jean de Vienne established the weekly votive Mass for the

---

77 Two documents from 1192 and 1299 name the *Rouelle* but not the altar; Sadler-Davis, 'The Sculptural Program', 37, note 8. The 1299 document is AMR, 2G 289, fol. 50v (transcribed in Ravaux, 'Les campagnes', 61, note 49).

78 '. . . ad honorem omnipotentis dei, beate marie virginis matris ejus, de beatarum marie magdalene et marie egiptiace ad altare sancti Nichasii ante Rouellam in ecclesia Remensis' (AMR, 2G 447, no. 3).   79 AMR, 2G 444, no. 2 (will of 25 September 1394).

80 Cerf, *Histoire et description de Notre-Dame de Reims*, vol. 1, pp. 81–6.   81 Ibid., p. 82.

82 Ibid., pp. 84–5. Cerf's statement that the altar on the left was dedicated also to Mary is founded on no documentary evidence (ibid.). (I am grateful to Donna Sadler for her opinion on the location of these two altars.)

83 A document from 9 May 1309 mentions a commemorative mass which was to be sung 'at one of the altars which are in the nave of our church in front of the stone of Saint Nicasius at the entrance of our choir' ('. . . ad unum altarium que sunt in nave ecclesie nostre ante lapidem sancti Nicasii in introitu chori nostri') (AMR, 2G 410, no. 3). Another foundation describes 'the altar in front of the stone or *Rouelle* which is said [to be] of Saint Nicasius on the left side of our choir' ('. . . altare ante lapidem seu rouellam qui dicitur sancti Nichasii a parte sinistra chori nostri') (AMR, 2G 445, no. 7 (28 November 1312)).

Virgin on Saturdays 'at the altar of the beautiful image next to the entrance of the choir of our church of Reims' in 1341.[84] This connection of the altar of the *Rouelle* with the Virgin was enhanced all the more by the appearance before 1343 of a new statue to her, a common sight in late medieval churches.[85] The first evidence of the new image is Canon Thomas de Cernay's foundation of a chaplaincy 'at the altar of the new image near the entrance of the choir and the *Rouelle* of blessed Nicasius on the right side of the said choir'[86] in this year. A document from 9 December 1363 likewise created a chaplaincy in honour of Saint Albinus 'at the altar of Blessed Mary in the nave of the aforementioned church of Reims next to the *Rouelle*'.[87] Even Charles V is thought to have made an endowment at this altar in 1364 in thanksgiving both for his coronation at Reims on 19 May and for his victory at Cocherel only a few days earlier. Unfortunately this foundation has not survived, but Charles Cerf, a nineteenth-century historian of Reims, records that the Masses instituted on this occasion were to be sung 'in front of the image of the aforementioned glorious Virgin in the nave of this church'.[88]

Endowments after Machaut's death in 1377 likewise continue to witness the use of the Marian altar near the *Rouelle*. In 1380, Charles V did provide for a Marian office, probably akin to a *Salve* service, at the *Rouelle* altar (Table 5.3).[89] Another

84 '. . . ad altare pulcre ymaginis juxta introitum chori ecclesie nostre Remensis' (AMR, 2G 357, no. 10). Prior to this time, the only reference to Marian Masses in a side chapel is to the daily Lady Mass. This service, by decree of Archbishop Guillaume de Joinville in 1221, was sung in the axial chapel of the church, dedicated to Saint James (AMR, 2G 408, no. 1). On the thirteenth-century chapel of Saint James, see Cerf, *Histoire de Notre-Dame de Reims*, vol. 1, p. 124; Reinhardt, *La Cathédrale de Reims*, p. 71, note 10; and Ravaux, 'Les Campagnes', 8–9. The latter author puts to rest Francis Salet's questions about the location of this chapel in 'Le premier colloque international de la société française d'archéologie (Reims, 1er–2 Juin 1965): Chronologie de la cathédrale', 364–5.

85 See the new study of Marian images in Michael Camille, *The Gothic Idol: Ideology and Image-Making in Medieval Art* (Cambridge, 1989), pp. 222–5. An altar to Mary in the nave or transept of a church was by no means an unusual sight in the fourteenth century. On the Marian altar in the transept of Tournai Cathedral, see Jean Dumoulin, Michel Huglo, Philippe Mercie, Jacques Pycke, eds., *La Messe de Tournai. Une messe polyphonique en l'honneur de Notre-Dame à la Cathédrale de Tournai au XIVe siècle: Étude et nouvelle transcription*, Publications d'histoire de l'art et d'archéologie de l'université catholique de Louvain 64 (Tournai, 1988), p. 21; and in the nave of the church of Saint-Donatian in Bruges, see Reinhard Strohm, *Music in Late Medieval Bruges*, Oxford Monographs on Music (Oxford, 1985), pp. 19–20. Numerous examples of altar statues of Mary can be seen in the exhibition catalogue *Les Fastes du gothique: le siècle de Charles V* (Paris, 1981), nos. 1–119.   86 AMR, 2G 442, no. 1 (26 April).

87 '. . . ad altare beate marie in navi ecclesie predicte Remensis juxta Roellam' (AMR, 2G 444, no. 1).

88 Cerf, *Histoire*, vol. 1, pp. 82, 348. The author quotes apparently from the original charter: 'Coram imagine dictae Virginis gloriosae, in navi ejusdem ecclesiae, et ad devotionem fidelium adaugendam decantentur.' Given the circumstances, there might well have been such a foundation in or shortly after 1364. Charles' later foundation of 1380, discussed below, seems in part to have restated this one.

89 AMR, 2G 1550, no. 1 (May 1380), published, though without identification of the original source, in Marlot, *Histoire de la ville, cité et université de Reims*, vol. 4, pp. 113, 631–5. A colour

foundation of 11 November 1387 established a service 'at the altar of the image of Blessed Mary the glorious Virgin in front of the *Rouelle* of our aforementioned church'.[90] On 22 April 1392, the canons of Reims acknowledged Succentor Denis de Méry's request for a daily Mass to the Virgin. This service was to be performed at the *Rouelle* altar while he was still alive and then replaced by a *Requiem* after his death.[91] The oratory was no less important in subsequent centuries, serving as the location not only of numerous services for the Virgin, but also of foundations which specifically mention polyphony.[92]

The altar of the *Rouelle* in Reims Cathedral was clearly the most important devotional site to the Virgin in the church in the fourteenth century. Regnault's discovery of the Machaut brothers' epitaph at this oratory moreover indicates that this was the place which they chose both for their foundations and for their burials, a common practice in the late Middle Ages.[93] At least one other canon, Guillaume Cauchon, was buried there in the sixteenth century,[94] and it was probably the final resting place of many of the church personnel who made endowments at the *Rouelle*.[95] Although these foundations undoubtedly included Masses and prayers, it is likely that no service at the *Rouelle* compared with 'the Mass which should be sung . . . with pious devotion' not only to Mary but also to the memories of Guillaume and Jean de Machaut.

The preceding discussion has treated five aspects of Reims Cathedral in the fourteenth century – liturgy, plainchant, choir, endowments, and the side altar of the *Rouelle* – and each section has depicted parts of the setting in which Machaut's Mass may have been heard. It is only the interaction of all five witnesses, however, that reveals the most plausible function for the work. What hypothesis can be proposed?

Machaut probably composed his polyphonic Mass in conjunction with a votive service that he endowed for the Virgin. He incorporated the work into the Saturday

facsimile of the beginning of this document is found in Paris, *La Chapelle du Saint-Laict* (unnumbered page at the end of the book). I treat this foundation in my forthcoming study of music and ritual in Reims.

90 '. . . in altari ymaginis beate Marie gloriose virginis ante Roellam nostre prefate ecclesie' (AMR, 2G 408, no. 5).

91 '. . . singulis diebus . . . quam diu vivet de beata virgine maria, et ipso viam universe carnis ingresso unam missam de *Requiem* vel aliam si festivitas vel dies solemnis hoc requirat . . . in predicta ecclesia nostra ad altare de Roella in navi' (AMR, 2G 357, no. 15); also found in a cartulary of Reims known as the *Livre rouge* (AMR, 2G 1650, fol. 340).

92 Treated in my forthcoming study of Reims Cathedral.

93 In his discussion of the Machaut's tomb, Jean Goy states that the *Rouelle* altar was situated next to the sixth pillar of the nave on the right, rather than at the altar to the right of the choir entrance and only a few feet away. He gives no evidence to support this location (Goy, 'Note', 153, and his Pl. I).   94 See his will of 13 June 1523, in AMR, 2G 358, no. 15.

95 These documents rarely tell where the testator was buried.

Mass for Mary at the *Rouelle* altar that Jean de Vienne had founded in 1341. In all likelihood, moreover, Guillaume and Jean's wills called for the continued performance of the Mass, specifying that a 'prayer for the dead' be added to the celebration of the work to give it the solemnity appropriate to their anniversaries. After Jean de Machaut's death in 1372 or 1374 and certainly by the time of Guillaume's passing in 1377, this polyphonic Mass would have been sung in front of the statue to the Virgin and now over the grave of the dead brothers as well.[96]

Support for this theory is found first in the language of the epitaph for the Machaut brothers, which virtually ensures that Guillaume and Jean wrote wills, and the foundations and testaments outlined in Table 5.3 show that canons regularly endowed masses. The singing of Machaut's polyphonic Mass could well have formed one of the provisions of the brothers' endowments, for the work conforms to what we know of the liturgy of Reims Cathedral and exhibits the musical variants found there in his day. Second, there were probably soloists available to give credible performances of Machaut's Mass. The epitaph states that the Mass was executed by 'skilful' participants, presumably trained singers, and the choir of the cathedral, placed on sound financial footing in 1352, was no doubt replenished beginning a few years later with a steady stream of soloists who were educated in its newly created *maîtrise*. This choir might have provided Machaut with the singers needed to perform a polyphonic work. Finally, the placement of the epitaph near the altar of the *Rouelle* indicates that the brothers were buried at this oratory to the Virgin, and the epitaph states that the Mass that Guillaume and Jean endowed should be performed there. A Mass for Mary was especially appropriate for the altar of the *Rouelle* in Reims Cathedral in the 1340s, after the arrival of her statue and following the establishment of the Saturday Lady Mass there by Jean de Vienne in 1341. Machaut's polyphonic Mass uses chants that have connections with the Virgin, and in addition, the *Vg* manuscript, copied under Machaut's direction, preserves the designation 'Mass of Our Lady' for the work. In sum, there is plentiful local, contemporaneous support for the theory of the function of Machaut's Mass just outlined.

Further corroboration comes from consideration of issues not yet treated. It has

96 Perhaps then it is understandable why none of the remaining manuscripts of the Mass, all of which postdate *Vg*, transmit the rubric for Mary (Table 5.3). Copied between about 1370 and 1372, *Vg* records the original intent of Machaut's Mass as a votive Mass for the Virgin. The next surviving manuscript that preserves the work is *A*, copied between the date of the composition of Machaut's *Prise d'Alexandrie* in 1370 and the year of his death in 1377. Since the designation 'Nostre Dame' does not appear in this manuscript, we may suggest on the basis of the evidence in the epigraph that *A* was copied after Jean de Machaut's death in 1372 or 1374. By this time, the principal connection of the Mass with the Virgin would have diminished slightly, because of the oration for the dead for Jean de Machaut. The rubric to 'Nostre Dame', hence no longer an entirely accurate designation, was perhaps forgotten.

long been thought that the Mass falls late in the composer's output, and the manuscript evidence indicates that it was written after the time of copying of C, which does not include the piece, and prior to the copying of Vg, the earliest version of the work (Table 5.4). Clement VI's newly uncovered bull of 1352 regarding the vicars and choirboys adds support to the notion of a relatively late date.[97] This act may have served as an impetus to Machaut, providing him for the first time with an ensemble of vicars and boys who, although probably not singing polyphony regularly in the choir, might at least have been able to perform polyphonic works at side altars.[98] Indeed it is probably no accident, in view of Clement's bull, that all but one of Machaut's Latin liturgical works likewise seem to date from after 1352.[99] Other factors push the likely time of origin of the Mass even later than this. The ferocity of the Black Death, which reached its height in Reims between 1348 and 1355, had hardly abated when the city suffered a devastating siege by the English in 1359–60.[100] At the end of this tumultuous decade, Machaut, now in his sixties, had reason to be acutely aware of his own mortality, and it is entirely possible that he and his brother made endowments and probably also drafted their wills in the early 1360s.[101] If this is the case, then the Mass was probably complete before 1365, and certainly prior to the copying of Vg in the early 1370s.[102]

How often Machaut's Mass would have been sung is related to the performance of the Saturday Mass for the Virgin in Reims Cathedral. This weekly votive service took place only on Saturdays when it was not displaced by a feast of nine lessons or

97 Machabey finds two documents witnessing Guillaume's presence at Reims in 1352 (*Guillaume de Machault*, vol. 1, pp. 47–8 (citing Pierre Varin, *Archives administratives de la ville de Reims*, Collection de documents inédits sur l'histoire de France, sér. 1, *Histoire politique* (Paris, 1848), vol. 3, p. 31, no. DCXXXV; and AMR, 2G 323, no. 15)).

98 Craig Wright likewise suggests that Du Fay's style of composition changed radically in the 1440s when he had an *a cappella* force of twenty to twenty-five singers at his disposal ('Dufay at Cambrai: Discoveries and Revisions', *JAMS* 28 (1975), 195–6.

99 Discussed in my forthcoming study of music at Reims Cathedral.

100 Desportes, *Reims et les rémois*, pp. 544–62.

101 In *Le Jugement du roi de Navarre*, he writes that he closeted himself in his house for a long time to avoid the plague; see R. Barton Palmer, ed. and trans., *Guillaume de Machaut 'The Judgment of the King of Navarre'*, Garland Library of Medieval Literature 45, series A (New York, 1988), lines 442–75. Machaut probably conducted as little official business as possible during the epidemic, since to do so would have necessitated his interacting with other persons. He says only that he hastily confessed his sins and prepared himself to meet death at any moment (ibid., lines 437–41). In any case, it is also likely that Guillaume made his will, and possibly his endowment as well, after the arrival of his brother Jean at the cathedral in 1355, and Daniel Leech-Wilkinson suggests in his forthcoming edition *Machaut's Mass* that the endowment/will was a response to Guillaume's illness of 1362.

102 On the basis of stylistic similarities between the Mass and two of Machaut's other compositions, Leech-Wilkinson has proposed a date of *c.* 1360–5 as 'probable', and *c.* 1362–4 as 'likely', *Machaut's Mass*, p. 103.

Table 5.4. *Proposed chronology of Machaut's Mass*

Date	Event		Chronology
1341	Jean de Vienne founds Saturday Mass for Mary at *Rouelle* altar		
1348	Black Death arrives in Reims		
1350		↑	
1352	Clement VI's choral foundation	Machaut MS *C* copied, Mass not present	
1356		↓	
1359	Siege of Reims		
1360			↑
1364	Coronation of Charles V		Guillaume (and Jean?) de Machaut augment Jean de Vienne's 1341 endowment of votive mass for Mary
1365			at the *Rouelle* altar with Guillaume's polyphonic Mass ↓
1370	↑ Machaut MS *Vg* copied, Mass rubricated for Mary		
1372	↓		
1374	Death of Jean de Machaut	Machaut MS *A* ↑ copied, no rubric for Mass here or in any other MS ↓	Mass now includes an oration *de defunctis* for Jean de Machaut
1377	Death of Guillaume de Machaut		Mass now includes an oration *de defunctis* for Jean and Guillaume de Machaut

some other special service. In reality, intruding masses replaced this service about a third of the time, and it is therefore likely that Machaut's Mass was actually executed on about thirty-five or forty, rather than fifty-two, Saturdays each year.[103]

To support the performance of a polyphonic Mass as often as this, we would expect to find evidence of a large sum of money. Indeed this is the case. Archbishop Jean de Vienne's original endowment yielded ten *livres* and eight *sous* annually. Though perhaps not as wealthy as an archbishop, Guillaume certainly had money and property of value to commit to the funding of a Mass in the 1360s and 1370s. He may be the 'Guille[me]te de Machaut' who was assessed for taxes in 1364 on a property in the nearby parish of Saint-Timothy,[104] and in 1371 he received three hundred gold *francs* from the Count of Savoy in payment for a manuscript.[105] Like other canons in the cathedral (Table 5.3), the Machaut brothers would have guaranteed the provisions in their endowments through sizeable donations, possibly equalling the same three hundred *florins* that the epitaph implies their wills also stipulated 'for the growth of the revenues of the said Mass' after their deaths. Each of these payments of three hundred *florins* would have yielded about 12 *livres* per year,[106] bringing the total of the three endowments after Machaut died to at least thirty-four *livres* annually.

Not only did this lucrative endowment continue to grow, Machaut's Mass apparently remained in the repertory of the cathedral at least until the early fifteenth century. Canon Laurent de Raillicourt gave two hundred *florins* 'for augmenting the Mass of the *Rouelle*' in 1407 (Table 5.3), and we noted earlier that Canon Jean le Verrier referred to the Machaut brothers' prayer in the Saturday Mass in his own endowment of 1411. By this time, the Mass had evidently become a permanent institution, one supported by at least forty *livres* annually.

The relative size of this amount can be gauged in comparison with other fifteenth-century endowments. In 1421 the polyphonic Lady Mass at Saint-Donatian's in Bruges, performed daily, was supported by eighty-four *livres* per year,[107] and Guillaume Dufay endowed the annual singing of his *Requiem* some fifty years later for only four *livres*.[108] Compared to these sums, the forty *livres*

---

103 This estimate is based on my study of thirteen calendars from Reims from the twelfth through fifteenth centuries.

104 AMR, 2G 191, fol. 141. Both Daniel Leech-Wilkinson and I came upon this hitherto unnoticed document in the Archives of Reims independently. Leech-Wilkinson believes that the first name reads 'Guillaumete'.   105 Machabey, *Guillaume de Machault*, vol. 1, p. 66.

106 See the two foundations in Table 5.3 from 1325 and 1368, which reveal not only the total amount of a foundation but also the expected yearly income. Based on these figures, a conservative estimate of the annual revenue from the 300 *florins* is about twelve *florins* (*c.* four percent).

107 See Strohm, *Music in Late Medieval Bruges*, p. 22.

108 Lille, Archives départementales du Nord, 4G 1313, p. 22. I thank Craig Wright for this reference.

destined for the Saturday Mass at the *Rouelle* altar, sung on the average a little less than once a week, is astonishing. Indeed, the magnitude of this foundation virtually excludes the notion that the 'Mass of the *Rouelle*' might have been a plainchant service; only a polyphonic Mass would have warranted an endowment of this size. Perhaps Laurent de Raillicourt and other canons who enriched the fund purchased the right to have their names added to the 'prayer for the dead' for the Machaut brothers.[109]

The Marian function of Machaut's Mass which has been outlined here was certainly typical of other Masses of the late Middle Ages and Renaissance. The editors of the Mass of Tournai have recently suggested that this work, the Gloria and Credo of which are similar to the corresponding movements in Machaut's Mass,[110] was compiled in 1349 as a votive service for use on the principal feasts of the Virgin.[111] Likewise, every fifteenth-century composer wrote Masses to the Virgin based on Marian chants. Even the dual Marian-commemorative orientation that the Mass took on after the demise of the Machauts finds ample precedent in works of the fifteenth century. Guillaume Dufay, for one, stipulated in his will that his Marian motet *Ave regina celorum* be sung at his deathbed.[112] He likewise composed a rhymed office in plainchant commemorating six Marian feasts, which was often celebrated in connection with memorial services.[113]

The situation in the fifteenth century differs in one respect, however, for composers were now writing works specifically called *Requiem* Masses and based on plainchants appropriate to this type of composition. If the polyphonic *Requiem* was an innovation of the fifteenth century, it was one that may have grown out of the two-fold nature of Machaut's polyphonic Mass, a piece intended to be Marian during his lifetime and commemorative 'by virtue of the prayer for [him]' after his death.

Just as polyphonic Masses to the Virgin existed both before and after Machaut's

---

109 The epitaph may even suggest this if the word 'amicorum' (line 5) is translated as 'friends' instead of 'loved ones'.

110 See Reaney, *Guillaume de Machaut*, Oxford Studies of Composers 9 (London, 1971), pp. 60–1.

111 Jean Dumoulin et al., eds., *La Messe de Tournai*, pp. 21, 56–7.

112 See Jules Houdoy, *Histoire aristique de la cathédrale de Cambrai, ancienne église métropolitaine Notre-Dame: Comptes, inventaires et documents inédits*, Mémoires de la société des sciences, de l'agriculture et des arts de Lille, 4th ser., vol. 7 (Lille, 1880), p. 91; and Wright, 'Dufay at Cambrai', 219. The notion of wills as the inspiration for the creation of sacred polyphony in the late Middle Ages is treated in Haggh, 'Music, Liturgy, and Ceremony in Brussels', 503–26, and 'The Medieval Obituary and the Rise of Sacred Polyphony in the Low Countries', paper presented at the meeting of the American Musicological Society in New Orleans, 1987.

113 The content and history of this feast, called the 'Recollectio Festorum Beatae Mariae Virginis', has been brought to light in Haggh, 'The Celebration of the "Recollectio Festorum Beatae Mariae Virginis", 1457–1987', *Studia Musicologica Academiae Scientiarum Hungaricae* 30 (1988), 361–73.

Mass, so the performance of polyphony at a side altar in a church and in the presence of a Marian image was commonplace. By 1349 the aforementioned Mass of Tournai was evidently sung at an altar in the transept of the church,[114] an oratory which was undoubtedly similar to the altar of the *Rouelle* in the nave of Reims Cathedral. In Brussels a polyphonic *Salve* service was performed at Saint-Goedele's by 1362,[115] and we have noted that Saint-Donatian's in Bruges executed a daily polyphonic Mass in the Lady Chapel behind the choir by 1421.[116] Later in the fifteenth century, Du Fay's Marian Masses and motets were sung in the cathedral of Cambrai in the apsidal chapel of the Trinity in front of a portrait of Notre-Dame de Grâce.[117]

Understood as a Marian-commemorative Mass for a side altar in Reims Cathedral, therefore, Machaut's Mass stands alongside a host of other Marian works of the fourteenth through sixteenth centuries. Armand Machabey was probably on the right track, then, when he said: 'the Mass of Our Lady might . . . have been composed for use in this chapel [the altar of the *Rouelle*] to which the two brothers seem to have been particularly attached'.[118] Unlike its predecessor in Tournai, Machaut's Mass is both coherent in harmonic and rhythmic language[119] and unified in terms of the choice of tenor chants. If the work was composed as a unit, it prefigures two kinds of fifteenth-century polyphonic Masses based on *cantus firmi* and inspired by the desire of composers to ensure their own salvation: the Marian devotional Mass and the *Requiem*. For the first time, it seems, a composer specifically intended that his Mass outlive him, that it be sung not solely as a votive service to the Blessed Virgin, but also in 'pious devotion to [his] memory'.

114 See the diagram of the church in Jean Dumoulin *et al.*, eds., *La Messe de Tournai*, p. 49.
115 Haggh, 'Music, Liturgy, and Ceremony in Brussels', 397–401, and 'Itinerancy to Residency', 360.   116 See Strohm, *Music in Late Medieval Bruges*, pp. 8, 22, 26–7.
117 Wright, 'Dufay at Cambrai', 199.
118 'La Messe "Notre-Dame" aurait donc pu être composée à l'intention de cette chapelle à laquelle les deux frères semblent avoit été particuliérement attachés' (*Guillaume de Machault*, vol. 2, p. 114). Machabey's suggestion has not gone unnoticed. It is repeated, though with new documentation, in Hoppin, *Medieval Music*, p. 420; Haggh, 'Music, Liturgy, and Ceremony in Brussels', 523; and in Leech-Wilkinson, *Machaut's Mass*.
119 Leech-Wilkinson, *Machaut's Mass*, chapter 4.

Appendix: List of sources cited in the musical examples

* = Kyrie troped with Marian Trope *Rex Virginum*

Manuscript Monophonic sources	Type	Century	Provenance	Kyrie IV	Sanctus XVII
F: AS 444	Missal	13, end	Arras, Saint-Vaast	16	
F: DOU 114	Gradual	14/1	Marchiennes (NE France)	58v	62v
F: LA 263	Festal liturgies, plays, etc.	12–13	Laon	26	82, 82v
F: LG 2 (17)	Gradual	14	?Fontevrault (near Tours)	246v	253
F: PA 110	Gradual	14	Paris	261v	264
135	Missal	13/2	London or Canterbury	228, 230	284v
*(135)					
197	Gradual	13, end	St-Victor	164v	
201	Missal	15/1	Roman	8v	
595	Missal/Breviary				
F:Pm 411(241)	Missal	13–14	Châlons-sur-Marne	247	243v
F:Pn, lat. 830	Missal	c. 1380	Paris, Notre-Dame	135v	138
842	Missal	13/2	St-Germain l'Auxerrois	295v	297v
845	Missal	14/2	Châlons-sur-Marne	196v	198v
861	Missal	14/2	Châlons-sur-Marne	208v	210v
904	Gradual	14/1	Paris	418v	
1107	Missal	13	Rouen	393v	267v
1112	Missal	1259–75	St-Denis	257	394
1337	Gradual	c. 1225	Paris	325	308
10502	Missal	13–14	Paris	12	
13255	Gradual	13/1	Sens	98v	
14452	Gradual	13, end	Paris, Cluniac	134	
15615	Missal	13	St-Victor	352	353
16823	Missal	13	Paris, Sorbonne	198v	
16828	Gradual	13	St-Corneille	173, 175	222
17311	Missal	14	St-Corneille	248v	
17312	Missal	14/1	Cambrai	192	
F: Psg 1259	Missal	13/1	Auxerre	267v	
F: R(m), A.233 (250)	Gradual	13/1	Ste-Geneviève	168v	
F: RSc 224	Missal	14	Jumièges	246	247
264	Gradual	14/2	Reims, Cathedral	72	75v
266	Gradual	13	Reims, St-Thierry	66v	69v
		15	Reims, St-Denis		
F: VN 759	Missal	13/1	Verdun, St-Vanne	266	268v

Manuscript		Century	Provenance	Kyrie	Sanctus
GB: Lbm, Add. 16905	Missal	14	Paris, Notre–Dame	351v	354
23935					
GB: Lva 1346–1891	Dominican Liturgy	c. 1260	Dominican, Paris	433v	434v
GB: Mr 24	Missal	1350	St–Denis	346v	368
	Missal	13/2	Sarum (Exeter)	9,	13
★(24)				10v	
I: Ac 695	Troper, 3 Prosers	13/2	?Reims (Troper)	6,	44v,
★(695)				9v	47v
I: Rvat 2049	Missal	13	Franciscan	10	11v

Manuscript Polyphonic sources	Century	Provenance	Kyrie	Sanctus
E: SC (no number = *Codex Calixtinus*)[1]	12	?Vezelay	190	
★GB: A 2379[2]	13	Scotland	2	
GB: Lbm 462	14–15	England		3, 22
GB: Lbm 463	14–15	England		4
GB: Lbm 40011B	14–15	England		9
GB: Ob D.R.3	14–15	England		5
★Hu (E: BU1h = *Las Huelgas MS*)[3]	c. 1300	Cistercian, Las Huelgas	1	
I: Bc, Q 11[4]	14	Central Italy		5v
I: Ma, M. 17. sup. (*Ad Organum Faciendum*)[5]	12	Laon	56	
Mo (F: MO, H196 = Montpellier MS)[6]	13/2	France, ?Paris	344	
OH (GB: Lbm, Add. 57950 = *Old Hall*)[7]	15	England		nos. 101, 118 120, 122
★W1 (D: W 677)[8]	13/1	Scotland, St Andrews	193	24v, 212v

[1]Facsimile edition in José Lopez-Calo, *La musica medieval en Galicia* (La Coruña, 1982).

[2]See the transcription of this fragment in Geoffrey Chew, 'A Magnus Liber Organi Fragment at Aberdeen', *JAMS* 31 (1978), 336–7. This example, along with the following four from British libraries, was brought to my attention by Peter Lefferts.

[3]Edited in Higini Anglés, *El Còdex musical de Las Huelgas* (Barcelona, 1931).

[4]Sanctus edited by Max Lütolf, *Die Mehrstimmigen Ordinarium Missae-Sätze vom Ausgehenden 11. bis zur Wende des 13. zum 14. Jahrhundert*, 2 vols. (Bern, 1970), vol. 2, p. 90, no. 28.

[5]Edited in Lütolf, *Die Mehrstimmigen Ordinarium Missae-Sätze*, vol. 2, p. 35, no. 1.

[6]Edited in Hans Tischler, *The Montpellier Codex*, Recent Researches in the Music of the Middle Ages and Early Renaissance 2–8 (Madison, 1978), pt. 3 (Fasicles 6, 7, 8), pp. 150-3, no. 299.

[7]Edited in Andrew Hughes and Margaret Bent, *The Old Hall Manuscript*, 3 vols., CMM 46 (American Institute of Musicology, 1969). No. 118 is attributed to Leonel Power and no. 122 to J. Tyes.

[8]Edited in J.H. Baxter, *An Old St. Andrews Music Book* (London, 1931).

6

SACRED POLYPHONY AND LOCAL TRADITIONS OF LITURGY AND PLAINSONG: REFLECTIONS ON MUSIC BY JACOB OBRECHT

M. JENNIFER BLOXAM

In the bull *Quod a nobis* of 9 July 1568, Pope Pius V announced the revision of the Roman breviary and mandated its use for all churches and dioceses that could not claim a liturgical privilege at least two hundred years old. Pius decried the deterioration of the divine Office that necessitated this unprecedented attempt to purify and standardize the liturgy of the Catholic rite:

Because the ordering of the divine Office, once piously and wisely established by the most supreme pontiffs, chiefly Gelasius I and Gregory I, and moreover reformed by Gregory VII, had turned away from the ancient customs long ago, the necessity was seen that it should be recovered, having been made to conform to the former model of worshipping. Indeed, some have disfigured the well-known order of the old breviary, which has been mutilated in many places, and altered elsewhere by certain vagaries and foreign elements.[1]

A Travel-to-Collections Grant from the National Endowment for the Humanities in 1989 and a Division I Research Award from Williams College enabled me to consult manuscripts and prints at the British Library in London, the Bodleian Library in Oxford, the Bibliothèque Royale in Brussels, the Museum Plantin-Moretus in Antwerp, and the library of the Grootseminarie in Bruges. I acknowledge with gratitude the help of David Crawford, Kristine Forney, Barbara Haggh, Barton Hudson, Anne Walters Robertson, Richard Sherr, Ruth Steiner, Reinhard Strohm, Rob C. Wegman, and Craig Wright in the preparation of this paper. The manuscript and printed service books referred to in this study are listed in the Appendix on pp. 175–7. Within this essay the system of abbreviation for manuscripts of liturgy and plainsong used is that of *The New Grove Dictionary*; printed sources of chant and liturgy will be referred to by short title and date. Manuscripts of polyphonic music are identified in the body of the paper and in the musical examples by the *sigla* employed in the *Census-Catalogue of Manuscript Sources of Polyphonic Music 1400–1550*, 5 vols. (American Institute of Musicology, 1979–88).

1 'Quae divini officii formula, pie olim ac sapienter a Summis Pontificibus, praesertim Gelasio ac Gregorio primis, constituta, a Gregorio autem septimo reformata, cum diuturnitate temporis ab antiqua institutione deflexisset, necessaria visa res est, quae ad pristinam orandi regulam conformata revocaretur. Alii enim praeclaram veteris Breviarii constitutionem multis locis mutilatam, alibi incertis et advenis quibusdam commutatam deformarunt.' *Bullarum diplomatum et privilegiorum sanctorum Romanorum pontificum*, 24 vols. (Turin, 1857–72), vol. 7, pp. 685–8.

Nine years later, in a brief of 25 October 1577, Pope Gregory XIII charged Palestrina and Zoilo with the revision of the chant melodies for the new editions of the breviary and missal overseen by his predecessor. He disparaged the debasement of the pure, true state of the plainsong:

. . . the Antiphoners, Graduals and Psalters that have been provided with music for the celebration of the divine praises and offices in plainsong (as it is called) since the publication of the Breviary and Missal ordered by the Council of Trent have been filled to overflowing with barbarisms, obscurities, contrarieties and superfluities as a result of the clumsiness or negligence or even wickedness of the composers, scribes and printers . . .[2]

At the heart of these post–Tridentine efforts to restore and regularize the liturgy and plainsong of the Roman Catholic church lay the desire to reform and reunite the church in the wake of the Protestant Reformation.[3] For centuries prior to the promulgation of a universal rite, however, the liturgy and plainsong of the Catholic rite existed in myriad local dialects, sometimes signalled at the beginning of pre-Tridentine service books by rubrics such as *secundum usum ecclesiae Antverpiensis* (according to the use of the church of Antwerp) or *ad ritum ecclesiae Cameracensis* (for the rite of the church of Cambrai). The degree of variation between the innumerable usages that proliferated in Western Europe during the late Middle Ages was immense, ranging from differences in the large-scale structure of the liturgical year to discrepancies in the small-scale details of a particular plainchant's text or tune.[4]

---

2 'Quoniam animadversum est, Antiphonaria, Gradualia et Psalteria quae ad divinas laudes et officia in Ecclesiis celebranda plano cantu, ut vocant, annotata prae manibus sunt, post editum breviarium et missale ex Concilii Tridentini praescripto quam plurimis barbarismis, obscuritatibus, contrarietatibus ac superfluitatibus, sive imperitia sive negligentia aut etiam malitia compositorum, scriptorum et impressorum esse referta . . .' Latin text from Raphael Molitor, *Die nach-Tridentinische Choral-Reform zu Rome: ein Beitrag zur Musikgeschichte des XVI. und XVII. Jahrhunderts*, 2 vols. (Leipzig, 1901; reprint, 1967), vol. 1, pp. 297–8. English translation by Oliver Strunk, from *Source Readings in Music History: The Renaissance* (New York, 1950; reprint, 1965), pp. 168–9.

3 The most thorough discussion of Counter-Reformation endeavours to address the liturgy and chant of the Catholic Church is Molitor, *Die nach-Tridentinische Choral-Reform*. See also Robert F. Hayburn, *Papal Legislation on Sacred Music, 95 A.D. to 1977* (Collegeville, MN, 1979), pp. 25–67, and Edith Webber, *Le Concile de Trente et la musique: de la Réforme à la Contre-Réforme* (Paris, 1982), pp. 61–153.

4 To further complicate the picture of late medieval and Renaissance liturgy and plainsong, liturgical usages themselves were not static and immutable; feasts could be added over time, the ranks of feasts could be changed and their liturgies embellished in response to endowments, and the components of some services might be revised or replaced. Whether copied by hand or printed, service books prepared for a particular place are bound to disagree in some details, especially in sources prepared many years apart. The evolution of the liturgical calendar of Brussels, for example, is explored in Placide F. Lefèvre, 'Le calendrier de Bruxelles avant la réform liturgique du XVIe siècle', *Archives, bibliothèques et musées de Belgique* 13 (1936), pp. 1, 15–38; Paul Perdrizet

The differences that pervaded the performance of the divine service from one locale to the next during the Middle Ages profoundly affected a community's and an individual's experience of the cycle of worship that shaped medieval life. The panoply of special local saints revered by a town's populace, often in services newly created in their honour, functioned as a powerful factor in creating a sense of communal unity and loyalty.[5] Chroniclers, notaries, and other medieval record-keepers noted the occurrence of events in relation to liturgical calendars that varied from place to place.[6] Certain hymns, antiphons, responsories, and sequences, often characterized by textual and melodic variants peculiar to a local usage, gained special popularity in particular cities through their frequent performance in processions, in the daily *lof* or *Salve* service in praise of the Blessed Virgin, and in other liturgical and votive services celebrated in churches throughout Europe.

For everyone charged with responsibility for the performance of the divine rite, from choirboy to canon, the local tradition of chant and liturgy governed the execution of daily musico-liturgical duties. A choirboy learned to sing the plainsong according to the usage of the ecclesiastical institution in whose choir he served.[7] As a grown man, a cleric might seek employment in other places, where he was expected to adapt to the usage of his new venue.[8] Ultimately, the Office and

traced changes to the calendar of Paris in *Le calendrier parisien à la fin du moyen âge* (Paris, 1933). Studies treating developments in the liturgy and plainsong of a particular institution include Craig Wright, *Music and Ceremony at Notre Dame of Paris, 500–1550* (Cambridge, 1989), and Anne Walters Robertson, *The Service Books of the Royal Abbey of St. Denis: Aspects of Ritual and Music in the Middle Ages* (Oxford, forthcoming 1991). The degree of similarity existing between the calendar, the structure of the Mass and Office, and the plainsong in books transmitting one usage will, however, far outweigh any differences when compared to the calendars, the structure of the liturgy and the chant of another usage.

5 See Donald Weinstein and Rudolph M. Bell, *Saints and Society: The Two Worlds of Western Christendom, 1000–1700* (Chicago: University of Chicago Press, 1982), especially the chapter entitled 'Place', pp. 166–93.

6 Reginald L. Poole, *Medieval Reckonings of Time* (London: Society for Promoting Christian Knowledge, 1935), pp. 12–16; see also F.K. Ginzel, *Handbuch der Mathematischen und Technischen Chronologie: Das Zeitrechnungswesen der Völker*, 3 vols. (Leipzig, 1914), vol. 3, pp. 88–287.

7 This obvious fact is implicit, for example, in an ordinance from about 1460 enumerating the duties of the *zangmeester* at the church of Onze Lieve Vrouw in Antwerp (Katedraalarchief, Antwerp, Capsa 19 Dominorum 48, published in J. Van den Nieuwenhuizen, 'De Koralen, de Zangers, en de Zangmeesters van de Antwerpse O.-L.-Vrouwekerk tijdens de 15e Eeuw', *Gouden Jubileum Gedenkboek van de Viering van 50 Jahr heropgericht Knapenkoor van de Onze-Lieve-Vrouwkatedraal te Antwerpen* (Antwerp, 1978), p. 63). The ordinance begins 'Primo est ordinatum quod magister choralium debet habere adminus octo chorales, quos bene instruere et docere debet in moribus, cantu et ceremoniis ecclesie.'

8 New vicars at the cathedral of Notre-Dame in Paris were required by the chapter to memorize the psalter and the *commune sanctorum* according to the usage of Paris; see Craig Wright, 'Antoine Brumel and Patronage at Paris', *Music in Medieval and Early Modern Europe: Patronage, Sources and Texts*, ed. Iain Fenlon (Cambridge, 1981), p. 39. But choristers were not entirely successful in

Mass of the Dead would be performed for his soul, according to the usage of the church in whose employ he died. These local dialects of chant and liturgy formed, therefore, an inescapable and integral part of daily experience for every person trained and employed by the church.

Composers of sacred polyphony could not help but be intimately familiar with local traditions of liturgy and plainsong. As singers, *magistri puerorum* and *magistri cappelli* in the choirs of sacred and secular establishments all over Europe, these men sang and taught the plainsong dialect of the institutions they served; some supervised the preparation of new chant books, rendered judgements on analytic debates pertaining to plainsong, and even authored original texts and melodies for newly created feasts.[9] The chant melodies and liturgical texts that formed the substance of a composer's daily musico-liturgical experience thus furnished an abundance of musical and textual resources upon which he could base the sacred polyphony created to adorn the services of the church, chapel, or confraternity that employed him.

This essay offers a preliminary exploration of two far-ranging questions arising from the realization that the liturgy and plainchant sung, taught, and embellished with polyphony by medieval and Renaissance composers varied tremendously between locales: 1) In what ways are local differences in the performance of late medieval liturgy and chant manifest in sacred polyphony of the period? 2) What can recognition of this interplay between plainsong and polyphony reveal about the purpose, context, and performance of particular Masses and motets, and about the chant on which these compositions are based? Answers to such ambitious questions as these emerge only from the accumulation of case studies of much more modest scope, of which this is one. Here the focus will be on three compositions by a single composer, Jacob Obrecht, whose choice and treatment of sacred *cantus firmi* often suggest close ties to local traditions of liturgy and chant. Two Masses and one motet will be placed against the backdrop of local usages that governed musico-liturgical environments in which Obrecht worked, an approach that brings the relationship of plainsong and polyphony in this period into sharp focus and so offers a range of answers to the general questions just posed.

absorbing the idiosyncrasies of local plainsong traditions; in Cambrai, for example, discordant performances of the *Salve regina* prompted the chapter to have the local version of this famous melody painted on a tablet placed against the wall (F-CA 1064, fol. 127v, quoted in Craig Wright, 'Performance Practices at the Cathedral of Cambrai 1475–1550', *MQ* 64 (1978), 304–5).

9 Dufay, for example, oversaw the preparation of new chant books at Cambrai during the 1470s (Wright, 'Dufay at Cambrai', p. 197), rendered a judgement on the mode of a problematic antiphon while visiting Besançon in 1458 (David Fallows, *Dufay* (London, 1982), p. 72), and composed the plainsong for a rhymed office celebrating a new feast endowed by a canon at the cathedral of Cambrai (Barbara Helen Haggh, 'The Celebration of the "Recollectio Festorum Beatae Mariae Virginis", 1457–1987', *Studia Musicologica Academiae Scientiarum Hungaricae* 30 (1988), 361–73).

Table 6.1. *Outline of Obrecht's career*

by April 1480–August 1484	*zangmeester*, guild of Onze Lieve Vrouw at Bergen op Zoom
September 1484–October 1485	*magister puerorum*, cathedral of Notre Dame at Cambrai
October 1485–January 1491	*succentor*, collegiate church of Sint Donaas at Bruges
October 1487–June 1488	guest of Duke Ercole d'Este at Ferrara
June 1488–July or August 1488	visitor to Bergen op Zoom while en route from Ferrara to Bruges
January 1491–January? 1492	whereabouts unknown
January? 1492–June 1497	*zangmeester*, collegiate church of Onze Lieve Vrouw at Antwerp
June or July 1497–December 1498	singer, guild of Onze Lieve Vrouw at Bergen op Zoom
December 1498–September 1500	*succentor*, collegiate church of Sint Donaas at Bruges
September? 1500–February 1501	*zangmeester*, collegiate church of Onze Lieve Vrouw at Antwerp
February 1501–June 1501	relieved of duties in Antwerp (probably due to illness)
June 1501–mid-1504	reinstated as *zangmeester*, collegiate church of Onze Lieve Vrouw at Antwerp
October 1503	visitor to the Habsburg court of Maximilian I at Innsbruck
	probably in Rome as member of the Papal Chapel sometime during this period
November 1503–September 1504	*maestro di cappella*, court of Duke Ercole d'Este at Ferrara
September 1504–February 1505	dies of plague in Ferrara
late July 1505	

This table is a collation of numerous studies about Obrecht's life; see in particular André Pirro, 'Obrecht à Cambrai', *Tijdschrift van de Vereniging voor Nederlandse Muziekgeschiedenis* 12 (1928), 78–80; Martin Staehelin, 'Obrechtiana', *Tijdschrift van de Vereniging voor Nederlandse Muziekgeschiedenis* 25 (1975), 14–15; Lewis Lockwood, *Music In Renaissance Ferrara 1400–1505* (Cambridge, MA, 1984), pp. 207–10 and throughout; Reinhard Strohm, *Music in Lat Medieval Bruges* (Oxford, 1985), esp. pp. 38–41, 144–8, 186; Kristine K. Forney, 'Music, Ritual and Patronage at the Church of Our Lady, Antwerp', *Early Music History* 7 (1987), 42–4; and Rob C. Wegman, 'Music and Musicians at the Guild of Our Lady in Bergen op Zoom, c. 1470–1510', *Early Music History* 9 (1989), 175–249. Information concerning Obrecht's probable tenure at the Papal Chapel and the greater precision of his death date are based on documents discovered by Richard Sherr treating the distribution of Obrecht's benefices following his death. I am grateful to Professor Sherr for generously sharing his discovery in a private communication.

A simple caveat governs the methodology here introduced and summarizes its obvious limitations: most composers travelled extensively, and we cannot be certain that they were not influenced by liturgies of locales for which no documentary evidence yet records their presence. In addition to comparing the liturgy and plainsong of usages known to have been familiar to a composer, therefore, as broad a survey of other local rites as feasible must also be undertaken. During the course of this study, numerous sources for many other northern usages besides those surely known to Obrecht were consulted, including Utrecht, 's-Hertogenbosch, Ghent, Brussels, Tournai, and Mons. Although it is not possible, for reasons of space, to include herein all the information accumulated, the broad spectrum of variation between local usages thus acquired has helped to place this more circumscribed comparison in perspective.[10]

Except for two brief sojourns to Ferrara in 1487–8 and 1504–5, an appearance at the Habsburg court in Innsbruck in 1503, and a probable association with the Papal Chapel in Rome in 1503–4, Obrecht pursued his career in the north, serving the Guild of Our Lady in Bergen op Zoom, the cathedral of Notre Dame in Cambrai, the collegiate church of Sint Donaas in Bruges, and the collegiate church of Onze Lieve Vrouw in Antwerp (see the outline of Obrecht's career in Table 6.1). Much is known about the musical establishments and the cultivation of polyphonic music in Antwerp, Bruges, Cambrai, Bergen-op-Zoom, Ferrara, the Habsburg court, and the Papal Chapel during the fifteenth and early sixteenth century thanks to recent documentary studies that afford an unusually rich perspective on the milieu in which Obrecht lived and worked.[11] The local liturgical usages and plainsong traditions of these centres have, however, enjoyed little or no attention.

---

10 The investigation of service books from locales in which a composer is not known to have been active can sometimes lead the way to new biographical information; just such an inquiry has shown that Pipelare drew *cantus firmi* for his *Missa de Sancto Livino* from an office for St Livinus indigenous to Ghent, a city this composer is otherwise not known to have visited. See M. Jennifer Bloxam, 'A Survey of Late Medieval Service Books from the Low Countries: Implications for Sacred Polyphony, 1460–1520', 2 vols. (PhD dissertation, Yale University, 1987), vol. 2, pp. 367–85.

11 On music and musicians in Antwerp, see Van den Nieuwehuizen, 'De Koralen', and Kristine K. Forney, 'Music, Ritual and Patronage at the Church of Our Lady, Antwerp', *Early Music History* 7 (1987), 1–57; Bergen op Zoom is treated by Rob C. Wegman in 'Music and Musicians at the Guild of Our Lady in Bergen op Zoom, *c.* 1470–1510', *Early Music History* 9 (1989), 175–249 (I am grateful to Mr Wegman for sharing his article with me in advance of its publication). Cambrai as a centre of musical activity is explored by Craig Wright in 'Dufay at Cambrai: Discoveries and Revisions', JAMS 28 (1975), 175–229, and 'Performance Practices'. On musical life in Bruges and Ferrara, see Reinhard Strohm, *Music in Late Medieval Bruges* (Oxford, 1985), and Lewis Lockwood, *Music in Renaisance Ferrara 1400–1505* (Cambridge, MA, 1984). Musical life under Maximilian I, the Habsburg emperor whose court Obrecht visited in 1503, is explored by Louise Cuyler in *The Emperor Maximilian I and Music* (London, 1973); see also Walter Senn, *Musik and*

Uncovering these obsolete usages is indeed a daunting task; natural disasters, iconoclastic destruction, war, and the inevitable urge to discard or recycle useless things have decimated the number of late medieval and Renaissance manuscript and printed books of liturgy and chant, and local traditions must often be reconstructed from a few motley sources. For the secular usage of Antwerp, for example, the full texts and tunes of the Mass are unknown for want of a single missal or gradual;[12] no complete antiphoner transmitting the chants of the Office as sung in fifteenth- and sixteenth-century Bruges has yet been recovered;[13] and even for Cambrai, with its relatively rich cache of service books, no complete gradual dating from these centuries has survived.[14] Comparing the plainsong and liturgy of different locales is therefore a matter of fitting together the few surviving pieces in a puzzle that will never be completed. Nevertheless, these neglected sources of late medieval and Renaissance liturgy and chant must be considered, for only they bear witness to a most important dimension of this era's music-making long overlooked in favour of the polyphonic repertory. And, as the ensuing discussion of three sacred works by Obrecht will show, the study of local traditions of liturgy and plainsong offers otherwise unobtainable insights on matters ranging from the general context to specific details of sacred polyphonic performance.

Theater am Hof zu Innsbruck: Geschichte der Hofkapelle vom 15. Jahrhundert bis zu deren Auflösung im Jahre 1748 (Innsbruck, 1954), pp. 19–47. The music and musicians of the Papal Chapel during the late fifteenth and early sixteenth centuries are treated by Richard Sherr in 'The Papal Chapel ca. 1492–1513 and its Polyphonic Sources' (PhD dissertation, Princeton University, 1975). Princeton University, 1975).

12 A twelfth-century missal from the Premonstratensian abbey of Sint Michiel in Antwerp, now in the church of Sint Willibrord in Berchem near Antwerp, has been shown to bear hallmarks of Antwerp usage, but the early date of the source and its monastic origin limit its usefulness to this investigation. See N.J. Weyns, 'Een Antwerps missaal uit de 12de eeuw', *Bijdragen tot de geschiedenis inzonderheid van het out hertogdom Brabant* (Brussel, 1966), pp. 5–42.

13 In the introduction to the *Missa de Sancto Martino* edited by Barton Hudson in the *New Obrecht Edition*, gen. ed. Chris Maas (Utrecht, 1983–) (hereafter *NOE*), vol. 3, pp. xxiv–xxv, a manuscript in the Seminary Library in Bruges (B-BRg, without shelf number) is misleadingly identified as an 'antiphonal from the former Church of St. Donatian'. This source, a large, two-volume antiphoner of the fifteenth century, was probably brought to St Donatian's from Italy in the latter half of the sixteenth century to replace antiphoners of local usage made obsolete by the post-Tridentine reforms, for the contents are entirely according to the usage of Rome, with no mention of any feast particular to Bruges.

14 The main corpus of service books for the usage of Cambrai are summarily and sometimes incorrectly described in Auguste Molinier, *Catalogue général des manuscrits des bibliothèques publiques de France*, vol. 17, *Cambrai* (Paris, 1891). The ornate gradual made by Martin Lescuyer in 1540 for Robert de Croy, Bishop of Cambrai (F-CA MS D 12), does not conform to the usage of Cambrai, as assumed by Alejandro Enrique Planchart in 'Guillaume Du Fay's Benefices and his Relationship to the Court of Burgundy', *Early Music History* 8 (1988), 155–7; the book contains no feasts particular to the usage of Cambrai, and differs significantly from the liturgy detailed in coeval manuscripts and prints for the usage of Cambrai, especially with regard to certain key sequences.

JACOB OBRECHT AND THE CULT OF SAINTS: MUSIC FOR ST DONATIAN,
ST BASIL, AND ST MARTIN

The cities and towns within the counties of Flanders, Hainaut, and Brabant venerated an extraordinary variety of local saints, whose numbers swelled throughout the Middle Ages thanks to the lively trade in relics.[15] Communities paid homage to their own unique array of local saintly heroes and heroines that might bear little resemblance to that of communities only a few kilometres distant. Compare, for example, the sampling of important local saints worshipped in Antwerp, Bruges, Cambrai, Brussels, and Tournai shown in Table 6.2.

St Donatian, to single out just one example, was the patron saint of the collegiate church of Sint Donaas in Bruges, where the relics of this fourth-century bishop of Reims were interred in the ninth century.[16] In Bruges the natal day of St Donatian was celebrated as a *triplex* feast on 14 October, with a full proper Office and sequence; his *translatio* on 30 August was observed at *magnum duplex* rank. In Tournai, the seat of the diocese to which Bruges belonged, St Donatian merited only a *commemoratio* on 14 October. But in Cambrai, the seat of the neighbouring diocese and the birthplace of the saint, the feast of St Donatian took place at *duplex* rank on 13 October, one day earlier than in Bruges. Both Antwerp and Brussels, only about 75 kilometres from Bruges, ignored this saint.[17] (Festal ranks did of course change; see Table 6.2 for the dates at which these ranks were in effect in the locales cited).

In the Low Countries as everywhere, feasts of high rank enjoyed the most elaborate celebration, in which music played a vital role. Not only did *duplex* and *triplex* feasts merit more extensive services with plainsongs proper to the feast, but processions accompanied by music further increased the solemnity of the day. Polyphonic Masses and motets constituted the most extravagant musical adornment lavished on a saint, whether for the regular liturgical observance of his or her

15 General studies treating the cult of saints and saintly relics include Heinrich Schauerte, *Die Volkstümliche Heiligenverehrung* (Munster, 1939); Patrice Boussel, *Des reliques et de leur bon usage* (Paris, 1971); Peter Brown, *The Cult of Saints: Its Rise and Function in Latin Christianity* (Chicago, 1981); Weinstein and Bell, *Saints and Society*; and A.G. Martimort, *The Church at Prayer*, vol. 4, *The Liturgy and Time*, translated by Matthew J. O'Connell (Collegeville, MN, 1986), especially section 2, chapter 4, 'The Veneration of the Saints', pp. 108–29. The *vitae* of saints held dear in Belgium are compiled in Joseph Ghesquière, ed., *Acta Sanctorum Belgii*, 6 vols. (Brussels, 1783–94).

16 For an account of the life and the translation of the relics of St Donatian, see *Acta Sanctorum*, 67 vols. (Paris, 1863–1925), vol. 54, pp. 487–519.

17 Neither did Reims, where St Donatian served as bishop in the fourth century, honour this saint in the later Middle Ages. Of twelve calendars from Reims surveyed by Anne Walters Robertson, only the earliest, a twelfth-century summer missal of the usage of Reims, F-RSc 221. includes mention of St Donatian. I am indebted to Professor Robertson for sharing this information with me.

Table 6.2. *A selection of local saints from northern liturgical usages*

Saint	Feast day	Tournai	Bruges	Cambrai	Brussels	Antwerp	Rome
Gudula	8 January	—	—	—	triplex	duplex	—
Fursey	16 January	triplex	triplex	duplex	—	—	—
Eleutherius	20 February	commemoratio	commemoratio	semiduplex	duplex	duplex	—
Gertrude	17 March	—	triplex	triplex	iii lectiones	iii lectiones	—
Basil	14 June	—	—	—	duplex[a]	duplex	—
Rumold	1 July	—	—	—	duplex	duplex	—
Gummarus	11 October	—	triplex	duplex[b]	—	—	—
Donatian	14 October	—	—	—	—	—	—

Calendars for the usages listed in this table are found in the following sources:

> Tournai – *Missale Tornacense* (1498)
> Bruges – *Breviarium Brugense* (1520)
> Cambrai – *Missale Cameracense* (1495)
> Brussels – *Breviarium Bruxcellense* (1516)
> Antwerp – *Breviarium Antverpiense* (1496)
> Rome – *Missale Romanum* (1474)

[a]Celebrated on 4 July in Brussels.
[b]Celebrated on 13 October in Cambrai.

feast day, or for the myriad privately endowed votive services addressed to saints held dear by an individual, a family, or a confraternity.[18]

One of the best known examples of polyphony inspired by the adoration of a local saint is the *Missa de Sancto Donatiano* by Jacob Obrecht, a piece first associated with Bruges by Fetis in 1864.[19] Subsequent research has brought to light the specific endowment that precipitated Obrecht's creation of this Mass, established on 14 March 1487 in memory of Donaes de Moor, a rich furrier of the city. The endowment provided for a polyphonic Mass to be sung at the church of Sint Jacob in the early evening on the feast of St Donatian, the patron saint of de Moor; six musicians were stipulated for the performance of the Mass, and the organist was also required to participate in the service.[20]

Three of the five *cantus firmi* embedded in this Mass derive from the liturgy for St Donatian in Bruges: the antiphon *O beate pater Donatiane*, and the responsories *Confessor Domini Donatianus* and *O sanctissime presul*.[21] Heretofore only the complete texts of these chants were known from the *Breviarium Brugense* (1520); now, a newly discovered fragment provides an unprecedented opportunity to compare Obrecht's use of one of these plainsong melodies, *O sanctissime presul*, to the very local chant that furnished his model. The resulting insights into this composer's manipulation of a chant tune whose precise details are known will open the way for a consideration of another Mass and a motet by Obrecht whose exact local chant models remain to be determined.

O sanctissime presul, the eighth responsory sung at Matins on the *natale* of St Donatian, serves as the principle *cantus firmus* for the Credo of the *Missa de Sancto Donatiano*. The tune of this responsory as sung in Bruges survives, along with other

18 The chapter of St Donatian's in Bruges, for example, established a new endowment in 1421 requiring the choirboys to sing a polyphonic Mass in honour of the Blessed Virgin (the *Missa de Salve*) every day, and to 'sing discant' at high Mass and Vespers when the rank of the feast required it (full text of document in A.C. De Schrevel, *Histoire du Séminaire de Bruges*, 2 vols. (Bruges, 1895), vol. 1, p. 31, note 4; for a discussion of this endowment see Strohm, *Music in Late Medieval Bruges*, pp. 22–3). In Antwerp, the Confraternity of the Holy Sacrament at the church of Onze Lieve Vrouw held a weekly devotional Mass whose extensive use of polyphony imitated that normally reserved for celebration of high feasts, as stressed in the foundation document of 1506 (full text in Forney, 'Music, Ritual and Patronage', pp. 54–7.)

19 François-Joseph Fétis, 'Obrecht (Jacques)', in *Biographie universelle des musiciens* (Paris, 1875), vol. 6, pp. 344, 346. The *Missa de Sancta Donatiano* was first edited by Johannes Wolf in *Werken van Jacob Obrecht* (Amsterdam and Leipzig, 1908–21), vol. 4: *Missen*, no. 15, pp. 41–84; a new edition by Barton Hudson is found in *NOE*, vol. 3, pp. 1–32.

20 Strohm, *Music in Late Medieval Bruges*, pp. 145–7; see also Strohm's contribution in the introduction to the *Missa de Sancto Donatiano* in Hudson, ed., *NOE*, vol. 3, pp. xiii–xv.

21 Hudson offers a detailed investigation of all plainsong materials in *NOE*, vol. 3, pp. xi–xiii; on their significance in relation to Donaes de Moor and his life, see Strohm, *Music in Late Medieval Bruges*, p. 146.

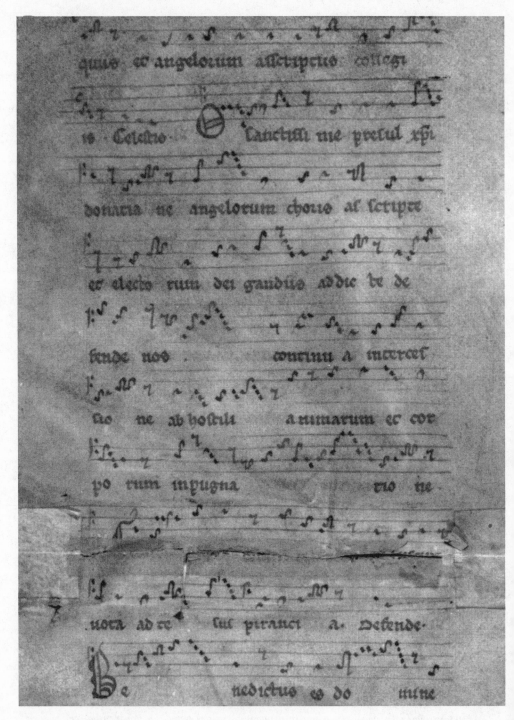

Figure 6.1 Responsory *O sanctissime presul* for the feast of St Donatian, from the fragmentary antiphoner B–Bra Oud Archief no. 538

portions of the Office of Matins and Lauds for the feast of St Donatian, only in the fragmentary antiphoner B-BRa Oud Archief no. 538, a fifteenth(?) century source in Messine notation (see Figure 6.1).[22] Although the particular church for which this antiphoner was made is unknown, the surviving portions correspond precisely to the selection and order of items contained in the printed breviary for the usage of Bruges, and the melodies contained therein are surely those sung at the collegiate church of Sint Donaas and other churches in the city on 14 October.[23]

Obrecht divided his plainsong model into three large sections (see Example 6.1). The first half of the responsory became the bassus of the Credo up to the *Et incarnatus*, which is free of borrowed material. In the *Et resurrexit* the composer continued in the bass voice with the second half of the respond, beginning *Defende nos*, while at the same time the tenor delivers the text and tune of another chant, the 'O antiphon' *O clavis David*.[24] Finally, the verse of *O sanctissime presul*, beginning *Exaudi preces coram*, provides the tenor for the concluding section of the Credo, *Et unam sanctam*. Modal integrity of the chant model was apparently not of paramount importance to Obrecht, for he transposed the verse of the responsory up a fifth upon the migration of the *cantus firmus* from the bass to the tenor.

The first of these three sections is remarkable for the facility with which the composer derives the bass line of a four-voiced polyphonic texture from a pre-existent melody: not only is the original tune left virtually intact, but the bass line is rhythmically integrated into the musical fabric for the first part of the section. In the second section, beginning *Defende nos*, the tune of the responsory is subjected to a range of treatments extending from utmost fidelity to the chant model to the freest paraphrase. This flexibility is in no way due to the constraints of combining the responsory's melody in the bass with that of the antiphon *O clavis David* in the tenor; indeed, the sections of the responsory most faithfully preserved by Obrecht coincide with equally rigorous statements of the antiphon's tune. The third and

---

22 I am indebted to Reinhard Strohm for generously informing me of his discovery of this important fragment during his research in Bruges, and to Noël Geirnaert, archivist of the Stadsarchief in Bruges, for kindly making this document available for study.

23 The usage of Cambrai also furnished an office for St Donatian closely resembling that known in Bruges. A comparative study of the extant texts and melodies for the Office as sung in Bruges and Cambrai remains to be done, but for the purposes of this inquiry it will suffice to note that the extant sources for the music of the Divine Office according to the usage of Cambrai (F-CA MS C 38 and the *Antiphonale Cameracense* of *c.* 1500–10) do not preserve the melody of the responsory *O sanctissime presul* under scrutiny here (F-CA MS C 38 lacks the Office of St Donatian due to a lacuna in the manuscript, and the *Antiphonale Cameracense* transmits only the tunes for first and second Vespers on the feast day). I am indebted to Professor Ruth Steiner for providing information on F-CA MS C 38.

24 The 'O antiphon' *O clavis David* was apparently chosen by Obrecht because of its text, which perfectly complements and completes the text of the Credo and the responsory sung with it. See Strohm, *Music in Late Medieval Bruges*, pp. 146–7.

Example 6.1 *Cantus firmus O sanctissime presul* from the *Missa de Sancto Donatiano* by Obrecht compared to plainsong from the usage of Bruges

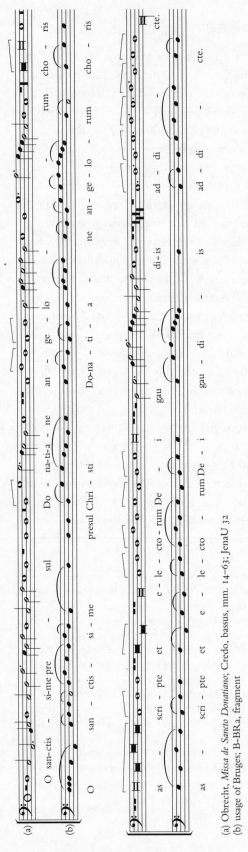

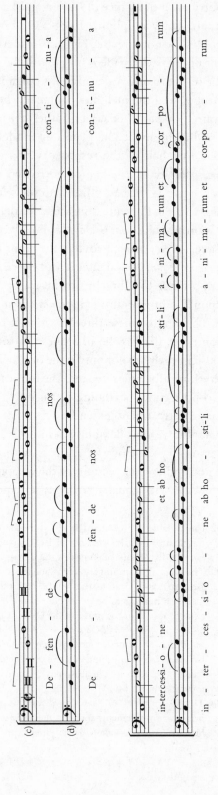

(a) Obrecht, *Missa de Sancto Donatiano*; Credo, bassus, mm. 14–63; JenaU 32

(b) usage of Bruges; B-BRa, fragment

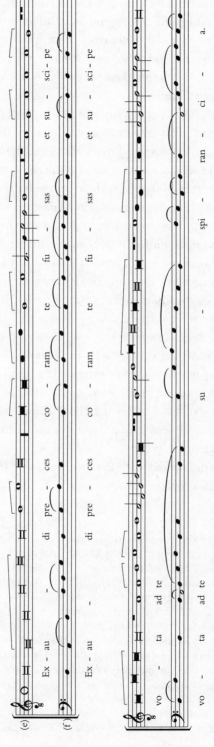

(c) Obrecht, *Missa de Sancto Donatiano*; Credo, bassus, mm. 91–152; JenaU 32
(d) usage of Bruges; B-BRa, fragment

(e) Obrecht, *Missa de Sancto Donatiano*; Credo, tenor, mm. 160–98; JenaU 32
(f) usage of Bruges; B-BRa, fragment

final section of the Credo presents a classic example of the structural tenor *cantus firmus*, in which the *cantus prius factus* adheres so rigidly to its model that it would appear to be copied directly from the antiphoner. Only at the penultimate and final melismas of the plainsong did Obrecht relax his hold on the chant melody.

From this extended example of Obrecht's transformation of a local plainsong melody into a *cantus firmus* for a Mass, a general guideline by which to gauge this composer's fidelity to a chant model can be deduced: the slower the rate of motion at which the *cantus firmus* proceeds, the more faithful that part of the *cantus firmus* is to the original plainsong. Phrases dominated by movement in breves or semibreves correspond almost note for note to the chant tune, while melodic lines dominated by motion in minims may include occasional notes superfluous to the model, or, less commonly, omit segments of the plainsong tune. Melismas within the plainsong, especially those of some length at the conclusion of sections, are unlikely to be translated literally into the polyphony; rather, Obrecht will sculpt a faster-moving phrase whose contour incorporates the tones of the chant but is not limited to them. Those portions of the *cantus firmus* that are set syllabically or neumatically are almost always melodically identical to the original tune.[25]

The discovery of the chant model for this *cantus firmus* from the *Missa de Sancto Donatiano* raises interesting questions regarding the text underlay of vocal lines based on plainchant for which the chant text was intended to be sung.[26] One need only compare the underlay provided for the bass line of Obrecht's Mass in JenaU 32, the only source of the work to include the Proper text of the responsory, with that of the original plainsong (both shown in Example 6.1), to realize the great extent to which scribes of polyphonic music and scribes of plainsong could disagree in the placement of a text.[27] JenaU 32 was copied c. 1500–20 in Saxony by a scribe probably unfamiliar with the local origin of the *cantus firmi* and possibly working from an incomplete exemplar, for large segments of the Proper texts elsewhere in

---

25 That Obrecht generally held the original form of his *cantus firmi* in great respect is confirmed by the excellent overview of Obrecht's *cantus firmus* technique in Edgar H. Sparks, *Cantus Firmus in Mass and Motet 1420–1520* (Berkeley, 1963), pp. 245–311.

26 A substantial body of fifteenth- and early sixteenth-century Masses survive for which sources indicate polytextual performance, that is, the *cantus firmus* retains its Proper text while the other voices sing the words of the Ordinary. A preliminary survey of this repertory is offered in Alejandro Enrique Planchart, 'Parts With Words and Without Words: The Evidence for Multiple Texts in Fifteenth-Century Masses', *Studies in the Performance of Late Medieval Music*, ed. Stanley Boorman (Cambridge, 1983), pp. 227–51. For a detailed consideration of texting problems in the Masses of Obrecht, including a discussion and list of works that seem to require the singing of texts extraneous to the Mass (including the *Missa de Sancto Donatiano*), see Barton Hudson, 'On the Texting of Obrecht's Masses', *Musica Disciplina* 42 (1988), 101–27, especially 122–5.

27 The new edition of the *Missa de Sancto Donatiano* by Hudson follows the example of JenaU 32 for most of the text underlay; see *NOE*, vol. 3, p. xviii.

the Mass are omitted.[28] In view of the fact that the *Missa de Sancto Donatiano* was originally destined for performance by singers well acquainted with the local liturgy of Bruges, it would seem desirable in this and similar cases to disregard the underlay of vocal lines based on plainsong made by scribes far removed from the local milieu, and to instead place our trust in the testimony of relevant sources of plainchant. Certain details in the transmission of this work support the idea that Obrecht intended, and the singers at Sint Jacob in Bruges realized, a performance of the Credo in which the vocal parts based on chant followed the underlay of the plainsong model. Three examples will illustrate this probability.

In addition to JenaU 32, the *Missa de Sancto Donatiano* survives in VatS 35, a manuscript copied for the Papal Chapel in 1487–89/90.[29] The two sources differ considerably in the extent to which the Proper text of plainsong *cantus firmi* are included, VatS 35 furnishing far fewer of the original texts. But Vat S 35 is temporally extremely close to the date of this work's composition, and a number of discrepancies in the musical readings of the two sources suggest that the Italian scribe had before him an exemplar in some respects closer to the composer's original text than that for JenaU 32. Example 6.2(a) shows that the version transmitted in JenaU 32 expunged repeated notes found in VatS 35 that perfectly accommodate a text underlay based on that of the responsory:

Example 6.2(a)   Variant readings in the *cantus firmus O sanctissime presul* from the *Missa de Sancto Donatiano* compared to plainsong from the usage of Bruges

(a) from *O sanctissime presul*; usage of Bruges; B–BRa, fragment
(b) Obrecht, *Missa de Sancto Donatiano*; Credo, bassus, mm. 22–7; VatS 35
(c) Obrecht, *Missa de Sancto Donatiano*; Credo, bassus, mm. 22–7; JenaU 32

28 For a summary of information and bibliography relating to JenaU 32, see *Census-Catalogue of Manuscript Sources*, vol. 1, pp. 296–7.
29 VatS 35 is briefly discussed and bibliography provided in *Census-Catalogue of Manuscript Sources*, vol. 4, pp. 41–2.

Similarly, VatS 35 contains a different arrangement of ligatures that allows placement of text identical to that of the plainsong model:

Example 6.2(b)   Variant readings in the *cantus firmus O sanctissime presul* from the *Missa de Sancto Donatiano* compared to plainsong from the usage of Bruges

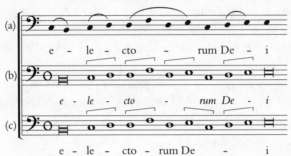

(a) from *O sanctissime presul*; usage of Bruges; B–BRa, fragment
(b) Obrecht, *Missa de Sancto Donatiano*; Credo, bassus, mm. 41–5; VatS 35
(c) Obrecht, *Missa de Sancto Donatiano*; Credo, bassus, mm. 41–5; JenaU 32

At several points in his manipulation of *O sanctissime presul*, Obrecht inserts rests between syllables of individual words or even within the melismas on single syllables. Was the text to be collapsed and repeated as needed, or were the syllables to be placed according to the chant model regardless of the resulting textual fragmentation? Example 6.2(c) suggests that the latter solution was preferred. Both VatS 35 and JenaU 32 embrace the first seven notes of *defende* in two ligatures, which by the conventions of texting would not normally accommodate more than two syllables;[30] furthermore, VatS 35 transmits a ligature pattern, indicated by brackets in the example, allowing text underlay that agrees with that of the chant:

Tracing this *cantus firmus* from the *Missa de Sancto Donatiano* back to its origin in a special plainsong for a locally venerated saint has thus afforded otherwise unobtainable insights into Obrecht's treatment of a *res facta*, clarified the text underlay of vocal lines based on chant, and distinguished preferred readings among musical variants in the sources of the Mass. The *Missa de Sancto Donatiano*, however, is exceptional in that the precise details of the work's genesis – the place, the occasion, the time – are documented; seldom can a polyphonic composition be so neatly associated with a specific tradition of liturgy and plainsong as this piece. In the absence of documentary testimony, the comparison of local usages familiar to a composer can provide valuable clues to the musico-liturgical context in which

30 Regarding the advice of theorists on text underlay, see Edward E. Lowinsky, 'A Treatise on Text Underlay by a German Disciple of Francisco de Salinas', *Festschrift Heinrich Besseler* (Leipzig, 1961), pp. 231–51, and by the same author, *The Medici Codex of 1518: A Choirbook of Motets Dedicated to Lorenzo de' Medici, Duke of Urbino*, Monuments of Renaissance Music, vols. 3–5 (Chicago, 1968), vol. 3, *Historical Introduction and Commentary*, pp. 90–107.

Example 6.2(c)   Variant readings in the *cantus firmus* O sanctissime presul from the *Missa de Sancto Donatiano* compared to plainsong from the usage of Bruges

(a) from *O sanctissime presul*; usage of Bruges; B-BRa, fragment
(b) Obrecht, *Missa de Sancto Donatiano*; Credo, bassus, mm. 91–100; VatS 35
(c) Obrecht, *Missa de Sancto Donatiano*; Credo, bassus, mm. 91–100; JenaU 32

certain compositions were created and performed, as the following examples will show.

According to the testimony of his *vita*, St Basil had no connection whatsoever with the Low Countries. Basil, one of the Doctors of the Church, spent his mortal life as the archbishop of Caesarea in Asia Minor during the fourth century.[31] But in the twelfth century, the relics of this saint were brought to the church of Sint Donaas in Bruges, and by virtue of the presence of his physical remains, Basil became one of the most highly venerated saints in the city. A chapel dedicated to him was built in the centre of the city, and the calendar of the *Breviarium Brugense* (1520) ranks his *natale* on 14 June as a *triplex* feast, thus comparable in liturgical solemnity to Christmas, Easter, and the major Marian celebrations. In nearby Antwerp and Brussels, however, St Basil's birthday was observed as a feast of only three lessons, and in Tournai, the seat of the diocese to which Bruges belonged, the feast was absent from the calendar, as was also the case in Cambrai (see Table 6.2). In light of the limited diffusion of interest in St Basil, it is not surprising that the complete Proper Office created in his honour, whose full text is transmitted in Bonnemere's printed breviary of 1520, apparently was sung only in Bruges.

No sources of plainsong preserve the melodies for the Office of St Basil, but one polyphonic motet, *O beate Basili/O beate pater* by Jacob Obrecht, extolls the saint through the combination of four antiphons from the Proper Office indigenous to Bruges.[32] The motet survives only in two Italian sources, Petrucci's *Motetti libro*

31 The life of St Basil and the translation of his relics are related in *Acta Sanctorum*, vol. 23, pp. 295–436.
32 The motet *O beate Basili/O beate pater* is edited by Wolf in *Werken van Jacob Obrecht*, vol. 6: *Motetten*, part 2, no. 9, pp. 85–96. Strohm first linked the piece to Bruges and noted the use of two Vespers antiphons from the feast of St Basil in *Music in Late Medieval Bruges*, p. 145.

quarto of 1505 (RISM 1505²), and FlorBN II.I.232, copied in Florence about 1515.³³ Both style and source evidence suggest that the motet dates from the composer's first period of activity in Bruges, from October 1485 to January 1491, and may well have accompanied him to Ferrara in the fall of 1487.³⁴

When Johannes Wolf edited *O beate Basili/O beate pater* for the first edition of Obrecht's oeuvre, he observed that the text was only fragmentarily transmitted and, lacking a source from which to complete or correct it, could supply only that text contained in the most reliable source, Petrucci's *Motetti libro quarto*.³⁵ *O beate Basili*, upon its introduction to Italy, had suffered the inevitable textual corruption at the hands of copyists and typesetters unfamiliar with the Proper Office in use in Bruges. From the *Breviarium Brugense* of 1520 we can now ascertain what the Italian scribes could not know – the liturgical identity of the various components here combined – as well as their correct and complete texts.

The *prima pars* of the motet is based upon the antiphon to the Magnificat for second Vespers on the *natale* of St Basil, *O Basili confessor Domini*, whose tune is presented in the superius, and upon the fifth antiphon of first Vespers on the same feast day, *O beate presul Basili*, whose melody is heard in canon between tenor and altus. Both sources furnish complete but corrupt texts for the superius and tenor voices, while text incipits indicate that the altus is to carry the text of *O beate presul Basili* and the bassus that of *O Basili confessor Domini*. A polytextual performance is thus made clear, combining the complementary texts of the two antiphons, both couched in the first person and both imploring St Basil to intercede with Christ. The texts of the *prima pars*, corrected according to the *Breviarium Brugense* of 1520, are as follows:

> *Superius (and Bassus)*
> O Basili¹ confessor domini venerande cui² probite³ meritis illuxit columna ignis incensa de celis exora⁴ pro tuis christum famulis ut nos suis condonet amicitiis.⁵
> *Tenor (and Altus)*
> O beate presul⁶ Basili pium⁷ dominum Iesum pro impietatibus nostris deposce.

---

33 Information and bibliography concerning FlorBN II.I.232 is provided in *Census-Catalogue for Manuscript Sources*, vol. 1, p. 216.

34 Petrucci's *Motetti libro quarto* of 1505 shows a marked preference for composers with connections to northern Italy, Ferrara in particular. Of the 35 attributed motets in this print, 23 – almost 64 per cent – are by composers either active in Ferrara or, like Gaspar van Weerbeke, well known there. The style of *O beate Basili/O beate pater* calls to mind that of the *Missa de Sancto Donatiano* of 1487, with which the motet shares a *cantus firmus*.

35 Wolf, *Werken van Jacob Obrecht*, vol. 6: *Motetten*, part 2, p. x.

[1]RISM 1505[2] and FlorBN II.I.232: *O beate Basili*

[2]RISM 1505[2] and FlorBN II.I.232: *cuius*

[3]RISM 1505[2]: *vitae*; FlorBN II.I.232: missing

[4]RISM 1505[2] and FlorBN II.I.232: *roga*

[5]RISM 1505[2] and FlorBN II.I.232: *amicis*

[6]RISM 1505[2] and FlorBN II.I.232: *pater*

[7]RISM 1505[2] and FlorBN II.I.232: missing

The *secunda pars*, for superius, altus, and bassus, is based entirely on *O beate presul Basili*; both sources provide the complete text only for the superius, with incipits sufficing for the lower voices.

Most problematic is the *tertia pars*. Both Petrucci's *Motetti libro quarto* and FlorBN II.I.232 supply the superius with the slightly corrupt text of the antiphon to the Benedictus for lauds on the feast of St Basil, *O virum digne colendum*. The scribe of FlorBN II.I.232 provides only the incipit of this text for the three lower voice parts, thereby suggesting monotextual performance, but Petrucci designates the bassus part with the incipit *Invisit sanctus sanctum Basilium*. Wolf, without a source from which to complete this text, had no choice but to revert to the words of the superius in order to furnish the bass line with text. Now, through reference to the local liturgy that inspired the creation of the motet, this mysterious incipit can be completed and the full polytextual performance of the piece realized. *Invisit sanctus sanctum Basilium* proves to be the first antiphon for Lauds on the *natale* of St Basil; the two texts for the *tertia pars* are as follows, according to the *Breviarium Brugense* of 1520:

> *Superius (and Altus, Tenor)*
> O virum digne colendum quem in columba spiritus sanctus[1] in gloria sua christus et cum sanctis virgo[2] invisit Maria: qui tyrannos qui demones deballavit et domuit mortem distulit cum voluit obiit et in celum abiit regnaturus in secula seculorum amen.
> *Bassus*
> Invisit sanctus sanctum Basilium effrem quem invenit ad sanctam procedentem viditquam pro os eius loquentem linguam igneam vere inquit magnus Basilius vere columna ignis Basilius vere spiritus sanctus loquitur in Basilio.

[1]RISM 1505[2] and FlorBN II.I.232: *quem in columbe specie in gloria*

[2]RISM 1505[2] and FlorBN II.I.232: *et cum sanctis suis virgo*

Without the plainsong models familiar to Obrecht, the underlay of these texts within the motet is largely a matter of editorial decision. In many passages, however, long note values and abundant ligatures result in melodic lines whose very appearance seems calculated to replicate the chant model, thus facilitating the underlay of the Proper texts. Indeed, so typically sparing is Obrecht in his embellishment of the chant tunes that a hypothetical reconstruction of the lost melodies can be deduced. The two Vespers antiphons furnishing the foundation of the *prima pars*, for example, prove virtually identical in their opening phrases (see Example 6.3(a)).

Example 6.3(a) Opening of *cantus firmi O beate Basili confessor Domini* and *O beate pater Basili* from the motet *O beate Basili* by Obrecht and their reconstructed plainsong models compared

(a) Obrecht, *O beate Basili*; *prima pars*, superius, mm. 1–7; RISM 1505[2]
(b) antiphon *O Basili confessor Domini*; hypothetical reconstruction; opening phrase
(c) Obrecht, *O beate Basili*; *prima pars*, tenor, mm. 5–12; RISM 1505[2]
(d) antiphon *O beate presul Basili*; hypothetical reconstruction; opening phrase

Further indication that Obrecht selected these plainsongs for their musical as well as their textual compatibility is found in the *tertia pars*, where similarity of contour at the outset of the two *cantus firmi* also obtains. The antiphon *O virum digne colendum*, as presented by the tenor, begins as shown in Example 6.3(b); *Invisit sanctus sanctum Basilium*, the antiphon sung by the bassus voice, duplicates the initial gesture of *O virum digne colendum*, thereby creating the effect of an imitative opening for this section of the motet (see Example 6.3(b)).

The discovery of the source of Obrecht's textual materials in the usage of Bruges thus illuminates not only aspects of this motet's construction and performance, but permits a partial recovery of plainsongs evidently unique to this usage. Still unknown are the specific requirements for polyphony on the feast day of St Basil, but endowments stipulating the performance of motets on various other feasts in Bruges suggest first and second Vespers, as well as processions, as the most likely

Example 6.3(b) Opening of *cantus firmi O virum digne* and *Invisit sanctus* from the motet *O beate Basili* by Obrecht and their reconstructed plainsong models compared

(a) Obrecht, *O beate Basili*; *tertia pars*, tenor, mm. 115–20; RISM 1505[2]
(b) antiphon *O virum digne*; hypothetical reconstruction; opening phrase
(c) Obrecht, *O beate Basili*; *tertia pars*, tenor, mm. 5–12; RISM 1505[2]
(d) antiphon *Invisit sanctus*; hypothetical reconstruction; opening phrase

occasions for the singing of motets.[36] That the texts and tunes of antiphons from the conclusion of first and second Vespers on the feast of St Basil dominate this motet may well reflect Obrecht's sensitivity to the performance context of the piece.

Throughout Western Christendom, certain feast days were everywhere observed. In addition to the universal celebration of events in the life of Christ that formed the backbone of the *temporale* and the five principal feasts in honour of the Blessed Virgin, services in praise of certain apostles, popes, and martyrs were mainstays in liturgical calendars, whatever the locale. Yet, their great antiquity and universal observance notwithstanding, these feasts varied widely in the details of their liturgical celebration, particularly in the selection and ordering of the plainsongs sung at the Office hours, and in the sequences assigned for their Masses. Large and small disagreements in the melody and texts of widely known plainsongs provide additional witness to the vigour of local traditions of liturgy and plainsong well into the sixteenth century. Local variations in the structure of universal feasts and the details of well-known chants had ramifications for the polyphonic repertory as well.

36 At the church of Sint Donaas in Bruges, an endowment of 1415 required the performance of motets at the conclusion of first and second Vespers on the feast of the Exaltation of the Cross, and another endowment of 1417 called for a motet to be sung during the procession on the octave of the feast of Corpus Christi. For these and other feasts requiring motets in the churches of Bruges, see Strohm, *Music in Late Medieval Bruges*, pp. 14–15 and throughout.

Table 6.3. *The Office of Matins for the feast of St Martin: a comparison of northern liturgical usages*

	Bruges	Antwerp	Brussels
A1	Martinus adhuc catechumenus	Martinus adhuc catechumenus	Sanctus Martinus obitum suum
A2	Sancte trinitatis	Sancte trinitatis	Cum repente viribus
A3	Ego signo crucis	Ego signo crucis	Domine jam satis est
R1	Hic est Martinus electus	Hic est Martinus electus	Hic est Martinus electus
R2	Dum sacramenta offerret	Domine si adhuc populo	Domine si adhuc populo
R3	Beatus Martinus obitum	O beatum virum Martinum	O beatum virum Martinum
A4	Confido in Domino	Confido in Domino	Sinite me inquit
A5	Tetradius cognita Dei	Tetradius cognita Dei	Scimus quidem te pater
A6	O ineffabilem virum	O ineffabilem virum	Artus febre fatiscentes
R4	Dixerunt discipuli	Oculis ac manibus in caelum	Oculis ac manibus in caelum
R5	Domine si adhuc populo	Beatus Martinus obitum	Beatus Martinus obitum
R6	O beatum virum Martinum	Dixerunt discipuli	Dixerunt discipuli
A7	Dominus Jesus	Dominus Jesus	Media nocte dominica
A8	Sacerdos Dei Martine aperti	Sacerdos Dei Martine aperti	Adest multitudo monachorum
A9	Sacerdos Dei Martine pastor	Sacerdos Dei Martine pastor	Exequie Martini
R7	Oculis ac manibus in caelum	O beatum virum Martinum	O beatum virum Martinum
R8	O beatum virum Martinum	Martinus Abrahae sinu	Martinus Abrahae sinu
R9	O quantus erat luctus hominum	O quantus erat luctus hominum	O quantus luctus erat omnium

The following sources were consulted:
Bruges – *Breviarium Brugense* (1520)
Antwerp– *Breviarium Antverpiense* (1496)
Brussels – *Breviarium Bruxcellense* (1516)
Cambrai– *Breviarium Cameracense* (1497)
Paris – F-Pn lat. 10482
Rome – *Antiphonarium Romanum* (1504?)

The Office for the feast day of St Martin, Bishop and Martyr, on 11 November typifies the diversity characterizing the local celebration of universal saints.[37] A comparison of sources preserving the usages of Bruges, Antwerp, Brussels, Cambrai, Paris, and Rome shows that first Vespers on the feast of St Martin is most variable, and heavily dependent on chants from the *commune sanctorum*. As indicated in Table 6.3, which juxtaposes the antiphons and responsories sung at Matins in these usages, certain segments of this Office recur between locales – for example, all usages surveyed place the responsory *Hic est Martinus* first, Antwerp and Bruges agree on the selection and arrangement of all nine antiphons, and Antwerp and Brussels concur on the choice and order of all nine responsories. Cambrai and Brussels intersect in the first antiphon of the first Nocturn and in all three antiphons

37 The life of the fourth-century St Martin, Bishop of Tours, is summarized in *Butler's Lives of the Saints*, ed. Herbert Thurston and Donald Attwater, 4 vols. (New York, 1956), vol. 4, pp. 310–13.

Cambrai	Paris	Rome
Sanctus Martinus obitum suum	Sanctus Martinus obitum suum	Martinus adhuc catechumenus
Tunc repente viribus	Cum repente viribus	Sancte trinitatis
Scimus quidem te pater	Scimus quidem te pater	Ego signo crucis
Hic est Martinus electus	Hic est Martinus electus	Hic est Martinus electus
Beatus Martinus obitum	Dum sacramenta offerret	Domine si adjuc populo
Dixerunt discipuli	Beatus Martinus obitum	O beatum virum Martinum
Domine jam satis est	Domine jam satis est	Confido in Domino
Artus febre fatiscentes	Artus febre fatiscentes	Tetradius cognita Dei
Sinite me inquit	Sinite me inquit	O ineffabilem virum
Domine si adhuc populo	Dixerunt discipuli	Oculis ac manibus in caelum
O beatum virum Martinum	Domine si adhuc populo	Beatus Martinus obitum
Cum videret	O beatum virum Martinum	Dixerunt discipuli
Media nocte dominica	Media nocte dominica	Dominus Jesus
Adest multitudo monachorum	Adest multitudo monachorum	Sacerdos Dei Martine aperti
Exequie Martini	Exequie Martini	Sacerdos Dei Martine pastor
Oculis ac manibus in caelum	Oculis ac manibus in caelum	O beatum virum Martinum
Martinus Abrahae sinu	O quantus erat luctus hominum	Martinus Abrahae sinu
O quantus erat luctus hominum	Martinus Abrahae sinu	O quantus luctus hominum

sung in the third Nocturn. No apparent pattern governs these replications, and despite the occasional duplication of some plainsongs between locales, the overall impression remains one of tremendous variety in the components of this Matins Office. Lauds and second Vespers are far more consistent in their structure, varying primarily in the choice of the fifth antiphon. According to late fifteenth and early sixteenth century calendars, these usages all accorded this feast a *duplex* rank.

Local differences in the cursus of plainsongs sung in praise of St Martin have consequences heretofore unrecognized for another of Obrecht's masses, the *Missa de Sancto Martino*.[38] Nine antiphons describing and praising aspects of this saint's life are unfolded one by one during the course of this remarkable composition, and the two surviving sources for the Mass indicate that the Proper texts of these antiphons were sung simultaneously with those of the Ordinary, thereby presenting an audible *historia* of the saint's life.[39]

38 For editions of this Mass, see Wolf, *Werken van Jacob Obrecht*, vol. 2: *Missen*, no. 8, pp. 117–64, and Hudson, *NOE*, vol. 3, pp. 35–72.

39 The plainsong basis of this Mass is discussed by Hudson in *NOE*, vol. 3, pp. xxiv–xxvii, where the chants are traced in several modern publications of chant and an assortment of fifteenth- and sixteenth-century service books. This effort to find models for Obrecht's *cantus firmi* is, however, of limited use, because the usages of the service books cited are not identified, and in fact none represent local traditions with which Obrecht is known to have been familiar.

Table 6.4. *Plainsong Cantus firmi in Obrecht's Missa de Sancto Martino and their function in local usages*

	Bruges	Antwerp	Cambrai	Paris	Rome and Ferrara
Martinus adhuc catechumenus	Matins	Matins	Vespers II[b]	Matins[e]	Matins
	A1	A1	MA	A1	A1
Dixerunt discipuli	Lauds[a]	Lauds	Lauds[c]	Lauds	Lauds
	A1	A1	A1	A1	A1
O virum ineffabilem	Lauds	Lauds	Lauds	Lauds	Lauds
	A3	A3	A3	A3	A3
Martinus episcopus migravit	X	Lauds	Lauds	X	X
		A5	A5		
Oculis ac manibus	Lauds	Lauds	Lauds	Lauds	Lauds
	A4	A4	A4	A4	A4
O beatum virum Martinum	Vespers II	Vespers II	Vespers I	Vespers II	Vespers I
	MA	MA	MA	MA	MA
Adoremus Christum regem	Matins	Matins	Matins	X	X
	IA	IA	IA		
Ego signo crucis	Matins	Matins	Vespers II[d]	Matins[e]	Matins
	A3	A3	MA	A3	A3
O beatum pontificem	X	Vespers I	Vespers II	X	Vespers II
		MA	MA		MA

Key to abbreviations used in this table:

A = antiphon
IA = antiphon to the Invitatory
MA = antiphon to the Magnificat

The following sources were employed in the compilation of this table:

Bruges – *Breviarium Brugense* (1520)
Antwerp – *Breviarium Antverpiense* (1496)
Cambrai – *Breviarium Cameracense* (1497) and *Antiphonale Cameracense* (c. 1500–10)
Paris – F-Pn lat. 10482
Rome – *Antiphonarium Romanum* (1504?)
Ferrara – GB-Lbm Add. 28025

[a] Unless otherwise indicated, all chants specified for Lauds occupy the same position in Vespers II.

[b] In the usage of Cambrai, *Martinus adhuc catechumenus* served as the antiphon to the Magnificat at Vespers II on the first day within the octave of the feast of St Martin, not on the feast day itself.

[c] The usage of Cambrai did not repeat the antiphons of Lauds at Vespers II, which had its own set of antiphons.

[d] In the usage of Cambrai, *Ego signo crucis* served as the antiphon to the Magnificat at Vespers II on the second day within the octave of the feast of St Martin, not on the feast day itself.

[e] In the usage of Paris, *Martinus adhuc catechumenus* and *Ego signo crucis* served as antiphons at Matins on the Sunday within the octave and on the octave of the feast of St Martin, not on the feast day itself.

Reinhard Strohm's recent discovery that Pierre Basin, Obrecht's colleague at the church of Sint Donaas in Bruges, endowed an annual Mass in discant for the vigil of St Martin's feast day on 10 November furnishes powerful documentary evidence associating this work with Bruges; indeed, the terms of the endowment, founded on 14 March 1486, explicitly charge the *succentor*, then Obrecht, with assembling the personnel and selecting the best singers. Strohm has suggested, and it seems indeed reasonable to assume, that Obrecht's *Missa de Sancto Martino* was written for the foundation of this endowment, first celebrated on 10 November 1486 at the chapel of St Martin in the church of Sint Donaas.[40]

One significant incongruity, however, forces a reconsideration of the proposal that Obrecht composed this Mass while in Bruges. Table 6.4 identifies the nine plainsongs treated as *cantus firmi* by Obrecht and their functions within the canonical offices for St Martin (including both his *natale* on 11 November and his *translatio* on 4 July) according to the usages of Bruges, Cambrai, Antwerp, Paris, Rome, and Ferrara. Two of the nine antiphons employed in the *Missa de Sancto Martino* were unknown in the usage of Bruges: *Martinus episcopus migravit* and *O beatum pontificem*. Obrecht apparently did not draw his *cantus firmi* for this Mass from the usage of Bruges, and so probably did not compose the mass while *succentor* there. On this basis Ferrara is also unlikely as the place of origin for this Mass, since, like Rome, Ferrarese usage did not include the antiphons *Martinus episcopus migravit* or *Adoremus christum regem*.[41] All nine antiphons were, however, sung in St Martin's honour at Cambrai and Antwerp, and although no documentary evidence has yet revealed the creation of a Mass specifically for St Martin at either Cambrai or Antwerp, a polyphonic Mass for the saint would have been entirely appropriate, since his feast day was celebrated at *duplex* rank in both cities.

From northern usages familiar to Obrecht, only the plainsong melodies from Cambrai survive, and they differ in a number of significant details from Obrecht's *cantus firmi*. Examples 6.4(a), 6.4(b), and 6.4(c) show three cases in which the *cantus firmi*, moving primarily or exclusively in breves and thus most likely to be true to their models, preserve melodic variants suggesting that the composer did not draw upon the usage of Cambrai for his *Missa de Sancto Martino*. Both melodic and textual variants distinguish the segment of *O beatum pontificem* given in Example 6.4(d), as indicated by bold type and brackets. Obrecht notated this *cantus firmus* in

40 The details of Basin's endowment and discussion of Obrecht's Mass for St Martin are found in Strohm, *Music in Late Medieval Bruges*, pp. 40–1.

41 A contemporaneous source for the divine Office as celebrated at the principal church of Ferrara, the cathedral of St George, is the partially noted breviary dating from 1400, GB-Lbm Add. 28025. The dependence of this liturgy on the Roman rite is explicitly stated in the rubrics commencing the *temporale*: 'Incipit ordo manualis ecclesie maioris Ferrariensis secundum consuetudinem sacrosancte Romane curie'.

Example 6.4(a)   Opening of *cantus firmus O virum ineffabilem* from the *Missa de Sancto Martino* by Obrecht compared to plainsong from the usages of Cambrai, Paris, and Rome

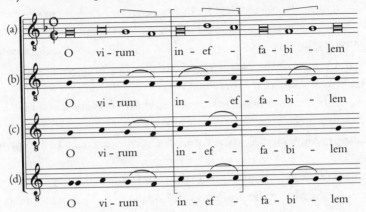

(a) Obrecht, *Missa de Sancto Martino*; Credo, tenor, mm. 13–20
(b) from *O virum ineffabilem*; usage of Cambrai; *Antiphonale Cameracense* (c. 1500–10)
(c) from *O virum ineffabilem*; usage of Paris; F-Pn lat. 10482
(d) from *O virum ineffabilem*; usage of Rome; *Antiphonarium Romanum* (1504)?

Example 6.4(b)   Opening of *cantus firmus O beatum virum* from the *Missa de Sancto Martino* by Obrecht compared to plainsong from the usages of Cambrai, Paris, and Rome

(a) Obrecht, *Missa de Sancto Martino*; Credo, bassus, mm. 188–91
(b) from *O beatem virum*; usage of Cambrai; *Antiphonale Cameracense* (c. 1500–10)
(c) from *O beatum virum*; usage of Paris; F-Pn lat. 10482
(d) from *O beatum virum*; usage of Rome; *Antiphonarium Romanum* (1504)?

Example 6.4(c)   Segment of *cantus firmus Ego signo crucis* from the *Missa de Sancto Martino* by Obrecht compared to plainsong from the usages of Cambrai and Paris

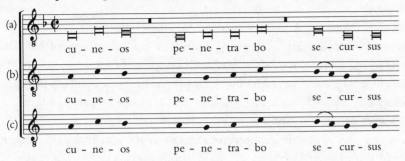

(a) Obrecht, *Missa de Sancto Martino*; Sanctus, bassus, mm. 84–95
(b) from *Ego signo crucis*; usage of Cambrai; *Antiphonale Cameracense* (*c.* 1500–10)
(c) from *Ego signo crucis*; usage of Paris; F-Pn lat. 10482

Example 6.4(d)   Segment of *cantus firmus O betum pontificem* from the *Missa de Sancto Martino* by Obrecht compared to plainsong from the usages of Cambrai and Rome

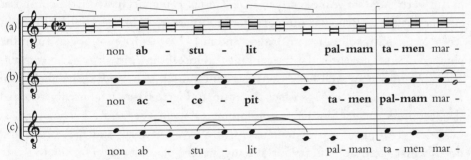

(a) Obrecht, *Missa de Sancto Martino*; Agnus Dei, tenor, mm. 93–109
(b) from *O beatum pontificem*; usage of Cambrai; *Antiphonale Cameracense* (*c.* 1500–10)
(c) from *O beatum pontificem*; usage of Rome; *Antiphonarium Romanum* (1504)?

proportio quadrupla (all the other voices proceed in *proportio dupla*), apparently in order to preserve the appearance of square plainsong notation within the polyphony.

Did the usage of Antwerp furnish the materials for this Mass? Without plainsongs from this city we cannot confirm the transmission of local melodic variants in the *cantus firmi*, but it may well be a significant indication of the local milieu of the *Missa de Sancto Martino* that only the liturgy of Antwerp embraced all the antiphons selected by Obrecht within the canonical hours of a single feast day, the *natale* of St Martin (shown in Table 6.4).[42]

How are the apparent incongruities between the documentary and musico-liturgical testimony to be reconciled? Without disassociating Obrecht's *Missa de Sancto Martino* from Basin's endowment, a new interpretation may explain the seemingly contradictory evidence. Although Strohm has suggested that the Mass was composed in 1486, the year in which the endowment was first established, the celebration was observed annually for at least the following decade, during which time additional funds were contributed to provide for more polyphony.[43] Obrecht might therefore have contributed a Mass at a later date, after he had ended his first term of service in Bruges on 22 January 1491 and assumed the duties of *zangmeester* in Antwerp later that year or early in 1492. Certainly contact between the composer and the chapter in Bruges continued after his departure in 1491: in 1491–2 Obrecht sent a Mass to his colleagues in Bruges, and in 1493–4 a group of singers from the church of Sint Donaas paid a special visit to Obrecht in Antwerp.[44] The *Missa de Sancto Martino* may well have been the composition delivered to the chapter in Bruges in 1491–2, perhaps as a special gesture to Pierre Basin, who briefly assumed the post of *succentor* at Sint Donaas following Obrecht's departure.[45] The liturgical evidence pointing, however tentatively, towards Antwerp, and the compelling documentary testimony in favour of Bruges as the place of origin for the Mass are therefore not mutually exclusive: Obrecht would have turned to the liturgy and

42 A special status for the feast of St Martin in Antwerp contemporary with Obrecht's service at the church of Onze Lieve Vrouw is suggested by the fact that, first in 1493, then in 1494, and intermittently thereafter, the choirboys were rewarded with wine, a treat reserved for important celebrations such as Circumcision, the feast of St John the Baptist, and the Assumption of the Blessed Virgin. My thanks to Professor Kristine Forney for sharing this information with me.

43 The full form of the endowment, reached on 17 August 1489, provided two Vespers motets in addition to the polyphonic Mass on the vigil and feast of St Martin's birth (11 November), a polyphonic Mass, sequence and Vespers motet for his *translatio* on 4 July, and processions on both feasts. See Strohm, *Music in Late Medieval Bruges*, pp. 40–1.

44 These contacts were reported by Edmond vander Straeten in *La musique aux Pays-Bas avant le XIXe siècle*, 8 vols. (Brussels, 1867–88), vol. 3, p. 187, with reference to Léon de Burbure, then archivist at the church of Onze Lieve Vrouw in Antwerp.

45 Pierre Basin served as *succentor* at the church of Sint Donaas from 13 August 1465 until 23 June 1466, and again from 17 January 1491 until 28 March 1491. See Strohm, *Music in Late Medieval Bruges*, p. 182.

chant of his immediate environment even while composing a piece destined for use in another locale.

THE MUSIC OF OBRECHT AND THE PERFORMANCE OF PLAINSONG

Thus far our attention has focused on the impact of local traditions of liturgy and plainsong on sacred polyphony; to what extent can the treatment of plainsong within polyphony inform us about chant? In the motet and Masses by Obrecht just discussed, a propensity to set the most literal quotation of the plainsong in long notes of equal value has been remarked; this procedure is evident in many sacred compositions throughout the fifteenth and early sixteenth century, and almost always entails retention of the original text.[46] Does this convention reflect the imposition of measured rhythm upon unmeasured melodies, or is this the echo of a late medieval performance practice of chant?

Many late fifteenth- and early sixteenth-century theorists, from Italy to Germany, define plainsong, or *cantus planus*, in terms of notes of equal value.[47] Franchinus Gaffurius, for example, related in his *Practica musicae* of 1496 that *cantus planus* is so-called by the Ambrosian and Gregorian clerics 'because they intone the individual notes simply, on one level in the even measure of a temporal breve'.[48] In 1518 Georg Rhau began his *Enchiridion utriusque musicae practicae (musica plana)* with a discussion of the different types of vocal music, choral and figural, noting that 'choral means plainsong or Gregorian, and it is referred to as old. Without any increase or decrease in prolation, it treats each note as of equal value.'[49] Seybald Heyden answered the question 'What is plainchant?', posed at the outset of *De arte canendi* of 1540, saying 'It is music in which a simple and almost uniform note-shape of one colour always retains the same value, excluding any augmentation or diminution. Examples are songs used daily in churches.'[50]

---

46 English composers at the beginning of the fifteenth century were the first to set entire chants as *cantus firmi* in long notes of equal value, and composers throughout the fifteenth and early sixteenth century resorted to this procedure; see Sparks, *Cantus Firmus*, pp. 10–13 and throughout.

47 The best discussion of the rhythm of plainsong in the later Middle Ages is provided in Molitor, *Die nach-Tridentinische Choral-Reform*, pp. 75–138.

48 Franchinus Gafurius, *Practica musicae* (Milan, 1496), facsimile reprint (Bologna, 1972), Book 1, chapter 1: 'Quod (licet improprie) Ambrosiani nostri atque Gregoriani clerici cantum planum vocant: quoniam simpliciter et de plano singulas notulas aequa brevis temporis mensura pronunciant.' Translated by Irwin Young, *The Practica musicae of Franchinus Gaffurius* (Madison, 1969), p. 12.

49 Georg Rhau, *Enchiridion utriusque musicae practicae (musica plana)* (Wittenberg, 1518): 'Una namque choralis quae et plana et Gregoriana seu vetus dicitur. Est quae in suis notulis aequalem servat mensuram absque incremento vel decremento prolationis.'

50 Seybald Heyden, *De arte canendi* (Nuremburg 1540), facsimile reprint (New York, 1969), Book 1, chapter 1: 'Choralis quae est? Ea est, in qua simplex et pene unica Notularum forma, eodem colore,

It is unlikely that the mode of performance described by these and other writers prevailed throughout Europe and for all categories of liturgical song.[51] The geographic and temporal spread of the theorists' testimony, however, confirms a widely used manner of performing chant in this period that finds further support in the contemporaneous *alternatim* literature for organ, in which the choral responses must have duplicated the delivery of the stately and equal notes of the chant tune by the organ.[52] And while the rendition of an antiphon in note values each roughly equivalent to a breve in *tempus imperfectum diminutum* (characteristic of many *cantus firmi* set by Obrecht and his contemporaries) would seem quite sluggish to a modern listener and may well exaggerate the stately pace of plainsong usually suggested by Obrecht's settings, the preferred speed for the delivery of the chant in Obrecht's time was slow. Admonishments directed to impatient choristers at the cathedral of Cambrai are typical. In 1504, for example, the vicars were told 'to sing and psalm more slowly', and in 1514 they were again remonstrated 'to execute the divine service more slowly and with more frequent pauses, especially in the psalmody and the singing of the antiphon *Salve regina* on Saturdays'.[53]

This concern for more frequent pauses in the performance of the chant enunciated by the chapter at Cambrai is mirrored in numerous sources of plainsong from the late fifteenth and sixteenth centuries in which the individual words or phrases are separated by vertical lines through the four-line staff. Frequent pauses between small text units of the chant implied by these lines find expression in some of the *cantus firmi* crafted by Obrecht.[54] The *cantus firmus* on the chant *Ego signo crucis* in the *Missa de Sancto Martino*, for example, shows a separation of words and phrases with the polyphonic framework that is closely akin to the chant as notated in the

eandem perpetuo quantitatem, extra omnem Augmentationem ac Diminutionem, retinet. Exemplo sunt Cantiones, quarum quotidianus usus in templis habetur.' Translated by Clement A. Miller, Musicological Studies and Documents 26 (Rome, 1972), p. 26.

51 The theorists are by no means unanimous in their descriptions of the rhythm of chant during this period. Tinctoris, for example, defines *cantus simplex planus* as a single melody 'in plain notes . . . which is made up of notes of indefinite value, like Gregorian chant'. (Johannes Tinctoris, *Terminorum musicae diffinitorium, c.* 1475, translated by Carl Parrish as *Dictionary of Musical Terms by Johannes Tinctoris* (London, 1963), pp. 12–13). An entirely contrary approach to the rhythmic realization of chant is first clearly described by Biagio Rossetti, whose *Libellus de Rudimentis musices* (Verona, 1529), edited by Albert Seay (Colorado Springs, 1981), discusses the barbarism of ignoring the value of long and short syllables, and assigns relative durational values to certain plainsong note shapes.

52 Mother Thomas More, 'The Performance of Plainsong in the Later Middle Ages and the Sixteenth Century', *Proceedings of the Royal Musical Association* 92 (1965–6), 124–6.

53 F-CA 1064, fol. 493 and 1066, fol. 264, cited by Wright in 'Performance Practices', p. 312.

54 The parallel between the vertical lines separating words in plainsong sources and Obrecht's treatment of several chants in the *Missa de Sancto Martino* was first noted by Hudson in the Introduction to *NOE*, vol. 3, p. xxvii.

Antiphonale Cameracense (*c.* 1500–1510) for the usage of Cambrai (for the usage of Antwerp, which is likely to have supplied Obrecht his model, no antiphons for St Martin survive) (see Figure 6.2).

Although it is impossible to gauge the rhythmic fidelity of a *cantus firmus* to its model with the same assurance that one compares a *cantus firmus* to its melodic model, both the witness of theorists and clues within plainsong sources themselves suggest that plainsong *cantus firmi* of Obrecht and others are the fragmented reflections of a lost performance tradition of chant. Indeed, when a composer set out to present a *cantus firmus* in such a way that the plainsong melody is unadorned and thus clearly recognizable, in a notation that closely approximates that of the chant sources, and with the original text, it would be strange indeed if rhythmic features of the plainchant were not also communicated within the polyphonic setting. Although the parameters of this study permit only this brief foray into the issue of the performance practice of plainsong, future inquiries in this direction will need to take into account the testimony of polyphonic music based on chant.

AFTERWORD

The symbiosis distinguishing the relationship between local liturgical usages and sacred polyphony of the late Middle Ages and Renaissance reached its pinnacle with Obrecht and his generation, and then diminished over the course of the sixteenth century. Composers lost interest in *cantus firmus* composition and turned less often to liturgical texts, choosing instead to borrow ideas from a pre-existing polyphonic composition in the making of a new piece and to set original texts often fashioned from disparate bits of Biblical quotations. And the advent of music printing on a commercial scale in the early sixteenth century directed the fruits of composers' labours to a much wider audience; sacred music with obvious and exclusive connections to a local liturgy would have had little meaning or use in printed collections destined to be distributed widely and used by a variety of people and institutions.

By the mid-sixteenth century, only faint echoes of local or regional fondnesses for certain saints and feasts can be heard within some publications. For example, in *Quatuor vocum musicae modulationes*, published in Antwerp by W. van Vissenaeken in 1542 (RISM 1542[7]), the motet *O bone Jesu* by Canis is introduced by the rubric 'in nomine Jesu', thereby associating the piece with the veneration of the Name of Jesus.[55] This popular devotion was not officially sanctioned by Rome until 1721,

---

55 *O bone Jesu* by Canis is transcribed in William Baird Wells, 'The Sacred Music of Cornelius Canis, Flemish Composer, 1510/20–1561' (DMA dissertation, Stanford University, 1968), vol. 2, pp. 36–9.

Figure 6.2   Notation of *cantus firmus Ego signo crucis* from the *Missa de Sancto Martino* by Obrecht in StuttL 47 compared to the notation of the plainsong in the *Antiphonale Cameracense* (*c.* 1500–1510)

but in the north pietistic fervour for adoration of the Holy Name was of such intensity that both Antwerp and Bruges celebrated a *festum nominis Jesu* on 15 January at triplex rank.[56] Lupus Hellinck, who spent most of his life in Bruges, composed the motet *Cursu festa dies sydereo* in praise of St Donatian; the text and

56 The adoration of the Name of Jesus intensified and spread throughout Italy, France, Germany, and the Low Countries in the later Middle Ages through the efforts of the Franciscan St Bernardine of

music of the piece do not, however, draw upon the local liturgy for this saint.[57] The motet *Plaude superna Sion* by Clemens non Papa, first published in 1553 at Louvain in Phalese's *Liber quartus cantionum sacrarum* (RISM 1553[11]), is a setting of the text for the ninth responsory for Matins on the feast of the *Recollectio festorum beatae Mariae virginis*, founded in Cambrai in 1457 and disseminated throughout northern France and the Low Countries in the century following.[58] And in the *Liber quartus ecclesiasticarum cantionum quatuor vocum* published in Antwerp by Tielman Susato in 1554 (RISM 1554[8]), the anonymous motet *Ave Gertrudis virgo grata* reflects the widespread affection in the north for the virtuous St Gertrude, though neither text nor music appear to draw upon local liturgical materials.[59]

After the Council of Trent concluded its deliberations in December 1563, the local usages themselves gradually became obsolete. The Council delegates did not mandate the suppression of local rites directly, but the process was set in motion: they charged the Pope with the responsibility of publishing a reformed breviary, missal, and catechism for the Catholic church, and they delegated to provincial synods the power to 'prescribe, according to the custom of the country . . . the right manner of chanting and singing that must be observed'.[60] Pope Pius V, who in 1568 declared the use of the reformed breviary obligatory for all churches and dioceses whose liturgical privilege was less than two centuries old, took the first big step towards the universal imposition of Roman usage, and subsequent provincial synods, including those at Gnesen in Poland in 1578 and at Antwerp in 1610, decreed the adoption of Roman chant throughout the diocese and called for the correction of old chant books or the creation of new ones.[61] In a fifteenth-century gradual copied for the church of Sint Donaas in Bruges, for example, a late sixteenth-century 'supplement' (so titled) provides Alleluias to replace many of those in the *temporale* (B-BRg MSS D7 and D8). By means of this appendix the

---

Siena (1380–1444) and his follower John Capistran (1386–1456), but the devotion was not officially recognized by inclusion in the Roman calendar until 1721. On the devotion to the Holy Name, see the entry by M. Kelley in the *New Catholic Encyclopedia* (New York, 1967–79), vol. 7, s.v. 'Holy Name, Devotion to', pp. 76–7; a study of this feast in England is found in Richard Pfaff, *New Liturgical Feasts in Later Medieval England* (Oxford, 1970), pp. 62–83.

57 Hellinck's motet was published in 1545 by Kriesstein in *Cantiones septem, sex et quinque vocum*(RISM 1545[3]); for a discussion of the piece and a complete list of sources see Bonnie J. Blackburn, 'The Lupus Problem', (PhD dissertation, University of Chicago, 1970), pp. 256–311 and 378.   58 See Haggh, 'The Celebration', pp. 369–70.

59 On the life of St Gertrude of Nivelles and her veneration, see Thurston and Attwater, *Butler's Lives of the Saints*, vol. 1, pp. 620–1.

60 See Weber, *Le Concile de Trent*, pp. 77–95, and Hayburn, *Papal Legislation*, pp. 25–31, for a discussion of these and other decrees of the Council of Trent relating to music.

61 An examination of the decrees of the local synods relating to music is provided in Molitor, *Die nach-Tridentinische Choral-Reform*, vol. 1, pp. 22–36.

book was made to conform with Roman usage, at least with regard to the one chant of the Proper of the Mass that varied most in northern liturgies.[62]

Powerful churchmen and an ambitious printer did much to eradicate local traditions of liturgy and chant in the Low Countries in the latter half of the sixteenth century. Between 1568 and 1570 the printer Christopher Plantin of Antwerp obtained, through the mediation of Cardinal Granvelle, archbishop of Mechlin, a papally sanctioned publishing monopoly to supply the Netherlands, Hungary, and parts of the German Empire with the reformed breviary and missal according to the usage of Rome.[63] In 1571 Plantin issued his first book of chant, the *Psalterium*, and in 1572 the *Antiphonarii Iuxta Breviarium Romanum restitutum* appeared; both were published with the encouragement and assistance of Cardinal Granvelle, Gilbert d'Oignies, bishop of Tournai, the bishop of Ghent, and the abbots of Hasnon and Marchiennes; Rembert de Malpas, *maître d'hôtel* of Cardinal Granvelle and cantor of the church of Sint Rumold in Mechlin, supplied exemplars of plainsong from Rome and supervised Plantin to ensure that the chant was correctly reproduced. Four hundred copies of the *Antiphonarii* were made, and although Plantin complained that sales were unsatisfactory, many churches in the Low Countries must have replaced their old books with these new volumes.[64]

The sacred relics of local saints remained, however, treasured possessions of churches all over Europe, and people did not easily forget their special heroes and heroines. In 1684, more than a century after Plantin distributed the *Psalterium* and *Antiphonarii* according to the use of Rome, his successor at the publishing house in Antwerp, Balthasar Moretus, printed the *Officia Propria Sanctorum Ecclesiae Cathedralis Antverpiensis redacta ad formam Breviarii Romani*.[65] This small book furnishes texts to the lessons and chants for Offices of local and regional saints held dear by the people of Antwerp, including Saints Gudula, Gertrude, Rumold, and Gummarus, and the preface to the volume stresses the necessity of continuing the

62 See Victor Leroquais, *Les sacramentaires et les missels manuscrits des bibliothèques publiques de France*, 3 vols. (Paris, 1924), vol. 1, pp. xxiv–xxvi, on the use of Alleluias as an aid to the determination of provenance.

63 Plantin's activities as a publisher of service books is explored in Leon Voet, *The Golden Compasses: A History and Evaluation of the Printing and Publishing Activities of the Officina Plantiniana at Antwerp*, 2 vols. (Amsterdam, 1969), vol. 1, *Christophe Plantin and the Moretuses: Their Lives and Their World*, pp. 3–122.

64 Detailed information about the background of the *Psalterium* and the *Antiphonarii* is given by Leon Voet in *The Plantin Press (1555–1589): A Bibliography of the Works Printed and Published by Christopher Plantin at Antwerp and Leiden*, 6 vols. (Amsterdam, 1980–3), vol. 4, pp. 1961–3 and vol. 1, pp. 78–82 respectively. The involvement of the prelates and Malpas can be traced in Plantin's correspondence; see Max Rooses and J. Denuce, eds., *Correspondance de Christophe Plantin*, 8 vols. (Antwerp, 1883–1918), particularly vol. 2.

65 Only one copy of this print is known to me, GB-Lbm 3505. de.2. Moretus published a similar volume for the cathedral of Sint Baaf in Ghent in 1661 (GB-Ob Vet.B3.3.60).

worship of these ancient and divine protectors. Gone, however, are the Proper plainsongs in their praise; instead, all the Offices draw extensively upon the Roman *commune sanctorum*.[66] So centuries-old local traditions of liturgy and chant gradually succumbed, and with their obsolescence a window on the sacred polyphony of the later Middle Ages closed. This window can only be thrown open by considering the Masses and motets of the period within the context of the late medieval traditions of liturgy and plainsong they adorned.

Appendix: list of manuscript and printed sources of liturgy and chant cited[67]

Many of the sources on which we must rely for the texts of the Mass and Office in the late fifteenth- and sixteenth-century liturgies are not manuscripts painstakingly copied by scribes well-acquainted with the local practice; rather, they are prints, often issued by presses far distant from their destination.[68] For example, the only extant breviary for the usage of Antwerp is a book published in 1496 by Johann Hamman in Venice, and the press of Antoine Bonnemere of Paris issued the only complete surviving breviary for the usage of Bruges in 1520 (see below). But these printers, like all who undertook to supply missals, breviaries, and books of hours to a local market, clearly worked from detailed exemplars supplied by local ecclesiastical authorities.[69] A sense of the integrity of their work can sometimes be gained through reference to manuscript sources of the usage in question. For

66 The replacement of Proper chants for the Offices of local saints with plainsongs from the *commune* was taking place centuries earlier; Robertson finds this process occurring in the liturgy at St Denis as early as the thirteenth century. See Robertson, *The Service Books*, forthcoming.

67 This list makes no attempt to catalogue all extant service books from these locales, even though many other sources from these usages were consulted. Only the sources referred to in the text, the tables, and the examples are given here.

68 A project entitled *Renaissance Liturgical Imprints: A Census* (RELICS), headed by David Crawford and James Borders at the University of Michigan, is well underway in amassing a bibliographic database of liturgical books printed between 1450 and 1600, and now supersedes the information available in previous published catalogues of liturgical imprints. See the communication, *JAMS* 42 (1989), 454. For the locations of the printed service books here listed, refer to RELICS.

69 The letters of Christopher Plantin bear frequent witness to the importation of exemplars for the liturgy and chant of distant usages needed for his publishing ventures. Regarding the source of the chant for the *Antiphonarii Iuxta Breviarium Romanum restitutum* of 1572, for example, Plantin reports in a letter of 22 February 1570 to Gilbert d'Oignies, Bishop of Tournai, that Rembert de Malpas, cantor of the church of Sint Rumold in Mechlin and *maître d'hôtel* for Cardinal Granvelle, Archbishop of Mechlin, '. . . avoit aporté de Rome le chant convenable audict Bréviaire, à l'usage duquel il m'escrit qu'il est fort exercité . . .'. See Rooses and Denuce, eds., *Correspondance de Christophe Plantin*, vol. 2, p. 115.

example, a comparison of the selection and order of Matins responsories for the Sundays in Advent, a highly variable component of the divine Office used to ascertain the usage of service books, shows that a manuscript ordinal made in 1417 for the collegiate church of Onze Lieve Vrouw in Antwerp (Antwerp, Katedraal-archief) concurs exactly with the *Breviarij secundum morem ecclesie sancte Marie Antverpiensis* printed by Hamman in 1496.[70] Likewise, the breviary printed at Paris for the usage of Cambrai in 1497 concurs in this test with an early fifteenth-century breviary copied for the cathedral, F-CA, MS A 97.

In addition to printed sources of the texts for the Mass and Office, printed books of chant, though uncommon, can be extremely important when manuscript sources of plainsong are lacking. For example, the *Antiphonale secundum usum Cameracensis ecclesie*, published in the first decade of the sixteenth century by the Parisian printer Simon Vostre, constitutes the only extant antiphoner for the usage of Cambrai that postdates the thirteenth century. The calendar is unequivocally that observed by the cathedral of Cambrai, as witnessed by the placement of the feast for the dedication of the church on 3 July. Moreover, the printed antiphoner duplicates the selection and ordering of chants as preserved in contemporaneous manuscript breviaries from the cathedral, including music for local saints such as Firminus and Fursey, and the plainsong melodies included therein agree to a remarkable extent with those of a thirteenth-century antiphoner from the cathedral, F-CA, MS C 38. Comparison of pre-Tridentine printed service books to their counterparts in manuscripts thus bears witness, at least in these instances, both to the integrity of local liturgical practices and to the adherence of early printed sources to local rites.

Usage of Antwerp

Breviarij secundum morem ecclesie sancte Marie Antverpiensis, 2 vols. (Venice: Johann Hamman for Cornelius van Bombergen, 1496)

Usage of Bruges

B-BRa, fragment – Bruges, Stadsarchief, Oud Archief no. 538. Includes fragmentary antiphoner from the fifteenth(?) century, containing portions of the office for the feast of St Donatian.

Breviarium ad usum insignis ecclesie sancti Donatiani Brugensis dyocesis Tornacensis (Paris: Anthoine Bonnemere for Canons of Sint Donaas, Bruges, 1520)

---

70 See R.-J. Hesbert, *Corpus Antiphonalium Officii*, 6 vols. (Rome, 1963–79), Rerum Ecclesiasticarum Documenta Series Maior, Fontes VII–XII, vols. 5 and 6, for a demonstration of the pertinence of Advent responsories in the determination of local usages; see also Victor Leroquais, *Les bréviares manuscrits des bibliothèques publiques de France*, 5 vols. (Paris, 1934), vol. 1, pp. lxxviii–lxxxi.

Usage of Brussels

Breviarii ad usum insignis ecclesie collegiate dive Gudile oppidi Bruxcellensis Cameracensis diocesis, 2 vols. (Paris: Desiderius Maheu for Jodocus Ascensio, 1516)

   Usage of Cambrai

F-CA MS C 38 – Cambrai, Bibl. Municipale, MS C 38. Antiphoner for the cathedral of Notre Dame from the latter half of the thirteenth century

Antiphonale secundum usum Cameracensis ecclesie (Paris: Simon Vostre, *c.* 1500–10)

Breviarium Cameracense (Paris: Ulrich Gering and Berthold Rembolt, 1497)

Missale secundum usum insignis ecclesie Cameracensis (Paris: Johannes Higman for Johannes de Campis, 1495)

   Usage of Ferrara

GB-Lbm Add. 28025 – London, BL, Add. MS 28025. Notated breviary for the cathedral of St George from 1400

   Usage of Paris

F-Pn lat. 10482 – Paris, BN, lat. MS 10482. Notated breviary for the cathedral of Notre-Dame from the early fourteenth century

   Usage of Rome

Antiphonarium secundum morem sancte Romane ecclesie completum (Venice: Lucantonio Giunta, 1504?)

Missale Romanum (Milan: Antonius Zarotus, 1474); a modern edition of this missal is Robert Lippe, ed., *Missale Romanum. Mediolani. 1474*, 2 vols., Henry Bradshaw Society, vols. 17 and 33 (London, 1899–1907)

   Usage of Tournai

Missale insignis ecclesie Tornacensis (Paris: Johannes Higman for Wilhelmus Houtmart, 1498)

7

THE PERFORMANCE OF CHANT IN THE RENAISSANCE AND ITS INTERACTIONS WITH POLYPHONY

RICHARD SHERR

It seems beyond doubt that singing Gregorian chant was the major task of all the singers and composer-singers of the Renaissance. Chant was also the first sacred music they learned, they sang it every day from their boyhood on, and it was a basic part of their musical lives. Furthermore, it turns out that the composition of chant continued to be cultivated well into the age of polyphony; not only were there many new settings of the Ordinary composed from the fifteenth to the eighteenth centuries, but no less a person than Dufay actually composed the chants for an entire newly instituted Office.[1] Yet, the performance of chant in the fifteenth and sixteenth centuries is not a subject that has inspired much serious scholarly discourse.[2] The arguments about chant melody and rhythm carried on by chant scholars concern mainly its quasi-mythical 'golden period' before about the tenth century; it is generally agreed that anything that occurred after about the eleventh or twelfth centuries, be it in melodic contour or rhythmic performance, is a hopeless corruption.[3] Students of polyphony, for their part, treat chant merely as a

The gist of this article was presented as a paper at the Fifty-Sixth Annual Meeting of the American Musicological Society, Oakland, 1990.

1 On settings of the Ordinary, see, for example, Otto Marxer, *Zur spätmittelalterlichen Choralges-chichte St. Gallens, Der Cod. 546 der St. Galler Stiftsbibliothek* (St Gall, 1908). On Dufay, see Barbara Haggh, 'Music, Liturgy, and Ceremony in Brussels, 1350–1500', PhD dissertation, University of Illinois, 1988; and Haggh, 'The Celebration of the "Recollectio Festorum Beatae Mariae Virginis, 1457–1987"', forthcoming in *Proceedings of the XIV Congress of the International Musicological Society*.

2 An exception is Mary Berry (Sister Thomas Moore), 'The Performance of Plainsong in the Later Middle Ages and Sixteenth Century', PhD dissertation, Cambridge, 1968 [hereafter, dissertation], and her article, 'The Performance of Plainsong in the Later Middle Ages and the Sixteenth Century', *Proceedings of the Royal Musical Association* 92 (1965–6), 121–34 [hereafter, article]. I am grateful to Professor Tom Ward for helping me to consult Berry's dissertation. See also Don Harrán, *In Defense of Music: The Case for Music as Argued by a Singer and Scholar of the Late Fifteenth Century* (Lincoln, 1989).

3 For a recent overview of the problem of rhythm, see Lance W. Brunner, 'The Performance of Plainchant: Some Preliminary Observations of the New Era', *Early Music* 10 (1983), 317–28.

source of pitches for *cantus firmi*.[4] The lack of scholarly concern also means a lack of bibliographical control which is only now beginning to be remedied.[5] This essay, then, cannot claim to be based on a thorough overview of sources, and its conclusions must be considered tentative. It will consider one aspect of chant performance in the fifteenth and sixteenth centuries that can illuminate and be illuminated by polyphony: rhythm. It will argue that there was some variety in chant performance practice, that chant notation was not always viewed as being entirely neutral with regard to rhythm, and that certain chants (particularly Credos I and IV of the *Liber Usualis*) were sung in a definite and widely transmitted rhythmic form (now obliterated in modern chant books), not always made explicit in chant sources, but faithfully reproduced in polyphonic settings. Thus, the actual performing tradition of certain chant melodies has been preserved in and can be extracted from Renaissance polyphony. That tradition thereby can be seen to underlie in a basic way many compositions, including hymns, numerous Credos, and all of Josquin's *Missa Gaudeamus*.

One reason for the lack of interest in the rhythm of chant in the Renaissance is the generally accepted notion that chant was performed then according to the 'equal note' principle, with each pitch basically receiving one beat, a practice presumed to have begun in the eleventh or twelfth century.[6] This theory can exist quite comfortably with Medieval and Renaissance *cantus fractus*, which was not so much the technique of 'singing Gregorian chant mensurally',[7] as it was the practice of *writing* it in true mensural notation or a quasi-mensural notation using minims to indicate short note values; as such, it was usually confined to newly composed chants or settings of metrical poetry.[8] Yet Renaissance theorists suggest that the equal note principle was not universally applied even to regular chant.

Johannes Tinctoris, for instance, seems to throw up his hands in despair when

---

4 And even in this regard, it is only recently that serious studies of local melodic traditions of chant have been attempted. See Edward Kovarik, 'Mid Fifteenth-Century Polyphonic Elaborations of the Plainchant *Ordinarium Missae*', PhD dissertation, Harvard University, 1973; and Jennifer Bloxam, 'A Survey of Late Medieval Service Books from the Low Countries: Implications for Sacred Polyphony, 1460–1520', PhD dissertation, Yale University, 1987.

5 *Renaissance Liturgical Imprints: A Census* is a computerized database that is only now being developed at the University of Michigan under Professors David Crawford and James Borders. I am grateful to Prof. Crawford for letting me share some preliminary material from the database.

6 Jerome of Moravia in his *Tractatus de musica* seems to argue for some sort of mensural performance of chant, but his rules are not easy to understand. See the translation in Carol MacClintock, ed. *Readings in the History of Music in Performance* (Bloomington, 1979), pp. 3–7.

7 See William Daglish, 'The Origin of the Hocket', *JAMS* 31 (1978), 12, note 35.

8 See Bruno Stäblein, *Schriftbild der einstimmigen Musik*, Musikgeschichte in Bildern, vol. 4, Lfg. 4 (Leipzig, 1975), pp. 68–9, and the study by Marxer cited above.

confronting chant notation. He has the following to say about it in his *Tractatus de Notis et Pausis*, chapter XV:

De notis incerti valoris

Notae vero incerti valoris sunt illae quae nullo regulari valore sunt limitatae. Cuiusmodi sunt quibus in plano cantu utimur quarumquidem forma interdum est similis formae longae, brevis et semibrevis, et interdum dissimilis ita quod pedes musicarum [*recte muscarum*] propter earum parvitatem a plerisque nominantur ut hic:

[Examples: Gaudeamus omnes and Salve sancte parens.]

Et huiusmodi notae nunc cum mensura, nunc sine mensura, nunc sub una quantitate perfecta, nunc sub alia imperfecta canuntur secundum ritum ecclesiarum aut voluntatem canentium.

(Albert Seay, ed., *Johannes Tinctoris Opera Theoretica*, CSM 22, (American Institute of Musicology, 1975), vol. 1, pp. 117–18.)

CONCERNING NOTES OF UNCERTAIN VALUE

Notes of uncertain value are those which are not limited to any regular value. Such are those we use in plainchant whose shape is sometimes similar to the long, breve, and semibreve, and sometimes dissimilar, as those which because of their small size are called flies' feet by most people as here:

And these notes are sung now with measure, now without measure, now under perfect quantity, now under imperfect, according to the rite of churches or the will of those singing.[9]

This hardly suggests a universally accepted rhythmic performance practice. Tinctoris may give an idea of the variety he suggests in his *Liber de arte contrapuncti*. Chapter XXI of Book II of that treatise speaks of how counterpoint, known as 'contrapunctus supra librum', can be improvized above chant (*cantus planus*) or mensural melodies (*cantus figuratus*). His examples of counterpoint on chant are revealing considering his other statement about the variability of chant performance. He seems to assume that chant can be rendered in any number of rhythmic

9 Also quoted in Berry, dissertation, pp. 126–7. Although the sources of Tinctoris's text may indeed have 'pedes musicarum' as in Seay's edition, it seems that the correct phrase must be 'pedes muscarum', a term used to describe the shape of single notes in Metz and Gothic neumatic notation (in German, 'Fliegenfuss'), and one which makes perfect sense in the context of this passage. Tinctoris would have been exposed to such notation during his youth in Flanders. See Lorenz Welker, 'Some Aspects of the Notation and Performance of German Song Around 1400', *Early Music* 18 (1990), 235–46, esp. 237; and Stäblein, *Schriftbild der einstimmigen Musik*, p. 68 (other references in the Index).

ways, and gives examples of the kind of counterpoint that might be sung over such rhythmicized versions (providing two-voice examples). He says that counterpoint can be effected when 'at the will of the singers' the chant is:

1 Organized so that each pitch equals a semibreve of major or minor prolation.
2 Organized so that each note equals a breve of tempus imperfectum.
3 Organized so that the notes are arranged in a repeating rhythmic cell: breve of three semibreves, breve of two semibreves, semibreve.
4 Organized in a rhythmic cell: breve of three semibreves, breve of two semibreves, semibreves, breve of two semibreves, breve of three semibreves.
5 Sung rhythmically by reading chant notation as if it were mensural notation.

Three of his tenors, furthermore, come from actual chant: *Victimae paschali laudes* (for no. 1), the *Alleluia Dulcis lignum* (for no. 2), and the beginning of the *Alleluia Concaluit* (for no. 5 – the ligatures in fact being read in mensural notation).[10]

Can he really have intended this to illustrate true examples of chant performance, or is he using the rhythmicization of chant merely as a device to help the improvizing contrapunctist (who of course had to be able to predict when the chant notes would change)? It is not exactly clear, but we would think that if chant were always performed according to the 'equal note' practice, there would have been no thought of mentioning the mensural choices, the strangest of which certainly is the reading of Gregorian notation as if it were mensural.[11]

In fact, later theorists who advocated equal note performance of virgae, puncta, and ligatures imply that mensural interpretations might influence singers. For instance, they admit that the notes that looked like semibreves (called *mediocres*) in the climacus or virga subtripunctis neumes often were sung twice as fast as the 'breves' (puncta) and 'longs' (virgae), although they clearly do not like the practice. Gaffurius, in his *Practica Musicae* (Milan, 1496), after having stated that the medial notes of a ligature should be sung in equal rhythmic values, goes on to describe *mediocres*, giving the notation in Example 7.1, and then continues:

Example 7.1   *Mediocres* in Gaffurius, *Practica Musicae* (Milan, 1496), sig. a iiii

Caeteris autem aequales sunt in pronunciatione & temporis mensura, licet nonnulli eas duplo strictius caeteris commensurent, quod non ratione sed cantoris arbitrio duximus concedendum.

---

10 Albert Seay, ed. *Johannis Tinctoris Opera Theoretica* CSM 22, (American Institute of Musicology, 1975), vol. 2, pp. 110–20. See also Berry, dissertation, p. 127.
11 Tinctoris also admits that the chant can be sung without any mensuration; he can give no examples of contrapunctus for this, naturally, and simply says that singers have to have a very good ear if they are going to predict when the notes will change.

These however are equal in pronunciation and rhythmic value, although some sing them twice as fast as the others, which we believe to be done not according to reason, but according to the whim of the singer.

Biagio Rossetti uses almost the same words to describe the performance of *mediocres* in his *Libellus de Rudimentis Musices* (Verona, 1529).[12] He, however, does suggest that in his day many people were in fact singing all notes of chant (including *mediocres*) in equal values:

sed multis in locis, et maxime hic in Italia, sunt multi qui omnes notulas cantant aequales ad modum brevium quando cantant festive, vel ad modum semibrevium quando strictius cantant, et tam ligaturas quam longas et mediocres, id est semibreves, omnes in eadem mensura. Et hoc faciunt quia omnes cantum non intelligunt figuratum, et non habent cognitionem de quantitate valoris notarum.[13]

But in many places, and especially here in Italy, there are many who sing all notes equally as if they were breves [i.e. slowly] when they sing solemnly and as if they were semibreves [i.e. more quickly] when they sing quickly, ligatures as well as longs and *mediocres*, that is semibreves, everything in equal measure. And they do this because not all understand [the notation of] polyphony and do not have knowledge of the quantitative value of the notes.

Rossetti seems to be arguing for the equal note theory, yet his argument curiously is based on the ignorance of the rules of mensural notation by most singers of chant, and this implies that those who did know mensural notation might have performed the chant different. In fact, singers with polyphonic training could not have helped noticing that the ligatures and basic note forms of chant were the same as those of mensural notation, and this might have had an effect on their methods of performance. A modern example of the problem might be to imagine performing a piece written in quarter notes, half notes, and eighth notes after having been instructed to treat them as if they were equal. It can be done quite easily, of course, yet there might be times when the very shape of the notes might cause subtle changes in rhythm, and the singer might even slip up on occasion and read the notes as written. I shall return to this question later.

Lanfranco and Zarlino when talking about text setting in chant also admit that the *mediocres*, called by them 'mezzane', were occasionally sung twice as fast as the other notes, and were sometime exceptions to the rule that only separate square notes can carry syllables in chant (both mention the Credo as a chant in which this was done).[14]

12 Caeteris autem, scilicet, notulis, aequalis sunt istae mediocres in pronunciatione et temporis mensura, licet nonnulli eas, scilicet, mediocres notas, duplo strictius caeteris commensurent, quod non fit ratione sed cantoris arbitrio. (Albert Seay ed., *Biagio Rossetti: Libellus de Rudimentis Musices (Verona, 1529)*, Colorado College Music Press, Critical Texts 12 (Colorado Springs, 1981), p. 17.)

13 See Don Harrán, *Word-Tone Relations in Musical Thought* (Neuhausen-Stuttgart, 1986), pp. 120–1.

14 On Lanfranco's definition of 'mezzana', see Harrán, pp. 145–6. It seems incorrect to translate 'mezzane' and 'middle notes', as many (including Harrán) do. For one thing, 'mezzana' is a

Ma nel Fermo solamente sopra le quadre si pone la sillaba eccetto alcuna volta: dove l'usanza porta di mandare le mezzane in Dupla proportione, come ne i Credo ed altri canti si vede. (Lanfranco, *Scintille di musica* (Brescia, 1533), p. 68; quoted in Don Harrán, *Word-Tone Relations in Musical Thought* (Neuhausen-Stuttgart, 1986), p. 416.)

But in chant, syllables are placed only on square notes, except occasionally where by custom the *mezzane* are sung in duple proportion [and have separate syllables], as can be seen in Credos and other chants.

. . . il che si osserva etiando nel Canto fermo, essendo che in ogni figura quadrata si accommoda la sua sillaba: eccettuando alcune volte le mezzane, che si mandano come le Minime; et anche come le Semiminime come si comprende in molte cantilene, et massimament nel Credo in unum deum il quale chiamano Cardinalesco. (Zarlino, *Le istitutione harmoniche* (Venice, 1558), vol. 4, p. 33; quoted in Harrán, p. 416.)

As may be observed in chant, being that every square note should have its own syllable, excepting occasionally [when] the *mezzane* [do], which are sung like minims, and also like semiminims, as can be seen in many chants, especially in the Credo in unum deum which they call 'Cardinalesco'.

Lanfranco and Zarlino tell us specifically that Credos were chants in which the equal note doctrine did not always operate (Pietro Cerone agrees; see Harrán, p. 416), and there is ample evidence of newly composed Credos; written in *cantus fractus* from the fifteenth to the eighteenth century.[15] Zarlino mentions the Credo 'Cardinalesco' or Cardinalis (Credo IV of the *Liber Usualis*, often called 'Credo Maior' in fifteenth- and sixteenth-century sources), a melody that was newly composed around the beginning of the fifteenth century. Gaffurius, too, singles out that Credo but describes what appears to be an unwritten performance practice tradition in which the rhythmic values of mensural music are imposed on 'neutral' chant notation in a setting of that Credo and in certain hymns and sequences, a practice he associates particularly with French singers (again, Rossetti uses almost exactly the same words):[16]

legitimate Italian word meaning 'flooring tiles', and was probably used because of its reference to the diamond shape of the notes, not to their position within ligatures.

15 See Tadeusz Miazga, *Die Melodien des einstimmigen Credo der Römisch-Katholischen Lateinischen Kirche* (Graz, 1976). In 1977, a dissertation by Bernhard Isenring, 'Das einstimmige Credo in den Choralhandschriften des 11. bis 16. Jahrhunderts', was listed as in progress at the University of Zurich, but I have been unable to determine if it has been completed.

16 Prosdocimus de Beldermandis seems to refer to something similar in one of the copies of his *Tractatus practice cantus mensurabilis ad modum ytalicorum*, although it is not clear whether he is describing an actual performance practice or whether he is trying to explain the creation of mensural values by claiming that they grew out of ways of reading chant notation. See Daglish, p. 12. Rossetti says: 'Sunt enim aliqui qui notas aeque describunt et commensurant figuris cantus mensurabilis, ut longas, breves ac semibreves ut constat in symbolo Cardineo vel Patriarchino, et in prosis et hymnis, quod Galli potissime ornatiorem modulorum pronunciationem pro ipsa diversitate concinnenda celeberrime prosequuntur.'

Sunt & qui notulas huiusmodi plani cantus aeque describunt & commensurant figuris mensurabilis consyderationis ut longas breves ac semibreves ut constat in Symbolo cardineo & nonnullis prosis atque hymnis quod Galli postissime ad ornatiorem modulorum pronunciationem ipsa diversitate concipiendam celeberrime prosequntur.   (sig. a iiii)

There are also those who write these notes of the plain chant all alike, and at the same time, count them in mensurable dimensions as longs, breves, and semibreves. This is evident in the *Symbolum cardineum* and in several sequences and hymns. Quite frequently this technique is followed by Gallic musicians especially for the purpose of expressing a more ornate articulation of their music by this very diversity.[17]

Let us consider the question of the Credo. Gaffurius seems to say that Credo IV is *written* in equal note values (suggesting something like the notation of that Credo in the *Liber Usualis*) yet *performed* as if the notes had mensural values. This implies that the actual melody had no definite rhythmic shape. Yet, the vast majority of the sources of this chant present it as a *cantus fractus*; in the Giunta Gradual of 1500, the notation includes longs, semibreves (including c.o.p. ligatures), and minims (there are no breves), and is even given a time signature of cut-C (it is the only chant with a time signature).[18] And, as the semibreves in this version not only move twice as fast as the 'square notes', but also carry syllables, they explain Lanfranco's and Zarlino's references to *mezzane (mediocres)* in Credos. Example 7.2 transcribes Credo IV as it appears in the Giunta Gradual of 1500.

The melody of Credo IV, as has been noticed, is remarkable for its clear first-mode profile. The major clauses of the text are generally divided into the smallest acceptable sub-clauses and these sub-clauses are set to similar melodic phrases delineating the pentachord or tetrachord of the first mode octave. The first phrases concentrate mostly on the d–a pentachord, clearly stated at the beginning of many of them, so that the sudden appearance at 'Et incarnatus est' of the top of the modal octave effectively draws the listener's attention to this important part of the text. The reiteration of the upper d' at the start of succeeding phrases ('Et resurrexit', 'Et iterum venturus est') also sets off melodically those sections of the text dealing with the events after Christ's birth from the beginning clauses which are annunciatory in nature.

The rhythm seems to have been generated by the natural speaking rhythms of the text; but because it is unambiguous, it makes clear the variations in treatment of syllables that might be obscured by a more 'equal-note, oratorical' performance. The beginnings and ends of each of the sub-phrases are emphasized by fast ornaments and by long notes; curious 'misaccentuations' also occasionally appear

---

17 Irwin Young, trans., *The Practica Musicae of Franchinus Gaffurius* (Madison, 1969), p. 20.
18 *Graduale secundum morem sancte Romane ecclesie* . . ., edited by Francesco de Brugis (Venice: Giunta 1499–1500). Credo IV is on fols. CCCLr–CCCLIIr.

Figure 7.1   Beginning of Credo IV from the *Graduale Romanum* (Venice: Giunta 1515):
London, British Library, MS c 35.1.2, fol. CCCLXVI^r

Example 7.2   Credo IV in the version of the Giunta Gradual (*Graduale Romanum* (Venice: Giunta, 1499–1500), fols. CCCL–CCCLII)

(as in 'vi-si-bi-li-ùm om-ni-ùm', 'Je-sùm'). The use of longer and shorter rhythmic values, which forces texts like 'incarnatus est' and 'iterum venturus est' into a kind of patter, tends to organize all the sub-phrases into six and eight-beat patterns (assuming the breve/virga to be the basic beat), so that a certain regularity of rhythmic phrase emerges and seems to have been intended. All this would have the effect, it seems to me (especially if sung at the fast tempo implied by the diminished time signature) of making it much more likely that the congregation would concentrate on the meaning of the text. An incisive rhythmic performance might have made their ears "perk up' in a way that an equal-note performance may not have.[19]

It has long been known that this Credo existed in this guise.[20] The chant was sometimes the basis of simple polyphonic elaborations found in some Italian sources dating from the beginning of the century; in these cases, the melody is transmitted in a mensural version that is almost identical to Example 7.2.[21] In fact, the melody and rhythm shown in Example 7.2 was so well known in Italy that it was possible in one source to copy a counterpoint to it without giving the chant at all.[22] But lest it be assumed that the mensural version is tied solely to the polyphonic setting, it should be stressed that it is also present, if we can believe Miazga, in 102 chant sources from Italy, Holland, Germany, and Eastern Europe, ranging in date from the early fifteenth to the eighteenth centuries.[23] Nothing shows more strikingly that Credo IV was a recognized mensural chant in the fifteenth century than the way it appears in BL, Additional MS 24687, a fifteenth-century Gradual from the diocese of Utrecht.[24] The manuscript is copied throughout in the expected Hufnagelschrift, yet when Credo IV appears on fol. 100r, Hufnagelschrift is abandoned and the Credo is copied in true mensural notation (it replaces the slightly anomalous longs of the Giunta Gradual with breves), in a rhythmic and melodic version that differs only slightly from Example 7.2. All this suggests strongly that Credo IV was not a

---

19 Anyone who has ever asked students what they 'feel' when listening to standard oratorical performance of chant, knows that the word 'calming' (a euphemism for 'soporific'?) comes up frequently.

20 Berry, dissertation and article; Bruno Stäblein, 'Credo' in MGG, vol. 2, cols. 1769–73.

21 An exception is a simply polyphonic version, Copenhagen, Det Arnamagnaeanske Institut, MS AM 80, 8-o, where Credo IV is presented mostly in virgae. As this manuscript is of Icelandic origin, it may with some justice be considered peripheral. See Angul Hammerich, 'Studien über isländische Musik', *Sammelbände der Internationalen Musik-Gesellschaft* 1 (1899–1900): 341–71.

22 See Giulio Cattin, Oscar Mischiati, and Agostino Ziino, 'Composizioni polifoniche del primo quattrocento nei libri corali di Guardiagrele', *Rivista Italiana di Musicologia* 7 (1972), 153–81, esp. note 15.

23 Miazga, *Die Melodien des einstimmigen Credo*, pp. 74–7; his earliest sources are from the beginning of the fifteenth century.

24 According to the notes in the front of the manuscript made in October 1903 by H.M. Bannister, the Sanctorale contains items peculiar to Utrecht usage.

chant on which rhythm was imposed, but that it was conceived in and transmitted with a definite rhythm. The Ur-melody and rhythm cannot be reconstructed without a filiation of all the sources, and it is to be expected that variants would crop up (especially regarding the ornamental ends of phrases), yet the basic archetype appears to be the one in Example 7.2. Credo IV is, in fact, one of the first of the hundreds of new Credo settings that were produced from the fifteenth to the eighteenth centuries, a phenomenon that has been noted, but little studied.[25] By the end of the sixteenth century, however, its rhythm and notation in Italy might have been changed under the influence of the reforms that led to the *Editio Medicea*. A Giunta Gradual in the British Library printed after the Council of Trent, possibly in the seventeenth century,[26] presents the melody without the ornamental semi-minims seen in earlier versions, and Zarlino, in his reference to this Credo, implies that it was not written with semiminims. It seems clear, though, that the *Liber Usualis*, in presenting this chant in 'equal notes' without many of its ornamental flourishes, deprives Credo IV of its original rhythm and melodic style.[27]

Credo IV may have always been mensural; hymns and sequences, also mentioned by Gaffurius, are better examples of chant that could have been written without mensural rhythm yet sung with it, for it seems that there were some hymns and sequences that were performed in rhythms inspired by their metrical texts, even though those rhythms do not always appear in chant sources. We can infer that this is true, because polyphonic sources of alternatim settings of hymns and sequences occasionally preserve the chant verses in mensural notation. There are not many examples, however; one of the clearest is the hymn *Conditor alme siderum*. Example 7.3 gives the notation of the hymn as it appears in a thirteenth-century chant source

Example 7.3 *Conditor alme siderum* in the version of the facsimile in Richard Hoppin, *Medieval Music* (New York, 1978), p. 111

Conditor alme siderum eterna lux credentium Christe redemptor omnium exaudi preces supplicum

25 See Miazga. It is not clear why, after approximately 500 years, there was this need to have new musical settings to replace the standard 'Credo I'.

26 It bears the call number L.18.f.6. The date is a problem, however; the title page has the date '1561', yet it also mentions the Council of Trent and Pope Clement VIII. The British Library catalogue says that the date 'has been altered from 1611'. Although I could see no evidence of that, it is clear that the print must date after 1561.

27 See Kovarik, p. 90. In other words, the process was exactly the opposite from the one assumed by Gastoué when he came upon some manuscripts with the original version of Credo IV which he took to be a corruption. See A. Gastoué, 'Comment on chantait le Credo en certaines églises au XVe siècle', *Revue du chant grégorien* 36 (1932), 48–9.

Example 7.4   *Conditor alme siderum* in the version of Bologna, Civico Museo Bibliografico Musicale, MS Q 15, fol. 314v

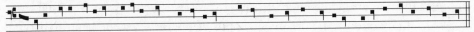

Conditor alme siderum eterna lux credencium Christe redemptor omnium exaudi preces supplicum

from Laon.[28] Example 7.4 shows the notation that is given for the alternatim section of Dufay's setting of the hymn in Bologna, Civico Museo Bibliografico Musicale, MS Q15 [hereafter, BolQ 15], fol. 314v. The mensural notation and triple rhythm of the chant in the polyphonic source are unmistakable.[29] If we believe Gaffurius, a singer reading from a source like Example 7.3 would have automatically sung it in the rhythm of BolQ 15.[30]

But not all hymn texts fit easily into a simple metrical pattern. For others, various solutions may have been available, including equal note performance. Most of the chant verses in the alternatim hymn section of VatS 15, for instance, do not have any trace of mensural notation. There are three exceptions, however. One is *Conditor alme siderum*, whose chant notation is identical to that in BolQ 15. Another is provided by the settings of *Ut queant laxis* on fols. 37v–39r of VatS 15. Two scribes copy the verses of this hymn, one (the main scribe of the manuscript) began on fol. 37v with chant and polyphonic settings, but the second scribe takes over on fol. 38v and copies verses of the hymn by De Orto along with the alternatim chant.[31] But whereas the chant in the hand of scribe A is written in undifferentiated longs, the chant of scribe B assumes a mensural guise, giving the rhythm shown in Example 7.5.

Example 7.5   *Ut queant laxis* in the version of Vatican City, Biblioteca Apostolica Vaticana, fondo Cappella Sistina, MS 15, fol. 38v

Gloria patri geniteque proli et tibi compar utriusque semper spiritus alme deus unus omni tempore secli

28 See Richard Hoppin, *Medieval Music* (New York, 1978), p. 111.

29 The same notation appears in the chant preserved in Vatican City, Biblioteca Apostolica Vaticana, Fondo Cappella Sistina 15 [hereafter, VatS 15], fol. 2r. Berry, dissertation, pp. 107–13, also mentions mensural chant sources for *Conditor alme siderum* and other hymns, but not *Ut queant laxis* and *Vexilla regis prodeunt*. [Compare also the examples cited by John Caldwell, above, Ed.]

30 Stäblein also mentions *cantus fractus* sources of hymns, but implies that they are mostly in Spanish sources. See *Schriftbild*, p. 69. See also the Berry article, 'The Performance of Plainsong', p. 125.

31 On scribes in VatS 15, see Richard Sherr, 'The Papal Chapel ca. 1492–1513 and its Polyphonic Sources', PhD dissertation, Princeton University, 1975, and Sherr, *Papal Music Manuscripts in the Late Fifteenth and Early Sixteenth Centuries*, forthcoming as Renaissance Manuscript Studies 5, published by the American Institute of Musicology, Hänssler-Verlag.

Then it appears as if the chant of Scribe A was edited to reflect this rhythm (certain of the stems of the Longs appear to have been emphasized by overlining), and this same rhythm is shown in the chant preceding Dufay's setting of the hymn preserved in Trent, Museo Provinciale d'Arte, Castello del Buon Consiglio, MS 92, [hereafter, TrentC], fol. 239v. This rhythm represents the 'Italian sapphic stanza' that we know better from the settings of certain odes of Horace by Pesenti and others.[32]

In the third example in VatS 15, radical alterations of the chant notation for the hymn *Vexilla regis prodeunt* on fols. 20v–23r (including the creation of a c.o.p. ligature) produces the rhythm shown in Example 7.6. Thus, the unwritten practice described by Gaffurius becomes a written one in these cases. It may not be a coincidence, of course, that the majority of the singers in the papal chapel at the time VatS 15 was copied were 'French'.

Example 7.6   *Vexilla regis prodeunt* in the version of VatS 15, fol. 20v

Vexilla regis prodeunt fulget crucis mi-ste-rium quo carne carnis conditor suspensus est pa-ti-bulo

What was the reaction of composers of polyphony when they set these chants? Normally, they respected the rhythmic forms of their secular *cantus firmi*; we might expect them to refer in some way to well-known rhythms of chants. Alternatim settings of hymns and other chants (sequences, Credos) were generally fairly simple compositions in which the original melody is made clear; we might expect fidelity to a rhythmic version to be strongest in such compositions. Indeed, as Ward's catalogue of hymns shows, practically every polyphonic setting of *Conditor alme siderum* begins by referring to the rhythm in BolQ 15 and VatS 15.[33] Example 7.7 shows how the rhythm imposed on *Vexilla regis prodeunt* in VatS 15 underlies every verse of Willaert's setting published in 1542.

The same is true for *Ut queant laxis*. Example 7.8 shows settings of the last phrases of the hymn as they appear in polyphonic compositions written over a period of about 100 years. The rhythm of the Italian sapphic stanza can be inferred in all of them. Even though the freedom with which the rhythms are treated suggests that they did not have the same authority as, say, the rhythm of the *L'Homme armé* tune, there seems little doubt that these hymns were, in certain places

32 See Francesco Luisi, *Del cantar a libro . . . o sulla viola: La Musica Vocale nel Rinascimento* (Torino, 1977), pp. 325–50.
33 Tom R. Ward, *The Polyphonic Office Hymn 1400–1520: A Descriptive Catalogue*, Renaissance Manuscript Studies 3 (Neuhausen-Stuttgart, 1980), pp. 118–23.

Example 7.7   The melody of *Vexilla regis prodeunt* as in the version of VatS 15, fol. 20v (staff 1), and as used by Adrian Willaert (staves 2–8; *Opera Omnia*, ed. H. Zenk, W. Gerstenbert, *et al.* CMM 3, vol. 3, p. 24). Chant phrases are separated by dotted lines. Quotations from the Willaert setting are taken from whichever voice part has the chant melody. The chant phrases may not follow one another immediately in the polyphony, and they may appear in different transpositions in different voice parts. Except for the chant excerpt, the level of transcription is semibreve = half note

Example 7.8   The melody of the last phrases of *Ut queant laxis* as in VatS 15, and as in settings of the hymn by De Orto, Dufay, Carpentras, Willaert, and Jacquet. Chant phrases are separated by the dotted lines. Quotations from the polyphonic settings are taken from whichever voice part has the chant melody. The chant phrases may not follow one another immediately in the polyphony, and they may appear in different transpositions in different voice parts. Except for the chant excerpt, the level of transcription is semibreve = half note

1 VatS 15, fol. 38v

2 Marbrianus de Orto (Ronald L. Miller, 'The Musical Works of Marbriano de Orto', PhD dissertation, Indiana University, 1974, vol. 2, p. 388)

3 Guillaume Dufay (*Opera Omnia*, ed. Heinrich Besseler, CMM 1, vol. 5, p. 61)

4 Elzéar Genet (Carpentras) (*Collected Works*, ed. Albert Seay, CMM 58, vol. 3, p. 147)

5 Adrian Willaert (*Opera Omnia*, eds. H. Zenk, W. Gerstenberg, et al., CMM 3, vol. 7, p. 94)

6 Jacquet of Mantua (*Collected Works*, eds. Philip Jackson and George Nugent, CMM 54, vol. 2, p. 57)

Example 7.9   Credo IV in the version of Trent, Museo Provinciale d'Arte, Castello del Buon Consiglio, MS 87, fol. 235v

in the fifteenth and sixteenth centuries at least, often sung in these rhythmic versions.

Settings of Credo IV tend to be more elaborate; very few exhibit the fidelity to the model of Example 7.1 that we find in the simple alternatim setting in TrentC 87, fols. 235v–238r (see Example 7.9). Yet a sampling of other polyphonic settings of the chant show that they too can be traced to a common rhythmic and melodic model that must have been close to Example 7.2 (see Example 7.10).

The preceding may not be entirely new or entirely surprising to those who have some knowledge of chant usage in the Renaissance. Nonetheless, it may be worth stressing that the practice of singing *mediocres* in duple proportion must have been widespread in the fifteenth and sixteenth centuries (or else the theorists would not have constantly complained about it), that there were independent rhythmic versions of certain chants that were the basis of polyphonic settings, and that composers of polyphony tended to be faithful in varying degrees to the rhythms of chant. Such things are easily demonstrated when the weight of the chant sources also comes down in favour of rhythmic interpretations, as in the case of Credo IV. I now want to suggest that similar things happened to the much older and formerly universal melody for the Credo, the so-called 'authentic Credo' (Credo I of the *Liber Usualis*, usually called 'Dominicalis' in the fifteenth and sixteenth centuries). This chant has a long history, with sources stretching back to the tenth century;

Example 7.10   Part of Credo IV as in the Giunta Gradual, and as in the settings by Weerbecke, Vaqueras, de Orto, la Rue, and Brumel. Chant phrases are separated by dotted lines. Quotations from the polyphonic settings are taken from whichever voice part has the chant melody. The chant phrases may not follow one another immediately in the polyphony, and they may appear in different transpositions in different voice parts. Except for the chant excerpt, the level of transcription is semibreve = half note

1 *Graduale Romanum* (Venice: Giunta, 1500)

2 Gaspar van Weerbecke, 'Credo Cardinalis' (*Fragmenta Missarum* (RISM 1505¹))

3 Bertrandus Vaqueras (*Opera Omnia*, ed. Richard Sherr, CMM 78, p. 133)

4 Marbrianus de Orto, Credo from the *Missa Dominicalis* (with Credo I in the Superius; Ronald L. Miller, 'The Musical Works of Marbriano de Orto', PhD dissertation, Indiana University, 1974, vol. 2, p. 252)

5 Pierre de la Rue, Credo from the *Missa de Beata Virgine* (*Monumenta Musicae Belgicae*, eds. René Bernard Lenaerts and Jozef Robijns, vol. 8, p. 8)

6 Antoine Brumel, Credo from the *Missa Dominicalis* (*Opera Omnia*, ed. Barton Hudson, CMM 5, vol. 2, p. 32)

Miazga lists 182 variant melodies in over 500 manuscripts, the earliest of which he dates *c.* 950–75.[34] All these melodies relate to an archetype, possibly of Greek origin, which sets the Credo text to arrangements of a few simple recitation formulae, the most striking including the half step motion e-f-e (a-b-flat-a) which either begins phrases or begins their second sections.[35] Credo I, unlike Credo IV, has been the object of much study by chant scholars, studies which have concentrated on the melody and its origins.[36] By consulting Miazga's incipits, however, it can be seen that a number of sources (very few in comparison to the total number) present Credo I as some kind of *cantus fractus.*[37]

Most of the *cantus fractus* sources are quite late, but a few seem to date from before the sixteenth century. That these early sources are roughly contemporary with the creation of the mensural Credo IV is surely not coincidental. We might want to argue that probably the venerable Credo I was given a rhythm in response to the increasing acceptance of Credos in mensural notation. An example of the rhythm of an early Italian *cantus fractus* setting of Credo I may be represented by Example 7.11, taken from the Kyriale appended to the fourteenth-century Missal/Gradual Vatican City, Biblioteca Apostolica Vaticana, Fondo Barbarini Latini, MS 657, [hereafter, BarbL], fols. 423v–425r; it bears a striking resemblance to the rhythms created for Credo IV (see, 'visibilium omnium' for instance).[38] While it certainly is not 'equal-note', it does come tantalizingly close in many spots to the 'oratorical' rhythm of the monks of Solesmes, yet (as in Credo IV) the very fact of the notation would encourage a more measured and un-oratorical performance of the chant.[39] In this case, however, it might indeed be argued that the version represents a purely local tradition since it is not supported by many contemporary chant sources, and also because there were other different *cantus fractus* versions in circulation; indeed, the

---

34 See Miazga, pp. 18–41.

35 See Willi Apel, *Gregorian Chant* (Bloomington, 1966), pp. 412–15.

36 See Miazga, *Die Melodien des einstimmigen Credo*; Dom André Mocquereau, 'Le chant "authentique" du Credo selon l'édition Vaticane', in *Paléographie musicale* 10 (Tournai, 1909–12), 90–176; Michel Huglo, 'Origine de la mélodie du Credo "authentique" de la Vaticane', *Revue grégorienne* 30 (1951), 68–78.

37 See in particular his numbers I.11, I.15, I.24, I.76, I.77, I.92, I.93, I.94, I.131, I.132, I.134, Berry, dissertation, pp. 115–18 also mentions examples of Credo I in *cantus fractus.*

38 This may be the earliest source. The Missal/Gradual has been dated *c.* 1368, but the appended *Kyriale* may be later (it is in a different hand, and is separated from the body of the manuscript by a blank folio). It contains another Credo, also in *cantus fractus.* See Billy Jim Layton, 'Italian Music for the Ordinary of the Mass', PhD dissertation, Harvard University, 1960, p. 353. The Utrecht Gradual in the British Libary also transmits Credo I as a *cantus fractus* combining Hufnagel neums and puncta with minims.

39 A Solesmes performance is in fact closer to Example 7.11 than the strict equal note performance of the Tallis Scholars, which presumably is supposed to represent the way the chant was performed in the sixteenth century. See *Sarum Chant: Missa in gallicantu*, Gimell CDGIM 017 (1988).

Example 7.11   Credo I in the version of Vatican City, Biblioteca Apostolica Vaticana, MS
Barbarini Latini 657, fols. 423v–425r

Example 7.11 (*cont.*)

lum se - det ad dex-te-ram pa - tris   et   i-te-rum ven-tu-rus est

cum glo-ri-a   iu-di-ca-re vi - vos et mor-tu - os   cu-ius re -

gni non e-rit fi - nis   et in spi-ri-tum san-ctum do-mi-num   et

vi-vi-fi-can - tem   qui ex pa-tre fi-li-o-que pro-ce - dit

qui cum pa-tre et fi-li-o si-mul ad-o-ra-tur et   con-glo-ri-fi-ca -

- tur qui lo-cu-tus est per pro-phe - tas   et   u-nam san-ctam ca-tho-li -

cam   et   a - po-sto-li-cam ec-cle-si - am   con -

fi-te-or u-num ba-pti - sma   in re-mis-si-o-nem pec-ca-to -

rum   et ex-pe-cto re-sur-re-cti-o-nem mor-tu - o - rum

et   vi-tam ven-tu-ri   se - cu-li A - men

Giunta Gradual, after having presented Credo IV and another Credo (de Apostolis) in *cantus fractus*, gives the chant for Credo I in undifferentiated virgae.

That the rhythm of Example 7.11 was in fact widely used for Credo I is demonstrated, however, by the polyphonic settings of the chant that begin to appear in the fifteenth century and continue well into the sixteenth. There are many more polyphonic settings based on Credo I than on Credo IV; not only are there those grouped by Petrucci in his *Fragmenta Missarum* under the rubric 'Credo de Village' (an appellation which has yet to be explained),[40] but Credo I is occasionally the basis of Credos within polyphonic Masses, particularly *Missae de Beata Virgine*. Often, the melody is used in its entirety, and is sometimes combined with other *cantus firmi*, as in the Credo of Compère's *Missa L'Homme armé* or Josquin's *Credo De tous biens pleine*; Josquin, in fact, had a habit of quoting from Credo I in his Masses, and he seems to have produced more single settings of the chant than any other composer. Space does not permit complete transcriptions of the versions of the melody I have found in polyphonic sources. Example 7.12 gives a few phrases of the text in thirty-five settings in *cantus fractus* and polyphony, ranging in time from the late fourteenth century to the late sixteenth and in provenance from England to Italy, in approximate chronological order. While it obviously does not include all *cantus fractus* and polyphonic settings, it does provide a large enough sample from which to draw some tentative conclusions.

One thing that emerges is that polyphonic composers never treat Credo I as an 'equal-note' chant *cantus firmus* (i.e. presented in undifferentiated long notes or in varying rhythmic structures). Instead, it is generally given a specific rhythmic form that can be discerned through different levels of note values and melodic and rhythmic elaborations, that is the same in simple and complex polyphony, and that is kept even when the Credo I chant is paired with another *cantus firmus*. Fidelity to this rhythm is strongest in the fifteenth century all throughout Europe. In the early fifteenth century, it can be found in Italy (BarbL 657, no. 1), at the papal court (Zacharia, no. 2), and in England (the Morgan Library MS and Old Hall, nos. 3 and 4), in the middle–late part of the century we find it in the Netherlands (BL, Add. MS 24687, Clibano, nos. 5 and 6), at the French court (Ockeghem, Compère, Févin, Mouton, nos. 11, 14, 24, 25), in Flanders (Regis, Busnois, Obrecht nos. 9, 10, 15), in Rome (Vaqueras, de Orto, possibly Josquin, nos. 12, 13, 16–18), in the monastery of St Gall (SGallS 546, no. 26), and in Vienna (Edlerawer, no. 8). Although there are exceptions, of course, where the chant is omitted or greatly distorted. It would be difficult to argue that the near identity of the basic rhythm of these settings from different times and places (particularly strong in 'et in unum

40 Charles van den Borren, 'L'Enigme des "Credo de Village"', in *Hans Albrecht Memoriam*, edited by Wilfried Brennecke and Hans Hasse (Kassel, 1962), pp. 48–54.

Example 7.12 Phrases from Credo I as used in many settings. Chant phrases are taken from whichever voice part has the chant melody. Quotations from the polyphonic settings are separated by dotted lines. The chant phrases may not follow one another immediately in the polyphony, and they may appear in different transpositions in different voice parts. Except for chant excerpts, the level of transcription is semibreve = half note. Blank spaces indicate that notes have been omitted in the transcription (either because they are ornamental or because the chant is not present)

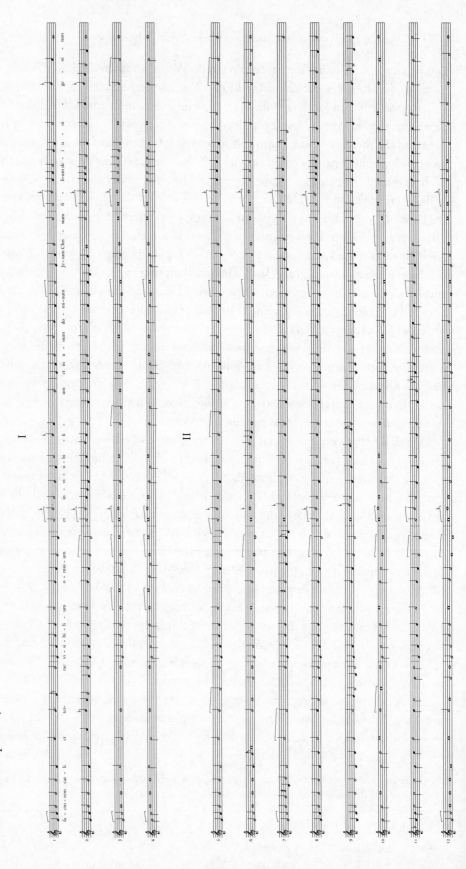

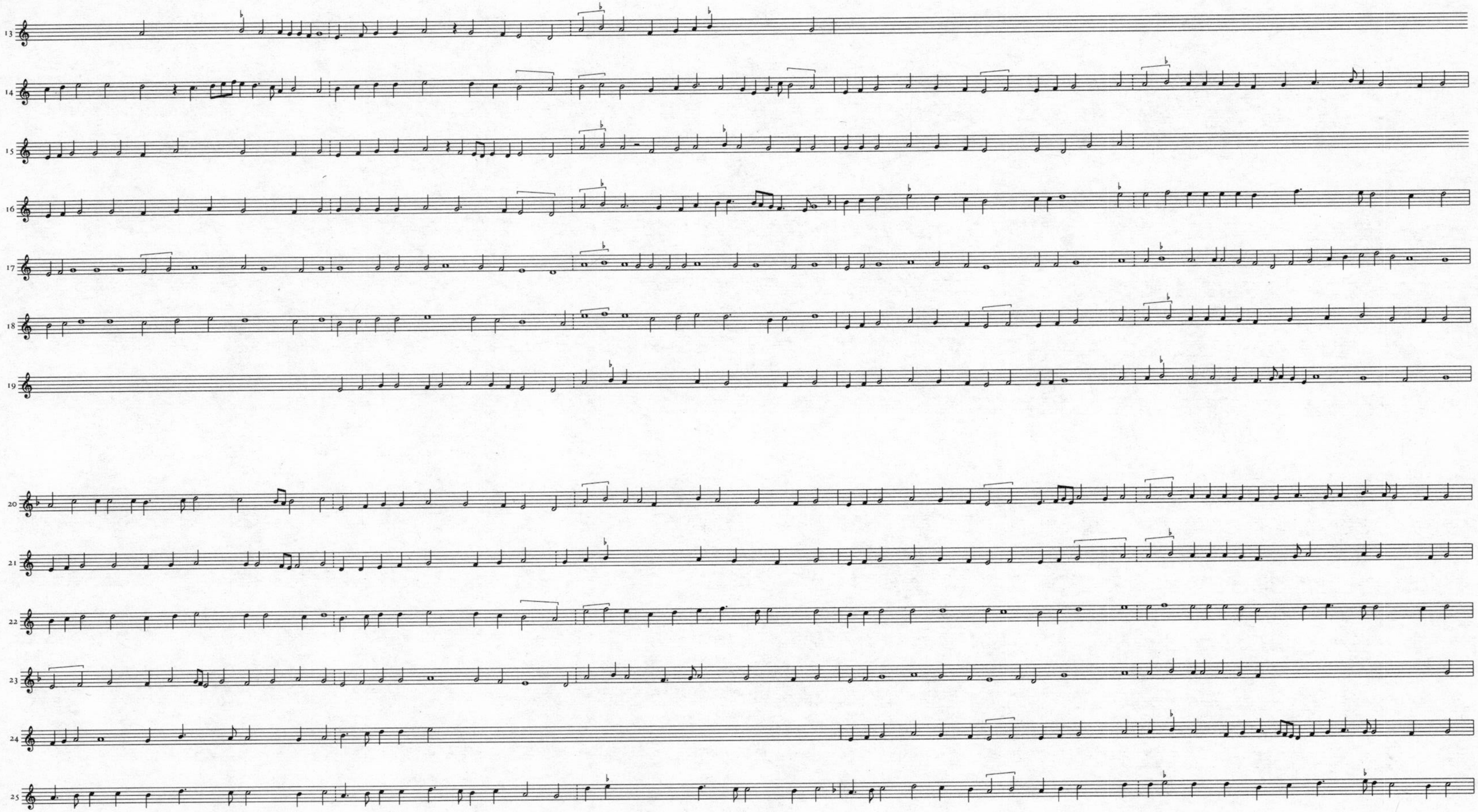

13
14
15
16
17
18
19
20
21
22
23
24
25

Example 7.12 (*cont.*)

III

IV

V

KEY TO EXAMPLE 7.12

Group I Late fourteenth to early fifteenth century

1 Vatican City, Biblioteca Apostolica Vaticana, MS Barberini Latini 657, fols. 423v–425r

2 Zacharia da Teramo, 'Patrem de Village' (*Polyphonic Music of the Fourteenth Century* (Editions de l'Oiseau-Lyre), vol. 13, ed. Kurt von Fischer and F. Alberto Gallo, p. 129)

3 Anonymous, from New York, Pierpont Morgan Library, MS M.978, p. 6 (from the reign of Edward III (1327–77); see Frank Harrison and Roger Wibberly, *Manuscripts of Fourteenth Century English Church Music* 26 (London, 1981), p. 206)

4 Anonymous in the Old Hall Manuscript (ed. Andrew Hughes and Margaret Bent, CMM 46, vol. 1/1, p. 152)

Group II Fifteenth century

5 London, British Library, Additional MS 24687, fols. 101r–102v

6 Nicasius de Clibano (in VatS 51, fols. 178v–180r)

7 Anonymous (in VatS 51, fols. 2v–5r)

8 Hermannus Edlerawer, 'Dominicale' (Munich, Bayerische Staatsbibliothek, Handschriften-Inkunabelabteilung, MS Latinus monacensis 14274 (*olim* Mus. 3234; Cim. 352c – 'St Emmeram Codex'), fols. 103v–105r)

9 Johannes Regis, 'Patrem de Village' (*Opera Omnia*, ed. C. W. H. Lindenberg, CMM 9, vol. 1, p. 62)

10 Antoine Busnois, 'Patrem de Village' (*Fragmenta Missarum* (RISM 1505¹))

11 Johannes Ockeghem, Credo sine nomine (*Collected Works*, ed. Dragan Plamenac, vol. 2, p. 59)

12 Bertrandus Vaqueras (*Opera Omnia*, ed. Richard Sherr, CMM 78, p. 112)

13 Marbrianus de Orto, Credo from *Missa Ad fugam* (Ronald L. Miller, 'The Musical Works of Marbriano de Orto', PhD dissertation, Indiana University, 1974, vol. 2, p. 308)

14 Loyset Compère, Credo from *Missa L'homme armé* (*Opera Omnia*, ed. Ludwig Finscher, CMM 15, vol. 1, p. 8)

15 Jacob Obrecht, Credo from *Missa Fors seulement* (*New Obrecht Edition*, Chris Maas, general editor, vol. 4, p. 31)

16 Josquin des Prez, in 'Patrem De tous biens plaine', from *Fragmenta Missarum* (*Werken van Josquin des Prés*, ed. Albert Smijers, Masses, vol. 4, p. 94)

17 Josquin, in 'Patrem de Village' 1, from *Fragmenta Missarum*, no. 19 (*Werken van Josquin des Prés*, Masses, vol. 4, p. 102)

18 Josquin, in 'Patrem de Village' 3, from CamBM 18, fols. 221v–224r (*Werken van Josquin des Prés*, Masses, vol. 4, p. 132)

19 Pierre de la Rue, Credo from *Missa de Feria* (*P. de la Rue Liber Missarum*, ed. A. Tirabassi, p. 205)

20 Alexander Agricola, Credo from *Missa Sine Nomine* (*Opera Omnia*, ed. Edward R. Lerner, CMM 22, vol. 2, p. 82)

21 Antoine Brumel, 'Patrem de Village' (*Opera Omnia*, ed. Barton Hudson, CMM 5, vol. 4, p. 106)

22 Brumel, Credo from *Missa de Beata Virgine* (*Opera Omnia*, vol. 4, p. 13)

23 Agricola, 'Patrem de Village' (*Opera Omnia*, vol. 2, p. 114)

24 Antoine de Févin, Credo from *Missa de Feria* (Edward H. Clinkscale, 'The Complete Works of Antoine de Févin', PhD dissertation, New York University, 1965, vol. 2, p. 89)

25 Jean Mouton, Credo from *Missa Alma redemptoris mater* (*Opera Omnia*, ed. Andrew Minor, CMM 43, vol. 1, p. 50)

Group III Early to mid-sixteenth century

26 St Gall, Stiftsbibliothek, MS 546 (O. Marxer, *Zur spätmittelalterlichen Choralgeschichte St. Gallens*, p. 147)

27 *Graduale Romanum* (Venice: Liechtenstein, 1551). p. 162

28 Claudin de Sermisy, Credo (*Opera Omnia*, ed. Gaston Allaire, CMM 52, vol. 6, p. 213)

29 Jacob Arcadelt, Credo from *Missa de Beata Virgine* (*Opera Omnia*, ed. Albert Seay, CMM 31, vol. 1, p. 65)

30 Pierre de Manchicourt, Credo from *Missa de Beata Virgine* (*Collected Works*, ed. John D. Wicks and Lavern Wagner, CMM 55, vol. 4, p. 160), combines Credo I (with its rhythm) with Credo IV (implying its rhythm)

Group IV Mid- to late sixteenth century

31 Cristóbal de Morales, Credo from *Missa de Beata Virgine* (*Opera Omnia*, ed. Higino Anglès, vol. 1, p. 11)

32 Giovanni Pierluigi da Palestrina, Credo from *Missa de Beata Virgine a 4* (*Werke*, ed. F. Espagne, F. X. Haberl, *et al.*, vol. 12, p. 145)

33 Palestrina, Credo from *Missa de Beata Virgine a 6* (*Werke*, vol. 11, p. 6)

34 Tomás Luis de Victoria, Credo from *Missa de Beata Virgine* (*Opera Omnia*, ed. Felipe Pedrell, vol. 2, p. 101)

Group V Late sixteenth to early seventeenth century

35 *Graduale Romanum* (Venice: Giunta, [1611]), p. 169–170.

dominum . . . unigenitum') is mere coincidence, or stems from one authoritative polyphonic work. Much more likely is that the polyphony reflects (as did settings of Credo IV and certain hymns) a widely accepted performance tradition in the fifteenth century, at least in the major European centres, of the chant of Credo I, one that is probably very close to the version of Example 7.11, as opposed to other *cantus fractus* versions. The general paucity of chant sources preserving this tradition suggests further that it was an unwritten practice which finds its confirmation only through the evidence of the preserved polyphony. Whether this performance tradition is in its origins related to polyphony is difficult to tell; in fact, the *cantus fractus* sources begin to appear precisely at the same time as the earlier polyphonic settings. We might view those sources as isolated attempts to fix an 'oratorical' performance practice in notation, the majority of chant sources treating Credo I as an 'official' chant by not presenting it as a *cantus fractus*. The polyphony proves that the composers actually did hear and remember the Credo I as a mensural chant.[41] It seems to have been sung that way for over 100 years, and I think we can say that the performance practice of Credo I in the age of Ockeghem and Josquin has now been 'recovered'.

Yet the consensus seems to break down in the sixteenth century. I have not included the Credo of Josquin's *Missa de Beata Virgine* and *Missa sine nomine* (both of which are based on Credo I) in Example 7.12 because both rhythmic and melodic structure suggest a different performing model, and late sixteenth-century Roman composers seem to be deliberately employing a new accentual pattern. This can be seen also in the Liechtenstein print of 1551 and in the Giunta Gradual of [1611], where the change of stress in 'dominum' probably reflects the humanistic reforming spirit that was to engulf all of chant by the seventeenth century. Only a study more inclusive than the present one will provide a surer picture of the situation.

The preceding discussion has used polyphony to demonstrate that the equal note doctrine did not apply to the performance of all chant in the Renaissance. But it is clear that the chants I have mentioned belonged to a very restricted group of melodies that entered the liturgy at a late stage. Nothing has been said about the main corpus of chant, which was never written as *cantus fractus*, and for which there is no evidence to suggest that, with the exception of *mediocres*, the equal note doctrine did not apply to its performance. Yet we have those puzzling statements by Tinctoris and Rossetti implying that chant notation could be read as if it were mensural notation. Can that have been a real performance practice applied to the

---

41 It seems unlikely to me that composers would rush to chant books to get the *cantus firmus* of Credo I, a melody they sang very frequently. In fact, some of the discrepancies in Example 7.12 might be due to the accidents of memory (such as the De Orto setting 'factorem caeli et terrae' to the melody of 'Patrem omnipotentem').

basic Gregorian repertory? On the face of it, that seems absurd; performing Gregorian ligatures as if they were mensural ligatures, for instance, will mean that almost all of them will end in a long, and this will produce a very strange rendition of chant. Nonetheless, I would like to suggest that it might have happened, or at the very least that there may have been a middle ground that might explain Tinctoris's and Rossetti's remarks. I would like to suggest that the ligatures might have been read mensurally or perhaps that the appearance of virgae either at the ends of ligatures or as isolated notes in the midst of puncta caused the same reaction among singers who knew mensural notation as an isolated half note in the midst of quarter notes might to us; they instinctively treated it as a longer note even if that meant overriding the equal-note doctrine. This highly speculative conclusion comes, as does everything else in this article from the observation that composers of polyphony respected the rhythms of chant when they used it as a *cantus firmus*.

For instance, the seemingly deliberate placement of virgae/longs in what looks to be non-mensural chant notation of the hymn *Ave maris stella* in VatS 15, as shown in Example 7.13, just might have suggested to the singers of an 'equal-note' performance the rhythm shown in Example 7.14, placing special emphasis on 'A-vè', àl-ma', and balancing by stress the first syllable of 'vìr-go' with the long melisma on the last syllable (something that singers might do naturally anyway).

Example 7.13   *Ave maris stella* in the version of VatS 15, fol. 42v

Ave maris stella dei mater al‑ma atque semper virgo   felix caeli porta

Example 7.14   Hypothetical transcription of Example 13

This, in turn, has certain affinities with the actual rhythm used in the simple setting of the hymn in Vatican City, Biblioteca Apostolica Vaticana, Archivio di San Pietro, MS B80 [hereafter, VatSP B80], fol. 183r in Example 7.15 (especially at 'virgo'), even though that setting stems from a different melodic tradition. That the hymn in VatSP B80 may also represent a particular rhythmic tradition can be seen by comparing its underlying rhythm with one that underlies the hymn as Josquin used it in the Kyrie of his *Missa Ave maris stella* (see Example 7.16).

But, as we have seen, hymns were occasionally open to mensural interpretations. A different case is drawn from the main Gregorian repertory. The Introit *Gaudeamus omnes* was well known in the Renaissance; it was set many times in

Example 7.15   *Ave maris stella* as used in Vatican City, Biblioteca Apostolica Vaticana, Archivio di San Pietro, MS B80, fol. 183r

Example 7.16   Rhythmic reduction of the melody in VatSP B80 compared phrase by phrase with a rhythmic reduction of the chant as used in the Tenor (transposed down a fourth) of the Kyrie or Josquin's *Missa Ave maris stella*

simple polyphony, and was used as the *cantus firmus* of Josquin's *Missa Gaudeamus*.[42] Example 7.17 gives the beginning of the chant in the Gregorian notation of two sources, one the *Liber Usualis*, the other the early fifteenth-century manuscript Bologna, Biblioteca Universitaria, MS 2216 [hereafter BolU 2216]. They both agree (as do many other, but not all, sources) in writing the first ligature with a virga at the end.[43]

42 See Frohmut Dangel-Hofmann, *Der mehrstimmigen Introitus in Quellen des 15. Jahrhunderts* (Tutzing, 1975).

43 See the examples in Solange Corbin, *Die Neumen*, Paleographie der Musik, Band I, Faszikel 3 (Cologne, 1977), p. 211, and Dangel-Hofmann, *Der mehrstimmigen Introitus*, pp. 190–4.

Example 7.17   *Gaudeamus omnes* as in the *Liber Usualis* and Bologna, Biblioteca Universitaria, MS 2216, fol. 1r

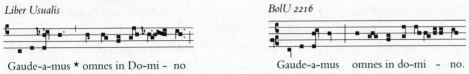

Liber Usualis   BolU 2216

Gaude-a-mus * omnes in Do-mi - no   Gaude-a-mus   omnes in do-mi - no.

Example 7.18 gives a transcription of both versions of the chant as it might have been considered by a composer who wanted to use it as a textless *cantus firmus* (therefore eliding notes that are repeated merely to enunciate the text), and who treated virgae as if they were longs, considering all other notes to be equal.

Example 7.18   Hypothetical transcription of *Gaudeamus omnes*

Example 7.19 gives a transcription of the chant reading the ligatures of BolU 2216 as if they were mensural (assuming tempus imperfectum – basically, this only lengthens slightly the already elided notes of Example 7.18).

Example 7.19   Hypothetical mensural transcription of BolU 2216

Example 7.20 gives the opening of the chant as it is actually used in the Kyrie of Josquin's *Missa Gaudeamus*.

Example 7.20   *Gaudeamus omnes* as used in the Tenor (transposed down a fifth) of the first Kyrie of the *Missa Gaudeamus* by Josquin

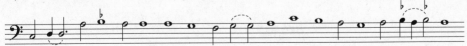

Is the remarkable similarity of the indisputable rhythm used by Josquin to the hypothetical rhythms in Examples 7.18 and 7.19 the result of mere coincidence? Or

has Josquin reacted to the melody of the Introit the way he reacted to the melody of Credo I and possibly *Ave maris stella* by reproducing in his polyphony the rhythm in which the chant was actually sung by him and his contemporaries? If he has, then his entire Mass becomes a monument to an unrecorded chant performance practice of the late fifteenth century, for not only is it one of the few polyphonic settings to utilize the intonation of the Introit, it quotes that intonation (using the procedures illustrated in Examples 7.18 and 7.19) so frequently that it becomes the true basis of the composition.

The influence of contemporary chant performance practices on the composers of the fifteenth and sixteenth centuries is surely a phenomenon worth noting. These practices seem not to have been as uniform as we have generally believed, and at least some chants, instead of being neutral repositories of pitches, were endowed with rhythmic life that made an indelible impression on singers and composers. We may therefore be grateful for those occasions where composers have preserved their performance traditions (traditions that may have been largely unwritten and that were in fact to disappear in later centuries) in their works of polyphony.

8

PATRONAGE, MUSIC, AND LITURGY IN RENAISSANCE MANTUA

IAIN FENLON

The most Christian princes . . . desiring to augment the divine service, founded chapels after the manner of David, in which at extraordinary expense they appointed singers to sing . . . praise to our God with diverse (but not adverse) voices . . . And since, if their masters are endowed with the liberality which makes men illustrious, the singers of princes are rewarded with honour, glory, and wealth, many are kindled with a most fervent zeal for this study.[1]

These remarks from Johannes Tinctoris's *Proportionale*, written about 1476 when the author was in the service of King Ferrante I of Aragon, offer a perceptive observation about one of the most important of all developments in the history of music in early Renaissance Italy, the formation of princely chapels. At Ferrara a sizeable *cappella* of singers had been established by Duke Ercole I d'Este as early as 1472; its further development during the next few years was perhaps stimulated by the example of Rome, where Sixtus IV had begun the construction of what was to become the Sistine Chapel and had established a new *cappella* of singers for St Peter's by 1473. Similar developments took place in the same period at the Sforza court in Milan, and at Naples where Tinctoris was working when the *Proportionale* was written.

It was presumably these developments that Tinctoris had in mind. Latent in his comments is also the idea that through such foundations rulers had to hand a new way of both competing for status with one another and with asserting their own *virtus* by projecting an image of themselves as model Christian princes, and in this they were supported and encouraged by contemporary political thought.[2] For

---

1 Cited and discussed in L. Lockwood, 'Strategies of Music Patronage in the Fifteenth Century: The *Cappella* of Ercole I d'Este', in *Music in Medieval and Early Modern Europe: Patronage, Sources and Texts*, ed. I. Fenlon (Cambridge, 1981), pp. 227–48.

2 For the rise of princely chapels in the late fifteenth and early sixteenth centuries, and the competition between them to secure the best musicians and composers, see Lockwood, 'Strategies of music patronage', and the relevant chapters of the same author's *Music in Renaissance Ferrara 1400–1505* (Oxford, 1984), both of which deal largely with Ferrara. A broader study which in

example, the humanist statesman and poet Giovanni Pontano (1422–1503), who also spent time in the service of the Aragonese Kings of Naples, devoted two treatises to the qualities of liberality and magnificence, and his *De splendore*, which specifies how princes should demonstrate their status and virtue according to well-defined rules, insists that a reputation for creating 'noble buildings, splendid churches and theatres' is a necessary demonstration of princely fame. From the last decades of the fifteenth century it increasingly became a part of what Italian princes considered to be a 'splendid church' that the liturgy should be ornamented with polyphony performed by a specially constituted body of singers. This theoretical emphasis, exemplified by Pontano's words, is not merely an endorsement of the values and concepts articulated by the earlier humanists, who had been concerned to analyse the *virtus* of the citizen body as a whole, but an adaptation of the traditional mirror-for-princes style to suit the changing situation in the Italian courts at the end of the fifteenth century. What would have been regarded earlier in the fifteenth century as inelegant and ostentatious personal behaviour, was now incorporated within a theory of courtly decorum.

The growth of choirs and of repertories in the court chapels in Ferrara and Milan, or in the pseudo-princely cathedral in Florence, are important questions which have received a good deal of scholarly attention. Liturgy, on the other hand, has largely been overlooked. As Robert Gaston has recently observed, liturgical history has remained one of the most isolated of disciplines; while liturgiologists have spent much of their efforts on defining the minute details of the Roman and other major European and Eastern liturgies, rarely have they investigated the wider historical significance of liturgy, or how it was understood and practiced in specific places in Renaissance Italy. Yet the question of liturgy is fundamental to understanding how the patronage of music and ceremony in religious institutions actually worked. Far from being a monolithic, rigidly formalized structure, capable only of being received 'passively', the liturgy could and often was appropriated or modified by those in power, whether autocrats like the Medici in Florence or the republican government of Venice. Festal calendars could be revised, civic and dynastic celebrations could be incorporated, and even liturgical reform itself, a central

addition to the Este court also considers those of the Sforza at Milan and the Gonzaga at Mantua is that of W.F. Prizer, 'North Italian Courts, 1460–1540', in *Man and Music. The Renaissance: From the 1470s to the End of the 16th Century*, ed. I. Fenlon (London, 1989), pp. 133–55. Information about the Aragonese Court Chapel can be found in A.W. Atlas, 'Aragonese Naples', in Fenlon, ed., *Man and Music*, pp. 156–73 and, treated at greater length, in the same author's *Music at the Aragonese Court of Naples* (Cambridge, 1985). For Florence in the same period, see F.D'Accone, 'The Musical Chapels at the Florentine Cathedral and Baptistry during the first half of the Sixteenth Century', *JAMS* 24 (1971), 1–50; for the Papal Chapel, see now C. Reynolds, 'Rome: A City of Rich Contrast', in Fenlon, ed., *Man and Music*, pp. 61–101.

concern for the Italian church during the sixteenth century, could be executed at a local level in a way which neatly conflated the terrestrial and celestial concerns of rulers, emphasizing their authority but at the same time consolidating their position as defenders of Christianity.[3]

In this context, the question of the retention of local liturgies in Italy in the period after the Council of Trent which, in the rather general way characteristic of its decrees, had attempted to move towards greater standardization and simplification of chant repertories, assumes a special interest. The three different and prominent cases of Milan, Venice, and Mantua immediately come to mind. In the first, where Carlo Borromeo adopted a strong interventionist approach towards reform at a local level, the Ambrosian rite was maintained in the face of the general trend towards greater uniformity of chant dialects.[4] The example of Venice is quite distinct. Since the early Middle Ages, the Republic had gradually evolved a distinctive civic liturgy, an annual succession of feast-days and ceremonies conducted by the patrician rulers for the entertainment of the population. These calendrical rites, an uniquely mixed cycle containing the major Christian feasts together with commemorations of important events in Venetian history, also functioned as a powerful instrument of social and communal stability. In its basic outline the Venetian calendar followed the conventions of Roman Christianity, but onto this framework was grafted a local liturgy, the *patriarchino*. An important feature of the rite was the importance given to the role of the doge, broadly analogous to that of the pope in the Roman liturgy; it was only on this authority that changes could be made. Until the fifteenth century the *patriarchino* was observed throughout Venice, but in 1456 it was abolished everywhere except in the Basilica of San Marco. These new conditions strengthened the social and political functions of the rite; as the exclusive property of the doge and signoria it became, in effect, a liturgy of state. It is not surprising that many of the most important feast-days in the Venetian year corresponded to the Roman calendar, though saints with a local significance, and above all St Mark, were given particularly elaborate treatment. But an unusually prominent feature of the *patriarchino* was its emphasis on significant events in Venetian history, many of them commemorations of important military victories. In this way the specifically Venetian was associated with the universally Christian; Patriotism and Faith were powerfully combined. As a liturgy under dogal control, the *patriarchino* was particularly susceptible to

---

3 R. Gaston, 'Liturgy and Patronage in San Lorenzo, Florence, 1350–1650', in F.W. Kent and P. Simons with J.C. Eade, eds., *Patronage, Art, and Society in Renaissance Italy* (Oxford, 1987), pp. 111–33.
4 The very particular case in the post-Trent period has been exhaustively dealt with in L. Lockwood, *The Counter-Reformation and the Masses of Vincenzo Ruffo* (Venice, 1970).

political influence, and most changes in its operations and emphases were a direct reflection of the changing fortunes of the Venetian state. Jealously protected by the Venetians, ever-suspicious of the motives and tactics of the papacy, the *patriarchino* continued to be used in the post-Trent period undisturbed by the general trend towards the abolition of local rites.[5]

The instance of the ducal basilica of Santa Barbara at Mantua is different again. Here, the foundation in the 1560s of a new church on a grand scale involved the 'invention' of a new liturgy based on a new calendar specific to the institution and on the codification of a repertory of chants based on Roman sources but revised in accordance with reformist principles. It is this case that will be considered quite closely, partly because rich archival documentation provides a detailed insight into the operations of the rite as it developed, and partly because the Santa Barbara chants themselves had a profound impact upon the style of polyphony that was specially commissioned for the basilica. And, since the basilica was clearly designed with the performance of polyphony in mind, a good deal of evidence is available about the arrangements for music in the building. Most of the composers involved were employed there, and their music, preserved for the most part in manuscripts from the Santa Barbara library, constitutes a distinct corpus which in the main travelled only to other Gonzaga strongholds and was not disseminated in print. As a body of sacred *musica reservata* it has a recognizable character of its own, distinguished by its use of Santa Barbara plainsongs as *canti firmi* and by its formal organization according to *alternatim* principles. Before considering the Santa Barbara liturgy and the polyphony that was composed for it, it may be useful to briefly review the history of the Gonzaga chapel from its foundation in the early years of the sixteenth century. The pattern that emerges is characteristic of the development of courtly chapels, in their cultivation of both chant and polyphony, in the early Renaissance.

MANTUAN TRADITIONS

Until the ducal basilica of Santa Barbara was built in the 1560s, the cathedral of San Pietro served not only as the major church of the diocese but also as the home of the major court chapel.[6] By comparison with other North Italian princely regimes such as those of the Sforza and the Este, the Gonzaga came late to the idea of a family

5 For Venice see E. Muir, *Civic Ritual in Renaissance Venice* (Princeton, 1981), particularly part III, and I. Fenlon, 'Venice, Theatre of the World', in Fenlon, ed., *Man and Music*, pp. 102–32.

6 The history of the Gonzaga chapel in the cathedral of San Pietro under the direction of Jacquet of Mantua is treated in I. Fenlon, *Music and Patronage in Sixteenth-Century Mantua*, 2 vols. (Cambridge, 1980, 1982), vol. 1, pp. 45–78 and the literature cited there; see also P.M. Tagmann, *Archivalische Studien zur Musikpflege am Dom von Mantua (1500–1627)* (Bern, 1967).

chapel with a permanent music establishment. The notion had first been mooted at the end of the fifteenth century, but it was not until 1510 that Marchese Francesco II Gonzaga, the husband of Isabella d'Este, finally established such a *cappella* in the cathedral. Neither Francesco nor Isabella were particularly noted for their piety, and the foundation of the new choir was probably prompted by the unexpected availability of experienced singers caused by Alfonso I d'Este's temporary disbanding of the court chapel at Ferrara. It was now arranged that Francesco's choir be attached to the chapel of Santa Maria dei Voti, which had been constructed in the cathedral by the Gonzaga between 1480 and 1482, and where there was already a tradition of chanted offices. A new organ was constructed to replace an earlier instrument of 1491, and direction of the choir was entrusted to Marchetto Cara. As far as repertory is concerned, the fortunate survival among the music books from the Santa Barbara library of a sequence of volumes published by Petrucci at Venice during the years 1502–9 provides some idea of what was performed. Mass music, mostly by the major Northern European composers of the period (Josquin, Isaac, Brumel, Obrecht) predominates in the collection, although there is also a copy of Petrucci's fourth motet book of 1505. Although no liturgical books from the chapel of Santa Maria dei Voti are known to have survived, it must be assumed that here, as elsewhere in Italy, the liturgy was chanted for the most part, and that polyphonic embellishment was occasional, probably being reserved for major feasts. And although the matter cannot be settled with any degree of certainty, since no surviving liturgical books either printed or manuscript can definitely be associated with it, it seems likely that the chants used in the Gonzaga chapel were taken from the Roman rite. It is certainly suggestive that chant books from the principal city churches of Sant' Andrea and San Pietro contain traditional Roman chants for, among other parts of the liturgy, the *Missa in Festis Beatae Mariae Virginis*.

In its essentials, the Gonzaga chapel in San Pietro followed a standard pattern. Its very location, in the principal church of the city and the seat of the bishop of the diocese, emphasized the identification of the family with both the church and the state. It was through such symbols that the seemingly natural authority of the Gonzaga as rulers was emphasized and reinforced. At the same time, the purpose of the chapel was also private and familial. As A.H. Lloyd has remarked of medieval English patrons of colleges: 'In most cases the main motive underlying the private munificence . . . was the priority enjoyed by [the founders] in the daily prayers and celebrations of such institutions.'[7] Whatever the interest of such family chapels for historians interested in their architecture or in the works of art that adorned them, it should not be forgotten that for the founding patrons their primary purpose was

---

7 A.H. Lloyd, *The Early History of Christ's College* (Cambridge, 1934), p. 30.

liturgical; in these settings, embellished with dynastic tombs and monuments, past members of the family were commemorated through liturgical acts, principally recitations of the Mass. Nor should we forget that, despite the understandable amount of attention which musicologists have given to the composition and dissemination of polyphony in the period, a phenomenon encouraged by the stronger impact made by music-printing from the middle decades of the century onwards, nearly all of the music performed in private chapels took the form of chanted services.

Although the traditions established in the chapel of Santa Maria dei Voti by Marchese Francesco continued after his death in 1519, the principal focus of musical performance in a liturgical context shifted in the 1520s to the cathedral proper. This was largely due to the influence of Ercole Gonzaga (1505–63), one of the three sons of Francesco and Isabella d'Este, who was appointed as Bishop of Mantua at the tender age of fifteen with the reluctant consent of Leo X.[8] After a period at the university in Bologna, Ercole returned to Mantua in 1525, and the next year was raised to the cardinalate by Clement VII. From this new position of power, Ercole quickly established himself as a skilful diplomatist in church business, a reputation which was to bring him close to the triple crown on two occasions. Nevertheless, while he was heavily committed in Rome and elsewhere, he was also involved with matters of both church and state in Mantua. From 1540 the government of Mantua was administered by a regency which included Ercole, and ten years later when the new duke, his elder brother Federico, died less than a year after taking control in his own right, it was again Ercole who took over the reigns of government. He remained in this position until his death, while also serving as president of the third session of the Council of Trent, beginning in 1563.

The conventional image of Ercole Gonzaga presents him as more of a prince than a prelate, more concerned with weighty affairs in Rome or with diplomatic missions than with the running of duchy or diocese. But this is to miscalculate the character of his position as regent and to underestimate his commitment to ecclesiastical reform. Together with other like-minded cardinals, Gonzaga became attached to the idea of reform through intervention at a local level; the institution of pastoral visits during the 1530s and his close supervision of the running of the Mantuan diocese both show a characteristic concern with reform. The aims of the reformers were pursued with increasing vigour after 1540, but as a result of Ercole's vision the available weaponry was not confined to the purely spiritual. His own position as a patron of the arts at personal, church, and state levels makes his patronage of considerable interest as an example of emerging ideas about the function of the arts in the service of the Catholic Reformation. Not surprisingly,

---

8 The following discussion of Ercole Gonzaga is based on the documentary material assembled in Fenlon, *Music and Patronage*, vol. 1, pp. 53–78, and on the secondary literature cited there.

the focal point of Ercole's artistic patronage was the local cathedral, and the most significant result of his interest the reconstruction of the building.

According to Giorgio Vasari, one of the Cardinal's main reasons for retraining Giulio Romano in Gonzaga service was so that he could be employed working on the project to reconstruct the cathedral, and it is tempting to view some details of the remodelling of San Pietro (begun in 1545) as the product of reformist thinking applied to ecclesiastical architecture and decoration. Although the Council of Trent's deliberately vague view of the reform of sacred art was not finally published until 1564, those decrees were the product of much thinking and writing about the subject that had taken place since the end of the fifteenth century. In its emphasis on a large interior space which would not impede observation of the liturgy, and in the arrangement of the high altar, Guilio's severely classical designs do seem to reflect reformist thinking; certainly they are in stark contrast to the ornate and often bizarre effects which he had produced earlier for the Gonzaga, notably in the highly hedonistic scheme at the Palazzo Te just outside the city. In spirit, the San Pietro project reproduces the interior of an early Christian basilica; more specifically it may well have been modelled on Old St Peter's in Rome, which Giulio himself had imaginatively reconstructed in the fresco of the *Donation of Constantine* in the *Sala di Costantino* in the Stanze in the Vatican. It is interesting that Vasari's account emphasizes that Ercole took a strong interest in the renovation, required since the old building was 'so badly constructed that very few people can hear, let alone see, when the divine offices are celebrated'. These emphases on accessibility and participation are firmly in line with reformist thinking.

The musical arrangements at San Pietro also attracted Ercole's attention. Between 1528 and 1565 the total number of choir clergy almost doubled, rising from eighteen to thirty-two men, and from documents it is clear that Ercole sometimes took a personal interest in the recruitment of new singers. The major figure to arrive was Jacques Colebault (Jacquet of Mantua), who is recorded in the city for the first time in 1527, and who remained there until his death in 1559.[9] The employment of a composer of Jacquet's abilities and international reputation marks a new departure in the history of Gonzaga patronage of music for liturgical performance, and the fact that the composer was paid directly by the cardinal rather than by the chapter emphasizes Ercole's personal involvement. The overwhelmingly liturgical character of Jacquet's compositions while in Ercole's service is suggestive of the cardinal's musical priorities; with the exception of a handful of secular pieces, his Mantuan output consists entirely of sacred music (particularly

9 The best treatment of the music of Jacquet of Mantua remains G. Nugent, *The Jacquet Motets and their Authors* (PhD dissertation, Princeton University, 1973); see also P.T. Jackson, *The Masses of Jacquet of Mantua* (PhD dissertation, University of North Carolina, 1968). A complete edition of Jacquet's music is in progress in the series *Corpus Mensurabilis Musicae*.

Masses, hymns, and motets), the majority of which was presumably written for performance at San Pietro. On this assumption it is possible to draw up a calendar on the basis of feasts for which Jacquet evidently wrote specific motets, and no doubt at Mantua, as elsewhere, these pieces could also be sung on other occasions. This might explain the absence of motets for major feasts such as the Annunciation, the Nativity of the Virgin, and All Saints, and the notable presence of feasts with a strong local resonance.

Jacquet's contemporary reputation owed a great deal to the growth of music printing during his lifetime, though his works were also widely disseminated in manuscript. The Venetian printer Scotto was Jacquet's main publisher, and the first to issue books devoted exclusively to his work – the two motet collections of 1539, both dedicated to Ercole Gonzaga. Between then and 1567 Scotto produced nine further volumes of Jacquet's music, copies of most of which survive in the Santa Barbara library. This substantial corpus indicates regular use of polyphony for the Ordinary of the Mass and for Vespers, at least for major feasts. For Holy Week Jacquet composed not only settings of the Ordinary, but also the Lamentations of Jeremiah and a Passion. Although the precise duties of the cathedral choir are undocumented, the liturgical texts which Jacquet set suggest that its role was similar in scope to that of similar institutions elsewhere in Italy whose functions are recorded in more detail.

The composition of liturgical music was clearly Jacquet's main preoccupation during his long Mantuan career, a time when he was effectively employed as Cardinal Ercole's personal *maestro di cappella*. The expansion of the musical resources at the cathedral during this same period also reflects the cardinal's conception of the function of polyphony in the service of the church, a church with whose moves towards liturgical reform Ercole was actively involved. And despite the attention which Jacquet's compositions for the cathedral, the first major body of Mantuan court sacred music, has inevitably received, it should be remembered that the daily staple of liturgical music still remained plainsong; here the cathedral followed Roman usage with modifications in the festal calendar to accommodate days with special local significance. In terms of musical practice, the picture at mid-century is, then, a fairly conventional one.

DUKE GUGLIELMO GONZAGA AND THE BASILICA OF SANTA BARBARA

Both literally and spiritually, Ercole's successor as ruler of the Mantuan duchy was Guglielmo Gonzaga.[10] Reared in the strongly reformist atmosphere of his uncle's

10 A detailed overview of the origins and early development of basilica of Santa Barbara during the period of Duke Guglielmo Gonzaga is given in Fenlon, *Music and Patronage*, vol. 1, pp. 79–117. For

court, he was a genuinely pious man for whom the construction, decoration, and liturgical operations of the Palatine Basilica of Santa Barbara was a constant preoccupation. A number of previous Gonzaga chapels were still in existence when he assumed power, though probably not all of them were in use; they included two small chapels in the Castello di San Giorgio (the fortified medieval heart of the Gonzaga palace), Marchese Francesco's chapel of Santa Maria dei Voti in the cathedral, and the small church of Santa Croce in Piazza in a more recent part of the palace complex. But by the early 1560s the demands of court ceremonial had outgrown these facilities, and Duke Guglielmo's pious temperament, nurtured in the strongly reformist atmosphere of mid-century Mantua, found natural expression in a scheme to construct a new chapel. The model here, as in many other things, may well have been Ercole, whose own project to remodel the cathedral of San Pietro, begun in the mid-1540s, had still not reached completion.

The first moves for a new court chapel were afoot by 1561, but this new building proved inadequate and, shortly after it had been completed, Guglielmo ordered the overseer of the ducal fabric, Giovanni Battista Bertani, to draw up plans for a larger structure to replace it. Papal approval was granted in 1562 through the Bull *Sincerae devotionis affectus* (see Figure 8.1). This new church (or more correctly Palatine Basilica) was dedicated, as its predecessor had been, to Santa Barbara and was constructed during the next ten years. The complex history of the building programme need not detain us, except where it has a bearing upon the theme of liturgy and patronage. It is certainly of some interest that the Mantuan church historian Ippolito Donesmondi, writing in the early seventeenth century, writes that the inadequate space for musicians in the first building was the principal motivation for the new project. Moreover, the Basilica itself was altered in the course of construction by demolishing the east wall and adding a semicircular apse and a passage connecting the sanctuary to the Sala di Manto in the ducal palace. These changes were principally designed to enlarge the ritual space and to emphasize its special character, and it is in keeping with this that the high altar was finally placed in the middle of the sanctuary where it still remains. An engraving by Frans Geffels to illustrate the official account of the obsequies for Duke Carlo II Gonzaga in 1666 shows the altar in this position with the officiating clergy ranged around the apse, an arrangement which allowed the celebrant to face the congregation, a rarely granted papal privilege (see Figure 8.2).

the chapel personnel, see also P.M. Tagmann, 'La cappella dei maestri cantori della basilica palatina di Santa Barbara a Mantova (1565–1639). Nuovo materiale scoperto nelli archivi mantovani', in *Civiltà mantovana* IV (Mantua, 1969), pp. 376–400. The relevant references in two older studies: A. Bertolotti, *Musici alla corte dei Gonzaga in Mantova dal secolo XV al XVIII. Notizie e documenti raccolti negli archivi mantovani* (Milan, [1980]) and P. Canal, *Della musica in Mantova* (Venice, 1881), can still be useful but must be used with caution.

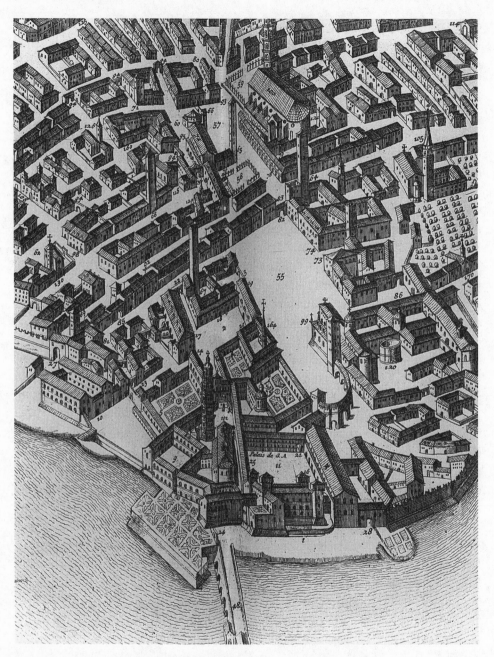

Figure 8.1   Pierre Mortier, *La ville de Mantoue*, engraving from J. Blaeu, *Novum Italiae theatrum* (Amsterdam, 1724–5). Detail of oblique view of Mantua (1704) showing the Gonzaga palace complex with: (1) Castello di San Giorgio; (2) Corte vecchia; (101) Santa Barbara; (164) Santa Croce in Piazza; also (55) the Piazza San Pietro with (99) the cathedral of San Pietro

Figure 8.2 Frans Geffels, *Veduta del altar maggiore della Chiesa Ducal di S.ta Barbara con l'apparto e fontioni funebri celebrate li VII genaro 1666 per la morte del Ser.mo Carlo II Duca di Mantoe Monferato*, engraving: Mantua, Biblioteca communale, Arm. 12 b. 11

This is not the only way in which the arrangements for Santa Barbara were somewhat exclusive. As a specially constituted and privileged institution, Santa Barbara was responsible not to the local diocesan authorities but to the Holy See: the main outlines of these special arrangements are specified in a further Bull from Pius IV, *Superna disposizione*. According to the *Constitutiones* drawn up in 1568, the establishment of the new basilica consisted of nine ordinary canons and six supernumeraries, four *mansionarii*, a number of chaplains, two *maestri di ceremonie* and a sacristan; in addition there were usually twenty or so aspirants (*chierici*), two deacons, two subdeacons, an organist, and a *maestro di cappella*. At full strength the institution employed sixty-four people, presided over by an abbot and six dignitaries.

A further sign of the exclusiveness of Santa Barbara was the development of a distinctive rite with its own separate missal and breviary based on reformist principles. The basilica's liturgy, which was carefully overseen by Duke Guglielmo himself, did not come into immediate operation but was the subject of long negotiations between Gonzaga and Rome. In 1571 a papal Bull of the new pope, Pius V, granted the Chapter of Santa Barbara the right to recite its own specially constructed Office, even though the chants themselves had not yet been fully compiled. That task took some ten years beginning in 1573, and it was not until 1583 that both the breviary and the missal finally received the Papal *imprimatur*. It was in that year that the breviary and the missal were finally published, and two years later the ducal printing-house of Osanna also issued the *Officium defunctorum*. This was largely done for the sake of prestige; the Santa Barbara liturgy did not operate outside the basilica, and for practical purposes the plainsong repertory was copied into large manuscript choirbooks, more than twenty of which survive containing Mass chants, propers, hymns, psalms, antiphons, and responses.

One of the most important of these survivals is the *Kyriale ad usum ecclesie Sancte Barbara* which, despite the various vicissitudes of the Santa Barbara library, is still in Mantua.[11] A large late sixteenth-century folio choirbook copied by a number of scribes and with many later changes, it is the only complete source for the chants of the Ordinary of the Mass as performed in the basilica. It contains the chants for ten Masses:

1 In Duplicibus maioribus Missa (Tone VIII)
2 In Duplicibus minoribus Missa (Tone IV)
3 In festis beate Mariae Virginis Missa (Tone VII)

11 Mantua, Archivio Storico Diocesano, Archivio della Basilica di Santa Barbara, MS 1. See Fenlon, *Music and Patronage*, Appendix III, where a brief summary description of the printed liturgical books and liturgical manuscripts from the basilica now in the Archivio Storico Diocesano in Mantua is given, and also P. Bersutti, 'Catalogo tematico delle monodie liturgiche della Basilica Palatina di S. Barbara in Mantova', *Le fonti musicali in Italia, studi e ricerche* 2 (1988), pp. 53–66, which provides textual and musical incipits for all the surviving chant manuscripts from the Basilica.

4 In festis Apostolorum Missa (Tone I)
5 In Dominicis diebus Missa (Tone II)
6 In Semiduplicibus majoribus Missa (Tone VI)
7 In Semiduplicibus minoribus Missa (Tone V)
8 In Simplicibus minoribus Missa (Tone I)
9 In simplicibus minoribus et feriis Temporis Pascalis (Tone IV)
10 In feriis per Annum Missa (Tone III)

The first eight of these Masses comprise the chants for all of the Ordinary; the ninth Mass omits the Credo, and the tenth both the Gloria and the Credo. Given the all-inclusive character of the manuscript, which clearly remained in use for several centuries as the main source for the Santa Barbara Mass chants, it must be assumed that these longer sections of the Ordinary were said rather than chanted on these less important days in the calendar. The Santa Barbara chants for the *Missa Defunctorum* together with the *Ordo sepeliendi clericum ecclesie nostre* (which also contains chanted sections) are contained in a separate manuscript, also still in Mantua.

Mass chants for part of the Ordinary can also be recuperated from two manuscripts of polyphonic Mass music which nevertheless contain chanted *alternatim* sections. The composition of *alternatim* Mass settings was something of a Santa Barbara speciality, a point that we will return to, but as far as the chants are concerned these two sources provide partial music for the Masses in *Feriis per annum*, *Domenicalis* and *Apostolorum*. Comparison of the notation in the larger of these two polyphonic manuscripts[12] with the *Kyriale* reveals differences of neumatic grouping, and occasionally melodic variants, suggesting that there is not a homogenous scribal tradition at work (see Example 8.1).

Example 8.1

12 Milan, Biblioteca del Conservatorio, S. Barbara MS 192. Most of the Santa Barbara polyphonic repertory, whether printed or manuscript, survives complete in the Conservatorio in Milan; it has now been catalogued in *Conservatorio di musica 'Guiseppe Verdi', Milano. Catalogo della biblioteca, fondi speciali I. Musiche della cappella di S. Barbara in Mantova* (Florence, 1972).

The Santa Barbara *Kyriale* differs radically from Roman use, not only in relation to the classification of feasts (with the subdivision of Duplex and Semiduplex), but also in other ways.[13] In order to preserve a single mode throughout a complete Ordinary, the compiler of the Santa Barbara *Kyriale* has composed new chants (and in some cases complete Masses), while at the same time incorporating elements from the Roman use. In the case of the *Missa in Festis Beatae Mariae Virginis*, for example, only the Gloria is taken directly from a Roman source, the rest of the Ordinary being recomposed, apparently in the interests of clearer declamation and modal purity. It is this latter concern which seems to be the overriding principle, as a comparison of the Christe from the *Missa in Dominicis* in both Mantuan and Roman versions makes clear (see Example 8.2).

Example 8.2

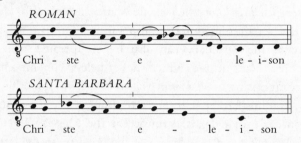

It is presumably in pursuit of this 'modal purity' that the Santa Barbara chants are modified from Roman use, or in cases completely recomposed, so that the total range of the modes never exceeds the octave. The ranges of the Mass chants in the *Kyriale* are seen in Example 8.3.

Example 8.3

From this it is clear that, with only occasional exceptions, the range of an octave is not exceeded in all modes and that in the fourth mode, used in two Masses in the

13 See K. Jeppesen, Preface to *Le messe di Mantova, inedite dai manoscritti di S. Barbara* (Rome, 1954), vols. 18 and 19, and R. Casimiri *et al.*, eds, *Le opere complete di Giovanni Pierluigi da Palestrina*, 29 vols. (Rome, 1939–61).

Kyriale, not even the full octave range is exploited. The restrained melodic style which results from this thinking and which is applied to the Santa Barbara Mass chants in a highly consistent, even pedantic way, is evident throughout the *Kyriale*. Consider, in Example 8.4, a moment from the Gloria of the *Missa in Festis Apostolorum* where the free and broadly arching melody of the Roman version has become transmuted into something far more prosaic.

Example 8.4

This apparent lack of sympathy for some of the most beautiful and characteristic melodic aspects of the older versions of the chant is typical not only of the Santa Barbara *Kyriale*, but also of the times; in the wake of the Council of Trent, 'reform' of the liturgy in accordance with humanistic principles was a major concern of the church. In practice this concern was principally aimed at more precise declamation, largely to be achieved through greater melodic simplicity so that the words of the liturgy might be more clearly heard; there is a clear analogy here with post-Trent architectural thinking, and with the simplified iconography sometimes advocated by churchmen for devotional pictures. Post-Tridentine graduals and antiphonals contain melodies with reduced melismas, with initial notes and cadential points modally regularized, and with text underlay simplified. These editions have been condemned as containing melodies which have been brutalized through distortion and abbreviation, and those text underlays follow the principles of Renaissance grammarians rather than those of tenth-century cantors. Whatever one's view, it is clear that the Santa Barbara chants are in keeping with a general trend. The result is a distinct corpus of chant which, while retaining elements of tradition, also includes much newly composed material.

On the question of who was to perform this repertory of chants, the *Constitutiones* of 1568 are quite unambiguous. It was the duty of the Prefect of the Choir to ensure that the correct chant was used as laid down in the liturgy, to teach the chant to other clerics, and to rehearse the celebrants who were to sing Mass and the other services. In these duties the Prefect was assisted by two canons who also taught chant, while the *mansionarii* were primarily responsible for the chanting of offices and for giving intonations. Constitutionally four *mansionarii* were required, and this strength seems to have been maintained a good deal more consistently than some of the other appointments in the basilica. The maintenance of the Santa Barbara rite was evidently taken seriously. None of these arrangements came within the domain of the *maestro di cappella* who was principally responsible for the polyphony required by the *Constitutiones* on feast-days, bringing in singers from the court as necessary.

The 'reformed' chants of the Santa Barbara rite inevitably lend a particular stamp to polyphonic works specially composed for the basilica, which use those chants as *canti firmi*. Again, it was the role of Duke Guglielmo Gonzaga that was crucial. The duke was himself a composer whose works were sometimes published, and from an early age he began the practice of sending his own pieces to other composers for criticism and comment.[14] The most celebrated of these contacts was with Palestrina, with whom Gonzaga began to correspond at the end of the 1560s just as Santa Barbara was being finished and its *cappella* established. Fortunately this exchange, which lasted for some twenty years until Guglielmo's death in 1587, can be reconstructed, and from it emerges a reasonably clear picture of the duke's own attitudes to sacred music in general, and to the composition and performance of music for the Santa Barbara rite in particular.[15] From a letter of 1568, the first in the series, it is clear that Palestrina had recently composed a mass for the new basilica on the instructions of Giaches de Wert, but the most specific information about the gestation of Palestrina's Mantuan Masses comes from a letter of 1578 written by a Mantuan agent in Rome; it describes the arrangement of the Cappella Giulia into two choirs of twelve singers and then continues:

If with the gracious permission of your Highness it may be so, Palestrina also wishes to have the second parts and to use them in the church in question [St Peter's] instead of the organ on occasions of high solemnity. For he affirms that Your Highness has truly purged these plainsongs of all barbarisms and imperfections that they contained. I trust that you will not do this [i.e. perform the finished work in St Peter's] without your permission, and as soon as his infirmity permits he will work out what has been done on the lute with all possible care.[16]

14 Duke Guglielmo Gonzaga's contacts with other composers are discussed in Fenlon, *Music and Patronage*, vol. 1, pp. 85–95; see also C. Gallico, 'Guglielmo Gonzaga signore della musica', in *Mantova e i Gonzaga nella civiltà del rinascimento* (Rome, 1978), pp. 277–81. For the Duke's own publications, see also R. Sherr, 'The Publications of Guglielmo Gonzaga', *JAMS* 31 (1978), 118–25.

15 For Gonzaga's protracted correspondence with Palestrina, see O. Strunk, 'Guglielmo Gonzaga and Palestrina's Missa Domenicalis', reprinted from its original version in *Musical Quarterly* 33 (1947), 228–39, in *Essays on Music in the Western World* (1974). Palestrina's Mantuan Masses are discussed by K. Jeppesen in 'The Recently Discovered Mantova Masses of Palestrina. A Provisional Communication', *Acta musicologica* 22 (1950), 36–47. On the same subject see also the same author's 'Pierluigi da Palestrina, Herzog Guglielmo Gonzaga, und die neugefundenen Mantovaner-Messen Palestrinas', *Acta musicologica* 25 (1953), 132–79.

16 Strunk, 'Guglielmo Gonzaga', pp. 100ff.

The sense of this becomes clear when it is remembered that during this same period Palestrina was at work composing a specially commissioned sequence of Masses for Santa Barbara, nine *alternatim* Masses based on Santa Barbara chants, and that the 'second parts' are presumably the chanted sections of Palestrina's settings. Only one of his Mantuan Masses was ever published during his lifetime; the remainder survive uniquely in manuscripts from the Santa Barbara library. It is clear from the printed books from the basilica's music collection that published music from the standard Mass and motet repertory was performed in Santa Barbara, but alongside these pieces a repertory of specially composed works, mostly written in *alternatim* style, was also gradually built up. With the exception of the single Mass despatched by the composer in 1568, all of Palestrina's Mantuan Masses were written during the years 1578–9 (that is precisely during the period that the manuscript chant books for the basilica were being compiled but before the rite itself had yet received official papal approval), on chants selected by the duke and at least in some cases 'purged of all barbarisms and imperfections by him, a procedure confirmed by comparing the chants themselves with Palestrina's *canti firmi*. The revisions (and in some cases recompositions) mostly consist of changes made to assist the declamation of text, to reduce melodic complexity and to impose a greater sense of modal uniformity, as comparison with 'unreformed' Roman sources makes clear.

Palestrina's Mantuan Masses constitute the largest body of Mass music specially composed by a single composer for the basilica, but the idea of a distinct repertory written in *alternatim* style and based on chants from the Santa Barbara liturgy is an earlier one which can be traced back to the foundation of the church in the 1560s. Many of the first clerics to be employed at Santa Barbara had previously been at the cathedral of San Pietro, and were no doubt attracted to the basilica by the more favourable conditions and prestige of the new posts, a pattern of transfer between the two institutions that continued throughout the century. (Among other arrangements made at the time of the foundation of Santa Barbara, Duke Guglielmo Gonzaga was granted Papal permission to transfer ten chaplaincies endowed by his father Federico II from San Pietro to the new basilica). Among the early appointees at Santa Barbara was Giulio Bruschi, a Piacenzan composer who had been at the cathedral since the early 1550s, and who was engaged in the early 1560s (before the arrival in Mantua of Giaches de Wert) to make some of the arrangements for the provision of music in the new chapel.[17] It was Bruschi who was involved in the commissioning of a new organ from the distinguished Brescian builder Graziadio Antegnati, and with the Veronese artist Domenico Brusasorci for the altarpiece showing the Martyrdom of Santa Barbara which was placed over the high altar. Bruschi was also among the first to compose Mass music for the Santa

17 For Bruschi, see Fenlon, *Music and Patronage*, vol. 1, pp. 103, 105–6, 107, 109n, 110 and 114–15.

Barbara rite and his two Masses, one *in semi duplicibus minoribus* the other *in duplicibus minoribus* are both written in *alternatim* style. So too are the five Masses written for the Basilica by the Brescian Giovanni Contino, a composer principally known to historians as the teacher of Marenzio. Contino spent two periods of service at Santa Barbara, the first in the early 1560s, the second in the mid-1570s. His five Masses on Santa Barbara chants, four of which remained unpublished during his lifetime are, like Bruschi's, composed in an *alternatim* manner.[18]

It would seem that the two most distinctive features of polyphonic Mass music composed for the basilica, namely its use of a unique repertory of chants and its deployment of *alternatim* style, were established from the 1570s. (It is significant that a tenth Mantuan Mass by Palestrina is not written for *alternatim* performance and stands apart from the other nine in a variety of ways; it is most likely this work which was sent to Mantua in 1568, before the details of the Santa Barbara *alternatim* practice had been worked out, and probably before the basilica's corpus of chants had been established). *Alternatim* style was hardly a new feature of composition. The earliest surviving source of Italian liturgical organ music (the Faenza Codex), compiled in the early fifteenth-century, contains music for *alternatim* performances of Mass and Office music, and more than a century later the practice was widespread. Biagio Rossetti, writing in the 1520s, commented that 'the organ is allowed in church so that the singers can relax during alternations with the organ and are not exhausted by continuously singing beyond the proper period of time, but are stimulated by it to sing together more alertly'.[19] And in the *Caeremoniale episcoporum* (Rome, 1600) issued during the pontificate of Clement VIII, the moments when the organ may be used during the Mass on Sundays (except during Advent and Lent) and on important festal days is laid down:

At the solemn Mass the organ is played alternatim for the Kyrie eleison and the Gloria in excelsis . . . likewise at the end of the Epistle and at the Offertory; for the Sanctus, alternatim; then more gravely and softly during the Elevation of the Most Holy Sacrament; for the Agnus Dei, *alternatim*, and at the verse before the post-Communion prayer; also at the end of the Mass.[20]

Although the *Caeremoniale episcoporum* does not specify where the texts of the Ordinary are to be divided for *alternatim* performance, there is considerable

18 Contino's masses for S. Barbara are also now available in a modern edition, see O. Beretta, ed., *Giovanni Contino. Cinque messe mantovane dal fondo Santa Barbara a cinque voci* (Milan, 1988), which has a useful preface. In addition to the biographical details given there, see also I. Fenlon, 'Cardinal Scipione Gonzaga (1542–93): "Quel padrone confidentissimo"', *Journal of the Royal Musical Association* 115, (1990), 234–5.

19 B. Rossetti, *Libellus de rudimentis musices* (Verona, 1529).

20 *Caeremoniale episcoporum iussu Clementis VIII Pont. Max. Novissime reformatum* (Rome, 1600), cap. xxviii.

consistency among Italian sixteenth-century organ Masses. A fairly standard arrangement is the following:

ORGAN	CHOIR
Kyrie 1	Kyrie 2
Kyrie 3	Christe 1
Christe 2	Christe 3

Celebrant
Gloria in excelsis Deo

Et in terra	Laudamus te
Benedicimus te	Adoramus te
Glorificamus te	Gratias agimus tibi
Domine Deus, Rex	Domine Fili
Domine Deus, Agnus	Qui tollis.. miserere
Qui tollis.. suscipe	Qui sedes
Quoniam tu solus	Tu solus Dominus
Tu solus Altissimus	Cum Sancto Spiritu

Celebrant
Credo in unum Deum

Patrem omnipotentem	Et in unum Dominum
Et ex Patre	Deum de Deo
Genitum	Qui propter
Et incarnatus est	Crucifixus
Et resurrexit	Et ascendit
Et iterum	Et in Spiritum Sanctum
Qui cum Patre	Et unam sanctam
Confiteor	Et exspecto
Et vitam venturi	Amen
Sanctus 1	Sanctus 2
Sanctus, Dominus	Pleni sunt
Benedictus	
Agnus Dei 1	Agnus Dei 2
Agnus Dei 3	

What is unusual about the Santa Barbara *alternatim* repertory is, firstly, its sheer size (particularly the large number of settings for the Ordinary of the Mass), and secondly, that the disposition of chant and polyphonic sections is quite different from the standard pattern shown above on p. 227. All of Palestrina's *alternatim* Mantuan Masses, and most of those written for the basilica by other composers, follow the same plan. It is clear that the repertory of Santa Barbara Masses built up during Duke Guglielmo Gonzaga's period was designed as a large and virtually unique corpus of choral Masses based on unique chants, disposed for *alternatim* performance in such a way that the polyphony provided a showcase for the chants themselves, heard either in their own right but also modestly encased in comparatively uncomplicated polyphony:

ORGAN	POLYPHONIC CHOIR
	Kyrie
	Christe
	Kyrie

Celebrant
Gloria in excelsis Deo

Et in terra pax hominibus	Bonae voluntatis
Laudamus te	Benedicimus te
Adoramus te	Glorificamus te
Gratias agimus tibi	Domine Deus, Rex
Domine Fili	Domine Deus, Agnus
Qui tollis.. miserere	Qui tollis.. suscipe
Qui sedes	Quoniam tu solus
Tu solus Dominus	Tu solus Altissimus
Cum Sancto Spiritu	Amen

Celebrant
Credo in unum Deum

Patrem omnipotentem	Factorem coeli et terrae
Et in unum Dominum	Et ex patre
Deum de Deo	Genitum
Qui propter	Et incarnatus est
Crucifixus	Et resurrexit
Et ascendit	Et iterum
Et in Spiritum	Qui cum Patre
Et unam sanctam	Confiteor
Et exspecto	Et vitam venturi
	Amen

	Sanctus 1
Sanctus 2	Sanctus, Dominus
	Pleni sunt
	Benedictus

OR, ALTERNATIVELY:

	Sanctus 2
Sanctus 1	Sanctus, Dominus
	Pleni sunt
	Benedictus

| Agnus Dei 1 | Agnus Dei 2 |
| Agnus Dei 3 | |

In practice, the Santa Barbara chants could have been performed in one of two patterns in *alternatim* works; either in an entirely choral scheme (with chant and polyphony heard alternately, or with the organ alternating with choral polyphony. A third arrangement, in which the organ alternated with chant may also have been used on minor occasions in the calendar. In all these cases it must be assumed that the organist improvised upon chant *canti firmi*, much in the manner illustrated in Adriano Banchieri's *L'organo suonarino* of 1605, which gives organ basses for chant melodies. That organ music was a prominent feature of liturgical services in Santa Barbara is clear from the *Constitutiones* of 1568 which specifies the day on which the instrument was played, but it does not follow that the instrument was used *alternatim* rather than simply at the offertory and the elevation. The truth of the matter is that it is not known whether or not the organ was used in the performance of the Santa Barbara *alternatim* repertory.

What is clear though, is that the arrangement of the ritual and performing spaces in the basilica (see Figure 8.3) firmly separated the clerics responsible for chanting from the organist, who was in turn separated from the musicians charged with performing polyphony. The latter were, on the evidence of Ippolito Donesmondi, situated in the gallery at the west end of the church (A), while the organ was accommodated in a small gallery on the north side of the building (B). There is no room in the organ gallery for performers other than the organist, and no evidence that the instrument was ever placed elsewhere. It is not entirely clear where the four *mansionarii* responsible for chanting would have been placed, but the most plausible location would have been in the sanctuary (C), so that whichever scheme of *alternatim* performance was followed at Santa Barbara, the physical separation of the various participants would have produced an excitingly stereophonic effect.

During the first few decades of the basilica's existence the Santa Barbara repertory of Mass music grew; in addition to Palestrina (9), Contino (5), and Giulio

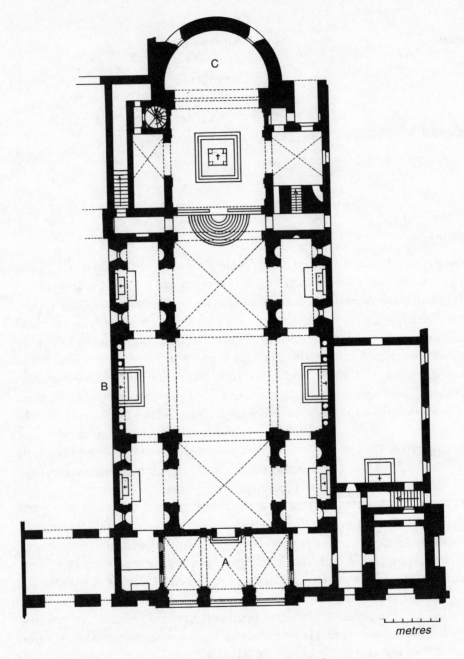

Figure 8.3   Mantua, basilica of Santa Barbara, ground plan

Bruschi (3), a number of other composers wrote *alternatim* masses for the rite during these years, and by the end of the century some forty-five settings had been composed. Apart from the set of *Missae Domenicales*, published, significantly enough, by the firm of Tini in the strongly 'reformist' city of Milan in 1592,[21] this substantial corpus of music remained in manuscript until its rediscovery in the present century. It includes mass settings by Francesco Rovigo (4), Alessandro Striggio (1), Duke Guglielmo himself (3) and, of course, the specially recruited *maestro di cappella* of the new foundation, Giaches de Wert (6). In terms of liturgical function the complete corpus is arranged as follows:

Missae in Duplicibus majoribus   4
Missae in Duplicibus minoribus   7
Missae in Festis Beatae Mariae Virginis   7
Missae in Festis Apostolorum   7
Missae in Dominicis diebus   7
Missae in Semiduplicibus majoribus   3
Missae in Semiduplicibus minoribus   1
Missae in Feriis per annum   1

Wert, one of the last in the great tradition of North European composers who had, since the early fifteenth century, travelled to Italy to live and work, arrived in Mantua, probably directly from Milan, in 1564.[22] Until his death thirty-two years later, he served the Gonzaga as their principal resident musician, spending much of this time as *maestro di cappella* at Santa Barbara. Although some of his church music was published during his lifetime, to his contemporaries he was primarily known as a composer of madrigals. While there can be no doubt that Duke Guglielmo Gonzaga's patronage of music and musicians is the most singular and best-documented example anywhere in sixteenth-century Italy of the extent to which a musically literate patron with an informed interest in liturgy could influence the style of sacred music, there is strong evidence that composers such as Wert, who was clearly alive to the new poetry and musical techniques of the 1580s, found the cultural atmosphere of the Mantuan court during the 1570s and 80s somewhat stifling. Nevertheless, while Wert's main artistic preoccupations during the last decade of Guglielmo's life were principally nurtured by his contacts with the court at nearby Ferrara, and with the composition of madrigals in a variety of progressive styles, he continued to write polyphony for the Santa Barbara liturgy throughout his career.

21 G. Pellini, ed., *Missae domenicales quinis vocibus diversorum auctorum* (Milan, 1592).
22 For Wert and his music for the basilica, see C. MacClintock, *Giaches de Wert (1535–1596). Life and Works* (n.p., 1966); his *Missa Domenicalis* for Santa Barbara is published in C. MacClintock and M. Bernstein, eds., *Giaches de Wert, Opera omnia*, 17 (Stuttgart, 1977), but the *canti fermi* are only there provided for the Gloria.

Mass composition forms a major part of Wert's output for the basilica. Altogether he wrote seven Mass settings, only one of which, the *Missa Domenicalis*, was published in his lifetime in Tini's collection. All survive among the Santa Barbara manuscripts as follows:

Missa in Duplicibus minoribus [MS 145]
Missa in Festis Beate Mariae Virginis [MS 143]
Missa in Festis Apostolorum [MS 192]
Missa in Duplicibus maioribus [MS 142]
Missa in Feriis per annum: Die Martis [MS 180]
Missa in Domenicalis [MS 192]
Missa Defunctorum [MS 164]

In terms of function, these liturgical categories are, with the exception of the *Missa Defunctorum*, all taken from the basilica's manuscript *Kyriale*, as are the chants on which they are based (see above). It is clear that *alternatim* Mass settings were performed in Santa Barbara throughout the year on both major and minor feasts including Sundays, saints' days and at least some ferial days, and this regular commitment makes the basilica one of the most important institutions for the performance of liturgical polyphony in the whole of late sixteenth-century Italy, comparable in its scope to the arrangements at St Mark's in Venice and at the Papal Chapel itself. Yet while this body of specially written Mass settings is certainly impressive, it forms only a part of the repertory performed there, and the Santa Barbara manuscripts also contain a substantial corpus of other liturgical music, notably hymns and psalms, written specifically for the basilica. It is through these pieces that it is possible to gain a more detailed impression of the way that both polyphony and chant were used to celebrate those feast-days which, while not unique to the Santa Barbara calendar, were given special emphasis in its rite.

Of the various collections of hymns Wert's magisterial cycle, preserved in manuscript in the Santa Barbara library, is the largest and most important. There are two main sources. The first, the older compilation of the two, contains a good number of pieces which are not present in the second, an illuminated folio choirbook, dated 1590, copied for the Basilica by Francesco Sforza, the principal scribe working there at the end of the sixteenth century and the early decades of the seventeenth. A third manuscript, also copied by Sforza, adds a handful of other hymns, mostly to be sung at Matins, which are not present in the other two. Taken together these sources contain 127 pieces, none of which were ever published during the sixteenth century.

In style, Wert's hymns resemble his other *alternatim* settings for the basilica. Among those written for use on saints' days, the following are prominent:

S Barbara: Vespers, Compline, Lauds, Prime, Terce, Sext, None
Octave of S. Barbara: Vespers

Chair of S. Peter: Vespers

Birth of S. John the Baptist: Matins, Lauds, Terce, Vespers, Compline

SS Peter and Paul: Vespers, Compline, Terce

S Margaret Virgin and Martyr: Vespers, Terce

S Mary Magdalene: Vespers, Terce

S Stephen: Matins, Lauds, Terce, Compline, Vespers

Beheading of S. John the Baptist: Vespers

S Adrian: Vespers, Compline, Terce

Dedication of the Basilica of S. Barbara: Vespers, Compline, Terce, Sext

S Sylvester: Matins, Lauds, Terce, Compline

From this it is clear that the feast-days of St John the Baptist, St Margaret, St Sylvester, St Peter, St Adrian and, of course, St Barbara herself were, together with a small number of others, of particular importance in the festal calendar. In addition to hymns for these saints, Marian feasts and the Finding and Exaltation of the True Cross also receive special emphasis in Wert's hymn cycle. A similar pattern is evident from the organization of a set of late sixteenth-century part books containing an anonymous sequence of polyphonic processional hymns to be performed on major feast-days when ceremonial was more elaborate. The books are arranged as follows:

1	In Processione S Crucis	O crux ave spes unica
2	In Processione Sacrarum Reliquiarum	Ad nos tenebris eructe
3	In Processione Sancti Joannis Baptiste	Plusquam prophete virginis
4	In Processione Sancti Silvestri	Silvester almus pontifex
5	In Processione Sancti Petri	Apostolorum principem
6	In Processione Sancti Adriani	Adest dies letissimus
7	In Processione Sanctae Mariae Magdalenae	Ut Magdalena lubrici
8	In Processione Sanctae Margaritae	Te Margarita quesumus
9	[A domenica Passionis ad feriam IV. Maj. heb.]	Vexilla regis prodeunt

It is not entirely clear why these particular saints held a special significance for the Gonzaga, though in a number of cases the reasons may have had to do with family history, St Margaret, for example, was the patron saint not only of Duke Guglielmo's mother, Margherita Paleologo, but also his great grandmother, Margaret of Bavaria, the wife of Marchese Federico Gonzaga. And St Barbara herself was not only the protector of the house of Gonzaga, but also recalled Barbara of Brandenburg, the Hohenzollern wife of Marchese Ludovico Gonzaga (1444–78). Guglielmo's susceptibility to associations of this kind is suggested by his choice of the names Margherita Barbara for his second daughter, baptized on 17 May 1565, only a few days before his new basilica was consecrated. As far as St Peter is concerned, the cathedral in Mantua is dedicated to him, and the fact that the basilica of Santa Barbara was responsible to Rome rather than to the local diocese made the celebration of his cult particularly appropriate; in this way the Gonzaga were able to emphasize their special status in relation to other Italian princes by drawing a parallel between Rome and Mantua. But beyond these considerations, the most likely explanation for the cult of these saints together with Adrian, Silvester, and Mary Magdalene is that their relics were already in the possession of the Gonzaga when the basilica was founded. A list of relics for the eight altars in Santa Barbara, including the high altar and the altar in the Sacristy, drawn up in 1564, arranges them as follows:

S Barbarae	S Crucis
S Martae	S Catherinae
S Lazari	S Galli
S Magdalenae	S Margaritae
S Eucarij	S Blasi
S Damiani	S Valerij
S Adriani	S Silvestri
S Mauritij	S Martini
S Cristiantiae	S Anastasiae
Gloriosae Virginis Mariae	S Johanis Baptistae
S Simeonis	S Cosmae
S Debeon	S Luciae

In each case the altars were dedicated to the first-named saint in each group of three, an arrangement reflected not only in the festal calendar and in the composition of polyphony designed to be performed on those saints' days, but also in the altarpieces which were commissioned to be placed above them. This scheme is also reflected in Guglielmo Gonzaga's own book of five-voice *Sacrae Cantiones* 'in festis duplicibus maioribus ecclesiae Sanctae Barbarae', published anonymously by Gardano in Venice in 1583. Here the *tabula* reads:

In festo sanctae Barbarae	De Spinis
Secunda pars.	In lege Domini
In festo Nativatatis Domini	Adest Christi
In festo sancti Stephani	Patefactae sunt
In festo sancti Iohannis apostoli & Evangelistae	Fluenta evangelij
In festo sancti Silvestri	O beatae pontifex
In festo Circuncisionis Domini	Puer qui natus est
In festo Epiphaniae Domini	Videntes stellam Magi

In festo Annuntiationis B. Mariae	Gaude Maria virgo
In festo Resurrectionis Domini	Exultemus omnes
In festo Inventionis sanctae Crucis	Crucem sanctam subiit
In festo Ascensionis Domini	Omnis pulchritudo Domini
In festo Pentecostes	Novae hodie
In festo sanctissimae Trinitatis	Gloria tibi Trinitas
In festo Corporis Domini	O sacrum convivium
In festo Nativitatis S. Iohannis Baptistae	Inter natos mulierum
In festo SS. Apostolorum Petri & Pauli	O beatae Petre
In festo Assumptionis Beatae Mariae	Quasi cedrus
In festo sancti Adriani	Felix sancti martyris
In festo Dedicationis Ecclesiae	Bendic Domine
In festo Translationis sacrarum Reliquiarum	Qui nos in corpore
In festo Omnium Sanctorum	Omnes sancti
Feria secunda Pentecostes	Sic Deus dilexit mundum

In terms of musical and liturgical practices, the exclusivity of what took place within the walls of Santa Barbara was secured in three main ways. Firstly, a sense of uniqueness was achieved here, as elsewhere, through the adoption of a specially devised festal calendar which was practiced there and nowhere else. With its emphasis on the early Church Fathers, notably SS Sylvester and Peter, the Santa Barbara calendar aimed to acquire an authority and even a somewhat spurious air of antiquity that would enhance the status of the basilica. Secondly, the reformed chants of the Santa Barbara liturgy are peculiar to that institution; their characteristics, which include melodic modifications and composition *ex novo*, lend them a distinct and unique quality thus further enhancing the exclusivity of the rite. Finally, it was largely through the vehicle of a specially commissioned corpus of liturgical polyphony, mostly organized on *alternatim* principles, that the chants of the Santa Barbara liturgy were displayed to the world, or rather to that privileged section of it that constituted the 'public' for the services held in the basilica. Through these means the Gonzaga displayed not only their piety, but also their power and authority in the troubled atmosphere of Counter-Reformation Italy.

INDEX